DOES TERRORISM WORK?

DOES
TERRORISM
WORK?

A HISTORY

RICHARD ENGLISH

OXFORD
UNIVERSITY PRESS

OXFORD
UNIVERSITY PRESS

Great Clarendon Street, Oxford, OX2 6DP,
United Kingdom

Oxford University Press is a department of the University of Oxford.
It furthers the University's objective of excellence in research, scholarship,
and education by publishing worldwide. Oxford is a registered trade mark of
Oxford University Press in the UK and in certain other countries

First Edition published in 2016

Impression: 1

Published in the United States of America by Oxford University Press
198 Madison Avenue, New York, NY 10016, United States of America

British Library Cataloguing in Publication Data
Data available

Library of Congress Control Number: 2015958818

ISBN 978–0–19–960785–3

Printed in Great Britain by
Clays Ltd, St Ives plc

For Maxine, Jasmine, and Arabella

Acknowledgements

Even an instinctively solitary scholar must acknowledge that lone-wolfing will not suffice when pursuing large-scale research. As with my previous books, the researching and writing of this one have been made possible and enjoyable by the kindness of many people. Their scholarship, advice, friendship, support, and insights have helped me hugely, and it is a pleasure to be able to thank the following individuals here: John Anderson, Ali Ansari, Javier Argomaniz, Abdul Haqq Baker, Eli Berman, Paul Bew, Roddy Brett, Peter Clark, Matthew Cotton, Martha Crenshaw, Audrey Kurth Cronin, Mark Currie, Gillian Duncan, Dennis Dworkin, Joseph Easson, David Eastwood, Joseph Felter, Page Fortna, Chloe Foster, Roy Foster, Conor Gearty, Andreas Gofas, Andrew Gordon, Adrian Guelke, Dipak Gupta, Mohammed Hafez, Chris Hawkesworth, Bruce Hoffman, Donald Holbrook, Bruce Hunter, Peter Jackson, Tom Johnson, Stathis Kalyvas, Jeffrey Kaplan, Michael Kenny, Dimitris Keridis, Desmond King, David Laitin, David Lake, Bob Lambert, Peter Lehr, Sarah Marsden, Julie Middleton, Diego Muro, Paul Newton, Luciana O'Flaherty, David Omand, Jonathan Phillips, Gilbert Ramsay, David Rapoport, Maria Rasmussen, Nick Rengger, Louise Richardson, Adam Roberts, Alex Schmid, Jacob Shapiro, Rashmi Singh, Joseph Skelly, Martin Stokes, Charles Townshend, David Veness, Paul Wilkinson, Caroline Winterer, and Tim Wilson. Colleagues and students at the University of St Andrews have made a great contribution to the ongoing scholarly debate on terrorism and I myself have certainly learned much from them. It has been a privilege to work at the University's Handa Centre for the Study of Terrorism and Political Violence (CSTPV), as it has been to gain insights from the large number of people whom I have interviewed regarding political violence over many years.

I'm also very grateful to those who invited me to speak on terrorism (and to those who offered responses and questions when I did so) at the following institutions during the course of working on this book: Stanford University; the University of Oxford; the London School of Economics; the University of Cambridge; the University of California, San Diego; Georgetown University; Copenhagen University; Boston College; the Naval Postgraduate School, Monterey; Chatham House, London; the National University of Ireland at Maynooth; the Royal Irish Academy, Dublin; San Diego State University; the University of Glasgow; the Swedish National Defence College, Stockholm; the International Centre for Counter-Terrorism in The Hague; the University of Birmingham; the University of Aberystwyth; Jawaharlal Nehru University, Delhi; the Institut Barcelona d'Estudis Internacionals (IBEI) in Barcelona (and the Ways Out project there); the University of Nevada, Reno; the University of Exeter; and the Olympia Summer Academy. A period based at the Stanford Humanities Center as a Visiting Scholar facilitated valuable conversations with many people within that intellectually iridescent setting.

As ever, the dedication of the book expresses my most precious debt of all.

Contents

List of Figures

Abbreviations

ANC	African National Congress
AQAP	Al-Qaida in the Arabian Peninsula
AQI	Al-Qaida in Iraq
CIA	Central Intelligence Agency
CIRA	Continuity Irish Republican Army
DOP	Declaration of Principles
DUP	Democratic Unionist Party
EOKA	Ethniki Organosis Kyprion Agoniston (National Organization of Cypriot Fighters)
ETA	Euskadi Ta Askatasuna (Euskadi And Freedom, or Basque Homeland and Freedom)
FARC	Fuerzas Armadas Revolucionarias de Colombia (Revolutionary Armed Forces of Colombia)
FIS	Front Islamique de Salut (Islamic Salvation Front)
FLN	Front de Libération Nationale
FWA	Free Wales Army
GAL	Grupos Antiterroristas de Liberacion (Anti-Terrorist Liberation Groups)
GCHQ	(UK) Government Communications Headquarters
GFA	Good Friday Agreement
GHQ	General Headquarters
GI	Gamaat Islamiya (Islamic Group)
HB	Herri Batasuna (Popular Unity)
HMSU	Headquarters Mobile Support Unit (RUC)
IDF	Israel Defence Forces
INLA	Irish National Liberation Army
IRA	Irish Republican Army
IRM	Islamic Resistance Movement
ISI	Pakistani Directorate for Inter-Services Intelligence
ISIS	Islamic State of Iraq and the Levant

JIC	(UK) Joint Intelligence Committee
JKLF	Jammu and Kashmir Liberation Front
JMB	Jamaat-ul-Mujahideen Bangladesh
JRA	Japanese Red Army
KAS	Koordinadora Abertzale Socialista (Socialist National Coordinator)
LeT	Lashkar-e-Taiba ('Army of the Pious')
LPA	Loyalist Prisoners Association
LTTE	Liberation Tigers of Tamil Eelam (Tamil Tigers)
LVF	Loyalist Volunteer Force
MIPT	Memorial Institute for the Prevention of Terrorism
MLN	Movimiento de Liberación Nacional (National Liberation Movement)
MLNV	Movimiento de Liberacion Nacional Vasco (Basque National Liberation Movement)
MPABA	Malayan People's Anti-British Army
MRLA	Malayan Races' Liberation Army
NLF	(Algerian) National Liberation Front
NORAID	Irish Northern Aid
OIRA	Official Irish Republican Army
OUP	Oxford University Press
PA	Palestinian (National) Authority
PIJ	Palestinian Islamic Jihad
PIRA	Provisional Irish Republican Army
PLO	Palestine Liberation Organization
PNV	Partido Nacionalista Vasco
PP	Partido Popular (Popular Party)
PRONI	Public Record Office of Northern Ireland
PSNI	Police Service of Northern Ireland
PSOE	Partido Socialista Obrero Español (Spanish Socialist Workers' Party)
RAF	Red Army Faction
RIRA	Real Irish Republican Army
RSF	Republican Sinn Fein
RUC	Royal Ulster Constabulary
SDLP	Social Democratic and Labour Party
17N	17 November
SICAT	*Studies in Conflict and Terrorism*
SLA	Symbionese Liberation Army

TNT	Tamil National Tigers
TPV	*Terrorism and Political Violence*
TUF	Tamil United Front
TULF	Tamil United Liberation Front
UDA	Ulster Defence Association
UFF	Ulster Freedom Fighters
UVF	Ulster Volunteer Force

Prologue

In the heart of Oslo, on the site where on 22 July 2011 Anders Behring Breivik exploded a van-bomb killing eight people at government buildings, the Norwegian state has established a dignified Centre commemorating the events of that terrible day. Breivik himself—a would-be crusader against what he took to be pernicious Norwegian multiculturalism and an increasing Muslim presence in the country—has been lengthily and deservedly imprisoned. And the 22 July Centre offers an elegiac window onto his atrocity. There are agonizingly silent photographs of most of the seventy-seven people he killed (after Oslo he murdered a further sixty-nine victims later the same day, at the Norwegian Labour Youth League's summer camp on beautiful Utoya island). And there is the actual wreckage of the van in which his Oslo bomb had been planted: a gruesome, mangled, sculpture-like relic of his blood-stained work.

It is hard not to be moved by the quiet gesture embodied in this 22 July Centre. But as I myself walked around it I was struck again—as I frequently had been while living for many years in violence-torn Belfast—that behind all such recollections of terrorism lies a question of very high importance, which we have nonetheless found it difficult to address adequately in relation to actions such as Breivik's famous operation. For all of its baneful effects, Does Terrorism Work?

Introduction

I

Does Terrorism[1] Work? It's an important, controversial, and difficult question. I think it's also one which requires a historically grounded answer, and a carefully crafted framework for assessment, if we are to address it as seriously as it deserves.

The question is important both analytically and practically. Any full understanding of a phenomenon which—like terrorism—is focused on the pursuit of political change, will necessitate analysis of how far such change has actually been achieved. In the case of terrorism, this issue is even more analytically important given its implications for explaining some of the central dynamics of terrorist activity: its causation (why does it occur where and when it does?); its varying levels across place and time (why does it endure for the periods and at the specific, differing levels that it does?); the processes by which terrorist campaigns come to an end (why does it dry up in some settings at some moments, but not in and at others?); and the patterns of support involved in terrorism (why are some people more likely to endorse and practise it than others?).

Despite the doubts of some,[2] a persuasive body of scholarly literature now suggests that those who engage in and support terrorism tend to display the same levels of rationality as do other people; that they tend to be psychologically normal rather than abnormal; that they are not generally characterized by mental illness or psychopathology (indeed, anyone who has met and got to know large numbers of people who have been involved in terrorist campaigns can testify to their striking normality). The argument here is not that terrorists act out of rationality alone, but rather that their decision-making processes are likely to be as rational as are those of most other groups of humans, and that even a seemingly incomprehensible act such as suicide bombing can be judged to be, at least in part, rationally motivated.[3]

This being so, the emergence and sustenance of terrorism centrally rely on the fact that perfectly normal people at certain times consider it to be the most effective way of achieving necessary goals. Since most people would probably prefer not to be engaged in violence than to be engaged in it, and would probably prefer peace to war, what has frequently happened is this: some people have judged terrorism to be necessary because they think their goal sufficiently important for it to be pursued through these violent means, and further think that it would be unattainable without them.

Indeed, those who have been involved in non-state terrorism often make precisely this claim, that the only way they could reach their justified objective was to use this form of violent politics. In Algerian National Liberation Front (NLF) member Saadi Yacef's words: 'It's our only way of expressing ourselves.'[4] Or there is the statement from one Tamil Tiger leader that 'The Tamil people have been expressing their grievances in parliament for more than three decades. Their voices went unheard like cries in the wilderness.'[5] In the phrasing of one Hamas leader, 'When all channels are closed to us, we use violence.'[6] Or, as one of the Provisional IRA or Irish Republican Army's most famous former members (Patrick Magee) put it very lucidly to me in interview: 'At one time that was all we *could* do, that was the only avenue open to us, was to engage in armed struggle.'[7]

This reflects a wider and very important pattern within the use of violence. In psychologist Steven Pinker's words, 'When a tendency toward violence evolves, it is always *strategic*. Organisms are selected to deploy violence only in circumstances where the expected benefits outweigh the expected costs.'[8] As the distinguished terrorism scholar Adrian Guelke has phrased it, 'success or, at any rate, the prospect of success is crucial to the legitimization of violence'; 'the assumptions that violent groups make about the likely consequences of their campaigns do seem to have an important bearing on whether and in what form any campaign will continue'.[9] Or, in the words of the fictional jihadist protagonist in one recent novel: given that he was going 'to try and change the twisted moral hierarchy of this world', then he had to recognize that his previous, non-violent political activity had achieved 'nothing...absolutely nothing...I too had no other option than armed struggle.'[10]

But if we are properly to understand the processes of non-state terrorism, then it is not enough to acknowledge that it occurs when sufficient numbers of people sincerely consider it likely to work, or when they believe it to be the only means of achieving change; nor is it enough for us to recognize that some forms of terrorist activity rather than others will occur because these particular forms are judged more likely to succeed in certain contexts (suicide bombing, for example, often being deployed when other violent tactics have been perceived to fail);[11] nor should we merely judge that terrorism is likely to dry up when enough of its adherents reject the view that it is the best way to achieve change. We need also to assess whether or not non-state terrorists are in fact *right* to consider this method to be the most efficacious way of achieving their various political goals. The issue of justifying the use of violence remains rightly prominent and complex.[12] With respect to such assessments in relation to terrorism, we need to know how far and in what ways terrorism actually works (or does not) in historical and political practice, and the precise dynamics that have been involved. If we want fully to understand terrorism analytically then we need not only to identify what people think to be the case, but also to assess systematically what has actually been the historical reality.

Among other things, terrorism is an instrumental business: people become involved in the terrorist process in order to achieve something else. To understand this process—to understand what terrorism actually *is*—we need to know how far such instrumentalism is justified by what has or has not been achieved. This involves taking non-state terrorism doubly seriously: treating it as the product of motivations and arguments which deserve serious, respectful engagement; and also assessing it as something worthy of honest, Popperian interrogation.

If 'Does Terrorism Work?' is an analytically and intellectually important question, I also think that it possesses a practical significance. If, for example, it proves to be the case that terrorism overwhelmingly has not led to the achievement of its practitioners' central goals; or that it has been a tactic which has tended repeatedly to appeal to people because it can achieve objectives of one kind rather than another; or that it tends to work least well in certain contexts, environments, or counter-terrorist atmospheres—then the practical importance of this for many people (terrorists and counter-terrorists among them) could be huge.

It is worth remembering that state responses to terrorism almost certainly do more to shape the world and its politics than do non-state terrorist acts themselves. States' reactions to the June 1914 killing of Franz Ferdinand transformed the world through the catastrophe of the First World War;[13]

state responses to the atrocity of 11 September 2001 altered the twenty-first century in decisive fashion also, with US priorities and policies, and international relations and conflicts, all being profoundly rearranged.

And if it is indeed responses to non-state terrorism (rather than terrorist acts themselves) which are decisively crucial, and if most of us think that a reduction in terrorist violence would improve the world by lessening human suffering, then a fuller understanding of the dynamics and effects of terrorism might yield some practical as well as analytical benefit.

This might be judged especially important if we admit with appropriate humility that our efforts to deal with non-state terrorist violence have often been deeply flawed. For example, the years of the post-9/11 War on Terror (easily the most extensive, ambitious, expansive, expensive attempt ever made to extirpate non-state terrorists and terrorism) in fact witnessed an increase in the numbers both of terrorist actions and of terrorist-generated fatalities. As economist Eli Berman has pointed out, in the years immediately preceding 9/11, the monthly global death toll from terrorism stood at 109 deaths per month. During the six years after 9/11 (years during which the War on Terror was aggressively pursued) this monthly figure rose from 109 to 158, even excluding terrorist attacks in Afghanistan and Iraq. If deaths from attacks in Afghanistan and Iraq are included, then the monthly death toll from terrorism rose from 109 to 529 (during the six War on Terror years which followed 11 September 2001). Whatever else it achieved during these years, the War on Terror clearly did not achieve a reduction in fatal terroristic violence. Quite the reverse. As Berman starkly stated: 'global terrorism is worsening.'[14] Again, as terrorism scholar Ekaterina Stepanova has put it, 'Since 1998, the main indicators of global terrorist activity (ie numbers of incidents, injuries, and fatalities) have increased significantly.' During the period 1998–2006, the annual total number of terrorist incidents rose from 1,286 to 6,659, the annual number of terrorism-related fatalities grew from 2,172 to 12,070, and the annual total of terrorism-related injuries rose from 8,202 to 20,991; the number of terrorist incidents for 2001 (1,732) is dwarfed by the figure for 2006 (6,659); and so 'one of the main stated goals of the US-led "global war on terrorism"—to curb or diminish the terrorist threat worldwide—has largely failed; all major indicators of terrorism activity show that the overall situation has gravely deteriorated since 2001, partly as a consequence of the "global war on terrorism" itself'.[15]

I am not arguing that if we had understood more fully the extent to which terrorism worked, then everything would have been fine in the post-9/11

effort to reduce terrorist violence. But it does seem to me strongly possible
that if states more fully knew how far and in what ways terrorism worked
(and does not work, and why) then they would be able to respond much
more effectively to it in practice. If it were demonstrated that the effectiveness of terrorism in changing the world in its perpetrators' favoured direction was not as great as is often feared, then the frequent and self-damaging
overreaction by states when they are provoked by terrorist attack might, to
some degree, be helpfully offset. There are those who think a certain kind
of terrorism to be 'the greatest danger facing the world today'.[16] Majority
scholarly opinion probably favours an alternative view (namely, that many
people exaggerate the threat or danger posed by non-state terrorism, consequently risking unwarranted panic or overreaction);[17] and there has certainly on occasions been a disjunction between degrees of anxiety and levels
of eventual threat. In the immediate aftermath of 9/11, for example, opinion
poll evidence showed that 49 per cent of Americans worried a 'great deal'
and 38 per cent worried 'somewhat' about further terrorist attacks in the
USA; two years later the respective figures had shifted to 25 per cent and
46 per cent. In reality, in the five years after 9/11 the annual number of
American deaths (worldwide) from terrorism never exceeded 100;[18]
'Terrorism is a peculiar category of violence, because it has a cockeyed
ratio of fear to harm.'[19]

Much has been written about the psychological processes which might
explain such an exaggerated anxiety,[20] and much has also been argued about
the dangers of state overreaction to terrorist acts.[21] But we will only fully
know whether we *do* in fact exaggerate and overreact regarding terrorism,
once we properly know the extent to which terrorism represents an effective and successful means of changing politics and society through terrible
violence. We might, after all, be right to over-attend to what are very low
probabilities, if those low-probability events repeatedly and significantly
succeed in forcing people into historical and political paths which they
would otherwise not have taken. But it is also true that if terrorism is shown
to succeed more in obtaining goals of one kind than of another, then our
responses to it might become more sharply focused and more proportion-
ately effective than they have sometimes proved to be in the past.

Again, if it were demonstrated that terrorism tended not to achieve its
central aims, then this would lend weight to practical arguments against its
use by non-state actors themselves. As Virginia Held argues, a potentially
promising 'argument against terrorism is that it does not achieve its perpetrators''

objectives and that other means are not only more justifiable but also more successful'.[22] There is suggestive evidence that terrorists themselves might at times exaggerate the possibility of terrorism working;[23] but we will only be able properly to judge this if we honestly and systematically examine the question in serious detail.

So there can be little doubt, I think, about the high importance of the question that we are addressing in this book; and this is reflected in the judgment of one of the greatest of all terrorism scholars, Professor Martha Crenshaw: 'Terrorism is assumed to display a collective rationality. The group possesses collective preferences or values and selects terrorism as a course of action from a range of perceived alternatives. Efficacy is the primary standard by which terrorism is compared with other methods of achieving political goals.'[24]

II

But within the literature on terrorism there has been less scholarly debate over the question 'Does Terrorism Work?' than there has been over issues of definition, causation, and appropriate response.[25] In part, this might be because of the numerous difficulties inherent in trying to answer the question (about which, more in a moment). Certainly, the question of whether terrorism produces better outcomes than might be reached through alternative methods, is one that is more often raised than it is satisfactorily answered.[26] In the debates that have emerged to date, opinions have ranged rather widely and, at times, controversially and in sharp-edged form. There are some, such as the eminent lawyer Alan Dershowitz, who have argued very strongly that terrorism has been allowed to work far too effectively in the past. 'The real root cause of terrorism', Dershowitz claims, 'is that it is successful—terrorists have consistently benefited from their terrorist acts. Terrorism will persist as long as it continues to work for those who use it, as long as the international community rewards it, as it has been doing for the past thirty-five years.' According to such a view, 'Terrorism will persist because it often works, and success breeds repetition,' and there is a need to alter our response as a result:

> the 'root cause' of terrorism that must be eliminated is its success...Before September 11, terrorism worked—not in every case and not for every group,

but often enough to be seen as a successful tactic for bringing about considerable change.... In all, the international community responded to terrorism
between 1968 and 2001 by consistently rewarding and legitimizing it, rather
than punishing and condemning it.... Any rational terrorist group that operates according to cost–benefit calculation will, at least in theory, be inclined to
opt for the tactic or tactics that hold the best prospect for furthering their
goals. At the moment, that tactic is terrorism.[27]

Other scholars have also suggested that terrorism has, historically, proven
to be successful. 'Terrorism often works. Extremist organizations such as al-
Qaida, Hamas, and the Tamil Tigers engage in terrorism because it frequently
delivers the desired response.'[28] Again, 'The main reason that suicide terrorism is growing is that terrorists have learned that it works.'[29] And other scholars too have suggested that terrorism has possessed considerable efficacy.[30]

In stark contrast, there are other students of the subject who have reached
very different assessments. Veteran terrorism scholar David Rapoport has
claimed that, 'By their own standards, terrorists rarely succeed';[31] another
very distinguished expert in the field, Conor Gearty, has pithily argued that
'terrorism has achieved little of any consequence. No government has fallen
because of its attacks, comparatively few casualties have been sustained, and
no terrorist group has achieved anything more than a fraction of its long-
term aims.'[32] Similar arguments can be found elsewhere in the field: 'terrorism ends, usually badly for the terrorists. Few terrorist groups achieve their
aims, and most enter a death-spiral, more often than not substantially of
their own making';[33] 'campaigns of terrorism—shocking and brutal as they
may seem—rarely succeed in achieving their stated objectives';[34] 'terrorist
groups rarely achieve their policy objectives'; 'terrorist success rates are
actually extremely low';[35] 'Violent non-state actors have historically had
limited success in achieving their strategic objectives... history shows that no
group pursuing an agenda of political violence has ever triumphed in a wealthy,
liberal democracy. They have rarely achieved much in non-democracies
either.'[36] Even a scholar such as John Arquilla, who very learnedly sets out
what irregular combatants overall have achieved historically, argues that,
'While it has been hard to extirpate terrorist organizations, it has proved just
as difficult to point to many cases in which they have achieved their aims.'[37]
Other leading experts too have tended towards the view that terrorists tend
not to achieve their goals and aims.[38]

Reinforcing such scepticism, other scholars have argued powerfully that
non-violent methods have proved far more successful than violent ones in

the pursuit of political change. According to this argument, civil resistance allows much better than do violent methods for attracting diverse, large-scale groups of activists, participants, and supporters to mass-based struggle; 'non-violent resistance has been strategically superior to violent resistance during the twentieth and twenty-first centuries'; 'Non-violent campaigns tend to succeed more often than violent campaigns in all regions of the world.'[39]

So we have here a subject on which scholarly opinion can be very sharply (at times, very controversially) divided. As terrorism scholar Max Abrahms succinctly puts it, 'Terrorism scholars are divided over whether terrorism is an effective tactic.'[40] And the situation becomes more complicated still when we note the thoughts of those people who have presented the issue as one open only to more ambivalent answer. One of the founding scholars in terrorism studies, Paul Wilkinson, for example, pointed out that terrorism 'has proven a low-cost, low-risk, potentially high-yield method of struggle', yet also that it has been one which 'very rarely succeeds in delivering strategic goals'.[41] He elaborated his view more fully elsewhere: 'the history of modern terrorism campaigns shows that terrorism as a major weapon has only very rarely succeeded in achieving a terrorist group's strategic goals'; 'However, there is a key difference between terrorists gaining all their strategic goals and terrorists having a strategic impact on macro-political and strategic events and developments. With careful timing and skilful planning terrorists can certainly have a strategic impact on international relations and politics from time to time'; 'although it is clear that terrorism rarely, if ever, wins strategic political goals, it has an impressive record in gaining such things as massive world-wide publicity, extortion of large ransom payments, and the release of considerable numbers of imprisoned terrorists'.[42] Another distinguished terrorism scholar, Professor Louise Richardson, has likewise suggested that 'Terrorist groups have been singularly unsuccessful in delivering the political change they seek, but they have enjoyed considerable success in achieving their near-term aims.'[43] Echoing this view, Dipak Gupta has lucidly argued that, 'while terrorist organizations are most often able to achieve their short-term strategic objectives, very few can reach their long-term goals'.[44]

In their meticulous study of terrorist attacks in Israel during 1988–2006, Eric Gould and Esteban Klor found that local terror incidents did render Israeli people more willing to yield territorial concessions to their Palestinian opponents, but also that if the levels of terrorism rose beyond a certain point then this prompted Israelis in fact to harden their opposition to such concessions; they also found that terrorism had the effect of making people more likely to vote for right-wing parties, but within a context of right-wing parties moving politically to the left against the background of terrorist pressure. As such, terrorism emerges from their work as a potentially 'effective strategy', but one which 'beyond a certain threshold can backfire on the political goals of terrorist factions'.[45]

III

As suggested earlier, it might be that there has been less extensive debate about terrorism's efficacy than about other aspects of non-state terrorism precisely because it is such a very difficult question to answer. I suspect that some of the fractious controversy within the existing debate has its origins in some of the same difficulties. For, if the question 'Does Terrorism Work?' is an important and a controversial one, then it is also a deeply difficult problem. My hope is that the approach adopted in this book will help to overcome at least some of the hermeneutical challenges involved here, and it is important to set out first what these main difficulties presented by our question actually are. I think that there are centrally five: the problem of defining terrorism; the difficulty of agreeing what it might actually mean to say that terrorism does 'work'; the problem of for whom the terrorism might be judged to work; the entangled nature of processes of causation in human behaviour; and the particular difficulties inherent in the sources pertaining to terrorist violence.

The notorious difficulty in defining terrorism[46] should not immobilize us. Many important phenomena (nationalism, revolution, empire, colonialism, class, fascism, Marxism, security)[47] elude consensual definition, but we do not consequently avoid analysing them or using these terms. As one leading authority argued many years ago, although an agreed and comprehensive definition of terrorism continues to elude us, 'To argue that terrorism cannot be studied until such a definition exists is manifestly absurd.'[48] This is not to ignore the problems involved. Elsewhere,[49] I have argued that the main definitional difficulties lie in the vast range of available, conflicting, existing definitions;[50] the issue of whether 'terror' is in fact more literally, definitively central to this violence than it is to other kinds of activity (such as criminal violence, or violence in orthodox warfare); the problem of whether terrorism is something done only by non-state actors, or whether state violence might also deserve the label;[51] the difficulty inherent in defining terrorist violence according to its targets (civilians, for example, or non-combatants); the similar problem of whether one can identify certain acts as inherently terroristic (suicide bombing, hostage-taking);[52] the difficulty in the overlap between terrorist activity and other kinds of violence (civil war, guerrilla war, insurgency, rebellion); the problem of change over time (could an anarchist bomb-thrower of the 1880s and a potential nuclear terrorist of the 2080s really be sheltered under the same umbrella term?); and the pejorative connotations so commonly involved in people's use of the word.

And these difficulties are not trivial when addressing the question 'Does Terrorism Work?' Should we, for example, ask the question only in relation to non-state actors, despite the fact that so much terrorizing violence with a political aim has been carried out historically by states? Are we, given the profound changes involved over the long history of terrorism, best to limit our discussion to a briefer rather than a longer time period from the past? Given that so many people assume that the term 'terrorism' necessarily refers to something villainous and unjustified, would we be better not using the term at all, but opting for a discussion under different phrasing altogether?

I'll address these and other concerns in a moment, after setting out the definition of terrorism to which I still hold:

> Terrorism involves heterogeneous violence used or threatened with a political aim; it can involve a variety of acts, of targets, and of actors; it possesses an important psychological dimension, producing terror or fear among a directly threatened group and also a wider implied audience in the hope of maximizing political communication and achievement; it embodies the exerting and implementing of power, and the attempted redressing of power relations; it represents a subspecies of warfare, and as such it can form part of a wider campaign of violent and non-violent attempts at political leverage.[53]

I believe that this definition substantially resolves the problems outlined earlier. The enormous range of competing definitions of the word 'terrorism' should not lead scholars to abandon a term which will continue to be widely used; rather, it should ensure that we clearly, honestly, and carefully define the term as we will use it. On the issue of how distinctively 'terror' is literally involved in terrorism, it seems to me fair to acknowledge the important role that terror is intended to play in producing its political effect in this kind of violence.[54] The issue of the state is a complex one. My definition above allows for the practitioners of terrorism to be state (as well as non-state) actors; and I have made clear elsewhere my view that much violence carried out in orthodox warfare deserves the term 'terrorism', even though it is practised by states.[55] I don't think this to be a particularly heterodox approach, in fact: many scholars have been explicit about the reality that states themselves have deployed violence to political purpose with deliberate, knowing, terrorizing effect.[56] The real question, it seems to me, is whether it makes sense to consider state and non-state terrorism synoptically or separately. I still think the latter to be the better approach, in terms of the main focus of a particular book. The dynamics of states (their scale, their origins, their ambitions, their inheritances) seem to me to differ so significantly even from those of very powerful non-state groups that a fully synoptic analysis of both kinds of actor in the same study would be impossible to carry out effectively. In this book, therefore, I will be considering that specific branch of terrorism carried out by non-state actors, even though I adhere to the view that much of what states have historically done and what they continue to do might be labelled terroristic (and though I will be making clear the role that terroristic violence by states has had in generating non-state terrorism by groups like al-Qaida, Hamas, the Provisional IRA, and ETA).

I am sceptical about how persuasively we can define terrorism according to particular kinds of target. Certainly, if acts of terrorism can indeed be 'easily and unsubjectively defined as organized violence that targets civilians',[57] then very many acts of formal warfare or organized crime throughout history would fit the description. More problematically, many acts of terrorist violence simultaneously kill civilians and others, but it would seem macabre and strange to suggest that some of those killed by a bomb were victims of terrorism, while others killed by the same bomb were not. Similarly, those violent acts which people most commonly identify with terrorism tend also to be methods which non-terrorists have used and continue to use.[58] So my definition allows for various kinds of targets and of acts.

The difficulty of related phenomena is a very serious one when asking whether terrorism works, since so many terrorist groups use multiple methods, both violent and non-violent. But if an organization at times uses terrorism, but at other points in its career can extend its activities to the level of what might be termed guerrilla or civil war, we need to be careful about which kind of violence is (or is not) working for them.[59] My definition addresses this issue by frankly acknowledging that terrorism can form part of combined and wider kinds of struggle; and this book will assess in context the varied effectiveness of different kinds of violence (and also of non-violent factors) in producing the actors' desired results.

Change over time will be addressed through a direct effort to recognize historical particularity over lengthy periods (vital for all four of our chapter-length case studies, for example), and it does seem to me that (as with many major political phenomena, such as revolution, or nationalism, or war) change over time need not rule out the usefulness of a term which is applied across decades or even centuries. There have been numerous periods in the past when observers have claimed to detect a decisively 'new' terrorism, so distinct from what preceded it that previous explanations and paradigms would supposedly fail to work. I tend to be sceptical about many such claims. As one of the greatest of all scholars of terrorism, Martha Crenshaw, has put it regarding recent arguments concerning the emergence of a supposedly new terrorism: 'the departure from the past is not as pronounced as many accounts make it out to be. Today's terrorism is not a fundamentally or qualitatively new phenomenon but grounded in an evolving historical context. Much of what we see now is familiar, and the differences are of degree rather than kind. . . . old and new have more in common than proponents of a new terrorism seem to think.'[60]

Finally, it is true that 'terrorism' tends to be a term used in deeply condemnatory fashion.[61] But my definition above allows us to use the word without assuming that those who practise such violence are necessarily making immoral or illegitimate choices when they do decide to deploy it. As with words such as imperialism, fascism, or colonialism, I think the appropriate scholarly approach should be to define and use the term in an analytically clarifying manner, rather than to use it in a necessarily pejorative way. Some will understandably resent the application of the term terrorism to the groups that are focused on in my chapter-length case studies. I understand and respect that view. But I don't suggest that only they have used terroristic violence in the conflicts within which they have been involved; so too, on occasions, have their state and indeed some other opponents. Nor do I imply necessary criticism by using the term terrorism in connection with them: I leave open the possibility that one might judge the violence of al-Qaida, the Provisional IRA, Hamas, or ETA to have been justified and legitimate. Moreover, I think that most observers would think that (whether legitimate or not, and whatever else they have done) these four groups have, at times, practised violence which might fairly be considered terroristic, and that their inclusion in this discussion is therefore justifiable. Even if one thinks that some al-Qaida-related violence has occurred within civil war settings, for example, a historically minded, contextual analysis makes it hard to deny that the group has on occasions practised terrorism.[62]

In any case, insofar as the word terrorism carries with it a suggestion of negative consequences, it might not be the most inappropriate term to use, when viewed from the position of its actual victims. Even if we were to judge a particular act of terrorism to be justified, it is very possible that its human consequences might be horrific to witness, and its malignity a very important element of the action; to use a term analytically need not mean that we lose the valuable sense of awfulness implied by its past or by its practical effects.

So much for defining 'terrorism'. Not much simpler is the issue of defining what it might mean to say that terrorism 'works', and this is the second main difficulty inherent in our question.[63] If (as is the case in the respective analyses cited above from very able scholars such as Dershowitz and Abrahms) people are using different senses of what the word means, then it is unlikely that we will get as decisive a debate as would be ideal. When Alan Dershowitz says that terrorism works, he clearly includes as terrorist success the gaining of world attention towards, or sympathy for, or recognition of a cause; or international approbation for individual terrorists; or the release of prisoners; or special treatment during incarceration for terrorists; or recruitment to terrorist organizations.[64] In contrast, Max Abrahms does not refer to success at 'an operational or tactical level' but rather focuses on terrorists' achievement of their 'core policy objectives': it is 'the notion that terrorism is strategically effective' that really interests him, though his fourfold categorization ('total success', 'partial success', 'limited success', 'no success') offers valuable subtlety to his analysis.[65]

Other scholars, assessing the efficacy of various methods of struggle, adopt different criteria again. So in Erica Chenoweth and Maria Stephan's excellent book on civil resistance and rival means of struggle, they make clear that: 'For our study, to be considered a "success" a campaign had to meet two conditions: the full achievement of its stated goals (regime change, anti-occupation, or secession) within a year of the peak of activities and a discernible effect on the outcome, such that the outcome was a direct result of the campaign's activities.'[66]

Now, if we are to treat terrorism as we treat other kinds of major human activity, then we should probably assume that it might work in complex, layered, very varied ways (as do so many of our activities as a species). Failure to recognize that potential complexity of 'working' will risk thinning out any answer that we might collectively reach. Terrorists will tend to set out more than one kind of goal for their violence (ultimate goals as opposed to short-term ambitions; a hierarchy of desired political changes); they may well be motivated by far more than their ostensible manifesto ambitions; as with so many kinds of human activity, success might need to be considered in terms not only of ultimate goals but also of more complex (at times, much more limited) outcomes; and understanding what 'working' means might vary from local and specific case to case, and from period to period, therefore necessitating very nuanced and closely focused assessment in context.

As my own definition of it suggests, terrorism is a heterogeneous phenomenon involving complex social behaviour, and so the extent to which it works is likely to involve heterogeneity also: 'Terrorism is a *method* which can be used for an infinite variety of goals.'[67] This being the case, we should probably beware answers which look suspiciously neat, and we should resist over-simplification. We will need to set out precisely a complex framework within which to judge (subtly, rather than mechanically) how far terrorism might be thought to have worked. This will involve reflection on how far terrorism has been effective when set against the alternatives available, at the time, to those who used it. Did it work better than other modes of struggle would have done in context?

It has been argued that 'Terrorist campaigns are frequently mounted by organizations that have failed to bring about their desired changes by other means, i.e., they are politically weak.'[68] If this is true, then in such instances were there really better means available for pursuing redress of important grievance? Not unrelatedly, one has to consider the degree to which success can be sufficient to have justified the damage done to lives and societies by terroristic violence. Can the achievements which seemingly vindicate terrorism really be considered to have done so when seen through the lens of broken lives and limbs? Put another way, even if it is established that terrorism produced greater progress than peaceful methods would have done in that context, was the difference between the two alternative outcomes sufficient to justify the awfulness of what the violent route actually involved?

A third difficulty lies in the issue of 'Does Terrorism Work—For Whom?' If a terrorist cause—say, that of the Basque separatists ETA—endures over a lengthy period of time, then one has to assess how far there might be a different sense of terrorism 'working' at different stages of the organization's struggle. Even if the group's personnel remained substantially the same, such people's goals and expectations might be expected to alter as their individual lives and group endeavours and contexts changed. Being a terrorist over a period of years is a different matter from becoming one in the first place; it is certainly possible that groups engaging in terroristic violence might begin with a set of political goals of which they partially lose clear sight when the dynamics of violent struggle become paramount in their day-to-day, combative vision.[69] Moreover, some terrorist groups think in very long timelines indeed. If one considers a struggle to be part of a centuries-long war, then assessing the extent of success even after a quarter of a millennium might be thought premature. This can work in numerous ways, of course. If a terrorist campaign aims at a political outcome and seems to achieve it in terms of the establishment of new political structures, can we really say that such terrorism has worked until we see how far those structures have in fact been able to deliver durably the kind of societal transformation which was the ultimate motivation of the violent actors? Attentiveness to historical context and period, and to the complex contours of change over fluid time, is therefore vital.

Relatedly, even at any one moment it is likely that different people within a non-state terrorist group will have differing motivations and goals, or at least varied priorities in terms of which of the organization's ambitions are most important to them. There could be variation between different locations of experience (al-Qaida operatives in 2003 in different countries, for example); between the various layers of a group (an inner ring might experience its campaign's success, failure, legacy, and achievements differently from those in more outer rings); and between different individuals even in one location and on the same organizational level. So there is a need to listen carefully to many voices as we assess terrorist success and failure and the gradations in between. It is not that we should establish simplistic divisions between analysis at the individual and group levels (since the two are so deeply interwoven). Rather, we should be sensitive to the ways in which the relationship between the two (and between different kinds of group level) can illuminate our reading of the true ways in which terrorism operates. Moreover, terrorism can work in unexpected ways, and might benefit people whom it was not even intended to advantage.

The fourth main difficulty in answering the question 'Does Terrorism Work?' is even more serious, and relates to the entangled nature of causation in human activity. Political change tends to be brought about by complex behaviour patterns of action and interaction, and by frequently multiple lines of causation. How can we be sure that it is terrorist violence which has occasioned the change in question, rather than other kinds of struggle carried out with the same purpose, or by factors (such as wider economic, or ideological, or technological developments) over which terrorist actors had little or no control at all? Separating out the effect of terrorists' terrorism from their own other activity (terrorists don't just do terrorism) and from the activity of other people is extraordinarily difficult, given the interlinking of so much human behaviour and thought. That so much of what occurs in the political past seems to do so according to contingency rather than close planning renders the issue more problematic still, as we try to identify the genuinely causal drivers of historical change.

Finally, there is the fact that in considering terrorism we are dealing with a subject for which there exist specific difficulties relating to evidence and sources. Even terrorist organizations from the past can remain to some degree opaque; this is clearly even more of an issue when we assess contemporary, still-active organizations and individuals. So gaining access to evidence can have its problems (and even some danger). A related problem here is that of secrecy (since no effective terrorist organization will be casual about access to its personnel or to its most honest assessments). Another concerns the issue of the potential difference between what groups and individuals publicly say and what they might privately think to be the case, between what they ostensibly value and what they privately prioritize. Yet another grows out of the understandably tendentious nature of so much terrorist and counter-terrorist argument; some non-state terrorists (though by no means all) have at times exhibited a near-Wagnerian tendency towards self-justification, as any serious reader of shelves of terrorist memoirs will be able to confirm. And terrorists and their counter-terrorist opponents have even stronger reasons than the rest of us, perhaps, to look back at previous achievements through lenses of comforting self-deception and post-hoc rationalization. So the sources and evidence relating to terrorist efficacy can be awkward in ways related to, but not limited to, their somewhat clandestine quality.

Given these serious difficulties (defining terrorism; agreeing what it means for terrorism to work; asking for whom such terrorism might work anyway; the entangled nature of causation; and the particular problems of sources in this field), we should approach our question with considerable humility and an appreciation of how partial any answer will probably prove.

But I don't think the difficulties are so great that we cannot move the debate forward by producing a more systematic and careful answer to the question than has yet been generated in the existing literature.

IV

In trying to produce such an account, and in order most effectively to answer our question, I argue in this book that we need to adopt an explicitly historical approach to the subject. Unlike most who have addressed this question in books and articles to date, I write as a political historian. The study of terrorism has long and rightly and fruitfully been multidisciplinary,[70] with mutual and beneficial learning between scholars of various traditions. So it is certainly not my contention that history[71] alone can offer the right answer to this question. For all of its failings, this book has benefited greatly from the insights and acumen of scholars from, as well as history, the disciplines of political science, international relations, law, psychology, medicine, theology, literature, sociology, geography, economics, anthropology, and philosophy. And, in a period of ever-increasing academic specialism, I hope that the argument of this book might engage readers from many different disciplinary parts of the intellectual world.

Moreover, history today is not divided from other disciplines by neat or uncrossable lines. There is a rather desirable blurring of boundaries, some important methodological sharing, and a willingness to be informed and influenced by ideas and approaches from other disciplines. As a result, many bibliographies in most disciplines are now effectively hybrid.

Despite this, each discipline has distinctive things to offer and it seems broadly accepted now (by people across a range of scholarly disciplines and hermeneutical approaches) that historical understanding and analysis are vital to any proper explanation of, and response to, terrorism.[72] So what is it that someone trained as a historian can distinctively and valuably bring to answering the question Does Terrorism Work? (Readers already convinced that historians can bring something of real value might choose to pass over this section! But I think that it's worth setting out here in detail the nature of that historically minded contribution, and I hope that some people will find it helpful.)

There's unlikely ever to be comprehensive agreement about exactly what constitutes the historian's method; and this is understandable enough, given the vast range of diverse, ever-evolving perspectives held by scholars regarding that process.[73] Yet I think it's worthwhile to set out briefly some key elements of what a historical method might be thought to involve, and then to apply this to our study of the question 'Does Terrorism Work?' And I want here to argue that there are five key elements of a distinctively historical approach which might be particularly stressed as of high importance for a book such as this.

The first concerns the vital importance of long memory and of properly understood change over time. If we're going to address the problem identified above, of terrorism working or not working for people at different periods of a lengthy struggle, then such an approach is undeniably essential. Sadly, however, much existing analysis of terrorism ignores the long inheritances of past experience from which we might draw important understanding. And if we are to avoid the potentially dangerous solipsism of the present, then historians' preparedness to attend to long-term frameworks, backgrounds, and developments is important. So my case-study chapters on the politics of al-Qaida, Hamas, the Provisional IRA, and ETA will attend to relevant long-term inheritances. This should not be a controversial point. I don't think it's plausible to suggest that, for example, we could adequately understand Hamas's violence in Israel/Palestine if we started our analysis with events in the 1980s with that militant group's establishment. Like so many other cases of terroristic violence, the roots here are too long-tangled in a complex, fluid past for this to be feasible. This is especially so given the problem already identified regarding when we can reasonably judge that terrorism has or has not worked, if those who are involved in it do (as here) think in terms of long time-frameworks.

Yet vast amounts of writing on the subject of terrorism display a very short-termist, even amnesiac, quality.[74] Much research on the subject focuses (understandably) on contemporary events and (less forgivably) on rather short-term assessments of what are really much longer-term phenomena.[75] No one scholar can command the whole range of the human past (and I readily admit my own limitations here). But I think that a strong attempt to draw on evidence relating to long pasts is essential if we are to answer our question satisfactorily. As we do so, historians' long obsession with the precise nature of change over time offers further advantages.[76] Such an approach necessitates recognition of developments and change at numerous interwoven levels (individuals, organizations, communities, nations, transnational phenomena). It also means that we have to be equally attentive to continuities in the past, to what has *not* changed. Carefully distinguishing between the continuous and the ephemeral lies at the heart of historical scholarship, and this often leads to a healthy scepticism about supposed historical watersheds. Clearly there can be huge shifts between periods, and recognizing this is of high importance.[77] But, given historians' frequent discovery of a complex mixture of change and continuity, such scholars often evince doubts about supposedly new eras or about allegedly new phenomena which turn out, on close interrogation, not to be anything like so novel. Reflection in a later chapter on how far even 9/11 inaugurated a new period of politics will provide one example. More broadly, our assessment of how far terrorism works will be helpfully informed by historians' recognition that even their own necessary periodizations ('the twentieth century', 'inter-war', 'post-revolutionary') disguise continuities across fault lines, and tend therefore to retain a certain artificiality and fragility (and to seem much more plausible when viewed from one place than from another).

For historical 'periods' do not tend to start or end neatly, and different aspects of life and politics can change at different paces. It has often been noted that there exist problems with any simple periodization of historical time,[78] and the possibility of multiple temporalities or overlapping time sequences is certainly significant. If rival actors in a violent conflict consider it to have begun at different times, or to have endured for different periods, then this will undoubtedly influence how one might read the degree to which terrorism has succeeded or failed.

As we reflect on such historical fluidity, issues of chronology and of narrative can prove very helpful. To some degree, the question 'Does Terrorism Work?' demands at least a partially chronological answer, since it addresses the issue of violent actions aimed at moving from earlier Point A to more desirable and later Point B. And, though many historians have shifted significantly away from narrative as the way of structuring their books, it remains true both that narrative has long formed a basis for explanations of the past as offered by historians,[79] and also that narrative remains for many scholars a vital backdrop to contextual assessment of the degree of change over time.[80]

This current book will certainly not adopt a crude approach to narrative history.[81] But it does recognize the value of understanding linear time and precise chronological sequences as we consider changing contexts and what has actually caused them to alter. Many terrorists cited in these pages have thought very much in terms of serial time and of the changes that they wanted to effect as they shaped particular political narratives; that historians are familiar with such details is therefore appropriate, and the solving of historical problems and the delivery of narrative developments can be mutually supportive endeavours.[82]

One of the benefits of close attention to historical time is the possibility of adopting a profoundly context-specific approach to explanation (and therefore a strong appreciation of uniqueness), and this is the second historical attitude of mind that I want to emphasize as we think about our method. If we want to know the different ways in which terrorism works for different people at one time and in one place, then attention to deep context is essential. And, paradoxically, subtle reflection on the diachronic (the study of something through its historical development as it changes over time) reinforces the interpretative necessity of analysing things synchronically (by focusing on studying a phenomenon at a particular period, and so understanding it fully in its contextual moment).

Some time ago, Professor Geoffrey Elton's truculent historiographical manifesto suggested that historians' work 'is "idiographic", that is, it particularizes, and not "nomothetic", that is, designed to establish general laws'.[83] Though many today would eschew much of Elton's historiographical approach, I think a large number of historians would still feel comfortable with the notion that we must ultimately respect the unrepeatable specificity of each event, struggle, person, context, setting, and episode that we seek to understand. Put starkly, historians still tend towards particularization.[84] (In this sense, ultimately, each of our four case studies in this book remains unique and, in key ways, different from the others.)

And the point is surely this: that the specific values and opinions held by people in particular settings of place and time are a vital ingredient for any recipe for understanding the efficacy of terrorism.[85] This is especially so given the residual locality of so much terrorism.[86] The motivations behind terrorist violence, and the assessment of how far such violence has actually worked, very often possess such local dynamics that the explanation of particular context is essential. If we are to deal with the problem of causation (raised above), then explaining events in contextual detail is absolutely necessary. And if we are to deal with the definitional problem that terrorism is often accompanied by other forms of violence and struggle, then again particular contextual explanation will be essential.

Emphasizing contextual specificity has tended to reinforce the importance of what is unique in terms of geographical and temporal context.[87] And contextual details often point up the decisive importance of small-group,

and even individual, action and initiative in practice[88]—something absolutely central to much terrorist activity. The importance of the individual,
and of individual-level explanations as part of our wider understanding, is
much evident in historians' thinking, and it tends at times towards a methodological individualism. In these pages, the vital role of key individuals will
again and again emerge into powerful prominence as a result.

As we think carefully about individual terrorists, we'll recognize the multiple, different roles that such a person can play, and therefore the complexity of the issues involved in terrorist efficacy. For contextual close reading
tends to reinforce in a powerfully distinctive way the idea of the complexity
of lived life: multi-causation, the tangled interrelations between people and
political processes, and the beguiling heterogeneity of even seemingly tightly
controlled groups of people. Many collectivities and groupings turn out, on
serious historical inspection, to be characterized by greater internal heterogeneity, and by much more porous relationships with supposedly antagonistic rival groupings, than is often assumed to be the case.[89] And this is
certainly evident in the study of terrorism (as we will see in each of our
detailed case-study examples).

This all underlines the need for caution when confronted with arguments
suggesting that terrorists might have 'won' or 'lost' in simple terms. Contextually
understood complexity of motivation, intention, and outcome between them
warn us against ideal-type or overly mechanical simplification.

As suggested, historical attention to complexity[90] might help as we try to
deal with the difficulty of the entangled threads of causation and change in
regard to how far terrorism works;[91] it will also allow us to address the myr-
iad ways in which 'working' might be understood in relation to actual, lived
practice. Such an emphasis will certainly complement the valuable contribution of more quantitative methodological approaches, the latter alone
probably being unable to tell us what we need—in all its contingent messiness—to know.[92]

So attention to change over time, and respect for unique context. Allied
to these instincts is (thirdly) the historian's distinctive approach to the range,
nature, and interrogation of sources and evidence (which will, I believe, help
us to address some of the distinctive problems alluded to above regarding
source material and the study of terrorism). One key point here is historians' keenness to examine what might be termed first-hand evidence: material drawn directly from the period and people actually under scrutiny.
This can involve a wide variety of materials, including memoirs, interviews,

newspaper sources, diaries, archivally housed documents (such as letters or memoranda), photographs, organizational files, buildings, economic statistics, novels, paintings, films, music, poems, radio or television programmes, tracts or pamphlets, speeches, governmental reports, and much else from the past. The oft-cited distinction between primary and secondary sources refers to the difference between this kind of evidence from the people and period under examination, and material written about the past in a later period by those engaging in analysis of it. Much discussion of terrorism at present involves regrettably little attention to the wealth of evidence directly generated by terrorists themselves. Identifying and interrogating what remains from the period under scrutiny does provide a significant basis for the fullest understanding of it.

Pursuing first-hand evidence can, for example, allow us to read the complexity of terrorist organizations and their achievements more attentively than is possible without it. One example here is the role of interview material. It still slightly surprises me that so many people who write about terrorists have never actually met one, not least because interviews can unveil otherwise unavailable and invisible views and experiences, through evidence acquired from people who are less salient and powerful than those who are usually quoted; such evidence can also lead one to re-evaluate other kinds of data in fresh and stringent fashion.

Oral evidence presents distinctive challenges, of course (relating to post-hoc rationalization, failures of memory, an instinct towards self-aggrandizement or self-justification, and the like). But these are not insuperable, if this evidence is interrogated in relation to other kinds of available source; and it still seems to me that historically contextualized oral evidence represents an important resource for the analysis of terrorism,[93] and a distinctively vivid and original one if it is carefully used. It is also a type of evidence with which historians have very long been familiar, in fact: both Herodotus and Thucydides drew on oral sources for their enduringly powerful histories. Indeed, interview and other kinds of first-hand evidence allow us to address the oft-lamented difficulty of a supposed lack of primary or adequate data about terrorism.[94]

Primary sources are not the only relevant evidence, of course, and historians (like many other scholars) recognize the need for vast reading across the secondary, academic, and other literatures relevant to the subject. Historical method might, in fact, be judged to necessitate the interrogation of an enormous, rich, wide, and varied range of different kinds of evidence and source materials, primary as well as secondary. Historical research has for many years encompassed far more than the straightforwardly political,[95] for example, and involves 'the use of multiple, converging, independent sources'.[96] Some of these will relate to individual or small-group and local experience; some will be broader in scope; between them, they will help to address the issue of for whom terrorism actually works in practice, allowing us to attend to different levels or units of analysis (individual, small-group, local, organizational, large-group, or transnational), while recognizing the complicated ways in which such different layers of terrorism are interlinked. Evidence, for example, about an organization's perception of success will often tend to be drawn from individual or small-group sources, and there is no neat or easy separation between the individual and the group as we study them.[97] Synoptic, exhaustive assessment of such a painfully broad range of sources will tend to undermine prior, ready-made answers—one of the elements making history such a subversive discipline, and one which relishes the complexity and uniqueness of human endeavour.

Historians' approach towards such varied (often original and direct) evidence also possesses distinctive elements: multiple sources need all to be treated with careful scepticism;[98] they are held to be mutually interrogative and challenging; they're considered in terms of their origins and flaws, their reliability and advantages;[99] they are deployed both in terms of what they compel us to say, and also what they allow us perhaps to suggest; they are read in relation to an almost necessarily multiple causation in human affairs; and they are read also in terms of what is *not* said in them, their silences sometimes being as telling as their noisier testimony.[100]

But how far do historians think that such a wide range of source materials can reveal decisive, consensual, definitive understanding? On a contentious, highly charged subject such as the one that is addressed in this book, there is unlikely to emerge from any discipline an interpretation considered to be final. Evidence is rarely so clear that this kind of question can be unambiguously decided by it, and so a measure of caution and humility is built into the claims that are offered in this book. I suspect that belief in historical objectivity becomes more difficult to sustain, the more seriously one considers the issue; and I fear that the pursuit of rigid neutrality in historians' work is probably rather Quixotic.[101]

Yet historian Peter Novick was surely right to suggest that 'At the very centre of the professional historical venture is the idea and ideal of "objectivity"....It has been the quality which the profession has prized and praised above all others.'[102] The difficulty, as Novick himself well knew, is that historical objectivity in its fullest or total sense (the idea of a scholar analysing a phenomenon entirely without bias on their own part, and with eyes only and neutrally on the independent nature of the thing under scrutiny) seems very unlikely to be attained. This is recognized by many historiographers (of varying historiographical backgrounds),[103] for there cannot be an absolute separation between the student and the thing being studied, between the researcher and the subject of their research;[104] and this tends to mean that there emerges no fully agreed past.[105] Political, social, religious, individual-personal, and other instincts and preferences will prevent a fully objective account emerging from anyone, as will the even more important factor of the date at which one writes, and also the geographical location, since the latter can play a major part in the generation and consumption of historical (as of other scholarly) knowledge,[106] and can do so in ways which particularize and bias author and audience alike according to culture.

Yet this isn't the end of the matter. Rigorous, honest, sceptical engagement with a very wide range of sources regarding the past might not be able to produce absolutely objective history; but it might enable us to offset some of the instincts which any observer might otherwise bring to the subject under study. The fact that historians cannot be fully neutral does not negate the value of being as neutral and disinterested as possible, rather than engaging tendentiously in debates over the past. In this sense, balance and fair-mindedness rather than party allegiance or political loyalty are the key things in the best historical research and writing. Similarly, while it is true that there can be no sheer separation between the observer and the observed, in historical analysis one must acknowledge that the latter did exist and happen whether or not the former decided to look at it, and this places limits on some of the more corrosive arguments against historical knowledge. In historical work, the centre of gravity does ultimately lie in the past, and there is respect for previous actors' prior independence of oneself and one's own world.[107] In this sense, the evidence might not compel agreement with any one interpretation; but serious, professionally detached, empathetic, systematic reading of such evidence might limit the range of authentic analyses which can credibly be sustained as reliable.

So, contrary to scholars like Keith Jenkins, I do not think it is true that 'we can all' legitimately draw from our studies of the past 'whatever conclusions' we like.[108] (Regarding the Rwandan genocide in the 1990s? Regarding the Holocaust? Regarding the history of rape?) The fact that we cannot definitively explain why something occurred—a revolution, for example, or a war—does not mean that all interpretations of it are necessarily equally valid. Carefully considered, the weight of evidence will favour some judgments more forcibly than others, despite ongoing and healthy historiographical debate. So it is *not* merely one person's opinion against another; there are strong scholarly reasons in many cases for judging one historical account more accurate, reliable, and persuasive than a rival.[109]

As one scholar has rightly argued: 'historical knowledge is not, and cannot be, "objective" (that is, empirically derived in its entirety from the object of the enquiry). [But this] does not mean, as sceptics might suppose, that it is therefore arbitrary or illusory.'[110] So the mutability of the past (to borrow an Orwellian phrase) actually has its limits, and historians' methodological debates and self-reflection on this issue offer rich resources, especially with such a highly charged and fiercely contentious issue as the efficacy of terrorism.[111]

So historiographical self-reflection tends to acknowledge that objectivity in any naive sense of full neutrality is unattainable.[112] But beyond a naive attachment to full objectivity there lies an important point regarding what the sources can still allow us to assert. I have argued elsewhere the vital importance of a dispassionate approach to the study of terrorism.[113] For our purposes in this book, the key issue must be to try to avoid inordinate partiality, through as even-handed an interrogation of as wide-ranging a body of evidence as is possible. Primarily, historians tend to ask what happened in the past, and why and how it happened.[114] In doing so, they need to reconstruct various competing experiences and views, as read through many source lenses. It is in this sense that historians still attempt (valuably, in my view) to get as close to objectivity as they practically can do,[115] to avoid self-serving polemic as a result, and to be prepared to reach—on the basis of vast bodies of different kinds of evidence—conclusions which they might initially have preferred not to reach.[116]

Fourth, historians perhaps tend towards scepticism about over-reliance on abstract theorizing, their work offering a helpful complement to the valuably theoretical abstraction more commonly found in some other disciplines engaging with our subject. There is something of a Burkean flavour to this, the past being considered more helpful than abstract philosophizing as one reflects on politics.[117] It is not that historians (and certainly not this one) are hostile to theory.[118] Far from it. But there is frequently a sense that the diverse and rich and complex reality of lived life undermines some of the explanatory power or descriptive illumination offered by Procrustean theoretical argument.[119] So, as hinted earlier, the fact that so much recent analysis of the efficacy or otherwise of terrorism has relied on game-theoretic models[120] might call for complementary attention to what humans have been known—through empirical evidence—actually to have done.[121]

One way of exemplifying this is to consider briefly the enormously important, conceptually sharp-edged contribution made to our subject by philosophers, and to see how history might add decisively to its insights. The wonderfully provocative Ted Honderich has wisely claimed that 'it would be irrational to come to a verdict about political violence without paying care-ful attention to the probability of its actually achieving ends of social change', further asking: 'Is violence never the best means to the end? That is obviously not obvious.'[122] But it might be suggested that to provide an answer to this question involves, among other things, a close reading of what we know about what people have actually achieved in the past in the realm of violence. Yet the striking book by Professor Honderich from which these quotations are taken is one largely innocent of detailed analysis of what has actually happened in the past. Fair enough, given the philosophical nature of that study. But it seems to me that a full answer to the philosopher's important question demands historical reflection and analysis too. Indeed, Honderich (with typical sharp-sightedness) suggests recognition of this himself:

> In the end, when the work of inquiry and reflection has been done, it may be that the strongest arguments against much or some political violence will indeed be those having to do with the probabilities of success. No doubt we can con-clude, now, that such arguments will sometimes be as conclusive as arguments in this area ever can be. No doubt there are situations in which political violence cannot be justified, because it is sufficiently unlikely to work.[123]

Another of Honderich's arresting books leads us to a similar point. There, he states his view 'that the Palestinians have had a moral right to their terror-ism' and further observes: 'Very obviously I take into account the question of whether Palestinian terrorism will work, which includes such considera-tions as its effects on opinions, attitudes, support of third parties, etc. This, presumably, is a political evaluation. So too, presumably, is a judgment of the necessity of Palestinian terrorism, the question of whether there are alterna-tives, no doubt negotiation.'[124] So Honderich—rightly, in my view—considers it inappropriate to assume that we can reach moral evaluations of such terrorism without consideration of these political questions. But these questions of whether terrorism works, and of whether it is necessary, are political questions which can only be answered satisfactorily if we engage also in systematic inquiry about what Palestinians have actually brought about through their violence (a question which a later chapter of this book will address in much detail). Such historical inquiry does not emerge in Honderich's own books; but it might sit usefully—even necessarily—alongside them on the scholarly shelf.

For it's important not merely to ask whether a violent act of terrorism might be justified in some abstract case of injustice, but also to consider this question on the basis of what we know to have happened in the many particular instances in which people have actually deployed such tactics in the past. If we are to assess the morality of political violence, then empirical engagement with the past is unavoidably significant. Yet numerous very sophisticated philosophical studies have often resorted to hypothetical examples when assessing the morality of terrorism, rather than to detailed consideration of actual experiences from the past.[125] Another route to such assessments, however, is the one adopted in this book: namely, to assess in detail what has actually happened in the past, rather than what hypothetical examples might suggest to be the case.[126]

Historians' tendency towards professional scepticism[127] is partly based on this process by means of which the messy, jagged actuality of human activity in the past repeatedly subverts neat, overly constricting models of abstract explanation. This reinforces their doubts about monocausal explanations of events,[128] and it allows varieties of experience and outcome to become more easily visible in our analysis, as complex developments can all be allowed to breathe.

It is also part of the reason why historians (fifthly) tend to be sceptical about notions of inevitability in human behaviour, and to prefer contingency instead within their analytical framework. Eric Foner has put it very crisply: 'events are inevitable only after they happen.'[129] And very many historians find that their research has led them towards scepticism about the notion of historical inevitability,[130] their close inspection of the past demonstrating instead the variety of choices and possibilities inherent within particular historical moments.[131] Indeed, while not all historians stress the importance of contingency,[132] the undermining of assumed inevitabilities and of predetermined outcomes towards which people will inexorably be moved is a very common aspect of historical work[133] (one of many things which make it such a subversive discipline in practice). Here, historians' longstanding emphasis on the role of chance, luck, and accident in the events of the past seems to be supported by recent psychological research,[134] and it usefully casts doubt on some of the political teleologies favoured by terrorist groups and by some of their state opponents too. While activists' pronouncements often suggest an inexorable directionality of progress in historical development towards a particular outcome, scholarly scrutiny of the evidence by contrast frequently suggests that both unanticipated futures[135] and 'unintended consequences'[136] play a major role in significant historical change over time.

Historians have very long reflected on the complex issues of progress and teleology within the human past.[137] But in the tension between contingency and necessity, historians' usual preference for allowing a role for the fortuitous and the unpredictable makes their work resistant to the attempted establishment of general laws possessing predictive reliability,[138] and that is an approach towards which I tend in this current book. Even the very question of what is popularly remembered, and what is not, reinforces our recognition about the unexpected in human activity.[139]

If the past involves so much of the contingent, then this partly explains why there has been something of a return to reflection on the counterfactual within historical scholarship in recent decades, especially in the USA and the UK.[140] This is a question of central relevance to the issue of terrorism's success, since what we are so often asking is whether another method of struggle might have produced a more effective outcome for those who practised the political violence in question. Moreover, contingency and the counterfactual urge us towards comparative reflection. If we are instinctively sceptical about the inevitability of the violence which occurred in situation A, then could the significant achievements brought about through peaceful resistance in situation B have worked instead in that former setting? Uniqueness is no barrier to comparison here, since the question really is whether the unique circumstances of situation A were such as to allow for a non-violent path to have been followed. If so, then why did people (contingently) not take that route? If not, then what were the particular differences between the two settings which drove them apart in their respective trajectories?

There are difficulties for us to consider here, of course, since the counterfactual is both based on contingency and undermined by it also. For a counterfactual narrative to begin, one needs to accept that at historical point H there was some contingency about a decision that was taken, so that the actual decision (H1) might have been rejected for an alternative (H2). The difficulty here is that the longer the counterfactual narrative proceeds forward from H2, the more contingencies there would subsequently be, with other counterfactuals suggesting themselves along the initial counterfactual route.[141] So if, for example, the ETA leadership had opted not to continue their terrorist violence after the 1970s shift to democracy in Spain, then our attempt to build a counterfactual narrative from that point until the present would be complicated by various hypothetical contingencies. ETA's members might have decided to follow this leadership decision, to reject it, or to split into two or more camps. Those who accepted the decision in the 1970s might then have held consistently to that peaceful path, or they might have decided in the 1990s that not enough movement was being achieved through constitutional politics and have sought a return to violence. That return to violence might perhaps have resonated with a sizeable number of Basques, or it might have met with resounding hostility and floundered. And so on. Each counterfactual starting point carries within it the possibility of future contingencies splintering into yet more counterfactuals. This does not, in my view, invalidate the entire counterfactual process; and it certainly does not imply a pervasive historical inevitability: one does not have to believe in the plausibility of long-term counterfactual speculation in order to recognize the vital role frequently played by contingency within the unfolding of the past. But such reflections do make counterfactual argument an endcavour to be engaged with rather humbly and cautiously.

In arguing that history has something distinctive to offer as we ask 'Does Terrorism Work?', I am not suggesting that only historians think critically about evidence, or that only historians evince scepticism about teleology. But I do hold that there is something distinctive in the combination of the elements of methodological approach adumbrated above, and which might be considered a valuable historical methodology as we try to answer the question we have set ourselves. Simultaneous commitment to considering change (and continuity) over very long pasts; to contextual particularization and a consequent acknowledgement of uniqueness and complexity even at small-scale or individual level; to the critical, intimate interrogation of a very wide range of mutually dialogic sources, including many that are first-hand or primary, and to the consideration of what we can (and cannot) therefore credibly claim about human activity; to the sceptical testing of abstract theorizing, setting the claims of the latter against the known knowns of the empirical record of the past; and to a recognition of the interconnected implications of contingency, the counterfactual, and the comparison of residually unique contexts—the *combination* of all of these methodological approaches seems to me to offer something from which the scholarly and public debate on terrorist efficacy might greatly benefit.

V

So, having argued that 'Does Terrorism Work?' is an important, controversial, difficult question, and one which we might profitably address through adopting a historical method, I want finally and relatedly in this Introduction to set out a detailed, systematic framework for understanding what we might consider it to mean to say that terrorism works. Such a framework is, I believe, particularly necessary if we are to overcome the problem identified earlier regarding the issue of what 'working' actually means in complex reality.

In stark terms, I would argue that there could be:

1. strategic[142] victory, with the achievement of a central, primary goal or goals

2. partial strategic victory, in which:

   (a) one partially achieved one's central, primary goal(s)

   (b) one achieved or partially achieved one's secondary (rather than central, primary) strategic goal(s)

   (c) one determined the agenda, thereby preventing one's opponent from securing victory

3. tactical success, in terms of:

   (a) operational successes

   (b) the securing of interim concessions

   (c) the acquisition of publicity

   (d) the undermining of opponents

   (e) the gaining or maintaining of control over a population

   (f) organizational strengthening

4. the inherent rewards of struggle as such, independent of central goals.

First, then, strategic victory, with the achievement of a central, primary goal or goals. Terrorism working in this sense would involve the securing of the group's or the individual's central war aim or aims. Focusing on this issue of central objectives should clearly be the starting point for our analysis, whether those goals involve freedom for a nation or a communal group; the ending of tyranny or of the oppression of one group by another; the expulsion of a foreign power; the achievement of a significant ideological change (to Marxism as society's dominant organizing political philosophy, for example); the achievement of major religious goals, or of social and/or political justice and/or equality; and so on.

Success here will turn decisively on questions of power, especially the attempted redressing of power relations which formed part of our definition of terrorism itself. Intuitively, one might expect strategic victory to prove rather rare. As Lawrence Freedman has noted in his powerful recent study, 'Strategy is often expected to start with a description of a desired end state, but in practice there is rarely an orderly movement to goals set in advance.'[143] As another world-leading expert in the field has similarly noted, governmental policies during war tend not to remain consistent: 'The actual outcomes of the war, even if still desirable from the point of view of at least one of the belligerents, are likely to have been very different from the objectives entertained at its outset.'[144]

Partial strategic victory might come in various forms, I think, including the partial achievement of one's central, primary goal(s). Terrorists might legitimately claim that their violence had worked if they had pursued 100 per cent and, through their activities, brought about what they saw as a very important achievement of a 60 per cent political change in the right direction. Most human ambition on a large scale falls short of full achievement of prior goals, so this possibility seems of high importance in any realistic and fair-minded assessment. A group might seek full independence for a nation state, fail to secure this, but nonetheless bring about the establishment of significantly greater autonomy for their national group than would otherwise have emerged. This might be only a diluted version of what was ultimately desired, but it is not necessarily something that we should judge to be an utter failure. And since the group's recognition of complex and constraining realities might grow during the years of struggle, what the real goals develop into might indeed prove closer to this more moderate outcome than early rhetoric and belief would have suggested. Change over time is again potentially crucial, and likely not to work in ways precisely anticipated by anyone in advance.

Partial strategic victory might also involve the achievement or partial achievement of secondary (rather than central, primary) strategic goals.

Revenge, retaliation, or hitting back at one's enemies rarely appear as the centrally declared objectives of terrorist groups. But, for some activists, they represent vital, motivating secondary ambitions; 'What appears to drive most terrorists...is not the desire or expectation of achieving the primary political objective articulated by their leaders but rather the desire for, and reasonable expectation of achieving, revenge, renown, and reaction';[145] 'If there is a single common emotion that drives the individual to become a terrorist, it is vengeance on behalf of comrades or even the constituency the terrorist aspires to represent.'[146] The vengeful, terrorizing punishment of people whom one hates, or with whom one exists in a state of deep enmity, might be one of the less attractive aspects of terrorist ambition. But it might also (perhaps) be one in which we find terrorists repeatedly succeeding fairly well, and it might be part of the explanation for escalation and cycles of sustained violence in numerous settings. Hitting back at people whom one holds to be (literally or representatively) responsible for prior wrongs lies at the heart of this; 'a major design feature in human nature, self-serving biases, can make each side believe that its own violence was an act of justi-fied retaliation while the other's was an act of unprovoked aggression'.[147] So the frequent self-presentation of a terrorist group's violence as a response to prior aggression represents a significant, attempted justification for activities within this possible terrorist arena of success.

Thankfully, truly exterminatory terrorism has not yet emerged (though it might yet do so).[148] On a smaller scale, however, revanchist violence has played a frequent part in terrorist activity. And it should not surprise us if this might be one area in which terrorism could work well, given that moti-vations towards terrorist violence (as towards so much else) interweave the rational with the visceral. The historian's attention to a wide range of differ-ent kinds of source material is likely to be important here, since without such evidence these layers of complex motivation will be much less likely to become clear.

Terrorism might also work in relation to the achievement of the second-ary strategic goal of sustaining a particular struggle. For some movements, the relevant cause is seen as one likely to endure for decades (even centu-ries) of endeavour. In this sense, mere group survival might embody success for terrorist activists, with the work done in one phase being seen as build-ing or consolidating foundations on which future labourers might work even more effectively. The flame might not be held up in triumph just yet, but its continued burning could—in itself—be seen to represent a significant achievement; and the capacity to carry out lethal terrorist attacks over a sustained period could be interpreted as a marked (if admittedly brutal) accomplishment. Keeping the tradition alive, revivifying it through violent struggle, maintaining a morally just cause, keeping resistance going for the future—all of this might involve a certain symbolic and recusant effectiveness, especially given the very long timeframe within which some terrorist believers do operate. Some hold there to be an inevitable teleology to human experience, and that their struggle will necessarily triumph at a later date; their own role as custodians, therefore, need not bring decisive victory yet for it to be judged to have worked. The seed now sown might only produce harvest for a later generation.

There are limitations to this, of course. Terrorists carry out acts at least partly with an ostensible intention that those acts instrumentally achieve end goals. In itself, therefore, sustaining the struggle might be seen as a rather limited success. So, while Hamas, Hezbollah, and the Taliban might indeed 'excel at violence and terrorism',[149] that still leaves open the issue of whether their violent actions work in terms of the declared goals of the movements in question. But if one does consider the existing political situation to be utterly unacceptable, and if one adheres to a long-term framework for the movement's victory, then avoiding defeat in one's own generation could perhaps, nonetheless, be seen as a form of success.

Partial strategic victory might, again, involve one determining the relevant agenda, thereby preventing one's opponent from securing victory. Your violence might stop an enemy from comfortably or uncontestedly controlling an area; it might spoil a peace or political process whose quality you despise; it might prevent certain settlements or compromises from being considered feasible as an end to the conflict in question (effectively, terrorism here securing you a political veto). More significantly still, I think, agenda-setting terrorist violence might determine how important the relevant issues and grievances are thought to be, and might frame them in a particular fashion that is to your liking. Again, terrorist violence has in the past often generated or deepened polarization between rival groups, thereby constraining the kind of integrated outcome for which some others might wish. And it can emphatically render the status quo untenable, costly, and problematic, through violent terror, chaos, and disorder. You might not win the future; but you can bloodily destroy the present. Moreover, your violence might gain for you a necessary role as a communal interlocutor when political endgames are ultimately arrived at.

If terrorism might work in terms of strategic victory or partial strategic victory, then it might also achieve various types of tactical success. Operationally, attacks can be carried out effectively in terms of their tactical planning: whatever one might decide about the strategic effect of the 9/11 atrocity, for example, there can be little dispute that it represented a dramatic success in tactical terms as an operation. We might also detect tactical success where terroristic violence secures interim concessions for its practitioners. The release of prisoners,[150] the acquisition of funds through ransom demands or other activities,[151] and other shorter-term concessions from opponents might all be considered here (and attention to this level of efficacy also partly offsets the problem of asking 'Does Terrorism Work—For Whom?' A prisoner who was released as an interim concession within a strategically unsuccessful struggle, might still consider that some of their group's violence had perhaps worked well enough).

Another kind of tactical success, potentially autonomous from strategic outcome, might involve the acquisition of publicity:[152] 'seizing attention', as one leading authority has aptly put it;[153] 'The success of a terrorist operation depends almost entirely on the amount of publicity it receives';[154] 'terrorism is a cost effective means of making a statement'.[155] If terrorist violence loudly proclaims a message—gaining headlines at local, national, and/or international levels amid so much news-hungry competition, and securing fame for one's grievance, cause, and demands—then it might be thought that terrorism has worked in magnifying one's own struggle and its significance. As so often with terrorism, relationships are vital here: the work of the media will be necessary to effectively high-profile publicity-seizure, and the nature of that publicity will vary greatly as a result of contingent media decisions after or amid the violence. Moreover, the publicity will vary in effect depending on the different audiences which receive the information.

Despite its comparatively low-level impact in terms of deaths,[156] terrorist violence has indeed often demonstrated a capacity to grab attention more emphatically than do most other forms of human activity (with people tending to focus on it far more than they do on the more lethal risks of, say, traffic accidents, drowning, or surgery).[157] The effect of any single act might be ephemeral, and publicity for certain kinds of horrific violence might work against and even discredit the perpetrators' various political causes.[158] Nevertheless, it can ensure that people who would otherwise have been unaware of one's cause now unavoidably know about it, and indeed that they remain conscious of it over (sometimes very) lengthy periods of time.

In this sense, terrorism might be thought to represent a kind of very aggressive preaching (Mark Juergensmeyer has referred to religious terrorism as a
species of 'performance violence').[159] Testifying publicly to a cause in this
manner can get one's message loudly and widely heard; and many terrorists
have sought precisely to use their violence tactically in this way, to achieve
maximum publicity for their actions and therefore for their precious cause.[160]
Such violent, symbolic proclamation can make sure that one's grievances
are not patronized with indifference. At an individual level, it might also
facilitate the reward of securing a certain fame, when such violence achieves
'renown'.[161]

Terrorist violence might also be judged to have worked tactically if it
variously secures the undermining of one's opponents. It might delegitimize a reviled regime in the opinion of different constituencies, and persuade people that the enemy government is less attractive or worthy of
support than had previously been thought to be the case; it might destabilize a previously comfortable political status quo and replace safe normality
with anxiety or fear; it might damage the reputation, credibility, or popularity of enemy authorities, especially through challenging their capacity to
offer security to their population; it could perhaps undermine the perceived
efficacy of rivals within one's own community; it might sustainedly deny an
enemy state its Weberian monopoly over legitimate violence within a particular territory; it could provoke clumsily counter-productive state reaction
(and overreaction);[162] and it might demoralize enemies through attritional
violence and/or inflict severe economic damage upon an opponent. The
threat of terrorist violence has clearly altered much behaviour in the past
(not least in transforming the experience of international travel significantly
for the worse. The prompting of tediously elaborate security checks and
interrogations at airports has ensured vast-scale time consumption across
the world: 'Whatever else terrorism had achieved in the past few decades, it
had certainly brought about a net increase in world boredom').[163]

For some groups, tactical success might also involve the gaining or maintaining of control over a population, often within very limited, local areas of
high significance. Terrorist violence (and the threat of further violence) can
help to enforce a group's authority within an area, and also to target people
within one's community who are collaborating with an enemy. Here, we
can try to respond in historical context to the problem of definition: for it
might prove that what we normally define as terrorism is less effective at
this level than larger-scale insurgent or civil war violence tends to be.

And tactical success might also take the form of organizational strength-ening. Clearly, a necessary element of terrorist group success involves the organizational sustenance of the group itself; and problems of unity and discipline have been repeatedly evident across violent organizations using terrorist violence.[164] Violence can attract support through demonstrations of strength and also through generating polarizing cycles of escalatory conflict which then render recruitment more probable; it can secure you important funds and material (a significant issue, given that 'Financial and material resources are correctly perceived as the lifeblood of terrorist operations');[165] and, over time, it can potentially secure for you a stronger hold on your own community than that of less bellicose, or muscular, rival groups.[166]

Of course, violence can also make organizational life problematic in dis-tinctive ways. Like other organizations, terrorist groups face managerial challenges. These might include the tensions between financial efficiency and security, and between tactical control and security: as Jacob Shapiro has powerfully suggested, the methods used to increase efficiency and control (record-keeping, increased communications) can make non-state terrorist groups more vulnerable to compromises of their operational security.[167] But durable groups have still sometimes found that the process of violent strug-gle has had intra-conflict benefits in terms of establishing and consolidating organizational power and resources.

In addition to strategic, partially strategic, and tactical successes (though sometimes related to them), terrorism might be said to work in offering some inherent rewards of struggle as such, independent of the instrumental pursuit of ostensible goals. These could take a wide variety of forms, and they reflect the fact that terrorism can involve far more than the violent pursuit of declared political goals. There might, for example, be opportun-ities for: prestige and status; an augmented sense of identity and pride, at individual and at group levels; power; lasting celebrity, renown, heroism, and even glamour; intense friendship and the meaningful belonging to a group—as one eminent terrorist put it about his comrades: 'we were all like brothers. And the mutual deep affection, the affection of fighters, than which there is no greater, was the source of our happiness';[168] money (terrorist careers can sometimes yield financial as well as other professional returns);[169] sex; right-eous, sanctified, altruistic, ennobling purpose, and even redemption;[170] adven-ture, excitement, drama, exhilaration, and the consequent emancipation from quotidian boredom into a liberated new life; the catharsis of exacting satisfying revenge upon hated opponents; imaginative and creative fulfilment

and expression, or inward and spiritual returns; the replacement of humiliation, degradation, worthlessness, and deference with proud defiance, dignity, and self-respect;[171] the empowering satisfaction of taking control of
one's own circumstances and replacing apparent helplessness with decisive
intervention; the rewards and appeal of Damascene conversion, of turning
decisively from one, wrongful path onto a more correct and uncompromising one, which will change the world in a righteous direction; and the satisfactions of being good at something, and of being utterly committed and
passionate. Close attention to a rich variety of historical sources can reveal
much about all this in context, and can partly offset the 'working for whom?'
problem: terrorism is very rarely a purely individual matter, and within even
the same small group of comrades, rewards such as those just outlined may
be experienced in very divergent manner and degree (as we will see). And,
importantly, we can attend here to complex causation and explanation, for
ideological motivation need not be the only factor in making people join
or remain in a terrorist campaign.

Nor need even strong ideological conviction preclude other, complementary rewards that can be acquired through the struggle itself. It might
seem strange (even immoral) to ask how far terrorism increases people's
happiness. But clearly for some people this has been the case, and not at all
trivially so (and if we are to understand why people continue to join brutal
terrorist organizations, then this represents an important insight). Not all
such rewards will relate to the ostensible, declared aims of an organization;
and so stated objectives should not be too neatly equated with causes, since
there may well be alluring goals which lie at least partly outside the circle
of a group's declared political aims. And these inherent rewards of struggle
can and do work at different levels, sometimes centred on an individual and
on other occasions involving group satisfaction. Moreover, as suggested,
tension within and between different units of analysis can be present here
too, with terrorism working differently for different people in the same
organization: one individual might gain greatly while another (even close)
comrade might find their trajectory less fruitful in terms of rewards; and
certain individuals might have a good war despite their organization or
movement ultimately failing to secure its major objectives.

So, in addition to the sense of terrorism working instrumentally (moving
you from unacceptable Point A to desirable Point B), there exist complementary, sometimes overlapping, emotional and psychological ways in which
terrorism might be said to work, and to carry with it intrinsic benefits. This

is not to argue (as some do) that non-state terrorists are primarily motivated by selfish ambition or desire for personal gain, but instead to point out that in complex ways there might be rewards from terrorist struggle as such—rewards which might affect our calibration of the ways in which terrorism does or does not work.

There are also other layers still of possible terrorist efficacy. For example, it is conceivable that terrorism might work for someone other than the practitioners—or indeed other than the practitioners' intended beneficiaries. Allies and sponsors can gain from terrorists' actions, as can unintended recipients of gain (the groups who perhaps gain concessions in one setting because their opponents fear that failure to grant such concessions might result in the kind of terrorism which has occurred elsewhere).

But centrally what has been established here is a systematic framework, within which to be able to assess more thoroughly whether terrorism has worked in practice in the past. Numerous of the above themes might emerge simultaneously in struggle (for example, revenge being achieved, through operationally impressive tactical manoeuvres, and as part of a series of actions which bring about the partial achievement of a central strategic aim, in a manner which simultaneously yields certain psychological rewards). So we will often detect a multiplicity of motivations and goals and achievements, just as we would with other aspects of human activity and striving. And they might exist in tension too. An organization might achieve a striking tactical-operational success which actually hinders the cause strategically because it backfires in terms of popular opinion at local and international level. In this sense, the claim that, 'Logistically...terrorism seems largely successful in achieving tactical aims'[172] will always need to be considered against the wider framework of outcomes, whether in terms of strategic success, partial strategic success, or inherent rewards. Again, practices which sustain an organizational strengthening might yet hinder the longer-term achievement of that organization's main objectives.[173]

VI

We've now seen that 'Does Terrorism Work?' can be a divisively controversial as well as an important question, and that there lie within it a set of serious difficulties as we try to answer it. There's the problem of defining terrorism; the difficulty of agreeing what it might mean to say that terrorism does 'work'; the problem of for whom the terrorism might be judged to work; the entangled nature of processes of causation in human behaviour; and the particular difficulties inherent in the sources pertaining to terrorist violence.

But we have also suggested that this question is too important—both analytically and practically—for it to be answered in a chaotic or cursory manner. My argument here is that a historical method, allied to an explicit and carefully nuanced framework for assessment, can help to mitigate these difficulties. A historically grounded recognition of the vital importance of long memory and of properly understood change over time will provide us with rich data from long pasts (thereby addressing some of the elusiveness and contemporary opacity of source material on this subject); it will also tend to draw on lengthy recognition of the subtle interplay of change and continuity over time, thereby helping to resolve questions of causation; and it will enrich our understanding of for whom terrorism might work, taking in longer frames of human life and cross-generational experience.

The adoption of a profoundly context-specific approach to explanation, and an associatedly strong appreciation of uniqueness, will help offset problems of definition, as the lines drawn between terrorist and other kinds of activity are understood in actual-life setting and detail; the tendency to particularize (together with the carefully layered framework of assessment in terms of the strategic, the partial strategic, the tactical, and the inherently rewarding), will facilitate not only the acquisition of complex detail of understanding, but also a nuanced awareness of the processes of complicated causation, since the connections between supposed cause and effect will be seen close up; the capacity to understand local, unique outcomes will open up intimate knowledge of multiple causation and outcome, thereby helping to resolve the problem of for whom the terrorism does or does not work.

The historian's distinctive approach to the range, nature, and interrogation of sources and evidence will help in terms of this latter difficulty too, as source richness and intimacy will allow for appreciation of different outcomes for different players, as seen through diverse sources. It will also offset the particular problems we have identified regarding evidence about terrorism, both by accessing a far larger set of (historical) data to complement the contemporary, and also through the emphasis on a professionally experienced engagement with first-hand evidence as interrogated by a richly varied range of other kinds of source. So the problem of gaining access to enough evidence will be addressed through the historian's utilization of so

wide and rich a source base; and the simultaneous interrogation of many
different kinds of evidence from competing sources, will offset the problem
of any bias that there is in any one particular piece of evidence. Again, long
historiographical debates on the objectivity issue will provide the basis for
securing as dispassionate and fair-minded an interpretation as possible in the
context of such a highly charged topic and body of data.

Historians' frequent scepticism about abstract theorizing (reinforced by a
very precise and layered framework for assessment) might help us to avoid
crudely simplistic assumptions about what terrorism 'working' might mean.
And historically grounded scepticism about notions of inevitability in human
behaviour, tied to a preference for contingency in analysis, will elucidate
outcomes in terms of the complexity of human causation, as chance, luck,
the unintended, and the unanticipated gain their deservedly prominent place
in our argument.

In all of these ways, I think that the approach adopted here might complement other scholars' work in a helpful manner, addressing some of the
real difficulties involved in our question, and hopefully using our capacious
framework of assessment as a way of evading the understandable tendency
of people to mean different things by the question and therefore to talk past
one another when true dialogue is what we require. The approach adopted
here will particularly address the difficulties of defining what 'working'
might mean, and of identifying proper answers to the question of exactly
'whom' terrorism benefits. The combination of a precise and complex framework, a historical method, and the use of both in reflecting deeply upon
historical case studies, offers something new within the debate.[174]

In drawing this Introduction to a close, it might be useful briefly now to
comment on the book's structure, and its intended audience.

It seems to me that our understanding of non-state terrorism requires both
that we look closely at individual, contextually understood case studies, and
also at the degree to which family resemblances exist between them. The
approach adopted here reflects this: an analytical, framing Introduction; four
in-depth, chapter-length case studies of particular organizations (groups which
are different from one another in some key ways, but which share some similarities also); and a Conclusion which looks synoptically across very many
other cases of non-state terrorism. Focusing chapters on individual organizations (al-Qaida, Hamas, the Provisional IRA, ETA) allows for sustained, detailed,
and systematic analysis; doing so within a consistent analytical and methodological framework allows for systematic comparison between cases.

And what we are ultimately studying is terrorismS rather than terrorism, so what is unique in each place remains central to any proper understanding of what is shared across different settings. Any case-study selection will prompt criticism (Why Hamas and not Hezbollah? Why ETA rather than the Baader–Meinhof group?), but I believe that the wider-angled reflections in the Conclusion, together with the insights acquired in each case-study chapter, will defend effectively against these assaults. If you don't look at the micro-historical example in detail then you lose what can be known from specific, deeply contextualized understanding; if you only look at one example of such specifics then you miss the possibility of wider and deeper insights and patterns. Both are therefore needed.

Recent historiography has increasingly recognized the value of combining an appreciation of national and local context with an eye also to the connections and echoes which exist between these settings; such transnational reflection does not eschew the national, but seeks to augment and enrich it, and this is the approach adopted here.[175] In particular, I hope that a focus on case-specific national settings will not only allow for consideration of similarity and difference between them, but also for the localized ways in which various actors themselves challenge national boundaries and assumptions in each of these settings. In Israel-Palestine, Ireland, Spain, and elsewhere, the fact of focusing on a national context does not imply a comfortable acceptance of any single national narrative, and various terrorist campaigns have done much to open such narratives to very brutal interrogation.

Who is the book written for? I think the subject is far too important to deserve only a scholarly audience. So, while I hope that a wide range of scholars from different disciplines will find something of value in my book, I also look forward to people from other walks of life responding to it and engaging with it. There's certainly a wide range of people with important insights and views regarding this subject, and I've written the book in the hope that it will prove interesting and informative for them. In that sense, the book is a deliberately public one, addressing one of the most vital questions that we face as we consider the challenges of the next century, and doing so with the intention of as inclusive a debate as possible. And if it helps to generate debate, dialogue, discussion, and the production of further insights and understanding by others in the future, then it will have served its central purpose. There's now a lengthy tradition of academic historians writing for an intendedly wide audience[176] and, as one of the greatest of them once put it, 'Historians should not write only for other historians.'[177]

I

Jihadist Terror

The Case of al-Qaida

I

If I had only ten qualities to enumerate in drafting a thumbnail biographical sketch of [Osama bin Laden], they would be: pious, brave, generous, intelligent, charismatic, patient, visionary, stubborn, egalitarian, and, most of all, realistic.

Michael Scheuer, head of the CIA's bin Laden unit 1996–9[1]

Few people concentrated their attention upon Osama bin Laden (Figure 1) more sustainedly or with a sharper focus or from a more ostensibly hostile standpoint than did the Central Intelligence Agency's Michael Scheuer (Figure 2). This book will again and again reflect the importance of the individual and of small-group initiative, and the case of bin Laden and al-Qaida provides a powerful (in some ways, perhaps world-changing) example. And, though incomprehensible to many, bin Laden and his violent politics probably make greater sense if we do assess what al-Qaida truly sought to achieve, if we offer an honest analysis of how far they have succeeded in practice, and if (in line with even former CIA man Michael Scheuer's frank outline) we are prepared to allow for the positive as well as the bloodily negative in reflecting on this troubling group's struggle.

Jihadism[2] has dominated debates on terrorism since the brutal attack on the United States of America on 11 September 2001. This has been especially and predictably true of the group behind that extraordinary assault: al-Qaida. Space allows here only for a brief narrative of the organization's life, before the rest of the chapter considers—as a case study in jihadism—that group's goals and its record of violent achievement.

Figure 1. Osama bin Laden, circa 2003

Figure 2. Michael Scheuer, former Chief of the CIA's bin Laden unit

Prior to 9/11, comparatively little academic research had been pursued into al-Qaida; after it, the pendulum swung dramatically (perhaps too dramatically) in the opposite direction.[3] So, despite much that remains murky, the broad outlines of the tale are now clear enough. Al-Qaida ('the base' in Arabic) was set up in Peshawar in Pakistan in August 1988 by Osama bin Laden, Abdullah Azzam, and a small number of colleagues; their initial aim for the new grouping was to continue their violent jihad beyond the anti-Soviet struggle then burning in Afghanistan. Following the Soviet invasion of the latter country in 1979, the struggle of the mujahideen ('holy warriors', indirectly CIA-backed and financed through the Pakistani Directorate for Inter-Services Intelligence (ISI)) had provided the context for the group's emergence. Horrified by the Soviet invasion, bin Laden himself had visited Afghanistan in the 1980s and began working for the anti-Soviet resistance; indeed, the violent Afghan jihad became his cause, his passion, his war, his driving struggle,[4] and the basis for his securing some renown within the Middle East. He had been enraged by the non-Muslim Soviets' invasion of Muslim Afghanistan, and his own involvement included both the collection and distribution of funds and also some actual fighting (apparently, quite brave fighting).

Al-Qaida effectively started business as a database of names of foreign fighters who had been involved in the Afghan war. But its role expanded after the end of the struggle in Afghanistan, with attacks on US forces in Yemen in 1992, and with support for the anti-American struggle in Somalia during 1992–4. It was, and has remained, a somewhat informal organization, a complex phenomenon, fluid and Protean, possessing at times a more organizational quality but also (perhaps increasingly) a diffuse-network character. So the relationship between al-Qaida and different attacks labelled under that name can vary considerably. Mitchell Silber's tripartite pattern—distinguishing between 'al-Qaida "Command and Control"', 'al-Qaida "Suggested/Endorsed"', and 'al-Qaida Inspired' assaults[5]—offers one helpful way, perhaps, of sifting between the different kinds of al-Qaida role involved in terrorist operations; it is sufficiently nuanced to allow for precision, but sufficiently capacious to allow for proper recognition of the role played by the group in context.

Pre-9/11 terrorist attacks included the al-Qaida-inspired bombing of the New York World Trade Center on 26 February 1993,[6] and a painfully evolving rhetorical and blood-stained threat from the group. Political temperatures were raised, and an ominous context provided, with two intended fatwas (Islamic judgments, rulings, opinions, interpretations). Osama bin Laden issued the first on 23 August 1996, declaring war on the United States in his rather grandly styled 'Declaration of War against the Americans Occupying the Land of the Two Holy Places'. Signed by bin Laden alone, this was then followed on 23 February 1998 with another fatwa (signed by numerous people, including bin Laden), this latter one presenting it as a duty of all Muslims to kill America's citizens and allies:'The ruling to kill the Americans and their allies—civilian and military—is an individual duty for every Muslim who can do it in any country in which it is possible to do it, in order to liberate the al-Aqsa Mosque and the holy mosque [in Mecca] from their grip, and in order for their armies to move out of the lands of Islam, defeated and unable to threaten any Muslim.'[7]

This call failed to resonate with most Muslims, but very destructive violence nevertheless ensued. On 7 August 1998 there were al-Qaida suicide bombings against US embassies in Nairobi in Kenya (killing over 200 people) and in Dar es Salaam, Tanzania (killing eleven). Two years later, on 12 October 2000, al-Qaida dramatically attacked the USS *Cole* while it was in harbour at Aden in Yemen, killing seventeen US naval personnel.

This violence fitted the pattern adumbrated in Osama bin Laden's 1996 'Declaration of War', with its plea that 'efforts should be concentrated on destroying, fighting, and killing the [American] enemy until, by the grace of Allah, it is completely defeated'.[8] And bin Laden himself was clearly the most stellar member of the al-Qaida band; in Rolling Stones terms, he and Ayman al-Zawahiri might perhaps be seen respectively as the Jagger and Richards of the outfit. The lead singer had been born in Riyadh in Saudi Arabia, on 10 March 1957: Osama ('lion') was the seventeenth son of a very wealthy, piously Muslim, strongly anti-Israeli building contractor, Mohammed bin Laden (who died in an air crash on 3 September 1967).

What were bin Laden's inheritances and influences as he emerged into his best-known role as al-Qaida's charismatically nefarious propagandist? In the late 1970s he attended King Abdul Aziz University in Jeddah, studying economics, management, and business administration. During his school and university education, bin Laden seems to have developed a deep love for and knowledge of Islam, the Koran, and Islamic history; 'Osama was more religious than the rest of us', as his older half-brother tellingly recalled.[9] And one particular influence on bin Laden was Abdullah Azzam (1941–89), a Palestinian-born, radical-Islamic ideologue, propagandist, and organizer. Trained as a teacher, Azzam was a follower of Sayyid Qutb (on whom, more later), joined the Muslim Brotherhood, gained a doctorate from al-Azhar University in Cairo, and in 1980 took up a job at King Abdul Aziz University, where he *perhaps* influenced bin Laden (the university was at that time very small,[10] which makes this influence more likely); Azzam certainly became in due course something of a spiritual mentor for Osama and greatly affected his thinking, though the two drifted apart during the later 1980s.

In terms of his ideology, Osama bin Laden might best be described as having become a Salafi jihadist. A strain of Sunni Islam, Salafism involves the thinking of those Muslims who want to emulate as far as is possible the 'pious predecessors' or 'pious forebears' (al-salaf al-salih) from Islam's first generations; they see themselves as following the authentic and unsullied Islam, and as trying to live as strictly as they can in line with the way that these predecessors lived. Trying to purify Islam, Salafis of bin Laden's stamp have believed violence against Islam's enemies to be both justified and required,[11] given that Islam had been corrupted; they have held there to be a need for the faith to be returned more strictly to its pure form, with a rather literal approach towards scriptural Islamic texts and a desire for the stringent application of sharia law to the Muslim community.[12]

After Afghanistan, bin Laden built upon this religious foundation a career as an inspirational leader of jihadist campaigns of violence. The period 1991–6 he spent in Sudan, returning in May of the latter year to Afghanistan and basing himself there until after 9/11.

Ayman al-Zawahiri (Figure 3), who was to become al-Qaida leader in the spring of 2011 after bin Laden had been killed, long held the role of deputy within the group (having first met Osama in 1986 during the Afghan struggle). Born in Cairo on 19 June 1951, al-Zawahiri was a medic who came from a prestigious Egyptian family (his father was a professor, his grandfather an ambassador). Less charismatic than bin Laden, he nonetheless brought with him ability in relation to ideology and strategy.[13] A radical Islamist and jihadist rather than a religious scholar, he had been deeply influenced by the arresting, simplistic arguments of Sayyid Qutb[14] and (tellingly) he had undergone an intensification of militant commitment while imprisoned and brutally treated in Cairo by the Egyptian state: 'they kicked us, they beat us, they whipped us with electric cables, they shocked us with electricity! ... And they used the wild dogs!'[15] Released in 1984, al-Zawahiri himself seems by then to have come to favour a pure Islamic state, and a need for revenge against the forces that had so abused him.

The grouping in which bin Laden and al-Zawahiri were such leading figures will probably always be most famous for the attack on the United States on 11 September 2001. The idea for that unmerciful assault seems to have originated with the Kuwaiti-born, US-educated, Pakistani militant, Khaled

Figure 3. Al-Qaida's Ayman al-Zawahiri, 16 June 2011

Figure 4. Mohammed Atta, a leading figure in the 9/11 attacks

Sheikh Mohammed (born 1965), who appears also to have been the overall commander of the scheme.[16] Later captured in Rawalpindi on 1 March 2003, Mohammed was then a senior al-Qaida figure, and he had earlier helped his nephew (Ramzi Yousef) put together the World Trade Center attack in New York in 1993. On 9/11 itself, the leading player in al-Qaida's most famous operation was Mohammed Atta (Figure 4). The 33-year-old son of an Egyptian lawyer, Atta had studied architectural engineering at Cairo University, had then worked (another vicious irony) as an urban planner in Cairo after university, before moving to Germany to study city planning and engineering at Masters level in Hamburg and arriving in Florida in June 2000.

9/11 (the 'Holy Tuesday' operation, as bin Laden himself termed it) saw four commercial aircraft hijacked at around the same time in the morning; the planes were going from one US coast to the other and were therefore full of fuel. Nineteen hijackers ('nineteen post-secondary students... who shook America's throne', in bin Laden's celebratory phrasing,[17] fifteen of them being Saudi nationals), between them then flew two of the planes into the towers of the World Trade Center in New York city, and one into the Pentagon in Washington DC; a fourth plane (United Flight 93) did not reach its apparent target of the US Capitol building in Washington, crashing instead into a field in Pennsylvania. Destroying the World Trade Center so utterly may not have been the anticipated outcome, and although there were people who appear to have thought along similar lines during the 1980s and 1990s,[18] none had come close to pulling off such a brilliantly executed, if humanly appalling, act. America's own 9/11 Commission judged 11 September to have been 'a day of unprecedented shock and suffering in the history of the United States'.[19]

The 9/11 victims were drawn from many nationalities, and the final death toll of 2,977 dying in New York, Washington, and Pennsylvania was overwhelmingly made up of civilians (as so often, terroristic violence targeting the defenceless and innocent). Despite prior suspicion about the possibility of hijacked aeroplanes being used by terrorists as missile-weapons,[20] the 11 September attack carried with it a shocking charge to world (and especially to American) opinion. There have been numerous other attempts at al-Qaida spectaculars after 11 September. Would-be shoe-bomber and al-Qaida conspirator Richard Reid (Figure 5; Abdur Rahim) tried unsuccessfully to bring down a flight from Paris to Miami in December 2001; the al-Qaida-affiliated Jemaah Islamiyah suicide bombing of Bali nightclubs on 12 October 2002 killed 202 people; al-Qaida-affiliated attacks in Iraq from 2003 onwards killed

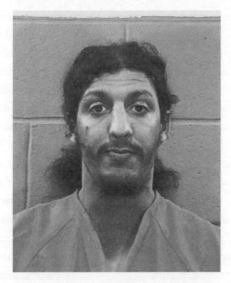

Figure 5. Richard Reid ('the shoe bomber')

very many more; the al-Qaida-inspired and al-Qaida-backed multiple train bombings in Madrid on 11 March 2004 killed 191 people and injured many others; Operation Crevice in 2004 saw the UK authorities foil a serious, al-Qaida-endorsed and al-Qaida-influenced conspiracy to bomb British bars, nightclubs, and shopping centres; the four bombs in London on the morning of 7 July 2005 killed 56 people (wounding over 500 more), should probably be categorized as an al-Qaida 'suggested/endorsed' endeavour,[21] and clearly possessed an al-Qaida dimension;[22] 21 July 2005 witnessed an al-Qaida-backed attempt to attack London's transport system with four bombs which did not in fact explode; an al-Qaida-backed plan to attack the New York subway with explosives in September 2009 did not come to fruition; and so on. But nothing could match the hideous jolt provided by Holy Tuesday.

There has been some sharp debate about the changing nature of al-Qaida's organizational identity (something to which we will return later in this chapter), and one's response to this issue will partly affect one's approach to the question of how far al-Qaida's terrorism has worked. For one thing, in the post-9/11 period it is probably true that groups inspired by or affiliating with al-Qaida have been responsible for more acts of terrorism than has any centrally conceived and controlled al-Qaida organization itself.[23] Some have argued that the decisive level of al-Qaida activity has moved to the grass roots; others have put the case that the group's core leadership continues to play a significant role; others again have stressed the importance of 'middle managers'—people who link the top of the organization with the grass roots.[24] Yet again, some scholars have presented al-Qaida as a jihadist network rather than an organization, as comprising adaptive systems which are self-organizing from the bottom upwards, decentralized and coalescent, tactically diverse, and lacking a systematically uniform ideological philosophy.[25]

Of course, the very notion of coalescence implies some resulting unity, and I suspect that the lines dividing various scholars in these debates are sometimes less stark than observers have at times assumed them to be. Moreover, while some people have presented contemporary jihadist terrorism as qualitatively different from other species of the terrorist phenomenon,[26] it should also be noted both that western anxiety about jihadism is not new in itself,[27] and (as we noted earlier in this book) that the dividing lines between old and new terrorisms in many cases tend to be rather blurred on close, careful, contextually rich inspection. Decentralized, self-organizing, adaptive, fluid systems of terrorists operating from the local ground upwards, characterized by various forms (rather than embodying a uniform version) of a particular ideology, marked by change over time and by some inconsistency and incoherence, and contingent rather than inevitable in their interactive complexity—such groupings are actually very well known from terrorism's long past (or, at least, they should be by now),[28] and they have been assessed as collective groupings in the past, reasonably enough.

Although far from monolithic and static, therefore, I think that al-Qaida can still be assessed in terms of its goals and achievements. It is a complex phenomenon, of course, and its objectives have changed over time.[29] But that Protean heterogeneity demands that we offer a nuanced and circumspect reading of it (fully aware of these dynamics), rather than that we should abandon the attempt to read al-Qaida as one entity for analysis. Despite al-Qaida's complexity (and the fact that different dynamics have operated at its various different levels, with complex results), it is possible to set out a family of goals for the grouping and to assess how far it has succeeded in achieving them through terrorism.[30]

II

There are two sides in this conflict, world crusaders allied to Jewish Zionists [and] led by the United States, Britain, and Israel, and on the other side the Islamic world. In such a conflict, it is unacceptable for the first side to

launch an aggression, enter my land, property and sanctities, and plunder
the Muslims' oil, and then say the Muslims are terrorists when it faces any
resistance from them.

Osama bin Laden (1998)[31]

Viewed synoptically (and on the basis of looking closely at what those
involved have actually said), al-Qaida's goals have certainly been ambitious.
In terms of central, primary, strategic objectives, I would suggest that they
have sought the overturning of what they consider to be apostate Muslim
regimes, the associated expulsion of the USA and US influence from
Muslim countries, and the renaissance of a particular kind of Islam.

A crucial intensification of Osama bin Laden's politics involved political
developments following Iraq's invasion of Kuwait in the summer of 1990.
Bin Laden offered to recruit a Muslim army to defend his homeland against
the Iraqi threat; but the Saudis turned instead to the United States of
America, inviting the USA to send hundreds of thousands of troops to protect Saudi Arabia against a possible Iraqi assault on that kingdom. On
7 August 1990 the first US forces were sent to Saudi as part of Operation
Desert Shield. These troops then remained in the country after the Gulf war
of 1990–1, and bin Laden was utterly outraged at such desecration of Islam's
holiest land, which contained the sacred cities of Mecca and Medina and
which was also his own homeland. Bin Laden's very deep hostility towards
the Saudi regime—as one which lacked appropriate piety—fitted a wider
al-Qaida pattern of ambition: to produce what they considered a more
authentic form of truly Islamic rule in such countries, with a strict application of sharia law being enforced. In the words of one of the leading experts
on bin Laden, the latter wanted 'to install Taliban-style theocracies from
Indonesia to Morocco'.[32] Osama saw it as a Muslim's duty to do all that they
could to take back the holy places and the lands controlled by enemies of
true Islam, to restore to Islam what had wrongly been taken from it, and to
replace human-made regulations with sharia law.

So the overturning of impious Muslim regimes has played a vital part in
al-Qaida's agenda (being a significant part, for example, of Ayman al-Zawahiri's
vision also). In this sense, there is clearly something behind the claims of
those who insist that the jihadist threat is primarily religious in character,[33]
although the pursuit of regime change also clearly has political dynamics
which are capable of being interpreted in secular terms. Bin Laden and his
comrades wanted a particular kind of Muslim theocracy to control the

Middle East's resources and politics and life. This was clearly religious politics; but it also embodied the desire of a humiliated Saudi to see his own role
and that of those who agreed with him politically to be enhanced. In itself,
the replacing of perceivedly corrupt, self-serving regimes with rule more
favourable to one's own world-view is not something immune to secular
political explanation; and it is clear that (for bin Laden, certainly) 'the religion of Islam encompasses all the affairs of life, including the religious and
the worldly, such as economic, military, and political affairs'.[34]

Yet it remains true that there has been a centrally religious pivot on which
this aspect of al-Qaida's politics has lastingly turned. Replacing allegedly corrupt regimes with ones in tune with Salafist ideas has, for example, been
evident in the arguments of the Palestinian-Jordanian ideologue Abu
Muhammad al-Maqdisi (a leading jihadist thinker; an influence on Ayman
al-Zawahiri—whom he appears to have known; and someone who has judged
many Muslim regimes to be insufficiently in line with proper Islamic conduct
and rules, and hence with true religion).[35] So the undermining and removal of
infidel, pro-western regimes from Muslim countries has been a central strategic goal for al-Qaida; 'I don't recognize the Saudi government as Islamic.'[36]

Relatedly, another of al-Qaida's central and primary strategic goals has
been the expulsion of the USA and of US influence from Muslim countries. Bin Laden was famously zealous to remove what he saw as a humiliating US military presence from Muslim territories: 'Osama bin Laden's
principal objective has long been the expulsion of American troops from
the Persian Gulf';[37] or, in bin Laden's own words, given US aggression and
injustice towards Muslims, 'we have declared jihad against the US, because
in our religion it is our duty to make jihad so that God's word is the one
exalted to the heights and so that we drive the Americans away from all
Muslim countries'.[38] And this has formed an important and durable part of
al-Qaida's central ambition; 'the Israeli forces are occupying our land and
the American forces are sitting on our territory. We no longer have any
choice but jihad.'[39] So the brutal 7 August 1998 al-Qaida attacks on US
embassies in Nairobi and Dar es Salaam occurred symbolically on the eighth
anniversary of the arrival of American forces in Saudi Arabia following the
Iraqi invasion of Kuwait. And they did so, it should be recalled, with appalling human consequences. One woman working at the Dar es Salaam embassy
at the time of the bombing recalled: 'Coming down the stairwell there were
all kinds of body parts'; of one person, she noted that, 'He didn't have any
skin left.'[40]

For his part, in 2000 bin Laden himself put his case with typically rhetorical self-indulgence in an al-Qaida recruitment video: 'The wounds of the Muslims are deep everywhere. But today our wounds are deeper because the Crusaders and the Jews have joined together to invade the heart of Dar al-Islam ("The Abode of Islam": our most sacred places in Saudi Arabia, Mecca, and Medina, including the prophet's mosque, and the al-Aqsa mosque and Dome of the Rock in Jerusalem, al-Quds).'[41] Additionally, Palestine was long a key issue for bin Laden, ever since his teenage years, with the need to liberate the region from western grip being vital to his world-view: 'The legal duty regarding Palestine and our brothers there . . . is to wage jihad for the sake of God, and to motivate our *umma* to jihad so that Palestine may be completely liberated and returned to Islamic sovereignty.'[42] Echoing this, al-Zawahiri also stressed the deep importance of the Palestinian struggle: 'Defending Palestine is a responsibility for all Muslims.'[43]

Much of the fire that has burned in terms of support for al-Qaida has been fuelled by perceptions that western powers have been aggressive towards, and at war with, Muslims, and even with Islam as such.[44] In bin Laden's own tendentious phrasing, 'After the end of the Cold War, America escalated its campaign against the Muslim world in its entirety, aiming to get rid of Islam itself.'[45] Indeed, as Robert Pape has strongly argued, hostility towards foreign occupation has played a key part in motivating suicide terrorism, and US occupation of (or military presence in) Muslim lands has been very important here.[46] The apparently ill-adjusted Richard Reid (who on 22 December 2001 feebly attempted to blow up an American Airlines flight to Miami with explosive devices hidden in his shoes) nonetheless put it starkly enough: 'what I am doing is part of the ongoing war between Islam and disbelief . . . I see it as a duty upon me to help remove the oppressive American forces from the Muslim lands . . . we do not have other means to fight them.'[47]

So damaging, undermining, weakening, and degrading the power of the USA (and ideally destroying it); doing so through violence; and driving American influence from the Muslim world—all of these interwoven themes have run through al-Qaida's bloodstream for years, and have done much to motivate its minatory, coercive actions. It seems clear that by 1993 al-Qaida 'conceived its central mission as attacking American targets';[48] and US allies—especially Israel—were also seen as part of this expulsion and demolition policy. Bin Laden himself was strongly, very deeply anti-Jewish, and American support for Israel against the Palestinians represented a grievance

of serious proportions for him during his career; damaging Israel and establishing a Palestinian state were undoubtedly important for him.

But the headline focus was on the USA itself, the supposed leader of the
worldwide conspiracy against Islam. The US-led west had supposedly
assaulted Muslims: 'They have attacked our brothers in Palestine as they
have attacked Muslims and Arabs elsewhere... The Blood of Muslims is
shed. It has become too much... We are only looked upon as sheep, and we
are very humiliated.'[49] The USA itself was 'the head of infidelity',[50] an
'unjust, criminal, and tyrannical' power.[51]

Though this anti-American politics carried with it some apparently
over-ambitious elements,[52] it seems that members of al-Qaida considered the
USA so corrupt and spineless that it could be beaten through violent acts. Bin
Laden certainly appears to have drawn inspiration from supposed terrorist successes in the past (such inspiration being one of the many reasons why careful
assessment of terrorism's actual degree of historical efficacy is so vital). He was
convinced that the violence of his comrades against the USA in Somalia had
proved effective, with the United States (he felt) being cowardly and weak in
1993–4 as it withdrew forces after eighteen of its soldiers had been killed in
Mogadishu in October 1993. Such episodes supposedly showed a weakness
which encouraged a jihadist belief in the effectiveness and power of
anti-American violence.[53] Of the Somali episode, bin Laden stated tauntingly
that 'when tens of your soldiers were killed in minor battles and one American
pilot was dragged through the streets of Mogadishu, you left the area in disappointment, humiliation, defeat'.[54] He drew a similar lesson from the US
response to Lebanese attacks in 1983. And his own Afghan apprenticeship was
crucial here too. Bin Laden tellingly considered that he and his Muslim colleagues had not only driven the Soviet Union from Afghanistan (the last Soviet
troops withdrawing on 15 February 1989), but that in doing so they had hastened the demise of that superpower state itself. Regarding this Afghan episode,
he claimed that 'the myth of the super-power was destroyed not only in my
mind but also in the minds of all Muslims'.[55] Al-Zawahiri held the same view:

> the jihad battles in Afghanistan destroyed the myth of a superpower in the
> minds of the Muslim mujahideen young men. The USSR, a superpower with
> the largest land army in the world, was destroyed and the remnants of its troops
> fled Afghanistan before the eyes of the Muslim youths and as a result of their
> actions. That jihad was a training course of the utmost importance to prepare
> Muslim mujahideen to wage their awaited battle against the superpower that
> now has sole dominance over the globe, namely, the United States.[56]

As one thoughtful terrorism expert has commented, 'From the perspective of the international brigade of jihadists who fought in the Afghan war, it appeared that the insurgency they had taken part in had exposed the rotten foundations of one of the world's two super-powers.'[57] So international relations could now be utterly recast again, with the same process being applied to the USA. In bin Laden's own words: 'We believe that America is weaker than [Soviet] Russia';[58] 'we believe that the defeat of America is something achievable—with the permission of God—and it is easier for us—with the permission of God—than the defeat of the Soviet empire previously';[59] 'We can conclude that America is a superpower, with enormous military strength and vast economic power, but that all this is built on foundations of straw.'[60]

Since America and their friends had been the aggressors ('It is no secret that the people of Islam have suffered from the aggression, iniquity, and injustice imposed on them by the Zionist–Crusader alliance and their collaborators';[61] 'It is now clear that the west in general and America at the forefront is carrying on indescribable Crusader's spite against Islam. Those who have lived these months under continuous bombardment from multiple kinds of American planes know that this is the truth'),[62] so there was a deep need to strike justly back. Part of this involved the attempt to produce heavy economic costs through inflicting violence upon the infidel Americans: 'bleeding America to the point of bankruptcy', as bin Laden put it in 2004;[63] as one commentator observed, 'The "bleeding wars" are the crucial first step. The al-Qaida leadership is convinced it can reproduce the communist collapse by defeating the western powers in Afghanistan and Iraq.'[64]

Even allowing for the fact that there is a propagandist element to much of this al-Qaida output, it remains clear from this evidence that al-Qaida saw the US led west as hostile to the Muslim world, that it instructively considered the struggle with the west to have been ongoing for centuries,[65] and that it thought violence essential in order to deal with this enmity: 'The jihad is part of our shariah and the nation [umma] cannot dispense with it [in fighting] against its enemies.'[66] In this sense, an instrumental view of necessary violence in response to perceived US foreign policy lay at the heart of al-Qaida's politics; and the aim had less to do with hatred of culture than with responses to US power, and with the desire that the USA should alter its role in the wider world: 'The evidence strongly suggests that al-Qaida has attacked the United States to change its foreign policies.'[67] One Palestinian teenager in 2003 explained his admiration for the 9/11 attackers

by saying, 'I don't hate American culture...What I hate is what their politics are doing. They are helping Israel with money, tanks, and guns against
the Palestinian people. So I support those who support us in our struggle
like al-Qaida.'[68] In bin Laden's own words, 'Every day, from east to west, our
umma of 1200 million Muslims is being slaughtered, in Palestine, in Iraq,
Somalia, Western Sudan, Kashmir, the Philippines, Bosnia, Chechnya, and
Assam.'[69] Something had to be done in response. 'Why are we fighting and
opposing you?...Because you attacked us and continue to attack us.'[70] So
al-Qaida sought that the USA should withdraw its troops from Saudi Arabia,
that it should end its support for repressive, pro-western rulers of Muslim
countries (in Pakistan, in Saudi Arabia, for example), that it should end its
backing for Israel, and that it should desist from engaging in wars that killed
Muslims.

   Al-Qaida's other central, primary goal seems to me to have been the
renaissance of a particular kind of Islam. This represents a layered goal, but
it centres on the adherence to and the defence of true Islam as they see it,
and the associated redemption of this authentic faith from what they read as
the humiliation of contemporary desertion and corruption. It relates to the
issue (already discussed) of replacing what are seen as apostate Muslim
regimes. But what is involved here is a specifically religious revival. The
minutes of al-Qaida's first meetings in 1988 made clear its deeply religious
identity: 'Al-Qaida is basically an organized Islamic faction; its goal will be
to lift the word of God, to make his religion victorious.'[71]

   Osama bin Laden himself, of course, was not formally trained as a religious scholar. But this lack of proper credentials did not mean that nobody
listened to him on religious matters or found inspiration in his views on the
need for Islamic rebirth (and nor did it mean that every al-Qaida operative
shared his intensity: as I say, this Islamic element reflects varied degrees of
commitment). Bin Laden's Salafist objective was the establishment of a particular kind of Islamic state, one which would strictly implement sharia law
(Islamic law as derived from a particularly stringent reading of the Koran
and of the actions, approvals, and comments of the prophet Muhammad). So
society would be cleansed; it would be arranged without tolerance of other
ways of living; and it would be run according to the supposedly God-given
Islamic system rather than human-made structures and rules.

   Ultimately, there has existed a geographically wide-ranging mission here:
'The global Salafi jihad is a worldwide religious revivalist movement with
the goal of re-establishing past Muslim glory in a great Islamist state stretching

from Morocco to the Philippines, eliminating present national boundaries';[72] and al-Qaida zealots are a 'vanguard trying to establish a certain
vision of an Islamist utopia'.[73] Global jihadism as sponsored by bin Laden
had the ultimate goal of an international theocratic system based on God's
direct rule, and the transnational extension of a particular, authentic form of
Islamic organization of society. This is seen in terms of the freeing of people
to live in a restored Caliphate[74] covering and uniting all Muslim territory,
liberated from western influence and control, and with the state being run
along the lines of sharia law. Previous Muslim glory would be restored in
what would amount to a rejuvenated Caliphate; according to such a view,
Islam is seen as the one true faith which should, therefore, dominate the
planet. Insofar as al-Qaida violence would hasten the enforcing of sharia
law in those areas where Muslims live and have historically lived, what we
see here is therefore (among other things) terrorism as attempted religious
salvation, and to ignore the religious motivation shared by many within
al-Qaida would hinder our understanding.[75]

It is hard to establish intellectual and other influences on groups' ideas in
a finally decisive manner, but it might be worth reflecting on the direct and
indirect effect on this Islamic renaissance goal that was wielded by the martyred Islamist ideologue Sayyid Qutb. Al-Maqdisi has certainly admired
Qutb, and we have already noted that the same is true for al-Zawahiri
(whose great-uncle was Qutb's lawyer). A case can be made that Qutb also
provided a measure of inspiration for bin Laden (though this is disputed by
some),[76] and Qutb's ideas have continued to have some effect in jihadist
circles and to be transmitted long after his execution.

With its quiet rage, Qutb's central argument does provide a fitting ideological foundation for al-Qaida's pursuit of the revival and revivified great-
ness of Islam. Despite the fact that many of his ideas had western sources,
Qutb was horrified at what he himself saw of the west;[77] for him, it was
essential to counter jahiliyyah (the state of ignorance of divine guidance), to
end the power of human over human, and to establish instead the rule of
God. Currently, he felt, 'the whole world is steeped in jahiliyyah... Our
whole environment, people's beliefs and ideas, habits and art, rules and
laws—is jahiliyyah.' But power and sovereignty should be God's alone: 'people
should not bow before anyone except God or derive laws from any other
source'; 'every aspect of life should be under the sovereignty of God'; 'Any
system in which the final decisions are referred to human beings, and in which
the sources of all authority are human, deifies human beings by designating

others than God as lords over men.... To establish God's rule means that His
laws be enforced and that the final decision in all affairs be according to
these laws.' This was an utterly uncompromising argument: 'Islam cannot
accept any mixing with jahiliyyah, either in its concept or in the modes of
living which are derived from this concept'; 'only Islamic values and morals,
Islamic teachings and safeguards, are worthy of mankind, and from this unchang-
ing and true measure of human progress, Islam is the real civilization and
Islamic society is truly civilized'.[78]

The text from which these quotations are taken (the compelling, though
rather unsubtle *Milestones*) is deeply redolent of ideas which al-Qaida itself
has celebrated; among other things, for example, it is a distinctly anti-Jewish
text.[79] And Qutb's envisaged recasting of society, law, and politics has been a
rich resource for deeply religious jihadists of a later generation. In a wider
sense, it is important to note both that al-Qaida's goals are not *either* political
or religious but, as they themselves would see them, necessarily interwoven
as religio-political; and also that the sources make clear how important religious motivation has enduringly been. In the words of Mohammed Sidique
('Sid') Khan, one of the 7/7 London bombers: 'I and thousands like me are
forsaking everything for what we believe. Our driving motivation doesn't
come from tangible commodities that this world has to offer. Our religion
is Islam—obedience to the one true God, Allah, and following the footsteps
of the final prophet and messenger Muhammad.'[80]

Al-Qaida's terrorism might also be judged to have worked if it achieved
a partial strategic victory, with the group partially achieving its central, primary goals, or achieving or partially achieving secondary strategic goals, or
determining the agenda and preventing its opponents from securing victory.
Most supposedly apostate Muslim regimes (the purveyors of a false Islam, in
al-Qaida's sharply zealous view) might survive, but one or two might fall, or
some might be weakened if not destroyed. The United States might continue to dominate certain Muslim countries, but it might be driven out of
one or two; America might survive as a superpower, but be economically, or
psychologically, or politically damaged by al-Qaida's violence. The Caliphate
might not be realized, but there might be spikes of newly revitalized Salafist
energy and devotion. These diluted versions of al-Qaida's central goals might
fall far short of the hoped-for, full ambitions of the group, but they might
represent significant success nonetheless.

Secondary goals might be significantly furthered also, whether revenge upon
enemies, the sustaining of the religio-political faith into a new generation, or

the securing of progress in terms of some locally specific agendas and conflicts. There is no doubt at all that revenge upon the USA and its allies has represented an important motivation behind some al-Qaida violence.[81] In al-Qaida's eyes, the USA and its allies have been the aggressors against the Muslim world. Hitting back violently and punishingly at them has offered significant rewards, therefore, in terms not merely of political instrumentalism but also of valuable retaliation in itself.

It is clear that the Hamburg cell which lay behind the 9/11 attack possessed deeply anti-Jewish and anti-American hatreds;[82] Osama bin Laden himself was viscerally clear on this point ('Every Muslim, from the moment they realize the distinction in their hearts, hates Americans, hates Jews, and hates Christians.... For as long as I can remember I...have felt hatred and animosity for Americans';[83] 'The hearts of Muslims are filled with hatred towards the United States of America and the American president');[84] and, in the words of one distinguished scholarly authority, 'The unifying element among the groups to which al-Qaida outsources its operations is not a mystical, retrograde form of Islam but a shared hatred of the US.'[85] One eminent expert who actually met the al-Qaida leader recalls from his first encounter with him that bin Laden's 'words were full of a raw hatred of the United States'.[86] So if some jihadists had come to see the USA as a 'global bully',[87] then hitting back seemed legitimate and desirable; 'The United States and their allies are killing us in Palestine, Chechnya, Kashmir, and Iraq. That's why Muslims have the right to carry out revenge attacks on the US.'[88] Those with more affiliative connections to al-Qaida have also reflected this pattern. On 22 May 2013 Michael Adebowale and Michael Adebolajo brutally killed British soldier Lee Rigby in London. Both killers had been in contact with al-Qaida in the Arabian Peninsula (AQAP) activists in the period before the killing, and they were clearly intent on brutal revenge for perceived western crimes.[89]

Partial strategic success might also be judged to have been achieved if al-Qaida's violence has enabled it to sustain jihadist resistance against the west, or to maintain a particular kind of jihadist ideology in vibrant form. Local agendas might also see some evidence of terrorism working for al-Qaida in a partial strategic sense, with progress made in these settings in relation to secondary objectives. In common with so many other terrorist campaigns, much of what al-Qaida engages with possesses distinctly local dynamics. These local accents have involved context-specific political ambitions (whether in Bosnia, Chechnya, Iraq, Afghanistan), and—as Bruce Hoffman put it in 2006—'The al-Qaida movement today is best described as a net-worked transnational constituency rather than the monolithic, international terrorist organization with an identifiable command and control apparatus that it once was.... [T]oday there are many al-Qaidas rather than the single al-Qaida of the past.'[90] Paradoxically, jihadist commitment and local nation-alist faith are not necessarily incompatible;[91] and al-Qaida has certainly been embedded in some very local concerns, settings, agendas, ways of operating, and aims of struggle.

This can take a number of forms. It might be judged a secondary goal, for instance, to influence the USA's allies in relation to their support for America's engagement with post-2003 Iraq. This seems to have been partly the case with the Madrid bombings of 2004,[92] and also the London attacks of 7/7 (which appear to have been influenced to some degree by the perceived success of the Madrid bombings in redirecting Spanish foreign policy).[93] 7/7's Mohammed Sidique Khan made clear his sense of trying to influence UK foreign policy itself (as well as wanting to punish Britain for its role in Iraq and Afghanistan) when he declared in his final video recording that: 'Your democratically elected governments continuously perpetuate atroci-ties against my people all over the world. And your support makes you directly responsible, just as I am directly responsible for protecting and aven-ging my Muslim brothers and sisters.... Until you stop the bombing, gas-sing, imprisonment, and torture of my people we will not stop this fight';[94] almost poignantly, Khan averred that, 'We are at war and I am a soldier.'[95]

In the Iraqi setting itself, what became al-Qaida in Iraq (AQI) was ini-tially formed during 2003–4 by Jordanian zealot Abu Musab al-Zarqawi (1966–2006). The group carried out extensive terrorist attacks during 2004–5, with the seeming aims of provoking a Shia backlash (and therefore a mobilized Sunni population rallying to the AQI flag amid a civil war esca-lation), of undermining the post-2003 Iraqi state, and ultimately of driving the USA out of Iraq in the specific context of post-2003 occupation.

Partial strategic success might also be detected, I think, if al-Qaida were judged to have determined the relevant political agenda, and to have pre-vented its opponents from shaping political outcomes. So bin Laden's hope that a dichotomized Muslim-versus-the-west conflict might be deepened, and that al-Qaida's violence would prevent comfortable western victory and supremacy, both merit close investigation.

What would al-Qaida tactical success look like? It might include opera-tional triumphs, and there seems to have been some direct thinking on their part about exactly this aspect of their work. Leading figure Ayman al-Zawahiri in 2001 argued for concentrating on martyrdom operations as a method because 'Suicide operations are the most successful in inflicting damage on the opponent and the least costly in terms of casualties among the fundamentalists.'[96] Indeed, there seems to have been an attempted learning process here, with al-Qaida deciding that suicide bombings might be more effective than other tactics, partly because of what they perceived as the efficacy of prior suicide bombings in Palestine (Hamas), Lebanon (Hezbollah), and Sri Lanka (Tamil Tigers). Again, therefore, we have the pragmatic emulation of supposedly successful past violence; and such patterns yet again show how utterly vital it is that we understand the extent to which terrorism has or has not *actually* worked in historical practice.

In tactical terms, terrorism might also succeed through the acquisition of publicity, something which bin Laden's propagandist gifts centrally played towards, and of which his colleagues were likewise very aware. As al-Zawahiri put it in 2005, 'we are in a battle, and . . . more than half of this battle is taking place in the battlefield of the media';[97] and, tellingly, al-Qaida has long placed propaganda at the heart of its activities. As one scholar has put it, there emerged a deliberately constructed 'symbiotic relationship' between jihadists' violence and their use of the media.[98] Al-Qaida violence might also work tactically through the undermining of opponents. It is clear, for example, that once the western engagement with Afghanistan began in 2001, it became a key al-Qaida goal that the USA and its allies be defeated there.[99] And it might succeed by means of the process of organizational strengthening. This last point is a general one, of course ('One does not become engaged in politics unless one's cause has a future,' as one scholar has put it);[100] but the specific questions of al-Qaida's survival and strengthening have been ones to which their smarter minds have certainly given thought. The group's most impressive strategist, the Syrian Abu Mus'ab al-Suri, clearly reflected carefully on the idea of changing al-Qaida's organizational structure in order to produce greater post-9/11 resilience.[101] Earlier, between the mid-1990s and late 2001, al-Qaida had aimed to become a properly bureaucratized organization (exhibiting the pedantic attention to accountancy, and to the appropriateness of colleagues' use of funds, that are customarily associated with such structures).[102]

In addition to strategic, partial strategic, and tactical success, al-Qaida terrorism might also be judged to work in terms of the inherent rewards of struggle as such. Given the well-established normality of decision-making that is typical of people who are involved in terrorism, it makes sense to concede that those opting for jihadism should, among other rewards, be on occasion partly motivated by the appeal of, for example, social endorsement, status among peers, and the like.[103] On the face of it, inherent rewards from al-Qaida terrorism might potentially include aspects of religious piety; the catharsis produced by revenge and by the expression of complicatedly generated rage;[104] opportunities for fame, or for material rewards; and the remedying of shame and humiliation (the connection between humiliation and rage having rightly been stressed very strongly in studies of terrorist violence).[105]

Clearly, these goals discussed above need not necessarily be discretely separated from one another. Hostility toward apostate regimes is interwoven with antipathy towards America and US influence. As bin Laden put it in an interview with regard to Saudi Arabia, 'Our main problem is the US government....By being loyal to the US regime, the Saudi regime has committed an act against Islam.'[106] Similarly, the removal of apostate regimes was seen as the basis for a revival of a particular brand of Islam; the pursuit of strategic victory in terms of a fully restored Caliphate might result in the partial establishment of what would ideally be a territorially more expansive Muslim realm; struggling for the revival of a particular form of Islam might bring with it inherent religious or psychological rewards; the secondary goal of revenge upon enemies might overlap with the strategic one of trying to destroy an enemy empire; tactical successes might be judged to move forward a strategic or partial strategic agenda; and so on. One founder member of al-Qaida who trained recruits for the group in Afghanistan recalled that 'some people will come to you and say "I want to be martyred, but not before I give the enemies of God Hell on this earth"'.[107] The allure of redemptive martyrdom here clearly overlapped with a vengeful desire to hit back at al-Qaida's hated enemies.

Equally, these different layers in our framework might exist in tension with one another for al-Qaida. The gaining of revenge upon enemies might backfire in terms of popular support or sympathy if the attacks were judged unwarranted or too brutal; and tactical success might prompt a political reaction which was strategically or organizationally damaging.

III

God has struck America at its Achilles heel and destroyed its greatest buildings, praise and blessings to Him. America has been filled with terror from north

to south and from east to west, praise and blessings to God. What America is
tasting today is but a fraction of what we have tasted for decades.

Osama bin Laden, commenting on 9/11[108]

So has al–Qaida's terrorism actually achieved the group's goals in practice?
Has terrorism worked?

Let's start with their central, primary, strategic objectives: overturning
what they see as apostate Muslim regimes, expelling the USA and its influence from Muslim countries, and achieving the renaissance of a particular
kind of Islam.

The relationship between Islam and war represents a very complex subject,[109] and the issue of the effect of al–Qaida's violence upon Muslim
regimes fits this pattern. At one level, there has been a very clear failure
indeed. The Saudi regime remains firmly in place; post-9/11 politics saw a
strengthening of the US relationship with some of the regimes most despised
by al–Qaida; and it might be argued that even where there has now emerged
a dramatic change of ruling power in Muslim countries (as in Libya or
Egypt, for example) this has not been due to al–Qaida violence nor in line
with setting up the kind of regime that has been and still is sought by that
terrorist group. Moreover, while post-9/11 international developments might
be read by some jihadists as confirming their world-view (of foreign, non-Muslim
powers militarily bullying Muslim peoples in places like Afghanistan and
Iraq), the fact remains that the authorities in most Muslim countries still do
not match the kind of regime which al–Qaida's violence was intended to
install and to encourage.

But historical processes are long term and contingent and very often
immune to reliable prediction. Is it possible that a neo-Taliban regime might
yet return to considerable power within Afghanistan, and that one might
judge that al–Qaida-supported terroristic methods in the Afghan conflict
had therefore helped to bring about such an eventuality?

It seems to me that there remains a wide range of possibilities for the
kind of political regimes that can be developed and legitimized in Muslim-
majority countries. (Though some people have argued that there exists an
inherent problem in reconciling Islam with democracy,[110] an argument by
which I remain largely unpersuaded, and one which surely has to be set
against the often problematic relationship which has existed historically
between certain Christian denominations and democratic politics.[111]) The
point is that, at present, al–Qaida has overwhelmingly failed to topple those

apostate regimes which it most sought that its terrorist violence would destroy.[112]

What, relatedly, of expelling the USA and its influence from Muslim countries? After (and because of) the al-Qaida attacks of 9/11, the USA invaded and occupied two Muslim countries (Afghanistan and then Iraq) with a very heavy military presence. It also deployed thousands of military personnel in other Muslim countries (Chad, Niger, Yemen) as well as influencing deeply the policy and politics and state-form of numerous other Muslim nations too (including the significant example of Pakistan). Regarding Palestine, if 9/11 did have an effect then it seems rather to have increased support for Israel within the United States.[113] In all of these ways al-Qaida violence might be judged to have been rather counter-productive (and productive of unintended consequences), since it reinforced heavy US involvement in the Muslim world, including military and very violent involvement.[114] Removing the Americans from Muslim lands was exactly what shoe-bomber Richard Reid emphatically failed to do, and the same has broadly been true even of more tactically effective jihadists also. Al-Qaida has, in practice, not driven the United States from the Muslim world. Far from it. For if 9/11 did make the United States rethink what its major threats actually were, and did lead it to redirect its foreign policy partly as a consequence, then this did little to bring about a withdrawal of US military presence and power from the Middle East and from other Muslim settings.

Indeed, while bin Laden cast his violent crusade in terms of defensive response to US and allied aggression (as he put it in the wake of 9/11: 'we ourselves are the victims of murders and massacres. We are only defending ourselves against the United States'),[115] the irony was that prior to 11 September it was far more difficult in any serious sense to present the United States as an invasive force against Muslims than it became *after* that brutal attack and directly because of it. Here, as so often, an accurate grasp of the actual nature of international relations did not represent a strong point in the thinking of bin Laden and most of his comrades. And their facile understanding stretched across many aspects of al-Qaida thinking, regrettably. As Michael Burleigh has sharp-sightedly pointed out, 'There is something narcissistic about this [jihadist] assumption that the west is obsessed with Islam and seeks to destroy it. It is not.'[116]

Bin Laden himself certainly underestimated the strength of the United States of America, and his hopes of destroying that superpower were clearly unsuccessful (ludicrously so, in truth). His comparison of the anti-Soviet struggle in Afghanistan with jihad against America was multiply flawed. He exaggerated the degree to which the 1980s Afghan imbroglio lay behind the collapse of the Soviet Union (and, in any case, his own role and that of other non-Afghan fighters there had been marginal in relation to the Soviet defeat,[117] something that he did recognize). Moreover, he had wrongly assumed an equivalence between Soviet vulnerability and what turned out to be resilient US strength. Washington represented a far sturdier opponent than had Moscow: ironically, indeed, it was the competitive *strength* of the USA which had in fact played a far more decisive role in defeating the Soviet Union than had Muslim resistance in Afghanistan; and—with further irony—it had been money and weapons from the USA and the Saudis which had helped enable the mujahideen to fight the Soviets there in any case.[118] So there simply was no appropriate analogy here with al-Qaida's assault on the United States, and this central foundation of bin Laden's thinking was disastrously flawed: at heart, the al-Qaida notion that America was not strong enough to resist Muslim violence was one that proved strikingly ill judged. The war with al-Qaida did not diminish the USA's status as the world's pre-eminent power.

It is important to note that the attacks of 9/11 themselves produced an intensified, more unified American nationalism: by early October 2001, 80 per cent of Americans were apparently displaying the country's flag; on 9/11 itself Wal-Mart sold over 100,000 flags, and a quarter of a million the following day;[119] and after 9/11 America became, if anything, more patriotically committed and cooperative and—for a time—it even became more likely to trust its own government (quite an achievement in itself, but not one that al-Qaida had sought after.[120] Unanticipated futures again). Not only did jihadist violence not constrain the USA's sense of its own unique role as a global power and, indeed, as a globally responsible arbiter; in fact, 11 September strengthened US determination to provide global leadership. It's arguable that America's response to 9/11 saw it stress even more strongly than before its own particular and special virtues, witnessed it strive for a more unified identity domestically, and led it to pursue more energetically a dominant role abroad in international relations.[121] The physical, military manifestation of this abroad might have been counter-productive in some cases (Iraq prominent among them, as we will see) but it hardly embodied a diminution of US global power or presence or role; 'Horrifying though the carnage of 9/11 was in New York, it left the international power of the US and its internal structures completely unaffected.'[122] Indeed, a long-term, historically informed judgment would probably maintain that the end of the Cold War brought about a much more significant set of changes in the shape of international relations than did the eye-catchingly memorable 9/11 attacks.[123] So here the problem of causation is partially solved, I think, by adopting the historian's longer-term sense of continuities when considering supposedly watershed-inducing change.

Of course, the matter is in part more complex than this, when we seek a full assessment of the effects of al-Qaida's violence. In terms of hurting and damaging the USA and its allies (rather than destroying them or driving them out of the Muslim world), al-Qaida terrorism could be judged to have had greater success. The grand hopes of Sheikh Omar Abdel Rahman, Khalid Sheikh Mohammed, and Ramzi Yousef in relation to the 1993 World Trade Center bombing in New York might not have been completely realized;[124] but that 26 February assault did kill six people and injure more than a thousand, it did represent the first jihadist hit within the USA itself (with appalling pre-echoes of future violence, as we now know), and it did cause understandable and extensive shock at the time.

Spectacularly, 9/11 itself inflicted horrific, symbolically powerful damage on the USA, something of which al-Qaida was openly proud. Ayman al-Zawahiri, for example, referred to how the 9/11 attackers had been 'able to inflict damage upon America, such as it had never before witnessed in its history';[125] bin Laden considered 9/11 to have demonstrated the 'fragile' nature of the United States.[126] So too the Madrid attacks of March 2004 and the London bombings of July 2005 did real damage to America's allies and, despite the resilience of these states in the face of terrorist threat, there is no doubt that some painful wounds were inflicted.

Though hard to calibrate, the psychological aspect of this is probably important and is certainly worth considering. The 9/11 attacks did make many in the United States begin to feel far more vulnerable and insecure and afraid. The unprecedented scale of the 9/11 assault on the USA itself was, for obvious reasons, extremely frightening for many, its sudden unexpectedness contributing greatly to this effect.

There are some who have seen 9/11 decisively as a historical watershed.[127] I myself remain broadly sceptical of this historical fault-line approach, since so much of post-9/11 politics and economics and culture and society has remained recognizable and familiar from the pre-2001 world.[128] But it is hard to deny that 9/11 created a new and shaking sense of vulnerability within the USA, and that as such it could be said to have had a damagingly morale-denting effect on al-Qaida's major enemy. 11 September caused many individuals in the United States considerable psychological harm, in terms both of the immediate terror, trauma, and distress caused by the events themselves (especially for those most directly exposed to the attacks), and also of the wider inculcation of a more enduring, anticipatory fear about possible future terrorism (though it is also true that much of the psychological trauma seeped away within a relatively short time).[129]

If the psychological damage was enormous, then it was also uneven. There is some evidence to suggest that terrorist violence such as al-Qaida's has its most painful psychological impact upon weaker and more vulnerable people in society, including the socially isolated, members of some ethnic minorities, the disabled, and the mentally ill.[130] More generally, 9/11 did have a significant effect on US society, self-image, self-narration, and contemporary life, at popular as well as policy and high-political level, as the tragedy prompted dramatic and enduring American responses.[131] Equally clearly, violence against America's allies (as in Spain in 2004 and the UK in 2005) also caused psychological damage in those respective countries, especially in the immediate aftermath of the terrorist atrocities.[132]

What about economic damage? Al-Qaida was certainly keen to achieve this, as we have seen, and 9/11 presents an intriguing case study for analysis. There was undoubtedly a short-term collapse of economic activity (the Dow Jones index losing 7.1 per cent of its value on the first post-9/11 day of trading).[133] And, while the attacks themselves seem to have cost something in the region of half a million dollars to carry out, the cost of the damage caused by those attacks has been variously estimated but includes assessments of around $50 billion,[134] and $200 billion,[135] and $500 billion.[136] Moreover, John Mueller and Mark Stewart's calculation that US spending on domestic security in the decade after 9/11 rose by over $1 trillion shows one of the key ways in which huge economic cost was inflicted by a comparatively limited (though shockingly spectacular) terrorist assault.[137] The USA was certainly not crushed economically by al-Qaida's most famous attack, and states' capacity for enduring the economic effects of terrorist violence have been rather impressive historically.[138] But jihadist terrorists did here cause significant economic damage to their enemy, one key example being that American domestic airline traffic and US tourism were hit hard and lastingly by the atrocity of 9/11. And it was not just 9/11, of course: the 12 October 2000 attack on the USS *Cole* in Aden caused a quarter of a billion dollars' worth of damage on the ship,[139] while the 2004 train bombings in Madrid have been estimated to have caused immediate material damage worth more than 17 million euros, and direct economic costs of over 211 million euros.[140]

Economic effects of al-Qaida violence have also involved, however, huge US investment in counter-terrorism in ways that have at times worked *against* jihadists. Post-9/11 especially, the United States has deployed a vast array of different skills and people to improve its security and to lessen its vulnerability to future terrorism. Much of this has involved technological innovation, and consequent, intensive economic investment and development (especially governmental investment in new security technologies); the post-9/11 period has seen aviation security improve as a direct result,[141] though clearly risks will persist. 11 September also prompted the reorganization of parts of the US state, with the January 2003 creation of the Department of Homeland Security arguably making the US more coordinated and coherent in its anti-terrorist activities. Much progress has undoubtedly been made, post-9/11 and in direct response to the jihadist threat, in re-tuning the USA's intelligence-based approach to challenges such as terrorism.[142]

Al-Qaida's 9/11 attacks prompted the USA and its allies to become lastingly involved in wars in Afghanistan and Iraq, and there were serious, direct, and damaging costs for these states in doing so. Many western military and civilian lives were lost. The British had already had some painful nineteenth-century experience of Afghan wars;[143] in the twenty-first century endeavour, by the time that UK forces withdrew from Afghanistan in 2014 after their thirteen-year campaign there, 453 of their service personnel had been killed and another 616 had been seriously or very seriously injured; there were huge economic costs incurred (£37 billion being the total cost of the war);[144] and drawing western powers like the UK into such imbroglios—though it clashed with al-Qaida's expressed desire to drive the USA and its influence from Muslim lands—did at least offer the chance for continued jihadist violence against it and its allies, and for the inflicting of many direct hits upon them as a consequence.

It should also be noted, however, that it was very heavily the Muslim populations of those countries which suffered direct violence most often. Crucially, we do have to reflect in historical context on the very varied answer necessitated by the question of for *whom* al-Qaida terrorism has supposedly worked; and historical attention to particular context here points to an extraordinarily different set of results in different settings. There has been vast and often fatal al-Qaida and al-Qaida-linked violence against

Muslims, and such terrorism against Muslim civilians has had a very damaging effect on al-Qaida's popularity and support base at local level across
much of the Islamic world;[145] between 2002 and 2009 even bin Laden's own
popularity, for example, dropped starkly in Pakistan (the country in which
he latterly resided).[146] Moreover, al-Qaida leaders have recognized the vital
importance of popular support for the ultimate success of their cause. Bin
Laden seems to have been distressed about the number of Muslims being
killed in al-Qaida's name and, in al-Zawahiri's own words, 'In the absence
of popular support, the Islamic mujahid movement would be crushed in the
shadows.'[147] Even in the comparatively non-violent context of the UK, one
of the effects of 9/11 and especially of 7/7 was to make the daily experiences of many Muslims more difficult, as polarization, exclusion, and suspicion grew in the wake of terrorist violence (violence for which very few
UK Muslims offered any support).[148] If it is true that jihadist violence has
produced a situation in which '"Britishness" has come to be constructed in
contradistinction to a new Islamist terrorist Other',[149] then this might be
judged a deeply ambiguous jihadist achievement as far as the daily lives of
British Muslims are concerned, both individually and collectively. For some
jihadists, the use of violence might have served (in part) as an explicit performance of a religious duty; but it has damaged many from within the
Muslim community itself.

And internationally, it is vital to note that al-Qaida's violence prompted
wars which led to the degradation, devastation, and destruction of Afghanistan
and Iraq, both of them major Muslim countries. At best, the western mission in Iraq resulted in very ambiguous outcomes for much of that country
politically; 'Iraq has disintegrated. Little is exchanged between its three great
communities—Shia, Sunni, and Kurds—except gunfire.'[150] And the Iraqi
lives lost, and the Iraqi culture and society ravaged by the violence, have
represented one terrible consequence of al-Qaida's 9/11 assault in historical
practice.[151] But even here the picture is complex. Al-Qaida's 9/11 assault
helped prompt an invasion of Iraq which generated resistance from (among
others) AQI; by 2014 AQI had metastasized (through a process of admittedly
complex causation)[152] into that much more formidable antagonist for the
west, the Islamic State of Iraq and the Levant (ISIS). ISIS's capture of Mosul
(Iraq's northern capital) on 10 June 2014 signalled the gravity of this new
threat, which is likely to prove enduring and which embodies considerable
tactical skill. The Sunni ISIS gained control of significant territory in Iraq
(and also Syria), reflecting the danger that (as Audrey Cronin has suggested)

terrorism might transform into something worse rather than better as matters evolve,[153] as far as damage to its opponents is concerned.

Terrorism is always changing, and some of its evolutionary developments
involve it bleeding into other phenomena. So ISIS has far more fighters
than al-Qaida, and controls territory in a manner that bin Laden never
managed; but its roots lay in the post-2003 violent resistance to an invasion
of Iraq which bin Laden and his colleagues had stimulated. Here, the
non-inevitability and unpredictability of political development are again
very telling: extraneous events (such as the instability of the Assad regime in
Syria from 2011 onwards) contributed to changing the al-Qaida-generated
story very markedly. So, while al-Qaida leader Ayman al-Zawahiri has been
critical of ISIS[154] and we cannot conflate the two groupings, there is no
doubt that the actions of the one set in motion events which organically
grew into the other. By prompting actions which spawned ISIS, al-Qaida
has undoubtedly created deep regional problems for the USA and its allies.
The fact that (as so often) the changes that terrorists wrought were not the
anticipated ones, does not mean that the outcomes have been entirely out
of tune with their overall wishes.

What of al-Qaida's other central, primary strategic objective, achieving
the renaissance of a particular kind of Islam? Again, on the surface, it seems
that there has been a spectacular failure here too, as we consider the effect
of al-Qaida terrorism on intra-Muslim power struggles and arguments and
dynamics. An al-Qaida-related thinker such as Abu Muhammad al-Maqdisi
(who remained committed to the deployment of violence against the USA
and against apostate Muslim regimes) has clearly failed to mobilize anything
other than a very small fraction of Muslim people behind his particular
version of Salafism.[155] And much of the religious thinking of al-Qaida
jihadists has been so muddled and lacking in credibility or authority that
such failure seems far from surprising: 'Research reveals that the majority of
Islamist activists, including the civil engineer Osama bin Laden and the
architect Mohammed Atta, are drawn not from people trained in theology
or religious studies, but from the ranks of graduates in modern faculties
such as medicine or engineering who combine a sophisticated knowledge
of the technical products of modernity with two-dimensional understand-
ings of their inherited faith tradition.'[156]

The hope of setting up an internationally extensive, sharia law-governed
Caliphate of the kind ideally preferred by al-Qaida certainly seems implaus-
ible, given current levels of support for it in the wider international Muslim

community.[157] Yes, ISIS's 2014 declaration of a Caliphate covering parts of
Iraq and Syria was a major development; but it fell far short of what al-Qaida
had hinted that it sought. Indeed, al-Qaida's Salafism has tended to remain
very much a minority taste, even among Sunnis,[158] with there seeming little
imminent prospect that the group's violence will work in terms of securing
a mass transformation of public opinion in its jihadist favour. Indeed, people
like Abu Muhammad al-Maqdisi have been explicit about what they have
seen as the damage done to the Islamist cause by some instances of indiscriminate or excessive al-Qaida violence.[159] The turbulence across so much
of the Muslim world (with dramatic political change in Tunisia, Eqypt, and
Libya in 2011, for example) seemed to involve very different goals and
methods from those espoused by al-Qaida, and to reflect a marginalization
of that group among Muslims. Whatever the multiple entangled roots feed-
ing the misnamed Arab Spring, the phenomenon was not one of al-Qaida's
creation or in tune with that grouping's approach to religious revival.

More broadly, and despite their ostensible anti-westernism, jihadist
ideas have been drawn significantly from modern, and indeed very western, sources;[160] when examined closely, they can also be seen to be
founded at times on very simplistic analyses (as with Sayyid Qutb's often
laughable reading of the United States of America); and they have relied
on some egregious distortion of holy texts in the hope of achieving
aggressive purpose.[161] It is important to remember that there are no neat
mirror images between major religions and that, for example, what happens in Islam and what happens in Christianity—though superficially
resemblant—might in reality involve very different dynamics.[162] But on
the point that we are currently considering, the dynamics do seem clear
enough at present: as things stand, it is distinctly unlikely that jihadist
ideas about religious revival will resonate sufficiently with enough people to gain the major historical momentum that has been sought by
al-Qaida; 'The fact is that al-Qaida is increasingly alienated from most
Muslims and even from most Islamists, having lost the strategic initiative
in Iraq, Indonesia, and elsewhere.'[163] Reinforcing this point, it might be
judged that the idea of setting Islam decisively against and apart from
other faith systems and their cultures runs against the traceable, longer-
term pattern of the human past in any case.[164]

If strategic victory has therefore largely eluded al-Qaida, might we judge
that their terrorism has worked in terms of at least *partial* strategic victory?
Have they secured diluted versions of their central, primary goals; how far

have they achieved their secondary goals; have they been able to determine the relevant political agenda through their violence?

The picture is complicated. It would be hard to make much of a serious case regarding the goals of a Salafist renaissance or of undoing apostate Muslim regimes, although the setting in motion of events which led to the ISIS-proclaimed Caliphate could be read as a diluted and vicarious success for al-Qaida, perhaps. More weightily, however, the evidence adduced in the discussion above offers some strong grounds for thinking that—while expelling the USA and its influence from Muslim countries, much less destroying the United States, have been mockingly distant for al-Qaida—the group's terrorism has indeed managed to inflict some very serious damage on its American and other enemies, whether personal, psychological, economic, cultural, or political. In this sense—the inflicting of painful damage upon opponents—al-Qaida's terrorism could be judged to have worked at partial strategic level.

Secondary goals have offered more returns still. Partly overlapping with the inflicting of damage is the secondary reward of securing revenge as an end in itself. This has surely been achieved repeatedly, and with some shocking human consequences for victims of the violence. From the pain of 1993's World Trade Center assault to the devastating humiliation of 9/11 and beyond, there has been frequent success in hitting back at the USA and other enemies for perceived, prior crimes against Muslims. In bin Laden's own view, all Americans could be considered legitimate targets: 'The American people are the ones who pay the taxes which fund the planes that bomb us in Afghanistan, the tanks that strike and destroy our homes in Palestine, the armies which occupy our lands in the Arabian Gulf, and the fleets which ensure the blockage of Iraq... That is why the American people cannot be considered innocent of all the crimes committed by the Americans and Jews against us.'[165] Similarly, al-Qaida in the Arabian Peninsula (AQAP) has had some success in striking vengefully at Saudi Arabian security forces and other targets,[166] and the killers of Lee Rigby in London in 2013 had been in touch with AQAP beforehand. This vengeful infliction of suffering carries with it unique personal tragedies, the awfulness of which has to be remembered when we assess terrorism's efficacy. Anat Rosenberg was killed by the 7/7 bombings in 2005 as she travelled to her work at a London children's charity. On the bus which Hasib Hussain's bomb destroyed that day, Ms Rosenberg was speaking on the telephone to her boyfriend John Falding as she died: 'I heard this dreadful scream in the background. Then after a few seconds her phone went dead.'[167]

The many instances that there have been of such blood-stained al-Qaida and al-Qaida-related struggle testify to the grouping's success regarding another secondary goal, the sustaining of a form of resistance (albeit one that is now arguably much attenuated, and one which in any case never involved the practical likelihood of genuinely committed mass support across the world).[168] Al-Qaida has elicited some sympathy and backing[169] and zealous adherence across many countries, with its strikingly expressed argument and its violent campaign possessing enduring allure for a minority of Muslims.[170] And the sustaining of a jihadist *ideology* has in itself, of course, represented a far from negligible achievement. As Bruce Hoffman and Fernando Reinares put it: 'while significant al-Qaida inspired terrorist activity occurred in the aftermath of the September 11 attacks, just as consequential were the proliferation and durability of its jihadist ideology'.[171] Nor did the al-Qaida brand lack some enduring popularity. A major poll conducted by the Pew Global Attitudes Project in March 2004 found Osama bin Laden to be viewed favourably by large numbers of people in Pakistan (65 per cent), Jordan (55 per cent), and Morocco (45 per cent)—all countries of significance in the battle for political sympathy.[172] Despite the broad rejection, therefore, of al-Qaida politics across most of the Muslim world,[173] there has been a significant degree of minority sympathy and sustained backing.

For some al-Qaida operatives, local agendas have represented what (for the group considered as a whole) might also be read as significant secondary ambitions. Especially after the post-9/11 US assault on al-Qaida, much that has gone under its networked flag has embodied very local action and motivation. So the AQI prevention of the stability sought by the USA in post-2003 Iraq could be seen as a secondary success, though it should be noted that public opinion turned starkly away from AQI from 2006 onwards. Still, between February 2003 and December 2010, AQI killed over 4,000 people (even excluding attacks on the military)[174] and this extraordinary violence did destabilize US and allied hopes for the country, with lawlessness and a measure of mocking chaos long enduring there.[175] The anti-US violence in Iraq during the post-2003 period was not by any means all al-Qaida-generated; but that grouping was clearly involved in it. As one al-Qaida-linked document tellingly expressed it in relation to post-invasion Iraq, 'If the United States is defeated this time—and this is what we pray will happen—the doors will open wide to the Islamic tide. For the first time in modern history, we will have an advanced foundation for Islamic awakening and jihad close to the land of the two mosques [Saudi Arabia] and Al-Aqsa mosque [Jerusalem].'[176]

Also related to Iraq were the Madrid killings of March 2004. In the run-up to the Spanish General Election of Sunday 14 March it had been expected that the PP[177] government led by Prime Minister Aznar (which was militarily supportive of the USA in Iraq, with some 1,400 Spanish troops having been committed there) would retain power since they were ahead in the opinion polls. But three days earlier, on the morning of 11 March, the commuter train bombings occurred at Atocha and other stations. Aznar's government wrongly and clumsily blamed the Basque separatists, ETA; public arguments ensued on the issue between the PP and the PSOE,[178] damagingly for the former, who were widely and angrily perceived to have tried to deceive the electorate; the PSOE won the election and the new Prime Minister (Jose Luis Rodriguez Zapatero) fulfilled his manifesto promise of withdrawing Spanish troops from Iraq. Did the al-Qaida-inspired and al-Qaida-linked bombers therefore win the election? That might be putting it slightly too strongly. But there is evidence that the Madrid atrocity and responses to it did between them help significantly to swing opinion away from Aznar's government,[179] and that this locally specific secondary goal (removing Spain from the US endeavour in Iraq) was secured through the blood-spattered, gruesome violence of 11 March.

In terms of the partial strategic issue of determining the political agenda, al-Qaida's record is again mixed, though it must be judged largely disappointing when viewed from their own zealous perspective. It's true that their violence (and especially that of 11 September 2001) greatly affected US and some other countries' priorities, making counter-terrorism an issue of much greater significance and prominence and importance;[180] but this, as we will see later on in more detail, was far from uniformly welcome in terms of its effects on jihadist organizational capacity. Bin Laden tried to present President Bush's War on Terror as a war against Islam;[181] but, as we have seen, he had limited success in persuading the majority of Muslims sustainedly to agree with him. Ironically, bin Laden rather welcomed Samuel Huntington's clash of civilizations thesis (in Osama's own pleading words, 'the clash is a clash of civilizations').[182] But the desire to establish a durably dichotomous world (Muslim; non-Muslim) through provocative violence largely failed, with the global Muslim community by no means displaying unanimous hostility towards the west (or anything approaching this), and with most Muslims remaining markedly non-jihadist in their politics.[183]

What of tactical efficacy? Has al-Qaida terrorism worked in that sense? I think that efforts to gauge success too neatly or mechanically in terms of the number of people killed probably fail to capture the nuanced complexity of effect here. But, operationally, there have been some cruelly successful al-Qaida ventures, and these have to be considered as at least part of our answer. 9/11 itself seems to have exceeded even bin Laden's own hopes in terms of the damage caused.[184] More broadly, suicide terrorism has been important as an al-Qaida tactical method: 'Suicide tactics are devastatingly effective, lethally efficient, have a greater likelihood of success, and are relatively inexpensive and generally easier to execute than other attack modes.'[185] As Pape and Feldman have suggested, during the period 1980–2001, more than 70 per cent of deaths due to terrorism have been caused by suicide terrorism, despite the fact that only 3 per cent of terrorist attacks during those years have used this method.[186]

Clearly, the most famous such attack was 9/11 itself, and one might very plausibly present this as having been a tactical success, despite its broader strategic failure.[187] The brutal operation cleverly enabled a weaker side to hit very symbolic and important targets that were deeply emblematic of enemy power. As we have seen, it was a comparatively inexpensive venture, and it involved an evasion of elaborate US law-enforcement efforts: the Central Intelligence Agency had formed a special unit in 1996 to pursue Osama bin Laden, and yet bin Laden's al-Qaida was nonetheless able to carry out the 9/11 attacks. Again and again when we consider the degree to which terrorism works, we see a mutually shaping relationship between non-state terrorists and their state adversaries. One aspect of that is the one which is echoed here: the degree to which terrorists in al-Qaida can tactically succeed will frequently depend on the extent to which their state opponents do or do not succeed in thwarting them. Important here is coordination, one of the most significant aspects of effective counter-terrorism, whether between different elements of one state or between different states facing the same terrorist threat.[188] As one of the foremost experts on American efforts in the field has put it: 'Forging American national security policy is a team game', but a game not always played as well as it might have been; 'the Central Intelligence Agency never succeeded in centralizing intelligence'.[189] It is clear that al-Qaida has at times benefited decisively in tactical terms from such coordination failings by states.[190]

Though no al-Qaida operation could approach 9/11 in terms of its tactical-operational success, there have been significant tactical wins on other occasions by the group. The February 1993 World Trade Center attack might not have brought down the North Tower into the South Tower as appears to have been intended. And there was a *Four Lions*-esque amateurism to parts of the episode.[191] One of the 1993 conspirators (Mohammed Salameh) had rented the truck that was used in the attack, and was caught having attempted—*after* the bombing—to regain the $400 deposit that he had paid for it, by claiming that the vehicle had been stolen. For all of that, the hideous loss of life and the shock of the assault marked something of a tactical success for the conspirators. October 2000 saw the tactically ingenious attack on the USS *Cole*; again, Madrid in March 2004 was a tactical triumph (tragically), and so too was 7/7 in London. Eliza Manningham-Buller, the then Director General of the UK's Security Service (MI5), appears to have told MPs immediately before 7 July 2005 that there existed no immediate terrorist threat to the UK.[192] On 7/7, however, three bombs exploded at around 8.50 a.m. on the London Underground, and a fourth at 9.47 a.m. on a bus in Tavistock Place. Fifty-six people (including the four bombers) were killed, and around 700 more were wounded. The entire operation seems to have cost around £8,000: a painful example of credit card-limit terrorism, and a devastatingly cost-effective, world-noteworthy tactical success. As the UK's own Report into the bombings made clear, 'the explosions were caused by home-made organic peroxide-based devices, packed into rucksacks'; 'Organic peroxide explosive . . . does not require a great deal of expertise and can be made using readily available materials and domestic equipment.'[193]

Clearly, however, many al-Qaida schemes have been tactically ineffective too, and it has been claimed of the group that 'the vast majority of terror plots end in failure for the conspirators'.[194] December 2001 shoe-bomber Richard Reid failed to detonate his explosive device while on his American Airlines flight from Paris to Miami. Indeed, this al-Qaida plot has pathetic failure running a long way through it: Reid himself was a London-born, repeated criminal, whose pre-jihadist career reflected a somewhat ill-adjusted pattern echoed in the tactical hopelessness of his attempted mass murder. Again, the jihadist plan which began in 2003, and which was unveiled in 2004 during Operation Crevice, saw the UK authorities discover and thwart would-be mass-casualty attacks in Britain—another operational failure for the terrorists. The most sustained scholarly assessment to date of AQAP's campaign in Saudi Arabia has judged it ultimately to have run out of tactical energy and to have been thwarted.[195] And tactical difficulties could be generated paradoxically by some earlier tactical successes. 9/11 made the day-to-day running of al-Qaida operations much more difficult during ensuing years, given the unprecedented attention subsequently devoted by bin Laden's enemies to thwarting him and his alliance of jihadists.

Another kind of tactical success is the grabbing of publicity and there is no doubt that—from the World Trade Center attack of 1993, to 9/11 itself, to Madrid in 2004, to London in 2005, and repeatedly beyond these cases—al-Qaida has achieved some extraordinary fame for its actions and its mission. And, in terms of causation, there can be little doubt that its extraordinarily high publicity status has been secured precisely and directly through its violence, and that the violence has allowed it to disseminate its ideas through various means on the basis of far greater salience than would have been the case without the terrorism.[196] Sometimes brilliant at utilizing the media, al-Qaida might indeed be thought to have engaged in a species of blood-stained preaching or proclamation, and in a defiant and terroristic declaration that this violently Salafist fundamentalism will not disappear and cannot be disregarded. Though bin Laden's arguments tended towards the derivative,[197] he did possess a Che Guevara-esque iconic style and presence and, regrettably, al-Qaida's murderous actions gained for him and his cause an extraordinary, unprecedented publicity. Even where the al-Qaida link seemed more sketchy, the publicity rewards could be huge. The *Charlie Hebdo* and subsequent jihadist killings in France in January 2015, for example, prompted vast, front-page-level, international attention: 'Al-Qaida Gunmen Execute Cop in Street';[198] 'Gunmen kill twelve in massacre at Paris magazine';[199] 'War on Freedom'.[200]

High-level publicity was often used to reinforce al-Qaida's politics in another area of tactical success, that of undermining opponents in various ways. There is little doubt that the leading figures in al-Qaida have closely studied and reflected on their opponents' manoeuvres and their vulnerabilities.[201] It could certainly be argued that 9/11 and associated al-Qaida violence and threats prompted a (contingent, rather than inevitable) US response which undermined the credibility and international reputation of the world's greatest power; 'The US invasion of Iraq, based on the false pretexts of the threat of weapons of mass destruction and the alleged link between al-Qaida, the 9/11 attacks, and Saddam Hussein, has caused the United States to lose nearly all credibility. As a result, any attempt at public diplomacy in the Middle East is met with deep scepticism.'[202] Many observers have considered the USA's post-9/11 efforts to undermine opponents within the Muslim world to have been far from successful.[203] And the Iraq endeavour certainly did—amid other consequences—generate considerable

international disaffection from US foreign policy. Indeed, there is considerable evidence that the US-led response to 9/11 helped to intensify a profound anti-Americanism across much of the world.[204] This should, of course,
be set against the revulsion that most Muslims have felt at al-Qaida's terrorist violence; most Muslims were, for example, horrified by 9/11.[205] Yet the
Iraq episode in particular did much to strengthen that jihadist threat which
it had ostensibly been intended to crush: 'Since 2003, the war in Iraq has
without question fuelled the process of radicalization worldwide, including
the United States.'[206]

Anxiety about the subsequent danger from jihadism existed for US allies
also. In October 2011 a senior UK intelligence source suggested that over
200 people in the United Kingdom were then involved in planning jihadist
suicide attacks in the UK.[207] Again, in the period immediately prior to the
2005 jihadist bombings in London, the UK's Joint Intelligence Committee
(JIC) had judged 'that western states could not be confident of identifying
preparations for attacks, and that there would probably be a successful attack
of some sort in the UK in the next five years'.[208] 7/7 brought that truth
bloodily home, and it was a threat which persisted as security and safety
continued to be undermined. In January 2015, following the *Charlie Hebdo*
jihadist killings of journalists and police officers in Paris, the Director
General of MI5 warned that: 'Al-Qaida continues to provide a focus for
Islamist-inspired violence and a significant driving force for extremists to
plot terrorist attacks against the West....We know, for example, that a group
of core al-Qaida terrorists in Syria is planning mass casualty attacks against
the west.'[209]

Part of this process of undermining the west was helped by the west's
own preparedness to transgress some of its precious rules of restrained
behaviour in terms of law and counter-terrorism. Here, it might be suggested that al-Qaida violence prompted liberal-democratic opponents partially to undermine their own moral legitimacy, and to degrade their own
liberty and culture. (As so often, this was non-inevitable: choices were made
from a range of possibilities about how to treat terror suspects, about
whether or not to extend legal powers, about how to approach the question
of torture, and so on.) Professor Alex Danchev has rightly referred to 'the
power of images in international affairs';[210] I suspect that the horror at photographs of 9/11 itself will be offset for future generations by the very memorable images of abusive treatment at Guantanamo Bay and Abu-Ghraib
Prison, where the imbroglio surrounding the treatment of detainees and

prisoners has lastingly damaged the reputation of the United States.[211] As one scholar has noted with particular reference to the post-7/7 UK context, 'al–Qaida strategists have the ability to prompt counter-measures that serve them better than the democracies they attack'.[212]

Indeed, Professor Conor Gearty has subtly argued that the 2001 atrocity reinforced an unwelcome trend for such states towards what he calls 'neo-democracy':'the modern tendency to see liberty as in reality a selective rather than universal entitlement and security as something that only those with liberty ought to have, even if it is at the expense of others'.[213] In Gearty's view, genuine democracy requires true equality of treatment before the law, and the egalitarian application of the concept of human rights.Arguably, neither of these emerged unbruised from the counter-terrorist reaction to 9/11 in the USA and among its allies. So terrorist violence can prompt states into undermining their own commitments to human rights, equality, liberty, and the rule of law, a process which long pre-dated al–Qaida but which has again risen to prominence in the wake of that group's very brutal violence.[214]

The mutually shaping, reciprocal, antiphonal, paradoxically intimate relationship between non-state terrorism and state counter-terrorist response can yield doubly unwelcome patterns here, with states and non-state actors reacting to each other in processes of spiralling degradation. Certainly, al–Qaida itself picked up eagerly on the ways in which episodes such as Guantanamo Bay seemed to discredit the United States,[215] and has had some measure of success in presenting the USA as abusive and illegitimate. Despite the dystopian anxieties of some, 9/11 and associated attacks and threats did not end the USA's accustomed way of life or that of its democratic allies, and nor did it produce a descent into the decisive abrogation of legal rights and duties. But (as so often in response to terrorist challenge) there was an erosion of certain democratically established norms and practices, in ways that might be seen both to discredit the states concerned and also to give propagandist gifts to their terrorist adversaries. Even in the process of bringing to trial the alleged architect of the 9/11 attack itself—Khaled Sheikh Mohammed—allegations made about US torture at secret CIA sites, and also about other supposed US transgressions, became prominent and occasionally embarrassing.[216]

It is clear that, in the wake of 9/11, the United States did deploy coercive interrogation methods and that on numerous occasions it transgressed basic principles of human rights as well as the principles of international law.[217] In this period, allegations of torture or of complicity in torture have tended to damage the credibility of the liberal–democratic state in its struggle against terrorism. This was the case, for example, with claims publicly made regarding al-Qaida suspects who had been arrested during 2003–7 and allegedly tortured by Pakistan's ISI, before then being questioned by an MI5 which was allegedly aware of and therefore complicit in this prior torture.[218] While the UK authorities emphatically deny that they have in fact condoned torture against suspected terrorists, allegations of collusion in the practice have been persistent and rather damaging, as have similar allegations made against the CIA.[219] A US Senate Select Committee assessment (made public in 2014) itself found that the CIA's use of 'enhanced interrogation techniques was not an effective means of obtaining accurate information', that the Agency's justification of the use of such extreme methods 'rested on inaccurate claims of their effectiveness', and that the CIA's interrogations of detainees 'were brutal and far worse than the CIA represented to policymakers and others'.[220] Indeed, the human costs of the brutal treatment of detainees by the USA can now be seen in a rich, evocative body of available evidence. So Mohamedou Ould Slahi's Kafkaesque account of having had to endure CIA rendition followed by both proxy and direct US interrogation (much of it brutally harsh and inhumane and degrading), and lengthy, isolated, and seemingly unjustified incarceration for years at Guantanamo Bay,[221] provides a powerful example both of the practical effects on some Muslims of the al-Qaida campaign against America, and also of the rougher, uglier aspects of the US response to terrorism from 9/11 onwards.

In another sense too, al-Qaida might be judged to have undermined the USA and its allies, by managing to draw it into conflicts in Afghanistan and Iraq from which western powers have disengaged without securing their proclaimed goals. If one takes a lengthy historical view of Afghanistan's past, then the challenges facing the US-led engagement from 2001 onwards certainly seem to have been very daunting indeed. Given the extraordinary complexity and fluidity of Afghan politics over the longer term, the difficulties in securing desired and pervasive political change there historically, the fact that the growing preoccupation with Iraq greatly distracted the USA and its allies from Afghanistan and somewhat undermined their work in the latter country, and the reality that political legitimacy for Afghan regimes is very difficult to sustain if they are seen by Afghans themselves as 'beholden to foreign masters'—given all of this, it might be thought that western ambition post-9/11 was tinged with naivety, and that the eventual elusiveness of success in Afghanistan might be judged unsurprising.[222]

Serious analysis of the post-9/11 Afghan conflict will necessarily result in complex findings, and much was undoubtedly achieved there by the USA and its allies. Yet al-Qaida is not without some successes in this process either, since US and allied accomplishments were overall rather disappointing and ambiguous. Even though much of the violence against the western powers in Afghanistan has been practised by groups other than al-Qaida, that latter organization can take credit for drawing the west into the maelstrom, and it has clearly played a notably violent role there in the post-2001 conflict.[223] Although the violence often took the form more of insurgency or civil war than of classically understood terrorism, terroristic methods were often deployed[224] and, as noted, it had been a striking act of terrorism which had prompted the USA and its associates to invade Afghanistan in the first place. Moreover, as noted in the Introduction, those practising terroristic violence are often (as here) involved in struggles in which other (sometimes grander) means of violence are also deployed; in the Afghan case, the insurgency which involved but also exceeded terrorism was the most effective mechanism for undermining al-Qaida's enemies.

At the time of their forces' departure in October 2014, there were profoundly mixed UK views about how successful the post-9/11 engagement in Afghanistan had actually been, especially when set against the very high costs incurred. 'It is actually really difficult to determine today what the results of this campaign will be' (Brigadier Darrell Amison, commander of the British Army's 102 Logistics Brigade); 'We've worked bloody hard to get here and a lot has been achieved, but there has been a lot of sacrifice' (Royal Air Force Group Captain Andy Knowles); 'This is a country that is a work in progress rather than a country that has been completed' (Brigadier Rob Thomson); 'Though we hear a lot about Afghanistan being a better place, no words could ever persuade a mother that it was worth the loss of her son.... The improvements will soon be swallowed up. It is already happening, as in Iraq. Even if some have benefited, it was not worth my son's life' (Patricia Quinlan, whose son Captain James Philippson was killed in Afghanistan in 2006 at the age of 29).[225] UK Defence Secretary Michael Fallon himself acknowledged that, as the British campaign ended in October 2014, 'there is no guarantee that Afghanistan is going to be stable and safe'; but, he argued, 'We have given Afghanistan the best possible chance of a safer future.'[226]

The USA and UK had shown little (almost certainly, too little) interest in Afghanistan after the Russians withdrew in 1989 and the Soviet Union collapsed in 1991; they then displayed insufficiently rigorous commitment (and lacked a seriousness of cultural and historical understanding) from 2001 onwards.[227] Both approaches (pre- and post-9/11) had pernicious consequences in terms of the effects of Afghan politics upon the west, and therefore helped al-Qaida to undermine western states.

Similarly, in Iraq from 2003 onwards, the successes of a complex set of violent actors against the USA and its allies have involved some al-Qaida terrorism which did (despite its flaws) undermine that group's opponents by significantly thwarting US and allied ambitions for the country.[228] Indeed, what one authority has termed the 'history of the strategies of cooperation, subversion, and resistance' that have long characterized Iraqis' engagement with their state perhaps hinted at the pattern which would evolve after the 2003 invasion: that of fragmentation, rebellion, disorder, persistent violence, and the thwarting of the will of those in authority. Iraq's past has been one in which 'neither the state nor those who have commanded it have managed to ensure that the multiple histories of the Iraqis are subsumed into a single narrative of state power'.[229] Just as the British creation of the state of Iraq in the first place had emerged through 'unintended consequences', following an otherwise-oriented invasion of Mesopotamia in 1914,[230] so again in the twenty-first century, invasion by a world-leading empire prompted a series of unanticipated trajectories.

Certainly, the ill-planned occupation of 2003 and afterwards reflected greater certainty of intention on the USA's part than it did long-term, well-informed recognition of the difficulties of what lay ahead in Iraq itself.[231] The 2003 endeavour in Iraq 'resulted in the destabilization of the country's security situation to such an extent that it [became] the new proving-ground for jihadist insurgent and terrorist operations'; 'Most jihadist strategists view the American military presence in Iraq as a blessing from God.'[232] So, while President Barack Obama hailed the 2011 ending of US military engagement in Iraq as having represented a 'moment of success',[233] the full picture had involved a considerable undermining of his super-powerful state.

And we must underline the fact that Afghanistan and Iraq exemplify a very important aspect of the question we are addressing in this book, for they relate to the complex and problematic relationship between different kinds of violence. The 9/11 attacks were—on pretty much any definition of the word—acts of terrorism; the US-led endeavours in Afghanistan from 2001 and Iraq from 2003 were clearly of a scale to justify the description of war;[234] within the conflicts which ensued in both countries, there were developments best described at times as involving insurgency and civil war; but there were also acts which fitted more orthodox definitions of non-state terrorist violence too. The points here are, first, that these different kinds of violence were organically and contingently linked together over a lengthy period (terrorism prompting war followed by civil war and insurgency and terrorism); and, second, that al-Qaida's violence therefore had its effects through the provocative effect of a clearly terroristic attack, whose consequences involved more than the kinds of violence that people would normally define as terrorism. If terrorism succeeded here in undermining al-Qaida's enemies, then it did so through processes which necessarily involved more than the initial terrorism itself.

The undermining of opponents could take other forms also, including those nearer home for western powers. So the vicious May 2013 killing of British soldier Lee Rigby in London set in train events which somewhat undermined the UK and wider western society also. The UK parliament's Intelligence and Security Committee Report of 2014 into the killing judged that inadequate liaison between online social networking Communications Service Providers and the UK authorities had contributed to a situation in which the brutal murder could take place; it also made certain criticisms of MI5 and other agencies (while making clear that the errors identified were not such as to have had a decisive effect in terms of facilitating the killing).[235] The 2014 Report, and the embarrassing problems identified within it, undoubtedly gathered high-level publicity and prominence.[236]

Tactical success might also involve a terrorist group finding that its violence generates an organizational strengthening, and great claims have certainly been made regarding the innovative reach of al-Qaida in terms of its geographical range.[237] The grouping has survived for nearly thirty years at the time of writing. This is a significant achievement in itself, especially given the extraordinary effort of so many powerful states against it. But, as noted earlier in this chapter, scholarly opinions differ sharply about the degree and nature of al-Qaida's precise form of survival.

Writing in 2006, Bruce Hoffman referred to al-Qaida's 'continued resilience, resonance, and longevity',[238] and in 2014 Professor Hoffman and Professor Fernando Reinares argued forcefully that al-Qaida had 'remained a clearly defined and active terrorist organization with an identifiable leadership and chain of command'; global jihadism had become 'a polymorphous phenomenon—not an amorphous one', and al-Qaida's leadership role remained significant and lethal. According to Hoffman and Reinares's careful argument, by the time of bin Laden's brutal death in 2011, his organization had come to comprise four interlinked parts: the enduring nucleus of 'al-Qaida Central or al-Qaida Core'; the group's 'Territorial Extensions or Branches', such as AQAP or AQI; 'Entities Affiliated and Associated with al-Qaida', such as the Afghan Taliban and Lashkar-e-Taiba (LeT); and 'Independent Jihadist Cells and Individuals'.[239]

In contrast, Dr Marc Sageman has suggested that the al-Qaida threat has changed far more greatly in nature, with jihadists embodying 'more fluid, independent, and unpredictable entities than their more structured forebears, who carried out the atrocities of 9/11'; in this view, al-Qaida had become 'a multitude of informal local groups trying to emulate their predecessors by conceiving and executing operations from the bottom up'.[240]

It is not disputed that the kind of al-Qaida organization which existed immediately prior to 9/11 has been attenuated and constrained in key ways. One of the clearest effects of 11 September was to make counter-terrorism a much higher priority for the United States and thus to ensure that 9/11 was less an inauguration of a new age of terrorism than the apotheosis of al-Qaida as a group. The late 2001 western assault on Afghanistan and overthrow of the Taliban decisively closed down the safe territorial space and consequent training possibility that had existed there for al-Qaida beforehand, with their Afghan training camps and headquarters being thumpingly brought to an end. Moreover, numerous key members were killed or captured by the USA and its allies. So, in one sense, 9/11 represented more of a watershed for al-Qaida than it did for any other political force. It might be that bin Laden and his comrades naively misjudged the likely response from the west (I suspect that this is true); 'The success of the 9/11 operation backfired on al-Qaida. There is some evidence that al-Qaida leadership anticipated a limited US response to the operation... This turned out to be a serious miscalculation.'[241]

But, like many bands, al-Qaida has continually reconstituted itself, and it would be wrong in any case to read it as having been a formal hierarchical organization in the way that (say) many western businesses or universities are. Post-9/11, with the international community of states more cooperatively focused upon them, they have had to develop as a more fluid and networked movement, or even as a set of (at times, agile) associations; as Hoffman has strongly pointed out, there remains an al-Qaida core, but it is not as definitively crucial as it was before 11 September 2001. Now frayed and torn, downgraded and constrained, al–Qaida's operational freedom and organizational bases have been somewhat eroded. The loss of Afghanistan was a very serious disruption and, although there has been something of a regrouping along the Afghan–Pakistani border and although the core element remains significant, the centre of gravity for al–Qaida has now moved partly towards those elements of its existence which involve looser mechanisms for inspiration, support, and brand-linkages.

These can prove lethal enough, however. And here one needs to keep in view the capacity simultaneously for overall strategic disappointment and for organizational resilience, improvised coherence, residual strength, and ingenuity.[242] Professor Hoffman, one of the world's leading terrorism scholars, has very recently referred to al–Qaida's 'operational durability or resiliency',[243] and this is an important point. By 2010, one of al–Qaida's most sharp-eyed UK opponents felt justified in claiming that 'the AQ strategy has failed. It has not led to the fundamental changes in policy that it sought';[244] but in the following year, the UK's new version of its *Prevent* strategy, unveiled in June 2011, still considered the most serious terrorist threat to that state to come from 'al–Qaida, its affiliates and like-minded groups', and recognized that levels of support for al–Qaida in some countries (Jordan, Nigeria, Indonesia, Eqypt) remained high.[245] Again, as one of the most distinguished of terrorism scholars put it in 2006: 'the al–Qaida movement, though seriously damaged by the extensive international measures against it, seems likely to continue to pose a threat through its global network of networks for some decades ahead'.[246] The al–Qaida of 2001 has been downsized, and its organizational dynamics contain many human flaws and weaknesses.[247] But the fact that the brand inspires, and that people still imitate violent actions and find aspects of the ideology appealing, means that something significant has been achieved in terms of the layered, organizational survival of resistance.

And the relationship between counter-terrorism and al–Qaida terror has involved a very complex set of dynamics. As noted earlier in this book, the War on Terror phase of world history witnessed an actual increase in the number of terrorist incidents and terrorist-generated fatalities worldwide, such that—in the view of one authority—'the paradoxical effect of the "war on terror" might well have been the increased proliferation of terrorism'.[248] Certainly, 9/11 and ensuing conflicts plainly did have some success in recruiting certain people to jihadist militancy.[249] But it should be registered that al–Qaida's survival has come to involve at times a self-starting, and not *necessarily* very centralized, flying of the al–Qaida flag: in these instances, it is episodic, and locally generated and sustained. In evolving al–Qaida plots against the west, there has tended sometimes to be a 'bottom–up' quality to the initiatives, in that 'individuals in the west sought out al–Qaida' rather than the other way around.[250] This continued existence should not be under-recognized in terms of terrorist success. In the view of the UK Ministry of Defence, al–Qaida 'has inflicted relatively little physical damage upon the military capabilities of the west. Its success lies mainly in its expert exploitation of the ideological and information arenas, where western governments are ill-prepared, combined with its ability to survive despite the most determined efforts of those governments to destroy it. For many non-state actors, including Hezbollah and al–Qaida, survival represents success.'[251] Moreover, despite fractures and downgrading of capacity, there remains the possibility that small numbers of people will be able to produce high-impact attacks and headline-seizing violence in al–Qaida's name, on occasions with support and direction from it.

So the group has both waxed and waned. There have been serious blows struck against al–Qaida organizationally, and these have involved some brutal acts. In addition to Osama bin Laden (killed by US forces on Monday 2 May 2011),[252] it should be borne in mind that, as mentioned, a series of the group's other important figures have been killed (Mohammed Atef 2001, Hamza Rabia 2005, Muhsin Musa Matwali Atwa 2006, Saleh al Somali 2009, Sheikh Sa'id al–Masri 2010, Abu 'Abd al–Rahman al–Najdi 2010, Ilyas Kashmiri 2011) or captured (Khaled Sheikh Mohammed 2003, Abu Faraj al Libi 2005).[253] It has become difficult for al–Qaida figures even to plan and meet, and the killing of bin Laden was (from the west's point of view) a sadly delayed but still powerful strike. 'The death of Osama bin Laden in May 2011 was a sledgehammer blow to al–Qaida core';[254] Barack Obama: 'The world is safer. It is a better place because of the death of Osama bin Laden.'[255]

That death did not kill off al–Qaida as such; but it did remove from the group someone whose charisma had been and remained an extremely important and pervasive resource,[256] and it brought to an end the embarrassingly long period during which the humiliating failure to find the al–Qaida leader had represented a propagandist success for the group. Had more US forces been deployed in late 2001 in Afghanistan on the Pakistan border, then it's possible that they would have succeeded in targeting bin Laden at Tora Bora in December 2001[257] rather than having to wait a somewhat embarrassing ten years to kill him. (Again, contingency rather than inevitability.) As so often with terrorism, state violence on its own has here had only partial effect: one should not exaggerate, for example, the degree to which the USA's use of unmanned aerial vehicles—drones—has incapacitated al-Qaida in practice,[258] nor ignore the possibility that the use of such technology will prompt terroristic blowback in the future. Overall, a strong measure of al-Qaida resilience has been maintained; but the group's survival has been a painful one and has left it a different kind of creature.

Beyond strategic, partial strategic, and tactical success, has al-Qaida terrorism worked in terms of the inherent rewards of struggle as such, at least partly independent of the grouping's central goals? Attention to particular contexts and to a range of sources suggests, of course, a complicated and varied and contingent set of outcomes here, as we consider the difficulty of assessing who it is for whom terrorism has or has not worked in practice. There is some clear evidence that a measure of personal, religiously inflected reward has been obtained by some of those associated with al-Qaida terrorism. It seems, for instance, that people involved in the 2004 Madrid plot had found a personal redemption in their prior, Islamist, religious awakening which had led them towards the bombing.[259] Likewise, Mohammed Atta's 'Final Instructions' (found in his suitcase after the 9/11 attack) seem to evince a calming sense of religious catharsis: 'Purify your heart and cleanse it of imperfections'; 'this action is for the sake of God'.[260] For some, as evident here, terrorism is also partly a matter of faith.

At an individual level again, there does appear to have been for some people a resolution through jihadist zealotry of a rather tortured cultural ambiguity and dislocation, especially perhaps the identity crises of certain Muslims in a European setting.[261] This is clearly not a widespread pattern among most Muslims in the west, or anything like it. But its rarity need not undermine either its occurrence or its importance, given the significant role of small-scale and even individual action in terrorist endeavours. If, at an individual level, jihadism has offered ways of dealing (among other things) with the centrifugal ambiguities experienced by some who find themselves caught between Islamic identity and western culture, then this is both a theme explored in a variety of intriguing ways in the recent period,[262] and also a jihadist echo of a pattern which can be tellingly found in previous, very different contexts of cultural ambiguity and terrorist activism.[263]

Yet again, there is evidence of some al-Qaida operatives making personal financial gain from the struggle,[264] and of some finding an alternative in it to unemployment;[265] there is no doubt that psychological and personal rewards (in terms of esteem, praise, renown, reputation, adventure, machismo, and so forth) have played a part in attracting some to the militant cause and that certain people did get a result (and success) here;[266] it is clear that there have existed for some the emotional, communal rewards of belonging to meaningful and identity-bestowing social networks of companions,[267] and there is evidence that the reinforcing of friendship ties can offer rewards to some violent jihadists, with intimate comradeship and mutual loyalty established in their violent struggle.[268] Social bonds can be as important as ideology in motivating and defining and giving meaning to people, even in such sacralized and violent struggles.

Again, online engagement—connected and related to al-Qaida violence, though partly autonomous from it—might offer rewards inherent within that very online experience and culture, whether imaginative, emotional, cathartic, fantastic, sub-culturally communal, or indeed in other ways that might also bestow meaning, prestige, or pleasure.[269] And for some al-Qaida people, there appears a strong sense that allegiance or opposition regarding jihadism indicates, respectively, a nobility of character or a cowardly laziness: that those who are against you are also morally degenerate or second-rate.[270] If dishonour, humiliation, and indignity have helped to generate al-Qaida violence, then engagement in that violence has at times offered a personal escape from those unwelcome conditions.

Yet many al-Qaida figures have been imprisoned and, as noted earlier, numerous of them have certainly not had a good war, in the sense that they have been brutally killed by the USA and its allies. So the picture is a varied one. But there can be little doubt that inherent rewards have been available for some al-Qaida activists, and that they have played a part in this terrorist experience.

IV

The walls of oppression and humiliation cannot be demolished except in a rain of bullets.

Osama bin Laden (1996)[271]

So al-Qaida's central strategic goals (the overturning of apostate Muslim regimes, the expulsion of the USA and its influence from the Muslim world, the renaissance of their strident version of Islam) have not been secured through terroristic violence. Even in partial strategic terms, the first and third of these goals seem far distant. But violence has at least hurt the USA and its allies in various ways, and the secondary goals of revenge and of sustaining a cause, and of driving local agendas, have seen greater success for them at times. Have they determined the wider political agenda? Not to the degree that they would have sought; but in preventing clear enemy victory they might justifiably claim some result here yet. Tactically, their achievements have been mixed, with operational successes and failures coexisting, with a mixture of both organizational attrition and resilient survival, and with a measure of success in acquiring publicity and undermining their opponents' legitimacy. Inherent rewards have been patchy, but not insignificant—though for many jihadists the war has been a painful one.

And al-Qaida have embodied an important theme within the wider study of terrorism: the capacity of small numbers of terroristic zealots to change the world, but not entirely as they would have wished or anticipated. That process has partly reflected the fatuous nature of much of their analysis and argument (their ludicrous underestimation of American power being a striking example). Despite considerable continuity of purpose, al-Qaida's aims and arguments have altered over time, as one would expect. So their agenda grew more globally ambitious, and their conception of what constituted a legitimate target significantly shifted (with the distinction between soldier and civilian becoming less important).[272] Yet the simplicity and lack of subtlety that have characterized their arguments have remained throughout much of their approach.

And at the heart of their violence has been the paradox of publicity. Yes, killings can seize the headlines. But, in doing so, they very often turn people against the cause in whose name such violence has been carried out. So, as noted, the *Charlie Hebdo* killings and ensuing drama in France in January 2015 undoubtedly grabbed world attention, and led governments and other elements within many states to think urgently about the jihadist threat. But the episode also stimulated mass revulsion against jihadist violence, prompted incredible levels of solidarity against the gunmen's actions in and beyond France (with over forty world leaders joining millions on protest marches in France itself),[273] and seemed to lead many in the west to redouble their commitment to defy those who would practise such 'barbaric', 'shocking',[274] 'vicious',[275] 'appalling', 'demonic',[276] 'evil',[277] 'sinister'[278] activity. Tellingly, there is some evidence from al-Qaida statements themselves that they have over time become rather exasperated with the lack of enthusiasm among

Muslims for their cause and violent struggle.[279] But deeper reflection on the history of terrorism would have left them unsurprised by it. For, while it is true that victims of terrorism inhabit a marginal and under-researched space within the study of terrorism,[280] it is also true that what terrorists distinctively do—brutally kill and injure people, very often civilian people, and very often people from the community in whose name the violence is practised—that this very activity is often what undermines terrorist groups so decisively. With al-Qaida, there is strong evidence for that having been the case. The victims, heterogeneous though their experiences have clearly been, can prove powerful fighters against the terrorists whose violence violated their rights so egregiously.

Could al-Qaida goals have been more effectively pursued through non-terroristic methods? Certainly, the group has failed to emerge as a possible centre for strategic agency at a global level. But then the kinds of goal that they have sought are not ones easily open to peaceful achievement either. Popular opinion is not sufficiently in their favour to allow for the revolution they desire. So while, for example, most Muslim immigrants to the west reject jihadist politics partly because they see them as ineffective,[281] it is also true that they fail to share the ultimate goals as a pressing ambition anyway.

Might the future overturn all these judgments? Ayman al-Zawahiri has clearly thought in terms of a long, trans-generational struggle,[282] and nobody has a basis for certain prediction of future trends over a very long term. If AQI was a response to the US reaction to al-Qaida, and ISIS embodies a complex development of AQI, then the lengthy struggle involving ISIS warriors might eventually embody a vicarious set of (as yet, unpredictable) outcomes for which al-Qaida could claim some responsibility. US leaders have certainly made clear that their assault on al-Qaida-linked enemies and ISIS fighters in Syria is likely to take a very long time ('I would think of it in terms of years,' observed Lt General William Mayville, Director of Operations for the US Joint Chiefs of Staff, in 2014).[283] Addressing the United Nations General Assembly on 24 September 2014, President Barack Obama himself made clear that his attempt to deal with ISIS was now a high and dangerous priority for him: 'As we look to the future, one issue risks a cycle of conflict that could derail so much progress. And that is the cancer of violent extremism that has ravaged so many parts of the Muslim world.'[284]

But at global level, the increasingly ambitious aims of Osama bin Laden and his comrades seem (probably) destined not to become fulfilled, given that his target audience is unlikely to be persuaded in majority numbers by the kind of simplistically zealous political analysis and violence that he offered. In his February 1998, co-signed fatwa, he had stressed the duty on every Muslim to engage in violent jihad if they could do so. Indeed, this was a familiar melody in his music: on 9 December 2001 he had argued that jihad had become obligatory 'upon each and every Muslim. . . . The time has come when all the Muslims of the world, especially the youth, should unite and soar against the kufr [non-believer] and continue jihad till these forces are crushed to naught, all the anti-Islamic forces are wiped off the face of this earth, and Islam takes over the whole world and all other false religions.'[285] In pursuit of these grand goals, al-Qaida's terrorism has not been able effectively to work.[286]

So bin Laden might indeed have become, as a leading authority has put it, 'one of the few individuals in modern times who had unequivocally changed the direction of history'.[287] And he and al-Qaida's violence persuaded other famous people that the world had indeed changed. So Tony Blair's personal, very frank account of his years as UK Prime Minister makes clear his sense of a fault line having emerged in human history with 9/11: 'It was an event like no other. It was regarded as such. . . . Above all, it was accepted that the world had changed. How could it be otherwise? . . . [T]his was not an ordinary event but a world-changing one. . . . September 11 threw the world's pieces into the air. It was accepted totally as altering our view of the world fundamentally.' Utterly altered, the world now had to be protected by a war against this new kind of threat: 'Unchecked and unchallenged, this could threaten our way of life to its fundamentals. There was no other course: no other option; no alternative path. It was war. It had to be fought and won.'[288] Neither Blair nor bin Laden were able to secure the victory that they most sought. But long after the planes flew so frighteningly into the New York towers in 2001, systematic analysis suggests that the main goals of al-Qaida, at least, remain genuinely elusive and evaporative.

2

Ireland and the
Provisional IRA

I

Operations like Mountbatten, Brighton, Downing Street, Bishopsgate, and Canary Wharf were too much for the British to ignore and ensured that they had to take the situation in Ireland seriously.

Ex-PIRA Volunteer, 2012[1]

The Provisional IRA attacks mentioned above took place across several decades (respectively, in 1979, 1984, 1991, 1993, and 1996). And, although the Irish nationalist past has arguably been typified far more commonly by constitutional reformism than it has by violent revolution,[2] there is no doubting the lengthy and rich inheritance upon which modern-day militant Irish republicans have been able to draw. Some, indeed, have traced the roots of their struggle over many centuries. In relation to the PIRA's late twentieth-century war I was informed in interview by one of the organization's US-based gun-runners that, 'The Brits—they're the problem, and will be. They have been since 1169 [the year of the Anglo-Norman invasion of Ireland], and will be until such time as they leave.'[3]

During the modern period, republican armed struggle has included nineteenth-century Fenian violence, the turbulent rebelliousness of the 1916–23 years, and the episodic campaigns of pre-Provisional IRAs during the period between the end of the Irish Civil War in 1923 and the 1969 foundation of the Provos. Much of this has involved violence that many would characterize as terroristic, and anxieties (for example) about Fenian threats to London in the nineteenth century pre-echoed much that has again concerned people in the jihadist era of 9/11, 7/7, and beyond.

In terms of terrorism's efficacy, this pre-Provo republican history of struggle embodies a complicated pattern. Founded in 1858 by a veteran from a rebellion that had occurred ten years beforehand, the Fenians were able to sustain republican resistance from one era into another, but not to secure through violence their sought-after independent Irish republic; they were able to exact revenge on the British, whom they considered to be denying Ireland its rightful freedom, and they left some powerful legacies for later generations through the writings of some of their key members and the martyrdom of others; they generated some operational successes, but also some dismal tactical disappointments; they acquired widespread publicity through acts of separatist violence, but much of that publicity was deeply negative; they added teeth to the parliamentary nationalism of Charles Stewart Parnell, but were less capable of determining the political agenda than he was able to do through his preferred and less aggressive methods (to which some of them shifted anyway);[4] they provided opportunities for many to enjoy otherwise elusive pastime pleasures,[5] while also prompting some mixed (and often unpleasant) experiences in terms of the incarceration and punishment of their members.[6] So while the Fenians' declaration in 1866 that 'England is loosening her iron grasp on Ireland'[7] was to prove unfounded, their violent politics was not without some of the successes that our framework in this book requires us to consider. The idea of achieving Irish independence through the coercive mechanism of force proved illusory, while lesser gains could, perhaps, be credited to the late nineteenth-century Irish nationalist physical force account.[8]

Of course, Irish nationalist (even specifically Irish separatist) politics never involved only violence as their method. Inheritances from previous generations gave early twentieth-century nationalists a rich cultural, literary, imaginative, and personality-adorned set of prevenient resources.[9] Moreover, some of the violence of the Irish revolution (during the 1919–21 Anglo-Irish War and the 1922–3 Civil War also) involved acts which some might regard as moving beyond terrorism. Yet, despite the delicacies involved with the term terrorism, there can be little doubt that the use of political violence with deliberately terrorizing effect was present in these enthralling years.[10] Some was practised by the UK state forces, and some by loyalists keen to preserve their place within the United Kingdom. But much was also evident in the record of Irish republicans, and evaluating its success is important if we are properly to situate the later Provisional IRA in appropriate context.

The dramatic Easter Rising of 1916 remains, even a century later, still a great inspiration to many militant Irish republicans. Having themselves been inspired so strongly by Robert Emmet's deeply unsuccessful 1803 rebellion,[11] it might seem unsurprising that strategic success eluded the 1916 rebels too: their sought-after independent Irish republic was deeply distant even after their often courageous, though tactically somewhat inept, efforts during that famous week of anti-British gesture. But, as with Emmet a century earlier, much longer processes were also involved here. The April 1916 rebels undermined their British opponents by prompting the state to act in a clumsy way: 'British coercion combined a provocative heavy-handedness with a counter-productive ineffectiveness.'[12] So, while the Rising was militarily suppressed by the British easily and quickly enough, its political effects were to prove much more difficult to put down. There was a post-1916 acceleration and intensification of Irish nationalist militancy, with a UK Cabinet memorandum the following month noting that, 'Throughout Leinster popular sympathy for the rebels is growing', that in Connaught 'among all sections of nationalists hopes are generally expressed that the dupes of the revolution will be dealt with leniently', and that in Munster 'general sympathy among all nationalists is becoming intensified in favour of the rebels arrested or sentenced'.[13]

Indeed, some of those who found the Rising and its legacy to be inspiring were to fight another day in even more serious fashion against the UK in Ireland. The 18-year-old medical student Ernie O'Malley, eventually to become one of the IRA's most famous warriors, later remembered the percussive effect that the rebellion had had upon him. 'Then came like a thunderclap the 1916 Rising', he recalled, with the British killing of the leaders being particularly powerful: 'When I heard of the executions I was furious.'[14]

The violence of 1916 carried with it also other layers of what might be considered success. There was apotheosis for some rebels (though this was accompanied by martyrdom for a limited yet long-remembered few); there was certainly some exhilaration and celebrity;[15] there was the creation of very powerful political legacies, and a significant sense that resistance against British rule had been sustained; there was the satisfying fusion for many of Catholic faith with Irish republican politics;[16] and, together with other developments during the later stages of the First World War, there was great damage done not only to the legitimacy of British rule in nationalist Ireland, but also to the constitutional, more moderate Home Rule politics that had seemed for a generation likely to prove victorious. More negatively still, the violence of 1916 of course caused significant and awful human suffering. The first victim of the Rising was an unarmed Irish police officer (James

O'Brien) who was mercilessly shot in the head at very close range by one of the rebels on 24 April in Dublin;[17] and Dublin's civilian population in particular suffered heavily in terms of fear as well as damage.

In all, over 400 people were killed in the brief conflict, with many more wounded and with considerable destruction done (to Dublin in particular). And 1916 also helped to reinforce the increasing likeliness and severity of Irish partition, just as the wider violence of 1916–23 made the partitioning of the island a much more deeply etched reality.[18]

That longer revolutionary era inaugurated so powerfully by Easter 1916 itself witnessed failure at strategic level: neither the IRA fighting the UK during 1919–21, nor the anti-Free State IRA of 1922–3, secured their preferred outcome of a united and independent Irish republic. It has been argued that the violence of the 1919–21 conflict produced a greater measure of freedom for what was to emerge as independent Ireland than would otherwise have been the case.[19] If true, then the IRA of that period could be read as having generated at least some partial strategic success (though opinions will differ regarding how far the violence was justified by the difference between what would have emerged without it, and what was generated by it). Likewise, in terms of secondary goals such as exacting revenge or sustaining resistance, some efficacy could certainly be attributed to Irish republican violence in these years. But again this came at a very heavy price: 1919–23 involved deep division in Ireland, between Irish nationalist and Ulster unionist, between exponents of force and those who eschewed its use, and also within the ranks of the violent nationalist movement itself. One undoubted effect of the use of violent means in these years was that polarization became more accentuated. This was true most painfully in the Civil War split of 1922–3,[20] but it was evident before that too.

The 1919–21 Anglo-Irish War certainly allowed for the cathartic expression of Irish republican Anglophobia—'the inborn hate of things English', as IRA man Ernie O'Malley would later pithily express it.[21] And, while I think that national self-determination must be seen as the centrally driving force behind Irish republican violence during the revolutionary years, there was also much pursuit of personal revenge against enemies. The 1922–3 Civil War witnessed vengeful violence originating from both sides (those who favoured the 1921 compromise Treaty with Britain, and those more uncompromising, anti-state republicans who resisted it), and certainly the non-state republican forces carried out a considerable number of attacks and acts of terrorizing intimidation against enemies and old foes (many of them civilians, and much of the violence being vicious and cruel in nature).[22] However noxious in its effects, this pervasive violence must be judged to have achieved something of its punishing, socially excluding, revenge-driven ambition.

There can be little doubt either that the IRA of those years kept republican militancy alive as a tradition of resistance. This is evidenced by the later Provisionals' celebratory identification with these revolutionary predecessors[23] (and also, incidentally, by the inspiration taken by activists elsewhere than in Ireland: a later generation of Jewish terrorists, for example, clearly drew comparisons with and some inspiration from the republican violence and activism of this Irish revolutionary period;[24] in turn, some later Irish republicans themselves looked back admiringly at the Jewish Irgun and Stern Gang.[25] The presumed efficacy of terroristic violence could have very lasting and global effect).

The sustenance of resistance at the time in Ireland was vital too, of course. There was a wide degree of support attained, for example, during the 1919–21 conflict itself. For it is clear that the IRA's violent campaign had been one which had gathered some very strong backing. In an October 1921 Report from General Barron, Divisional Commissioner of Police for Munster, No. 1 Division (which included the turbulently difficult counties of Clare, Limerick, and North Tipperary), it was suggested that that part of Ireland was characterized by considerable IRA sympathy: 'The general attitude of the civilian population is, in almost every case, more truculent and less conciliatory'; 'Practically every male of fighting age has willingly or unwillingly become a member of the IRA.'[26] And, to a degree, IRA violence also determined the political agenda, making Ireland more of a pressing issue for London in the build-up to the flawed partitionist settlement of the early 1920s.

At a tactical level there were also some successes, sufficient in number for the IRA to challenge during 1919–21 the UK state's Weberian upholding of a successful monopoly on the legitimate use of force within their Irish territory. A very high-level UK government meeting in October 1921 (chaired by the Prime Minister and attended by, among others, the Secretary of State for the Colonies, the Lord Privy Seal, the Lord Chancellor, the Attorney-General, and the Secretary of State for War) heard Neville Macready (who commanded UK forces in Ireland) comment that 'in the event of a renewal of hostilities [in Ireland], the continuation of drilling [by Irish republicans] might tempt the Sinn Feiners to come out and fight, which would be an advantage';[27] so the IRA's preference for ambush and terroristic tactics was plainly something which was judged to cause greater problems for the UK state than would non-terrorist methods.

Through IRA violence, publicity was achieved, and there was a certain measure of undermining opponents involved too. British forces during the Anglo-Irish War engaged in some clumsily counter-productive violence, and lost political ground among Irish nationalists as a consequence. So there was some plausibility to Ernie O'Malley's later claim regarding the UK authorities in Ireland in 1921 that 'Their campaign of terror was defeating itself';[28] and this was a point echoed by another leading IRA man, Michael Brennan, in relation to the same year: 'the British reprisals, instead of turning the people against us as the cause of their miseries, had thrown them strongly behind us.'[29] In less effective manner, but still significantly enough, the anti-Treaty republicans of 1922–3 did undermine for a time the stability and normality of the nascent independent Irish state.[30] Likewise, IRA violence in both phases of the 1919–23 conflict helped them to achieve a degree of control over wide groups of the nationalist population.

Were there also inherent rewards from this violence? There were certainly costs (over 1,500 people were killed during 1919–21, and many republicans spent grim days in jail during that war and also the ensuing Civil War conflict).[31] But it is also true that some of the revolutionaries found these years to be glory days in terms of their professional careers,[32] and that there were aspects of the struggle in itself which appealed, whether in terms of manliness, defiance, soldierliness, the exciting escape from quotidian boredom and family restrictions, or the fusion of the spiritual and the national.[33] Some of these people had a good post-war phase also, on the basis in part of their revolutionary exploits, though some experienced post-revolutionary damage and melancholia too.[34] The generation which moulded the violent Irish revolution of 1916–23 embodied a vast range of divergent ambitions and hopes, many of which were disappointed when the post-revolutionary Irish states, north and south, emerged in the 1920s and settled into a largely conservative range of enmities and structures.[35] As so often during political struggle, people assumed a future which did not actually arrive, whether that involved socialism, feminism, the ending of sectarian division, or imaginative and intellectual and creative freedom.[36] The mordant recollection of one Civil War republican captures something of this rather well: there had been 'practically as many visions of what "The Republic" entailed as there were people—and most of them completely unrealistic'.[37] Such views are echoed by scholarly judgments such as that of Charles Townshend that 'Republicanism, for most of its adherents, was about achieving separation—sovereign independence—rather than implementing any concrete political programme.'[38] The range of detailed visions sheltering under that large separatist umbrella could be broad (a pattern that we will see again when we consider the Provisional IRA themselves).

One very striking aspect of the 1919–21 republican campaign against UK rule in Ireland was that the violence of the IRA represented only one, partly interwoven, element of a wider repertoire of struggle. The methods deployed by republicans included electoral politics, and indeed the creation of an alternative infrastructure of government and of state administration,[39] including the setting up of a parliament in Dublin in 1919 in the form of Dail Eireann. Widespread support for the Sinn Fein political party did not overlap at all completely with support for IRA violence; but it did represent a very powerful expression of disaffection from UK rule across much of nationalist Ireland, and parliamentary abstentionism (together with other, cultural and communal, modes of resistance, including widespread social ostracism) played its important part in complementing the aggression of the Irish Republican Army. Moreover, even for those whose involvement was aggressively oriented, it might not actually be the violence that possessed the greatest efficacy. The publicly supportive reaction upon Terence MacSwiney's hunger-strike death in 1920 dwarfed the kind of mass displays that could have been elicited in support of violent acts by the IRA of which he was a member.

Again, women's role in the sharp-edged military aspects of Irish republicanism was comparatively limited in these heady years, but their political work played a significant part in a wide range of activist endeavours contributing momentum to the republican struggle. Unless these efforts are to be ignored, or the careful case put forward by historians for their significance is to be disregarded, then one must judge here that literary, linguistic, journalistic, economic, social, electoral, theatrical, propagandist, and speaking activity—as well as violence—played its role in bringing about what change was secured for nationalist Ireland in this period.[40] So the Irish republican struggle of the revolutionary period was very much that of a complex movement, rather than purely of an armed wing; disentangling the causal processes involved is therefore, as with the later Provisional movement, far from straightforward.

Moreover, it is vital to stress the contextual point that (while this chapter focuses on Irish republican violence), in the Irish revolution of the early twentieth century as in Northern Ireland much later on, others as well as republicans deployed violence. It was the mobilization for violence by unionists in Ulster that decisively tilted Irish nationalists towards political violence in the post-1912 period. More broadly still, without the effects of the First World War, that republican shift towards aggression would almost certainly have been much more restrained.[41] So the roots of causation were very tangled.

Between the end of the Irish Civil War and the birth of the Provisional IRA in 1969, there were stuttering IRA efforts to destabilize and undo what remaining members felt to be two illegitimate states across a now-partitioned Ireland. Such activists sustained resistance, and displayed considerable commitment, energy, and ideological zeal.[42] But the momentum was hard to sustain in large numbers: 1952 police estimates suggested there to be only about 200 IRA members in Dublin, and another 50 in Cork.[43] Unionist majority opinion dominated politics in Northern Ireland, and the growing legitimacy of independent, southern Ireland undermined the politics of the mid-century IRA there also.

There was a 1956–62 border campaign, aimed at the ultimate undoing of partition. But not only did this clearly fail to secure its central, strategic goal, it also dimmed into feeble disintegration owing to there being such low-level sympathy for an IRA assault on the existing order.[44] A later Sinn Fein politician, looking back at this 1956–62 episode, referred with admirable frankness to it as 'a very disastrous and ill-conceived border campaign, a non-supported border campaign in the late fifties and early sixties'.[45] And in 1962 itself it seemed to many that IRA violence might have had its final day. Overall, the IRA of 1956–69 was rather fissiparous, small-scale, marginal, and ineffective, finding its priorities and methods largely at odds with the wider Irish nationalist community. It did sustain organized, militant republican resistance for another generation, albeit with the effect of helping to stimulate a later conflict of a kind that they had neither anticipated nor sought to bring about.[46] Unexpected futures, yet again.

So there had been other IRAs before the Provisionals[47] were established. But the PIRA[48] conducted by far the most sustained IRA campaign to date, and it offers a very rich case study concerning the efficacy of non-state political violence. The organization was born in December 1969, emerging out of a split within the pre-existing Irish Republican Army—a split which helps begin the process of establishing what the Provisional IRA wanted to achieve through its violent actions.

II

The armed struggle is the cutting edge of the campaign to remove British
forces and achieve a united Ireland.

Provisional IRA spokesperson (1984)[49]

There are two clear candidates for consideration as the Provisional Irish
Republican Army's central, primary goals: communal defence, and the
achievement of a united and fully independent Irish republic. If they were
to achieve strategic victory, then these objectives were the crucial ones.

In the context of inter-communal violence between Ulster Protestants and
Northern Catholics at the end of the 1960s, and in the absence of effective
protection from the forces of the Northern Ireland state, there was an understandable urge among sections of the Catholic community for self-defence.
The unsurprising desire of the Northern Irish Catholic minority to pursue
fairer treatment within the northern state during the 1960s had resulted in an
overwhelmingly peaceful civil rights movement; but the latter had prompted
the existing, inherited inter-communal enmity in the north to become more
sharply and violently charged. When this tension resulted in inflammable
violence between rival communities in 1969, there were significant attacks on
Catholic areas by members of the Protestant community, and it was felt by
some nationalists that the existing IRA had offered insufficient defence. So the
logic of communal protection and the urgent need for defence decisively
helped to generate the republican split which gave the world the Provos.

This is richly evident from contemporary and later first-hand sources alike,
and it remained deeply and lastingly embedded in militant republican thinking.
The PIRA's first Chief of Staff, Sean MacStiofain (Figure 6) (clearly a well-
placed source of evidence), claimed that after loyalist attacks on Catholics in
August 1969, northern republicans 'were determined that they would not be
caught defenceless again'.[50] A Belfast Provisional leader, interviewed in February
1971, asserted the PIRA's preparedness 'to use force to any extent required to
protect the minority in Belfast from attack from any sources—be it the British
Army, the RUC [Royal Ulster Constabulary], or Protestant bigots'.[51] The Irish-
born, US-based, long-time Provo gun-runner referred to earlier in this chapter
(George Harrison) was equally clear about the priority of the matter: 'you had
to defend the ghettos...the thing to do now is to get weaponry in to the people
who are willing to defend the nationalist ghettos.'[52]

Figure 6. Sean MacStiofain, the PIRA's first Chief of Staff

This goal of defence long remained central to the PIRA's self-image (reinforced once clashes with the British Army ensued), and it was one repeatedly highlighted by Irish republicans. As Sinn Feiner[53] Francie Molloy claimed in 1997, the PIRA had been 'the defenders of our people for the last twenty-five or thirty years'.[54] One PIRA man, looking back to the early 1970s, put it this way: 'We saw ourselves defending people against an occupying army which was coming into our district every day, wrecking all round them.'[55] Whether or not early Provisionals had a republican family background, therefore, one of the motivating goals which led many of them to join up and get involved in the new group was the objective of providing defence for their Catholic streets and people. This had been an inherited goal and self-image in relation to previous IRAs; but it took on a very new and urgent dimension with the scale of inter-communal violence in the later 1960s.

The other central, primary goal was the realization of Irish national self-determination through the achievement of a united and fully independent Irish republic. This was a pivotal, strategic goal for the Provos. It would involve the destruction of the Northern Irish state, the removal of the Irish border which had been established in the 1920s, and the creation of a new political entity utterly free from British sovereignty and control. The PIRA's first public statement, issued on 28 December 1969 in Dublin, unambiguously set out what they considered 'the fundamental republican position': 'We declare our allegiance to the thirty-two-county Irish republic, proclaimed at Easter 1916, established by the first Dáil Eireann in 1919, overthrown by force of arms in 1922 and suppressed to this day by the existing British-imposed six-county and twenty-six-county partition states.'[56] The legitimacy of the existing, late twentieth-century Dublin and Belfast parliaments, and of the partitioned states over which they presided, was here resoundingly rejected by republicans.

As Sinn Feiner Alex Maskey later put it, 'In 1969, I was like a lot of other young nationalists who decided that this state [Northern Ireland] was fatally flawed and had no right to exist. The injustice in this state was not going to go away on its own; the state had to be removed.'[57] The Provisionals themselves certainly set their cause, resolutely and centrally, against the acceptance of a partitioned Ireland, considering it to be a transgressive mutilation of Irish national self-determination and a denial of true Irish democracy. Patrick Magee (imprisoned during 1985–99 for his part in the 1984 PIRA Brighton bombing) put the matter very lucidly: 'I believe that the political reunification of the island of Ireland is a prerequisite for the fullest development of democracy.'[58] And, when examined in context, it is clear that the PIRA expected to succeed in this pursuit of a united Ireland: 'we shall win, because we regard British disengagement from Ireland now as inevitable', as one-time leading Provo Ruairi O Bradaigh confidently put it.[59]

The PIRA's nationalism was a very recognizable and explicable one in terms of wider patterns of nationalist community, struggle, and power that are familiar in nationalist politics elsewhere.[60] Irish republicans strongly identified themselves as a political community whose national freedom had been wrongly denied them, and for whom violent struggle was a necessary means of putting things right. For the central reason given, for the war in which the PIRA were engaged, was British refusal to put right the wrongful partitioning of Ireland: as leading Provo Daithi O'Connell put it in 1974, 'The British government have simply to say we are not going to stay in Ireland, we are going to disengage from Ireland.'[61]

Repeatedly, republicans made clear that only British withdrawal and the establishment of a united Ireland could provide the basis for an acceptable solution to the Irish problem. As one sharp-sighted activist phrased it in

March 1977 in a valuable contemporary source, 'The republican movement regards British colonial presence in Ireland with its gross exploitation of the Irish people and Irish resources, not only as illegal but as the basis for most of our economic and social problems today.' So Northern Ireland could not be reformed: 'The six counties is a politically contrived and manipulated "state" designed specifically to allow the permanent domination of one section of the community over the other. Any reforms which it is forced to accept are only cosmetic in nature and in essence not worth the paper they are written on.... The republican movement will not settle for anything less than British withdrawal.'[62] Ten years after they had killed their first British soldier, the Provisional IRA issued a statement clearly linking Irish self-determination with British withdrawal: 'the war in Ireland could be ended very quickly if the British government acknowledged the democratic right of the Irish nation to self-determination, and announced a British withdrawal from Ireland.'[63]

And violence was the means to bring this about: 'The IRA strategy is very clear. At some point in the future, due to the pressure of the continuing and sustained armed struggle, the will of the British government to remain in this country will be broken. That is the objective of the armed struggle.... [W]e can state confidently today that there will be no ceasefire and no truces until Britain declares its intent to withdraw and leave our people in peace.'[64]

From their own political perspective, it was entirely reasonable that the IRA should be so tenacious and insistent about this point, about the necessity of destroying Northern Ireland and replacing partitioned Ireland's states with a united and independent republic. In the words of the Provisionals' most significant player of all, Gerry Adams (Figure 7), the 1920s establishment of Northern Ireland had 'resulted in the creation of a sectarian state in which nationalists have always been treated as second-class citizens';[65] 'the north of Ireland state was a state based upon the violent suppression of political opposition'.[66] The north was illegitimate, unfair, factitious, undemocratic, and irreformable; in the PIRA's strongly made case, it had to be removed by the pressure of force, as equality would only be achievable once the northern state had been destroyed; 'Half a century after its foundation, Northern Ireland had grown into a political entity that could not reform itself.'[67]

Indeed, both states in Ireland (the British north and the independent south) had to be undone and replaced. As the Provos' Belfast-produced paper *Republican News* put it in the context of 1975, 'It is the stated intention of the republican movement to destroy the colonial and neo-colonial states

Figure 7. Gerry Adams and Brendan Hughes in prison, 1970s

in Ireland.'[68] And this strategic goal endured for many years. In the early
1990s a spokesperson for the PIRA's GHQ Staff stated clearly that the 'only
possible lasting solution' was full British disengagement from Ireland.[69] The
Provisionals' New Year message for 1993 made a similar claim: 'there is but
one solution and that solution is based upon British disengagement.'[70] So a
return to Stormont[71] rule was unacceptable: 'That is never going to happen.
Partition in Ireland was founded and sustained on injustice and a denial of
democracy. It has failed and failed utterly.'[72] So, although there was more to
the PIRA's political ambitions than ending partition, it remains true—in the
words of one of their most articulate former members, Tommy McKearney—
that 'ending the union [of Great Britain and Northern Ireland] and establishing a 32-county [Irish] republic was always a core and headline demand
of the organization'.[73] A rich range of first-hand sources makes this very clear.

Why pursue this demand violently? When asked about support for the
Provisionals among the nationalist population, one leading Irish republican

(Sinn Fein politician Conor Murphy) suggested persuasively that people had turned to a physical-force approach because of the belief that constitutional politics had been shown not to work, and that pursuing constitutional methods would have produced only irrelevance to the situation. On this reading, Murphy argued, the emergence of the PIRA was born of a view held by many people that only armed force would have any effect. When the Provos were born:

> Was the [northern] state capable of engaging, was it capable of change? And I suppose the effect of the [1960s] civil rights movement showed that it probably *wasn't* capable of change. There was no dynamic within the British state to come over and impose anything other than a managing exercise. So even when [Northern Ireland Prime Minister Terence] O'Neill tried his limited reforms and was swept aside, I suppose that was a strong signal that *this* state was not capable of any degree of change.... All of that, I suppose, sustained the notion that the only way to deal with this was through armed action, that a political way and building a mass movement, attempts to create class consciousness... that that wasn't likely to catch on, it wasn't dealing with what was confronting people in the here and now.[74]

Expanding lucidly this point, Murphy suggested of the early 1970s that 'There would be people that would have been in the [Provisional] IRA that would have had a very fixed view that armed struggle was necessary. So really the strength of their argument and their ability to recruit and sustain an effective armed force and to build a struggle around that was probably due to how immovable the state was, or how effective politics—or constitutional-type politics—could be against what the state was doing.... So if those who had advocated (SDLP-types[75] and civil rights-types)... advocated constitutional change were proving some success, it probably would have robbed the more militant factions then of the ability to recruit people.'[76] Standing in the 1984 European Parliament Election, Sinn Fein's Danny Morrison made clear the view that 'It is impossible for real progress to be achieved by peaceful appeal or by involvement in British constitutional politics and that is the real reason why armed struggle has been necessary to wear down the will of the British government in occupying our country.'[77]

And it's important to note that the PIRA for years seemed confident of violently secured success. 1972 was going to be 'The Year of Victory'.[78] The PIRA's Belfast Brigade leadership in 1976 asserted bravely that British defeat was definitely coming: 'Make no mistake about it... Britain's days in Ireland are numbered; the Irish people recognize it, the world at large recognize it, and the Irish Republican Army certainly recognise it.'[79] In June 1979 Gerry Adams (then Sinn Fein Vice-President) made clear his own confidence: 'That the British face military defeat is inevitable and obvious';[80] and such belief in 'the inevitability of Irish unity'[81] long endured in the Provisionals' thinking. One PIRA figure in 1993 colourfully set out their commitment to maintaining armed struggle until British disengagement had been secured: 'It's the gun and the fuckin' ballot box and that's the way it's goin' to stay till Britain leaves.'[82] In June 1984, leading republican Martin McGuinness (Figure 8) made clear his own strong view of the central role that PIRA violence would play in securing British withdrawal: 'The Irish Republican Army offers the only resolution to the present situation. It is their disciplined, well-directed war against British forces that will eventually bring Britain to withdraw. . . . We recognise that only disciplined revolutionary armed struggle by the IRA will end British rule.'[83] McGuinness has not always been entirely reliable in his claims about the PIRA;[84] but his undoubted importance within the organization, and the fact that his statement here resonates with so many other

Figure 8. Former Provisional Irish Republican Army (PIRA) leader Martin McGuinness in 2011

first-hand sources from the movement, between them make this a reliable index of Provisional republican thinking.

Gerry Bradley, a Belfast PIRA man between 1971 and 1994, had clearly been confident of his organization's victory: 'I genuinely believed that one day the IRA would be chasing the British Army down to the docks, firing at them, and the last British officer would be backing up the gangway onto the boat with his pistol in his hand.'[85] For such Provos, PIRA violence was essential in order to bring about the necessary transition to a fully independent and united Ireland; and for the Provos the Irish fight for independence was part of a wider pattern of anti-colonialism and anti-imperialism.[86] Moreover, in the words of an eminent Sinn Feiner, regarding those young people who had joined the PIRA in the early 1970s, 'It was quite obvious to them that constitutional politics was having no real success. It was really tinkering around the edges but it wasn't likely to change anything radically.'[87] As the PIRA themselves put it in their 1981 Easter statement: 'Only through armed struggle will we be listened to, only through the struggle waged by the Irish Republican Army can we win national freedom and end division and sectarianism in Ireland.'[88] This was essentially a Clausewitzean argument: the war with the British was to be made more oppressive for the latter than it would have been for London to give the Provisional IRA what they demanded; not for nothing have so many republicans from this period referred to the Prussian soldier-intellectual.[89]

If the achievement of effective defence and the bringing about of a fully independent and united Ireland would represent strategic victory, what would partial strategic victory for the PIRA involve? Clearly, if it could be shown that PIRA violence had brought about partial defensive security for the Catholic community in the north, or that it had secured a diluted but significant and otherwise unobtainable degree of political equality, power, and freedom for Irish nationalists, then some would make the case that the Provos' political violence had worked—imperfectly, perhaps, but importantly. The kind of national self-determination envisaged for so long by the Provisionals might have proven elusive; but could PIRA terrorism be judged to have brought about a milder form of self-determination, whereby the majority of Irish people—admittedly still dichotomized into two separate states—had endorsed a rearranged Northern Ireland which itself offered greater capacity for northern nationalists to determine their own political affairs?

I think that a balanced assessment of the PIRA would also have to consider whether the organization's violence worked in terms of securing secondary strategic goals. A full reading of the Provisionals would have to acknowledge that the group was never just about defence and a united Ireland. There was also, for some members, the appeal of hitting back at enemies, of revenge, and retaliation. As one ex-PIRA man honestly put it, 'the sectarianism was there...Protestants were a target in the eyes of people'.[90] Their Protestant loyalist paramilitary opponents were certainly clear that inter-communal hatred and the escalatory, tit-for-tat sequences of mutual Ulster violence had helped to strengthen the PIRA. Leading loyalist Jackie McDonald put it very crisply in interview: 'If you think what made the Provies...If there had been no loyalist paramilitary retaliation to what they were doing, and no intern-ment, it [the Provisionals' campaign] might have lasted two or three or four or five years. But there were major events that happened, that swelled the ranks of the IRA...with the UDA and UVF killing Catholics; internment; Bloody Sunday—all those things made the IRA.'[91]

And there is no shortage of PIRA evidence to support such a view, namely that Provisional IRA members were in part and at times motivated by a desire to hit back violently in response to prior violence against their own commu-nity: 'We have met violence with violence';[92] 'People were very, very much interested in defence [in the early 1970s], and very much interested in retalia-tion as well 'cos people were very, very angry. They really were angry.... There was a real rage there, amongst young people.'[93] Fitting this rage, republicans did on occasions seek to lash out at Protestant enemies as such.[94] It is not that revenge alone motivated PIRA members or explains their activity; but no explanation of what the organization did will be complete without recogniz-ing the role that a desire for hitting back did historically play in context. They and their community had been attacked; hitting back could be seen to make some sense. Belfast republican Sam Millar sharply describes his own initial experience of the British Army in the early 1970s: 'At seventeen, I met my very first Englishman as he kicked in the door of our home in the early morning hours, and forcefully dragged me out of bed using my ears as a rope.'[95]

Here again we see that it is impossible to ignore the role of state violence (some of it clearly terrorizing in its effect and political in its motivation) in generating and sustaining non-state violence. A chronological, richly sourced, contextualized reading of the PIRA cannot avoid recognition that the UK state's sometimes terrorizing violence played a part in making the Provos seem legitimate and necessary to their supporters and members in Ireland.

Secondary goals might also involve maintaining a tradition of resistance to British rule itself. One of the Provos' most conspicuous figures, Ruairi

O Bradaigh, claimed in 1970 that the republican movement of the day maintained 'direct organizational continuity from Fenian times, through the Irish Republican Brotherhood, past 1916 and the First Dáil to the present day'.[96] Another man with pre-Provisional IRA work experience on his curriculum vitae, Dan Gleeson (who had fought during the 1919–21 Anglo-Irish War), was long held by the Provos to embody the links between previous republican phases of struggle and the modern-day PIRA campaign; and Gleeson himself long concurred with this view, commenting in 1985 that 'while there is a British presence in our country there will never be peace...And while they hold guns to the throats of Irish people, there will always be an IRA to fight them.'[97] Some PIRA members were indeed from militant republican families, continuing a tradition of proud resistance which their own parents and other relatives had handed on to them.[98]

Socialism represented a commitment for many Provisionals, and should be seen as a significant secondary goal of the organization. Inspired by the powerful example and ideas of figures such as 1916 rebel James Connolly (even now the pre-eminent Irish socialist-republican political theologian), many within PIRA ranks had what one former member called 'grandiose dreams of finally freeing Ireland from 800 years of British imperialism, and liberating mankind from the yoke of capitalism into the bargain'.[99] Like other IRAs before them, the Provisionals in many instances saw their struggle as one which would revolutionize economic and social relations in socialistic manner.[100] For its part, the PIRA of 1970 was at least rhetorically committed to the ultimate objective of a socialist republic, and from these early days there existed what Danny Morrison has nicely called an 'instinctive affinity with working class politics'.[101] Ex-PIRA woman Marian Price's father had been 'a very strong socialist', and in Price's own view socialism and republicanism were inextricably interwoven: 'I really don't think you can have one without the other.'[102] Again and again, from different kinds of source material, we find instances of PIRA members for whom socialist republicanism clearly played a significant role: 'Connolly was a big influence in my life';[103] 'We stand opposed to all forms and all manifestations of imperialism and capitalism. We stand for an Ireland, free, united, socialist, and Gaelic';[104] 'the dominant ideology among republican prisoners in the H–Blocks in the 1980s was that of a revolutionary, left-wing, socialist, Marxist orientation'.[105] And Sinn Fein politics exuded a lastingly leftist quality. Paddy Fitzsimmons, a candidate for the party in the June 1983 Westminster elections, made clear in his contemporary election literature that Sinn Fein were 'the only party that will look after its people and bring about a thirty-two-county socialist republic'; he listed the 'effects of British rule' as negative regarding unemployment, housing, education, agriculture, and other economic issues, so his declaration that 'Sinn Fein is the only political party who have consistently opposed British rule in Ireland' possessed a distinctly social and economic dimension to it.[106]

Other secondary goals for some included the cultural, whether linguistic ('Learn Irish, speak Irish, be Irish': 'Sinn Fein members have a duty to encourage the use of Irish among themselves and the public at large'),[107] or Catholic.[108] Despite the elements of deep communal, devotional, symbolic, cultural Catholicism among many Provos, they remained ostensibly committed also to producing an Ireland beyond sectarian division: they intended their violence to 'win national freedom and end division and sectarianism in Ireland'[109]—the latter being in practice another of their secondary goals.

Beyond such secondary goals, PIRA partial strategic victory might also be identified in the determining of the political agenda, and the prevention of opponents from securing their preferred outcome to the Northern Ireland conflict. If the Provos could prevent the kind of resolution that was anathema to them, and ensure that no settlement was reached which excluded them from the finally arrived-at political structures in the region, then their violence might be seen to have worked in some measure. In Gerry Adams's words from January 1989, republican violence 'sets the political agenda'.[110]

At a different but important level, tactical success might also see Provo violence working. This might variously involve operational efficacy (the successful bombing of a target, assassination of an individual, killing of military personnel, and so forth). But it might also involve the securing of interim concessions (in terms of the day-to-day improvement of prison conditions for their incarcerated members, for instance, as a means of further legitimizing the IRA's armed struggle; or in terms of gains made as part of a complex negotiating process taking place at the end of the conflict); or the acquisition through violence of otherwise unattainable publicity for the IRA's cause; or the undermining of opponents (whether unionist, British, or rival-nationalist); or the gaining and exerting of control over a population or community through violence or its threat; or the organizational strengthening of the movement itself—in this case, through the refinement and bolstering of the PIRA, and the development also of its important political wing, Sinn Fein. On this organizational point, if violence ensured that republicans were necessarily involved in making and partly determining the nature of the final settlement, then it might have been seen to have had some tactical efficacy. One leading republican's statement that 'there will be no settlement until republicans are included in a solution'[111] reflects this crucial point.

There exists clear evidence that the Provos were sharply conscious of these tactical priorities. That publicity was important to them is evident from the fact that the first issue of their Dublin-based paper (*An Phoblacht*) appeared in early 1970 and that, similarly, their Belfast organ (*Republican News*) emerged also in that year—right at the start of their long campaign. The undermining of opponents was something which they equally clearly sought, whether those opponents were a clumsily overreacting UK state, a set of non-violent but also some violent Irish nationalist rivals, or the forces of organized, pro-UK unionism in Ulster. The last of these—political unionism and loyalism—was presented by many Provos as fascistic or quasi-fascistic,[112] in a clear effort to delegitimize and undermine it.

Finally, I think that we should not ignore the potential for inherent rewards of struggle as such, operating at least partly independently from the group's political and other goals. As with so many political movements from the past, it would be wrong both to exaggerate the programmatic coherence of the PIRA's ideological thinking as it was understood by all individual members, or to present the political-ideological case as the sole motivation for people's having joined and fought with the Provisionals. The desire to satisfy a Fanonist rage ran through much PIRA activity. (It was not coincidental that Frantz Fanon has been so frequently read and quoted by the IRA,[113] nor that hatred emerges from PIRA-related sources so frequently.) Bobby Sands: 'At eighteen-and-a-half I joined the Provos. . . . I went out to meet and confront the imperial might of an empire with an M1 carbine and enough hate to topple the world.'[114] But it is worth asking also how far the appeal of personal and communal dignity, strong comradeship within the movement, societal prestige, adventure, and so forth played at least some part in motivating people towards sustained engagement with the Provisional IRA.

III

The IRA forced the British government to the negotiating table. . . . They were a revolutionary force who, when an opportunity to advance the struggle for Irish unity through peaceful means was established, removed themselves from the political equation.

Sinn Fein's Martin McGuinness, Easter 2011[115]

Given our layered assessment of their goals, therefore, did the Provisional IRA's violence work?

The strategic goal of defending the Catholic community was largely unfulfilled. Gerry Adams has argued that by 1972 the Provisional IRA had 'created a defensive force of unprecedented effectiveness'.[116] The evidence is, however, strongly against him here. In this period, during the Provisional IRA's first three years (18 December 1969 to 17 December 1972), 171 Catholic civilians were killed by loyalists or by UK security forces in the northern conflict.[117] During much of the conflict, indeed, Provisional IRA violence tended—among its other effects—to prompt retaliatory violence against Catholics from Protestant loyalist paramilitary groups.[118] According to one authoritative record, there were 1,236 Catholic civilians killed during the Troubles between 1969 and 2000; in the same period 394 republican paramilitaries were also killed (another heavy blow to the Catholic community).[119] The notion that PIRA violence effectively protected Catholics in the north cannot withstand such evidence, tragically.

Indeed, detailed consideration of specific cases rather underlines this broader point. One consequence of the PIRA's January 1976 Kingsmills killing of ten Protestant civilians in south Armagh, for example, was the convincing of Billy Wright to sustain a career of significant loyalist terrorism. The sequences of violence generated by his subsequent UVF and LVF paramilitary violence involved large numbers of lives being ruined, many of those victims being the very northern Catholics whom the PIRA wanted to protect and defend.[120] If Wright was indeed, in UK Secretary of State Mo Mowlam's words, 'one of the most efficient and ruthless killers on the loyalist side',[121] then his vicious killings were partly set and sustained in motion by the actions of the Provisional IRA.

Even more important than defence, arguably, for the Provisional IRA was their central strategic goal of establishing a fully independent and united Irish republic. They ended their armed struggle in 2005 without having secured this central war aim. During their campaign of violence the PIRA repeatedly made clear that their interpretation of achieving the fulfilment of Irish national self-determination involved British withdrawal from the north, the ending of British sovereignty over any part of Ireland, the dismantling of the partitioning border, and the establishment of a sovereign and fully independent united Ireland.

They had again and again—and, from an Irish republican perspective, entirely understandably—rejected the idea that a majority in Northern

Ireland represented a legitimate veto on the establishment of Irish unity. Unionist consent had not been thought essential to the ending of the border, and in the Provos' long-held view it was Ireland as one single unit (and not as two units deciding simultaneously but separately) that should represent the national self that did the determining. Moreover, the destruction of the irreformable Northern Ireland state was long considered an integral part of this trajectory, and one which PIRA violence was explicitly intended to bring about. All of this has been clearly demonstrated earlier in this chapter, and it shouts out unambiguously from a wide range of important evidence: 'The six-county state and those institutions which maintain it are irreformable and corrupt, and as such they must be confronted and destroyed';[122] 'Outside of a thirty-two-county sovereign, independent democracy the IRA will have no involvement in what is loosely called constitutional politics';[123] 'the six-county statelet could not be reformed...I am dogmatic and unapologetic in my opposition to the loyalist veto'.[124]

The 1998 Belfast or Good Friday Agreement (GFA)—the deal which substantially defined the terms on which the Northern Ireland conflict drew to an end—was one which diverged in key respects from this central aim regarding the fulfilment of Irish national self-determination as the Provisional IRA had for so long interpreted it. The GFA affirmed a commitment to recognize the northern unionist veto that had for many years been denounced by the Provos as undemocratic and unacceptable. For the Agreement clearly recognized 'the legitimacy of whatever choice is freely exercised by a majority of the people of Northern Ireland with regard to its status, whether they prefer to continue to support the union with Great Britain or a sovereign united Ireland'. Any future united Ireland must therefore, on these terms, come about subject to northern majority endorsement, since the GFA further and explicitly recognized 'that it is for the people of the island of Ireland alone, by agreement between the two parts respectively and without external impediment, to exercise their right of self-determination on the basis of consent, freely and concurrently given, north and south, to bring about a united Ireland, if that is their wish, accepting that this right must be achieved and exercised with and subject to the agreement and consent of a majority of the people of Northern Ireland'.[125]

There can be no doubt that such commitments undermined the traditional PIRA understanding of self-determination, as they themselves made limpidly clear in their response to the GFA in April 1998. The PIRA leadership said that it had 'considered carefully the Good Friday document. It remains our position that a durable peace settlement demands the end of British rule in Ireland and the exercise of the right of the people of Ireland to national self-determination. Viewed against our republican objectives or any democratic analysis, this document clearly falls short of presenting a solid basis for a lasting settlement. In our view the two imminent referenda [on the Belfast Agreement, north and south] do not constitute the exercise of national self-determination.'[126] This statement was fully consistent with what the Provos had long believed and argued. Yet the GFA notion that Irish self-determination had to be exercised on a partitioned basis—with the northern majority having an effective veto over any shift away from membership of the UK—was one that had become deeply embedded in the Irish peace process (it was emphatically there in the UK and Irish governments' December 1993 Downing Street Declaration, for significant instance);[127] and, despite their understandable reservations about the GFA, that latter document was to become one on which the Provisional republican movement came to base its ensuing politics. This reflected some real political courage on their part, for the 1998 Good Friday Agreement did not endorse the outcome which their violence had long and crucially been supposed to achieve.

It is undoubtedly true that the issue of Irish self-determination had been made more pressing and famous and urgent of attention because of PIRA violence. That was the reason for its repeated salience within peace process documents. And, taking the longer historical view, it is also important to stress that a united Ireland could still emerge in the future, that many republicans from the Provisional tradition remain very strongly committed to it, and that if the current political journey were indeed to result in future Irish unity then they could presumably argue that their earlier violence had represented one necessary stage in bringing that process about in the first place. Accordingly, Gerry Adams stressed in 1998 that republicans saw the GFA as 'transitional': 'And it could become a transitional stage towards reunification.'[128] Former PIRA Chief of Staff Joe Cahill read the deal in similar terms: 'The Good Friday Agreement is not a settlement. It's not perfect, it has faults, but it's a basis for progress. It could and should be a stepping stone to a thirty-two-county republic. I see it as a new line of strategy.'[129]

Scholarly opinion varies greatly regarding what was achieved by the PIRA's campaign.[130] But in terms of what had actually been secured by the time that the Provos' armed struggle ended in 2005, it is clear that strategic success regarding the goal of Irish unity had so far eluded the group. Indeed,

while there had been occasions during the Troubles when representatives of
the UK state had seemed to suggest to republicans the possibility of British
withdrawal from Northern Ireland, in reality the evidence suggests that
such a withdrawal never emerged as the policy of the UK government at
any point in the conflict. For it was repeatedly recognized in London that
realities such as political opinion in Northern Ireland (and indeed in the
Irish Republic) would not allow for Irish unity in the foreseeable future; so
withdrawal from Northern Ireland never became UK government policy.[131]
As one disenchanted ex-PIRA Volunteer put it to me in an interview (again,
reflecting the way in which interview evidence can bring to light voices
other than those of a movement's leadership, and words which would not
otherwise very easily be heard):[132] 'To what extent did the IRA achieve their
strategic goals? I would have to say they failed dismally'; they had pursued:

> the strategy of the long war, until such times as the British conceded a declar-
> ation of intent to withdraw from Ireland, and this was not some woolly con-
> cept dreamed up by a couple of individuals: it was a strategic goal widely
> discussed within the Republican Army and was accepted throughout the
> Army as *the strategic goal*, which was not negotiable under any circumstances.
> Taken from that viewpoint, the IRA completely failed to achieve its strategic
> goal, which was to force a British declaration of intent to withdraw.[133]

Another ex-Provo was equally clear in his negative view of what had been
achieved, referring to:

> the truth that the outcome of a quarter century of war was not worth a single
> drop of anybody's blood. Was it all then a futile, useless waste of lives?
> Probably.... [T]he success of an undertaking must be judged against its reasons
> for beginning and its end, and, thus seen, the IRA failed utterly, its closing
> position on how to achieve British withdrawal and Irish unity by then identi-
> cal to that of the successive British governments it fought against.[134]

Other ex-PIRA voices have made a similar case. Anthony McIntyre, for
example, has forcefully, lucidly, and starkly argued that post-1998 Northern
Irish political arrangements represent a defeat for Provisional republicanism:
'The political objective of the Provisional IRA was to secure a British declaration of intent to withdraw. It failed. The objective of the British state was
to force the Provisional IRA to accept—and subsequently respond with a
new strategic logic—that it would not leave Ireland until a majority in the
north consented to such a move. It succeeded.'[135] In the words of another
ex-PIRA member, 'The ceasefires can be viewed as a victory for the British

government... the IRA wasn't able to achieve its demands through armed struggle.'[136]

But the PIRA was a heterogeneous organization and so opinions vary among its former members about what it achieved, and there is certainly another line of argument available, very different from the views cited above. And this more positive argument leads us to the issue of partial strategic victory. As noted, it is hard to claim that PIRA violence diminished levels of anti-Catholic violence during the 1969–2005 period, given the mutually sustaining hostilities between the various actors in the conflict, and the appallingly high levels of violence inflicted on so many northern Catholics during it. But while that central, defensive goal was therefore not, I think, partially achieved, a stronger claim could be made that in relation to Irish self-determination the PIRA's violence did drive politics further in their preferred direction than things would otherwise have moved.

As noted before, full strategic success eludes most of us much of the time.[137] And, while full strategic victory clearly eluded the PIRA, this need not mean that they had achieved nothing significant through their sustained violence. Indeed, in the process of the republican transition towards more moderated politics, a number of leading voices expressed a shrewd sense that compromise would ultimately be needed, as the basis for securing some of their objectives. Again, here, the wide range of available sources allows for a sense of how varied republican opinion began to be. In jail in August 1990, leading republican Danny Morrison reflected on the effect that the death of communism had had on his own political thinking: 'If there is one thing last year in Eastern Europe should have taught us it was the bankruptcy of dogmatism, of communism, which couldn't put food on the table. The lesson has certainly helped me rethink my politics and taught me to be more pragmatic and realistic in terms of our own struggle. If we all lower our demands and our expectations a peg or two we might find more agreement.' The following month he observed tellingly that 'Republicans now are fed up glorifying past defeats and are determined to show something substantial for the sacrifices. I can't see it being resolved until... everybody agrees to come down a few rungs.'[138]

So the GFA-based deal hammered out in the 1990s did not yield the fulfilment of self-determination as the Provos had long argued for it. But it did provide the foundation for a greater capacity for northern nationalists to determine the kind of society in which they lived, through the political institutions which ensured strong representation from them in the power

structures of the new Northern Ireland. Taken together with the extensive
reforms of the north and the ongoing amelioration of the Catholic experience there, it could be argued that the peace process allowed for a much-im-
proved nationalist relationship with the Ulster state.

If, as one ex-PIRA member put it, 'the IRA's armed struggle brought the
Brits to the negotiating table',[139] then the eventual shape of the northern
compromise could—to some eyes—be read as having been prompted by
Provo violence. Long-time PIRA man Eamon McGuire, looking back at
the Provisionals' long campaign and what it had achieved, suggested that
'the question arises: was it worth the price to get this far? I believe it was.
One must think about how bad things were prior to 1969 before answering
that question.' For the struggle, according to McGuire, necessarily involved
different phases. 'The nationalists rose up against an unjust system, and this
was the first step in the struggle; the destruction of Stormont was the second. The third step has to be political because we must unite all our people
and move on.'[140] The evidence suggests that much of the fire-centre for
Provisional politics had come from deep communal disaffection from a
northern state which they considered unfair as well as illegitimate. If the
Provos' armed struggle forced the UK to amend the shape of the north as
significantly as it eventually did, then for some of its members PIRA violence had achieved something major in the process.

The arguments here will never be finally conclusive. As noted, the Provos
had long rejected reform of the north as a solution, so some people will
judge that they have so changed their view as to have become politically
unrecognizable. Others will point out, as eminent Sinn Feiner Tom Hartley
has lucidly done, that (like other political movements) Irish republicans have
been fluid and responsive rather than static:

> What people, I think, don't realize about us is that really we've always been a
> party of change. We changed our attitude towards elections. We changed our
> attitude towards [the Dublin parliament in] Leinster House. 'No return to
> Stormont'—now we're in the building. People often see us as a very central-
> ized, fixed entity but in fact we have been consistently able to bring our con-
> stituency into new political spaces. Republicans don't have a static view of
> politics. This generation knows that you're in there, you're ducking and weav-
> ing, you're shaping. Some days you win, some days you lose, but all the time
> you're in there shaping the agenda.[141]

Moreover, while the Provos seem pragmatically to have accepted for some
time that a united Ireland would not emerge as part of the 1990s peace

deal,[142] there was a positive way for them nonetheless to interpret their trajectory. If Sinn Fein were to end up in power both in Northern Ireland and
in the Republic of Ireland (sharing power with other parties in each case)
then, while a united Ireland still eluded them, a republican influence on governmental power across every part of Ireland would yet have been brought
about. Given the historically deep ties linking Sinn Fein to the Provisional
IRA, it is hard to see this development as independent of Provo struggle.

Again, if effective strategy is about building coalitions,[143] then the capacity of republicans to forge alliances (even sullen ones with former opponents
such as the Democratic Unionist Party or DUP) indicates an ability to build
on the central prominence within negotiation, and within power structures,
that PIRA violence had ensured for the movement. Significantly, however,
that constructive politics of coalition has been dependent upon the disap-
pearance of the PIRA from the political stage. It is only with a *post*-PIRA
Sinn Fein that the DUP has begun to do enduring business.[144]

Those from the enduringly constitutional-nationalist tradition might powerfully argue that much that was on offer at the end of the Northern Ireland
conflict had been available much earlier, and that Provisional IRA violence
therefore caused unnecessary damage and pain to many people. Indeed, the
SDLP had bravely suggested that non-violent means had existed all along for
pursuing the kind of change which eventually emerged. In 1974 the party
declared that 'The Provisional IRA can achieve nothing by carrying on their
campaign of violence but they can achieve almost anything they desire by
knocking it off.'[145] Similarly, the eminent Irish Catholic cleric Cahal Daly had
(long before the Provos stopped their campaign) expressed his clear view 'that
political change is possible without violence, but is impossible unless violence
is rejected'.[146] Scholars too have argued strongly that the 1998 GFA deal was
very different from the central goal long pursued by the PIRA, and that what
emerged in the later 1990s could have been achieved without their violence
(which was aimed at something very different anyway).[147]

Yet other voices have argued that only PIRA violence drove people
towards addressing crucial problems. Sinn Fein politician Conor Murphy,
for example, reflected that the Provos' armed struggle had 'changed the attitude of the British government...A constitutional-political approach to
this [Northern Ireland] would have allowed the British government to put
a lid on it—it wasn't a problem for them, really...and it was only really
when things are happening [i.e. violence] that made people say, "No there's
something wrong here".'[148]

And one outcome of the violence was that when the political deal to end the Troubles did arrive, the party that had been the PIRA's party was the one which emerged to dominance within the northern nationalist community. People frequently assume that politics in the north of Ireland embodies the victory of violent extremes. In truth, during the period from the 1960s to the second decade of the twenty-first century, northern nationalism has tended to see the majority of its adherents back parties which did *not* espouse the use of violence. For it was only after the PIRA began bringing their violence to an end that their political party, Sinn Fein, managed to eclipse the non-violent SDLP as the favoured party of most northern nationalists.[149]

Much of what was secured in 1998 might, perhaps, have been available much earlier (in the 1973 Sunningdale Agreement, for example);[150] but the party that came to dominate northern nationalism after the GFA was the Provisionals' party, and this was partly because PIRA violence gave Sinn Fein much greater punch than their non-violent SDLP rivals possessed, when the long peace process was being developed and shaped. The evidence demonstrates this plainly enough. Jonathan Powell (Prime Minister Tony Blair's Chief of Staff and chief negotiator during the process which produced the GFA, so a very significantly placed source) has made clear how central the ending of the PIRA's campaign of violence was as a motivation behind the British government's crafting of the peace process.[151] Relatedly, Powell has clarified the realities that possessing weapons can involve in terms of augmenting groups' leverage. He recalls that the SDLP's Seamus Mallon 'complained that the British government was talking to Sinn Fein rather than to them because the republicans had guns. That was exactly right. If you want to stop violence then you have to talk to the men with guns, rather than only to those who act purely politically.'[152] Reinforcing this, Tony Blair himself has made clear that more attention was indeed paid to Sinn Fein than to the SDLP at least partly because the former represented part of a violent, armed movement: 'The SDLP thought that they often got ignored because we were too busy dealing with Sinn Fein. "If we had weapons you'd treat us more seriously" was their continual refrain. There was some truth in it. The big prize was plainly an end to violence, and they weren't the authors of the violence.'[153]

The Provisional IRA's shift from war to peace facilitated the ending of what had often seemed a perpetual conflict and (as well as undermining any sense of inevitability in the ongoing level of the Irish struggle) their change of approach reflects a pragmatism deeply rooted in militant Irish republican history.[154] Pragmatists can, of course, also be principled and there is rich evidence pointing to the long-term ambition of Sinn Fein towards an independent and united Ireland, as well as towards the advancement of nationalist communal interests in the north. And, in assessing how much the Provisionals secured through their 1969–2005 campaign, it is worth reflecting on evidence from those against whom they were strongly opposed. In a telling interview, one eminent former officer in the RUC Special Branch (than whom there was probably no more hostile organization, as far as the Provos were concerned) reflectively considered what Provisional republicans have been able to secure:

> While it would be difficult to say that the events of post-1998 have been a total victory for Sinn Fein as they have not obtained their overall objective of a united Ireland, they have probably gained more than anyone else and established themselves as the largest nationalist party in Northern Ireland at the expense of the SDLP. They have managed to do this whilst generally maintaining relative cohesive discipline within their organization. Although the [anti-peace process republican] Dissidents continue a campaign of sorts, they do not have the same support as PIRA or generally the same quality of volunteer. However, this could change either by defections from PIRA or new blood being recruited into the organisations.[155]

It is important to ask also *why* it was that one of the world's most impressively sustained and committed non-state rebel groups decided to compromise and to endorse a deal which fell short of its ultimate demands. There's little doubting the central significance of Provisional leaders Gerry Adams and Martin McGuinness in shaping the PIRA's approach to the evolving peace process, and it was a process which eventually removed the PIRA from the political stage. It was noted in the Introduction that close attention to historical context points to the decisive importance of small-group, and even individual, action and initiative in practice; I think the crucial role of Adams and McGuinness and their close colleagues in altering the direction of the PIRA offers a historically significant example (and the contingency rather than the inevitability of their decisions is important here too). Moreover, the development of that process of transformation was a long one, stretching over many years in all its jagged unpredictability. In their peace process careers McGuinness and Adams helped bring to an end the vicious violence which they and their PIRA comrades had done so much previously to sustain. Why?

Much of the explanation lies with Irish people's own political opinions. As noted, the Provos sought to apply Clausewitzean pressure upon the UK government, using violence to make the war more oppressive and painful for London than it would be for the latter to yield up a united Ireland. But the main obstacle to a united Ireland actually lay in Ireland, rather than in London or in Britain. Most Northern Irish people clearly, unarguably, and lastingly preferred (and still prefer) to stay in the UK than to be expelled from it into a united Ireland, as has been made unambiguously clear in repeated surveys and elections.[156] Neither political argument, nor the pressure of impressively sustained PIRA violence, has shifted Ulster unionist attitudes on this point. Indeed, it may have hardened unionist opposition still further. People in Ulster can possess multiple identities, of course. But, in common with many other settings of ethnic antagonism,[157] so too here when inter-group conflict strains the tension between a person's different identities, they often feel compelled to jettison one and opt decisively for the other. In the Northern Ireland case, this has been reflected in the way that the PIRA's violence contributed to a diminishing of the proportion of Ulster Protestants who have identified as 'Irish' (20 per cent in 1968, but only 3 per cent by 1986),[158] since Irishness seemed increasingly to be associated with an aggressive and threatening separatism.

Such unionist opinion put severe constraints on what any UK government could do in response to Provisional IRA violence. Pro-union, loyalist terrorism provided evidence that British withdrawal would hardly be followed by a peaceful shift towards Irish unity; and the long record of unionism and loyalism makes forcibly clear that Northern Irish majority opposition to absorption in a united Ireland has very deep historical roots, and rests on autonomous and sturdy opinion rather than on an easily evaporative false consciousness. Against this background, the Provisionals' violence never came close to persuading unionists to sympathize with their central strategic goal. As one very insightful and intelligent ex-PIRA member himself put it, PIRA 'bombs in cafes and restaurants that took civilian lives, whether accidents or not, were understandably viewed by unionists as murderous attacks on their community rather than military operations'.[159] Whatever the PIRA said or actually intended, what they *did* often looked to Ulster Protestants as though it had much to do with sectarian enmity and revenge. And that was hardly likely to encourage unionists to consider absorption into a republican Ireland to represent a benign development. As one (admittedly disenchanted) ex-PIRA man put it, 'The IRA campaign forced many progressive Protestants into hiding and made the majority unite behind the most reactionary and conservative elements.'[160]

Here there were deep historical patterns at play. Modern-day Irish republicans' understandably iconic eighteenth-century hero, Theobald Wolfe Tone, had himself found in his own day that there had existed a tension between, on the one hand, seeking to separate Ireland from England through violence and, on the other, trying to unite Ireland's divided Catholic and Protestant communities.[161] Ireland's more recent past also offered informative suggestions that the ending of partition would prove extremely difficult. The long-dominant nationalist party in independent Ireland during the twentieth century, Fianna Fail, had repeatedly failed—from its inception onwards—to overcome (or even to acknowledge and understand) the depth of north-eastern opposition to a united Ireland; formally committed to undoing partition, the party had been entirely unable to produce a way of moving practically towards that goal.[162] The Provos' inheritance from previous nationalist endeavours, therefore, suggested that they faced a Sisyphean task in trying to secure Irish unity and independence in the face of Irish unionist hostility.[163] British withdrawal from Ireland and the ending of partition turned out not, after all, to be inevitable.

Moreover, even among modern-day Irish nationalists themselves (north and south) there have existed diverse views about the best solution to the Northern Ireland problem. As noted, during most of the period when the PIRA was carrying out its full-scale violence, it was their non-violent and constitutional-nationalist rivals in the SDLP who had the political support of most northern nationalists; moreover, while opinion in the Republic of Ireland has clearly favoured a united Ireland, it has not done so as any kind of high-level priority for most people there.[164] Indeed, the available archives make clear how longstanding has been the reluctance, in practice, of Dublin politicians and civil servants to favour any immediate moves towards Irish unity, certainly as pursued by force.[165] So, between the strong hostility of Ulster unionists, the reformist tendencies of so many northern nationalists, and the tepidity of southern Irish irredentism, there existed serious popular-opinion obstacles, among the Irish people themselves, for the Provos in their march towards a united and independent Ireland.

In this sense, the PIRA's focus on trying to break British commitment to remain in sovereign control over the north had limitations to its effectiveness, since arguably the most important obstacles to Irish independent unity lay not in Britain, but rather among the people of Ireland. And some of those Irish people who opposed Irish unity and independence—northern loyalists especially—represented a potentially very violent opposition to any British plans for disengagement. Probably rightly, the UK government was firmly of the view that withdrawal would occasion far worse violence, rather than a solution. Secretary of State for Northern Ireland James Prior, at a meeting in the House of Commons with the Number 10 Policy Unit in 1984, recognized the complex social and political difficulties of the north, but was clear on this point about withdrawal and its likely consequences: 'The Secretary of State made clear that the security situation in Northern Ireland was aggravated by the problems of high unemployment, particularly among young people, and the difficulties of finding an acceptable political way forward'; but he also made clear that 'if steps were taken which threatened the sovereignty of Northern Ireland and which led to a British withdrawal, a violent and highly organized civil war would ensue'.[166]

Moreover, the Provisionals' capacity to effect a decisive change in British opinion anyway probably fell far short of what they had hoped for and expected. Crucial to the PIRA's argument was the idea that their violence would force British public opinion towards pressurizing the UK government to disengage from the north of Ireland. In the event, pressure in Britain for withdrawal from Northern Ireland never gained sufficient momentum for this part of the PIRA's plan to come to fruition. Even the lengthy campaign in England itself (the most directly painful part of the PIRA's work for the majority of British people to bear), failed to generate as much pressure as had been hoped. Despite over 500 PIRA incidents in England, over 100 deaths, and thousands of injuries, little progress was made in relation to securing British popular pressure towards a united Ireland: 'While the organization may have achieved significant publicity as a result of their actions in England, there is much evidence to suggest that their impact on British public opinion and British government policy was minimal.'[167]

The Provisionals represented an enduring and credible threat to the normal security of Britain, and this should not be underestimated. But the degree to which that threat made British people sufficiently prioritize disengagement from Ireland was another and very different matter. One aspect of this was the seeming reality that the longer a violent threat endures, the *more* bearable and containable (rather than less bearable) it seems to become.

In addition to Irish popular opinion and British indifference, there was also the matter of economics. Much evidence points towards the profound economic problems that would be involved in any speedy shift towards a united, independent Ireland.[168] And, as the archives again tellingly make clear, this was recognized by sharp-sighted republicans themselves during the conflict.[169]

Intelligent pragmatism also led key republicans to note the effect that international developments were having in variously pushing towards the pursuit of a compromise deal. These included the greater role of the USA in contributing towards a fair outcome in the north, the effective death of millenarian Marxism with the associated collapse of the Soviet Union, the examples of other peace processes (such as that in South Africa) as evidence that long-held enmities could fruitfully be overcome, the capacity of the UK and Irish states as European Union friends to put together a meaningful context for conflict resolution in Northern Ireland, and the fact that a post-9/11 world was one in which serious politicians had to be seen to show their renunciation of what looked like terroristic methods.[170]

It is also true that the UK state showed no obvious signs of leaning towards giving the Provisionals what they centrally wanted any time soon. And the state had displayed an increasing capacity, not to defeat the PIRA, but certainly to limit its tactical effectiveness and the levels of violence that it could pursue. By the beginning of the 1990s, it was clear that the Provisionals could not be beaten in the sense of being stamped out; but it was equally clear that their violence was being somewhat contained, and that this severely limited the likelihood of its yielding imminent victory for them. So, for example, the PIRA could clearly continue their violence at a significant level during and beyond the 1990s; but the evidence suggests also that they had been damagingly infiltrated by the UK and Irish states in ways that undermined their capacity to pursue victory in a meaningful manner.[171] In the words of one of the Provos' police adversaries, regarding the condition of the PIRA by the end of the Troubles: 'They were being contained. . . . It became stalemate.'[172] And, if informers were crucial here, then so was technical surveillance through the use of bugs: the latter, in the words of one ex-RUC man, 'was massive. It was absolutely crucial to it.'[173]

Some ex-Provos themselves have been admirably lucid on this issue of their having become monitored and somewhat undermined by the state: 'There is little doubt that many IRA operations were compromised by information being leaked to British authorities.'[174] In the early days of the Troubles, the clumsiness of the British Army had played substantially into the Provisionals' hands. Regarding early 1970s Northern Ireland, for example, Lieutenant General Sir Alistair Irwin commented that 'A lot of what we did was more than just a nuisance to people; it was positively contributing to hostility.'[175] In time, however, that Army did come to play a role in keeping a lid on what would have become a more awful and more bloody conflict and in thwarting much PIRA activity.[176]

The RUC were very important here too, not in preventing all PIRA operations, of course, but certainly in frequently frustrating the Provos' intentions. As one ex-Special Branch officer put it, the Provisionals

> realized that they had major internal security problems, taken together with the lack of quality of a large proportion of their volunteers, and this also emphasized the importance of going down a political road. Although the security forces had penetrated PIRA and had scored successes over the years—mid-eighties, mid-nineties, it has been reported that four out of five attacks were thwarted by the security forces—PIRA still had the capability to carry out successful high-profile operations. Overt and covert actions by the security forces could never 100% prevent all terrorist actions.[177]

According to another ex-RUC member, two out of three of the Provisional IRA's planned operations were, towards the end of their campaign, being thwarted by the state on the basis of prior intelligence.[178]

And, as suggested, part of this involved the role of informers. Historically, there had long been difficulties for Irish republican organizations in terms of informers and spies,[179] and the same kind of problem now plagued the Provos. As one ex-PIRA man frankly put it: 'All the [PIRA] players were marked by the mid-eighties. The Brits noted where they were seen, where they were coming from, and where they were going.'[180] One UK intelligence document has claimed that half of the PIRA's senior members and a quarter of their total membership during the Troubles were, in fact, agents for state intelligence services.[181] Even if one treats such claims with scepticism (and they do here come from a very engaged point of origin), there is sufficient evidence to make clear the corrosive effect on the Provos' campaign of state counter-intelligence work. To know that people close to you were informing on you to the authorities could do damage to operations and to morale alike. As one ex-PIRA member candidly put it: 'someone close to me who knew my intentions must have informed on me. This was a very bad feeling.'[182]

In addition to the RUC and the British Army, the UK Security Service was also involved in this anti-PIRA intelligence war. In the words of one former Director General of that Service, MI5 eventually built up 'a large and very successful intelligence operation against terrorism in Northern

Ireland'.[183] Long-term and large-scale imprisonment of so many PIRA members also helped to constrain what the movement could do, and so the *political* calculations about what a putative peace process might offer to Irish republicans have to be read in light also of the fact that the UK state was partly thwarting their armed struggle and what it could achieve. By the late 1980s and early 1990s the intelligence capacity of the state was strengthening the logic of the Provos seeking some kind of compromise deal; in this sense, intelligence was 'absolutely fundamental'.[184]

With all of this in view, one reading open to sharp-sighted Provos by the beginning of the 1990s was that they were in a rather fruitless stalemate.[185] It was not that the Provisionals could not have continued with their campaign, nor that the PIRA leadership committed itself at once unambiguously or inevitably towards peace. The Provos' relationship with the UK state was one which evolved over years of posturing, listening, negotiating, bargaining, and compromising—some of it open, and some if it necessarily hidden at the time.[186] But the Provisional leadership did become shrewdly aware that their violence was not producing the intended victory, and that greater momentum towards republican goals might be available through an alternative, less aggressive form of politics. Indeed, leading republicans were explicit about the stalemate context. Danny Morrison in June 1990 referred to there being 'a military stalemate',[187] just as others in the movement had earlier made a similar point.[188]

The leadership's success in bringing so many of their movement along with them as they shifted political approach remains one of the most remarkable features of the Irish peace process, and the capacity of people like Gerry Adams to prompt extraordinary loyalty from his comrades[189] offers partial explanation, though republican discipline and command structures and more than a hint of organizational authoritarianism and repression also played their part.[190]

Also crucial was the impressively evolving nature of the Provos' political party, Sinn Fein, which changed from its initial role as a subservient mouthpiece to being the dominant partner in the republican relationship. In interview, one of the party's most talented figures (Conor Murphy) cogently reflected on this long-term shift towards Sinn Fein salience: 'Sinn Fein, or the republican movement, recognized that they needed to grow a political body.... Everyone who supported republicanism could not be involved in the IRA...So you had to have a movement capable of attracting people, of creating demands, of broadening [to] social issues, political issues, cultural

issues.'[191] And there is now an impressive literature attesting to the pragmatism and the complex gradualism involved in this development of Sinn
Fein-led republican activism.[192] Regarding the Provisional IRA's 1980s movement towards a peace process politics, again it is worth listening to Conor
Murphy's thoughtful argument:

> From a purely military point of view, the various initiatives that had been tried
> by the IRA, a series of initiatives to try and *really* step up the war: some of those
> had their successes, but not perhaps on the level that people had expected. The
> IRA was suffering casualties. There were more people going into jail. . . . Suddenly
> people are seeing husbands going in, and then the next generation is going
> into jail as well or being killed. I'm not saying that the will to resist was being
> eroded, but had no new dynamic been entered into that, perhaps that could
> have been the case. . . . If it was becoming fairly clear that armed struggle wasn't
> going to drive people onto boats and out of Belfast harbour, then you had to
> have another dynamic which opened up the possibility of great political
> change, and then therefore the political and the party and the elected people
> and the elected representatives suddenly became more the shop-front end of
> things, the shop-window end of things, and more and more the cutting edge.[193]

The Provisional IRA had not secured strategic victory, but its jagged movement towards a different kind of politics allowed for Sinn Fein to attempt
to bring about partial strategic success in the wake of the armed struggle.[194]
And they were only able to engage in the peace process politics which
delivered their partial success because they did gradually jettison political
violence. For the UK government had long made clear that sustained
involvement with Sinn Fein would require them to distance themselves
from armed struggle. As one memo from the UK authorities in Belfast put
it in 1985, 'the reason for our animus towards Sinn Fein is their expressed
support for terrorism'.[195] Earlier in the same year another UK document
had made a similar point: 'The government's policy on its relations with
Sinn Fein has been made very clear. Unless Sinn Fein renounces the use of
violence Ministers are not prepared to have dealings with them.'[196] Similar
points had been made previously. One 1984 statement drafted for James
Prior when he was Secretary of State for Northern Ireland put it crisply
enough: 'Until and unless Sinn Fein renounces violence, neither my
Ministerial colleagues nor I will meet Sinn Fein MPs or Assembly members,
and we shall not reply personally to letters from them.'[197]

Another layer of partial strategic victory might involve the attainment of
secondary goals, among which the PIRA could be seen to list hitting back

against their enemies. There can be little doubt that they had much, bloodily repeated success here. Although I think revenge cannot in itself explain PIRA violence, at times it is clear that the Provos did succeed in exacting it, whether against the British Army, the British ruling elite,[198] or other more locally rooted opponents (for there was clearly some cathartic violence carried out against Protestants, the evidence making clear that some sectarian aggression was indeed practised by the PIRA,[199] though admittedly not as much as they could have pursued had they wanted to do so more extensively). Border Protestants felt themselves especially vulnerable (suffering some life-changingly awful damage at the PIRA's hands),[200] and the cycle of violence in County Armagh during the mid-1970s embodied an episodic pattern of sectarian hitting back.

The scale of the success in targeting enemies can be traced in various kinds of evidence, from the stark figures of those killed,[201] to poignantly poetic and evocative accounts of the Northern Ireland conflict such as that from former member of the British Army Nigel Pantling, whose work gently and movingly records the vulnerability of the individual soldiers in post-1960s Northern Ireland.[202] And, regarding the Army, it is important to reflect on the relationship between the problem of definition, the historical method, and our assessment of terrorism's efficacy. This book has adopted a capacious definition of terrorism which allows for recognition of state actions, as well as the acts of non-state groups, as potentially falling under that heading. In Northern Ireland, it's hard to explain the PIRA's popularity, or to understand the nature of their partial strategic success, without acknowledging that many within their republican community considered British military violence to be terroristic, and that such people thought state violence therefore to justify a vengeful process of hitting back (at which the PIRA was repeatedly successful). Listening closely within the Irish context to first-hand sources (to ex-PIRA member Marian Price's assertion that 'the real terrorism' is what states do, for example)[203] helps us to explain the Provos' desire for revenge, and to appreciate the degree to which their violence did therefore serve a serious, albeit secondary, goal in practice.

It is easy to forget now the horror that violence (from all sides) produced in the Northern Ireland conflict. And much of this violence was carried out by the Provisional IRA. A large Provo bomb on 20 May 1985 outside Newry killed four young RUC officers and prompted the RUC Chief Constable (John Hermon)—who had visited the scene of the explosion—to describe the actions involved in the attack as 'sub-human and so horrific that no sane or civilized person could be associated with them in deed or thought'.[204]

Did the Provos' violence succeed in helping them to sustain resistance into the future? They saw themselves as part of a long chain of struggle against what they considered the wrongful rule over Ireland by England and Britain; and it is clear that, in producing an armed campaign which the UK state acknowledged that it could not extirpate, they did achieve something of this secondary goal. But the ongoing longevity of the republican struggle also owed much to the non-violent aspects of the movement's work. This— whether in written argument through newspapers and other media, or through prison resistance, or through the increasingly important election work and other popular engagement by Sinn Fein—also forms part of a complex causal pattern. As I write in 2015, the most vibrant part of the Irish republican movement has clearly become the emphatically political one of Sinn Fein, rather than the armed political activism of the PIRA. The strength of the political party derives much from the energy and force and momentum and personnel that the armed struggle had drawn together. But it would be simplistic to suggest that violence had by itself succeeded in sustaining republican resistance into the future. Indeed, it was long the case that non-violent activity by republicans contributed crucially to their popularity and momentum. The archives again are useful here regarding contextual politics. When standing for election in the 1984 European Parliament Election, Sinn Fein's Danny Morrison combined 'an unapologetic stand in support of national reunification' with a stress also on his party's setting up of advice centres which dealt with housing and welfare problems in a practical, day-to-day manner.[205]

The secondary goal of socialism—certainly in the hard-left version so strongly favoured by many within the PIRA during the 1970s and 1980s—is harder to read as having been successfully achieved at all. When I read through the books gathered into prison by the PIRA themselves during the conflict, many of the volumes that they were reading (Progress Publishers editions of Marx, Engels, Lenin, Trotsky) were the same books that I myself had been reading as a left-wing student at Oxford in the 1980s. (My own copies are here on the shelves of my study as I write.) But, for ex-prisoners and ex-students alike, the late 1980s death of communism limited any room for thinking that a hard-edged socialism such as that evident in these readings would be able to determine the shape of the world.[206]

And, once again, there were long and telling pre-echoes from the Irish republican past at work here. Earlier generations of IRA activists had also espoused with commitment, eloquence, energy, and considerable intelligence an intended fusion of hard-left politics with republican separatism, only to discover that their millenarian social hopes would fail to resonate with enough Irish people, and would therefore not come to fruition.[207] The fact that earlier socialist republicans had been frustrated in their similar political ambitions did not make it inevitable that the Provisionals would experience the same disappointment; but it does provide a significant and pertinent pre-echo, and reinforces the sense that Irish conditions might prove unpropitious for such radical ambition. Sinn Fein and the republican movement still celebrate the most iconic of all Irish republican socialists, the deeply impressive James Connolly;[208] but his kind of radical socialism is now far less prominent within their thinking than it had been before, and it shows no sign of being implemented in Ireland in practice.

What of secondary, cultural goals, and of the ending of sectarianism? There is no doubt that many PIRA members found their struggle comple- mented and enriched by an Irish-language enthusiasm, evident not least in the Irish-speaking wings of the jails;[209] and, although there developed much hostility towards the role of the Catholic Church, and much individual scep- ticism about Christian faith more broadly among latter-day PIRA members, it is also true that at periods in the struggle the intensity of their violent conflict reinforced for some members an individual but also a communal faith.[210] This could do nothing major, of course, to stop the late twentieth and early twenty-first-century decline of the influence of the Catholic Church and faith within Ireland.

And that faith, of course, was one which faced considerable enmity from some within the Ulster Protestant community. And, despite the genuine and admirable post-conflict efforts of many ex-PIRA figures in the direction of reconciliation (in one former member's words, 'This is what we have to do. When the war is over, you have a responsibility to make peace. It's work that won't stop. It's work that will continue'),[211] there can be little doubt that the Provisionals' violence greatly intensified sectarian division during the con- flict itself. There were instances, as they themselves have acknowledged, when they became involved in sectarian violence; there were periods of struggle, such as the 1980–1 hunger-strike phase, when inter-communal comity was further eroded amid deepened sectarian polarization;[212] there was the sectarianizing impact of some particularly shocking episodes, such as the November 1987 Enniskillen bombing at a Remembrance Sunday service, in which the PIRA killed eleven Protestants; and there was the unintended effect that, for example, the loyalist UDA were convinced that 'the Provisionals intend to drive forcefully from Ulster any Protestants who survive their terrorist campaign'.[213] The appalling details of the effects of the PIRA's violence have been thoroughly documented elsewhere.[214] But it is important not to forget the precise horror of episodes such as the 17 February 1978 La Mon House bombing at a hotel on the outskirts of Belfast: twelve people (eleven of them civilians) were killed by a Provo incendiary bomb which had cans of petrol attached to it and which dispersed terrifying fire through the building; most of the bodies were burned beyond recognition.[215]

Ireland's past contains numerous, poignant examples of republican activists attempting to end sectarianism, while their actions actually intensified sectarian division in practice.[216] Regrettably, the Provisionals have tended to fit this pattern. For PIRA violence contributed to an enduring and much deeper communal polarization between the two communities in Northern Ireland, the legacy of which is likely to remain for many years to come, and understandably so amid scarred memories and the destruction of inter-communal trust.[217]

Did Provisional IRA violence have the partial strategic success of determining the political agenda? It's clear that many Ulster unionists would have preferred a very different kind of outcome for the politics of Northern Ireland from that which has latterly emerged.[218] In this sense, the Provisionals' capacity to drive muscularly before and during negotiations for some key concessions (prisoner release, extensive police reform, north–south dynamics) could be seen to involve them having ruled out some of what their enemy wanted. Moreover, the paradoxical effect of violence such as that practised by the PIRA is that anyone wanting to end it is likely to have to produce a process and a solution which at least partly involves such groups within it. Whether or not Provo violence brought about political changes that would not otherwise have been possible, it did have the effect of necessitating that Sinn Fein would be involved in the power politics behind the making and implementing of a new Northern Ireland deal.

On the other hand, highly intelligent republicans such as Gerry Adams thoughtfully recognized the difficulties that the PIRA's violence involved in terms of determining a wider agenda. Long aware of the need for serious political momentum, Mr Adams had observed of the 1970s that for the Provisionals, 'Armed struggle had dominated the movement to the extent of being considered almost the only form of struggle.' He further commented of this era that 'the biggest weakness of Sinn Fein in the north was our failure to build either alliances with the SDLP or a party political electoral alternative'.[219] And the dominance of PIRA violence within the republican movement did help to explain their problem with alliances and with party political growth. As noted, the SDLP of that earlier era had been vehemently critical of the blood-stained violence carried out by the PIRA, both from a moral and from a tactical point of view; and the capacity of Sinn Fein to develop its support base to higher levels was limited by the hostility of many people within the northern Catholic constituency towards their movement's violence.

As so often, therefore, what we see in close context is a complex picture. Provisional IRA violence certainly did grab attention and headlines in ways that made their reading of the situation in Ireland seem very urgent, and in ways that helped to shape the political agenda; but it simultaneously con-strained for years their capacity to develop broader and more effective polit-ical alliances and strategies which would allow them to fulfil that ambitious agenda effectively through the pursuit of fuller politics.

When we move from strategic considerations towards tactical ones, I think the evidence suggests a greater degree of efficacy for the Provisionals' violence, even though the human consequences of that violence for the victims were so often horrific and brutal. Operationally, the Provos had many tactical successes, enabling them to kill, for example, 638 military personnel, 273 Northern Ireland police officers, and 23 members of the Prison Service during the conflict. They also killed over 600 civilians,[220] however, many of them unintentionally. In these latter instances, appalling human suffering was complemented by tactical mistakes or ineptitude. Moreover, as noted, while the PIRA continued for decades an impressive capacity to sustain a violent campaign against a state which possessed powerful resources, that state did manage to curtail republicans' intended violence significantly as the armed struggle went on year by year. One illustration of this was the very different capacity on the Provos' part to kill British soldiers at different phases of the conflict. During the years 1971–82, 564 British military per-sonnel were killed in the Northern Ireland war (an average of 47 people per year); but during the later phase of the Troubles, between 1983 and 1994, only 197 military personnel were killed (an average of 16 per year).[221] Clearly, this is still a very high total in terms of the awful human cost for those killed and for their families and friends. But it does reflect the increasing problems that the PIRA had in successfully targeting an Army and a state which had grown more sophisticated in their response to the conflict. Indeed, as one ex-PIRA man rather candidly later put it, 'After '76, the number of ops dropped dramatically. You couldn't have an op every day. The Brits knew all the tricks by then and who to look out for.'[222]

And contextual consideration of particular PIRA operations—even operationally successful ones—can itself produce a complex image. On Monday
27 August 1979 the Provisionals killed Queen Elizabeth's cousin, Lord
Mountbatten, together with three people who were with him on his boat
in County Sligo (including his 14-year-old grandson, Nicholas Knatchbull);
on the same day a cleverly planned PIRA operation in the north at
Warrenpoint killed eighteen British soldiers through the use of two bombs.
So here was, in one sense, a major operational double success, reflecting
considerable tactical skill. A figure at the heart of the British establishment
had been killed, as had a large number of British soldiers; worldwide attention had been seized; and tactical acumen had helped to produce the
result. Yet even a day such as this had ambiguous colours to it, tactically.
The Mountbatten and Warrenpoint killings prompted the UK state's
intelligence response to PIRA violence to become more integrated and
coordinated than it had previously been,[223] and this was one of the ways
in which a more successful counter-PIRA campaign could be waged by
the British. And, in time, Nicholas Knatchbull's brother Timothy produced a remarkably powerful memoir about the loss of his identical and
uniquely intimate twin in the Mountbatten attack; for Tim Knatchbull
the 1979 bomb left 'a legacy of mental and emotional wounds which
refused to go away'; he referred openly in his very moving book to 'the
hole in my life left by Nick's death'.[224] As so often in the Troubles, the
victims here (including this 14-year-old child) had been defenceless when
they were attacked, and the operational efficacy of the bombing has to be
set against the longer-term effect on the republican cause of, for example,
a well-publicized account like that of Tim Knatchbull: one that was manifestly lacking in bitterness, despite the PIRA's having cruelly killed his
brother, his grandfather, and his grandmother, as well as seriously injuring
him himself in the attack.

   Did the Provisionals' violence bring them tactical success in terms of
interim concessions? I think the evidence from the long peace process suggests that the enduring threat and/or use of violence allowed them to wring
more from that process than would otherwise have been probable.[225] Did
their armed struggle succeed in achieving publicity? Not as decisively as they
would have hoped, in terms of bringing about unbearable pressure on the
UK government. But, without question, Provo violence did secure for the
group and its cause far greater attention—locally, nationally, internationally—than they would have gained without it. After the Provos' campaign,

the issue of Irish national self-determination could not be considered marginal. Bombs in England often generated more of a response than did attacks in Northern Ireland itself; the Provisionals developed a sophisticated public relations, publicity, or propaganda operation to make their case as effectively as possible; and some of their violence generated lastingly memorable publicity effects (the 1984 Brighton attack, for example, which came close to killing UK Prime Minister Margaret Thatcher; or the 1979 bombing in County Sligo which did kill Earl Mountbatten).

Some might counter that PIRA publicity and support were generated not merely by their violence, but by other activities too: so the 1981 hunger strike gained far more attention for Bobby Sands than had the violent actions on his part which had led to his incarceration,[226] and that strike itself generated significant recruitment to the movement. This was the view of republicans themselves,[227] but also of their British opponents: the UK authorities were clear that among the effects of the hunger strike (even before the painful 1981 sequence had ended) was 'a sharp increase in the influence of the Provisional IRA in Catholic areas, the alienation of much of the minority community in Northern Ireland from government, and the disruption of political life.... The Provos and INLA have gained a new batch of recruits.'[228] So the non-violent hunger strike in defence of PIRA violence had itself gained much momentum. And many people also encountered the republican movement's argument through their books rather than their bombs.[229] Again, however, the hunger strike was an attempt by the prisoners to legitimize their comrades' armed struggle beyond the jail, just as people's attention to republican writing (and, of course, hunger striking) grew significantly from their fascination with an armed movement producing such gestures and drawing on them so vividly.

It is certainly true that the PIRA (and INLA) hunger strikes of 1980–1 gained widespread international fame, that these were campaigners who were in jail because of their engagement in republican armed struggle, that what happened in these jail protests was directly intended to legitimize the violent campaign beyond the prisons, and that—despite both strikes ending without the authorities having ceded prisoner demands—the post-1981 jail regime in the H-Blocks, for example, involved considerable interim concessions yielded to the inmates.[230]

Yet it is also true that much of the momentum during the late 1970s and early 1980s in relation to prisoners' demands took the form of a wider mobilization against the criminalization policy of the UK government; this was essentially non-violent, and it involved many more people than just PIRA activists. The process of causation again, therefore, proves on contextual inspection to involve violence being only one part of a more complex set of dynamics. Significantly, it was also the case that this wider anti-criminalization movement was often driven from the grass roots rather than from leadership level, that the building up of wide and communal support for the prisoners was actually made more *difficult* on occasions because of PIRA killings (from which some people understandably recoiled), and that many of the broader, radical hopes for societal change which were evident within this broader mobilization ended up being thwarted and disappointed in any case.[231] Moreover, even the PIRA hunger strikers themselves were, in that strike, engaging in a different form of struggle from violence. As noted, Bobby Sands became famous not for the violence he had practised prior to imprisonment, but for the world-renowned self-sacrifice that he engaged in so bravely while in jail, in order that his comrades' ongoing violence would be read as political rather than criminal in nature.

In terms of the tactical undermining of opponents, a more complex picture emerges, whether one considers Ulster unionists, the British state, or the Provos' rivals within northern nationalism. The unionist state had existed for nearly half a century by the time that the PIRA were born at the end of 1969. Within a few years, the violence in which the Provos had played such a decisive part had led to the proroguing in 1972 of the Belfast parliament at Stormont and the introduction of direct rule from London. This was a huge blow to unionist confidence and power: nationalists tended to celebrate the apparent demise of Stormont and (relatedly) unionists were profoundly dismayed by it.[232] As one ex-Provo starkly put it, 'The abolition of Stormont had been a key IRA demand and no one was in any doubt that we had brought about its demise.'[233] In a short period of aggression, it seemed, the PIRA had undermined the power at the very heart of the hated unionist state of Northern Ireland. Much later, as part of the eventual deal to end the conflict and to persuade the PIRA to desist from their violence, the Royal Ulster Constabulary was replaced by the Police Service of Northern Ireland: again, a powerful element of unionist identity and authority had been undermined. Moreover, the violent undermining of unionism involved both the recasting of the Northern Ireland state that had existed since the 1920s, but also an erosion of identification between the wider British population and northern unionists. As one leading ex-PIRA member sharp-sightedly put it, 'What the armed struggle did was bring down the Orange state. As well as that I believe it has changed the context in terms of the attitude of the British. People in England do not see people in this part of the world [the north of Ireland] as part of their cultural tradition.'[234]

There is certainly evidence of ex-PIRA people being delighted at unionist disarray, disorganization, confusion, and lack of direction; and of their taking pleasure in the conflict having wrong-footed unionists; moreover, it seems that many ex-PIRA members still hold to their previous ideological interpretation of the politics of Ireland and its relationship with the UK, and to their fundamentally inimical reading of Ulster unionism and loyalism.[235] So undermining unionism and the old Northern Ireland were and remain important goals, and the conflict of ideas and legitimacy persisted for many years and still does. Even after the campaign had been concluded, republicans such as ex-prisoner Sam Millar were further undermining unionist reputations. Millar's fascinatingly Chandleresque Belfast novels include one in which a group of Northern Ireland prison officers with strong police connections have been involved in running a brutally violent prostitution ring during the late twentieth century:

'He and a few of his mates pimped some of the women prisoners, those on drugs, leasing them out to high-placed establishment figures at private functions.'
'What kind of establishment figures?'
'The usual shit-bag collection of politicians, judiciary, clergy—and *cops*.'[236]

Corrupt and dishonest Northern Ireland police appear also in Millar's other fictional work,[237] and these writings reflect a strongly held view—here made very public—that the unionist state was deeply marred by corruption.

It could be countered, however, that those latter contributions towards the undermining of unionism were secured through the pen rather than the bomb. And it should also be noted that the 1998 Good Friday Agreement, to which the PIRA eventually reconciled itself, recognized that as long as a majority of people in the six counties wanted to remain within the United Kingdom then they would be able to do so. While the old unionist state had been reinvented in much more agreeable shape, therefore, the central element of unionist politics—their right to remain in the UK—had been sustained, despite all of the PIRA's ingenious and violent efforts to the contrary.

How well did the Provos undermine the wider British state? They certainly provoked its military forces into some counter-productive overreaction in the early years. So, famously, episodes such as the 1970 Falls Curfew in Belfast or the January 1972 killings on Bloody Sunday in Derry drew recruits to the PIRA and opprobrium upon the UK state in powerful meas-ure. The latter violence by the British Army generated a very public humil-iation even decades later: the UK Bloody Sunday Inquiry (set up in 1998) published its ten-volume Report in 2010, concluding that British soldiers had (on 30 January 1972 in Derry) unjustifiably and fatally shot people who had not been posing a threat to them.[238] There is no doubt that the fatal violence practised by the Provisionals in the period before Bloody Sunday had contributed to the febrile atmosphere within which the Army's awful killings on that day actually occurred; similarly, there is no doubt that, more widely, Provo violence prompted much of what British soldiers coun-ter-productively did themselves in the early 1970s among the Catholic com-munities of the north. As so often in other settings, what we see here is state forces acting harshly in response to non-state challenge, and thereby actually damaging their own reputation and strengthening the cause of their non-state enemies. In the words of one ex-PIRA member in interview, the British Army represented the PIRA's 'best recruiting agents'.[239]

It is sometimes held that the enmity between the Catholic working class of the north and the British Army was inevitable, but I am sceptical about whether the evidence compels such a view. Contemporary accounts suggest that there was—even well into 1970—some basis for building relationships between British soldiers and working-class Belfast Catholics, even in areas which were later to become focal points for conflict.[240] The decisions taken about British military activities in the early 1970s were contingent ones, and critical assessment of them involves more than merely hindsight-informed wisdom. As the archives reveal, concerns were expressed at high-political level in the very month of the July 1970 Falls Curfew itself, about the dan-gers of the authorities acting in damagingly one-sided, rather than helpfully impartial, manner towards the respective northern communities.[241] Anxiety was expressed *at the time* about the counter-productive rough-handedness of the Parachute Regiment (who carried out the Bloody Sunday killings) and about the dangers of deploying them in sensitive contexts in that very period; tellingly, indeed, such concerns were vocally expressed even by other regiments in the British Army itself.[242] Again, there is little doubt that the introduction of internment in 1971 undermined rather than strength-ened the British state's authority in Northern Ireland; as one British soldier evocatively later put it, internment was: 'a complete disaster . . . in any inter-nal security operation—and that's what Northern Ireland was—hearts and minds are the most important part of it. And internment destroyed it.'[243] But doubts had been expressed in advance here too about the wisdom of introducing this policy at the time (not least by the UK Prime Minister and Home Secretary of the time).

So British Army friction with the Catholic community in the north does not look to have been inevitable, certainly at the high levels at which it actually, depressingly emerged. If this depth of violent enmity was indeed contingent rather than unavoidable, then there seems an extra layer of tragedy to it. For evidence from the period of PIRA mobilization makes utterly clear the effect that British Army interventions did make in a negative direction, when the soldiers were directed wrongly. So, for example, internment was introduced on 9 August 1971: during the pre-internment phase of that year the PIRA killed ten British soldiers; during the briefer period between internment's introduction and the end of the year, they were able to kill thirty. The Provisionals' violence had, of course, pre-dated and helped to produce the context for these British Army engagements, so the process of causation was deep and multiply layered. When in January 1970 the Army Council of the PIRA opted to pursue a sustained, offensive engagement with the British, their decision came long before the Falls Curfew, internment, or Bloody Sunday had occurred. But there can be little doubt that heavy-handed activity by the British Army in Northern Ireland heightened levels of PIRA support and sympathy.

This is vividly evidenced also in other kinds of material, including the reflections of ex-PIRA member Seanna Walsh, whom the organization's leadership chose to deliver their end of campaign statement in July 2005 (so clearly an authoritative voice). What had been the process of Mr Walsh's becoming a PIRA activist? For him, as for many others of his generation, the role of the British Army was important. 'There was no real republican politics in my family background. The hassle really started in the late 1960s— the protest marches, the reaction from the state and from loyalism. All of that began to have an impact on me.' Initially there was 'almost ambivalence' to the British Army. But that changed, with the Army beating up people in the area, with Walsh's Belfast Short Strand community being effectively 'under siege' from loyalists and the military, and with a series of key episodes: the 1970 Falls Curfew, 1971 internment, 1972 Bloody Sunday. 'After internment, the war really started between the IRA and the British Army in nationalist areas. With internment there was a step change in the relationship with the British Army.' It became clear that 'The only way we would resolve this whole problem would be to get rid of the British. For myself, Bloody

Sunday was the key moment. That was when I decided I would have to do something.' But Walsh's view, supported by the kind of evidence mentioned above, was that this affected a wider number of people also: 'In terms of motivation, the actions of the British Army in the early stages were what determined the mood of the area.'[244]

The Northern Ireland conflict involved mutually stimulated bouts of appalling violence from various sides, and this included some collusion between members of the UK security forces and loyalist paramilitary groups. The extent of this is sharply disputed,[245] though it seems clear (and surely unsurprising, given the context of anti-state violence?) that some collusion did occur; there is no doubt, however, that debates and consideration about this topic have tended to damage the reputation of the UK state.[246]

And the PIRA's campaign did attract some international sympathy which caused headaches for the UK state and somewhat embarrassed it. This was true during the 1980–1 hunger strikes, but also at other times. A 1985 letter from US Congressman Mario Biaggi and numerous colleagues reflected this, with its expression of support for Irish Northern Aid (NORAID) activist Martin Galvin in his desire to visit Northern Ireland (against the clear wishes of the UK authorities).[247] But the issue of Northern Ireland becoming an international embarrassment for the UK authorities was a longstanding and problematic one, reinforced by PIRA activities and some state reactions to them.[248]

Did PIRA violence undermine their Irish nationalist rivals? The evidence is ambiguous here. As noted, for many years the Provos' constitutional-nationalist rivals in the SDLP tended to dominate northern politics in terms of electoral support; it was only after the Provisionals had moved to a different, essentially non-violent form of politics that their party, Sinn Fein, managed to eclipse their SDLP rivals here. Yet there is also no doubt that PIRA violence had been one of the elements strengthening Sinn Fein's muscular hand during the peace process engagement with the British, and that this helped them to eclipse the SDLP over time. Former SDLP leader John Hume had frequently been very critical of the Provos; they had, in his words, the 'hallmarks of the fascist'.[249] And it might be judged that the Provisionals eventually, if tacitly, did acknowledge that there was much in the alternative approach that had long been espoused by their constitutional-nationalist rivals. The irony has been this: the benefits of an SDLP-style emphasis on the non-violent assertion of Irish nationalist politics, pursued with a serious eye towards unionist preferences in Ulster, have indeed drawn the PIRA away from violence; but the Provos' ongoing threat of violence enabled them to eclipse the SDLP politically as they have made that move into constitutional politics themselves.

PIRA violence had earlier enabled the group to establish itself as the pre-eminent republican army when set against (for example) the Official Irish Republican Army (OIRA) or the Irish National Liberation Army (INLA).[250] And this intra-communal rivalry reflects our next point: that PIRA muscle enabled the group to gain influence and a significant measure of control over members of their community. This point should not be simplified. Much, possibly most, of the support that accrued to the Provisionals came from a shared sense of political grievance and purpose. But there were very many, and very brutal, instances of violence by the Provos against members of their own community. And non-fatal as well as fatal violence could have an intimidatory effect on neighbours in the community: republicans carried out, for example, 1,228 punishment shootings between 1973 and 1997, and a further 755 beatings between 1982 and 1997.[251] Did this mean that everybody in their community obeyed the PIRA's wishes? Obviously not. But the frequency, brutality, and pervasiveness of this alternative set of mechanisms of enforcement did make conformity to Provisional preferences less costly in some areas than hostility towards them.

Such control could only be sustained if the organization was strong enough to maintain that threat credibly. Did PIRA violence work to tactical effect in making the Provisionals organizationally more robust? There was certainly a marked success in the way that the Provos initially established themselves organizationally, becoming strong enough to see off the OIRA and then other republican rivals throughout their lengthy armed struggle, and keeping larger numbers of supporters with them than joined or defected to other groupings.[252] And some of this definitely involved the self-sustaining processes of violent conflict. The PIRA saw their violence as a response to loyalist attacks and as resistance to British military repression; in turn, the Provisionals' own violence prompted British Army reaction and a sustenance of UDA and UVF aggression; and recruits were drawn in, and organizational robustness was developed, as a consequence.

But the Provos were always more than just an armed group, and as the relationship with their political party, Sinn Fein, evolved into the peace process period, that latter organization also gained from PIRA violence, though not without costs. It is clear that the UK government's keenness to deal with and to appease and to maintain peaceful relations with Sinn Fein

owed much to the violent threat that their PIRA alter ego embodied. So, to
the extent that Provo violence ensured that Sinn Fein were key interlocutors, it could be judged to have had tactical-organizational efficacy.

But this was a complex process. Provisional violence had led to the Provos
meeting leading Conservative Party and Labour Party politicians all the way
back to the early 1970s. What was different in the peace process era was that
the costs of PIRA violence for republican momentum meant that violence
both propelled Sinn Fein into a position of greater significance, and also
threatened to place limits on their long-term momentum if that party did
not shed the violence at some stage. Violence could provide you with leverage, but you would only gain lasting political benefits if you were to move
towards the kind of non-violent politics that the peace process eventually
demanded. So it is true that Sinn Fein are now apparently indispensable
within the reformed Northern Ireland; but it is also true that that political
role has only become workable because the PIRA has effectively left the
stage. Violence gained you intra-communal and also inter-communal salience, but it also set a ceiling upon levels of popular support and opportunities for governmental authority and for involvement with other powerful
political actors. The then Taoiseach (Prime Minister) of the Republic of Ireland,
Albert Reynolds, made clear shortly before the 1994 PIRA ceasefire that the
abandonment of violence by the Provisionals would be a prerequisite for
Sinn Fein's involvement in real political progress towards a solution: there
needed, in his words, to be 'a permanent cessation of violence'.[253]

As noted, there has emerged a strong political pragmatism within Sinn
Fein's approach. And part of this indeed involves shrewd recognition that
there were limits as well as rewards to the politics of armed struggle. If Sinn
Fein is to achieve real power in the south of Ireland as well as in the north
(and its National Chairperson, Declan Kearney, has been admirably clear that
'the prospect of government in the north and government in the twenty-six
counties is very much part of the trajectory'[254] for the party), then a post-
PIRA Sinn Fein is the only way that such a goal could be moved forward.

It should also be noted, of course, that much of the momentum achieved
by Sinn Fein has been achieved by means other than violence. Election
work, local advice centres, the public process of political argumentation and
debate, media and other publicity activity—all of this has played an increasingly important role in moving their politics forward.

In addition to any strategic and tactical efficacy, did PIRA violence work
in the sense of delivering inherent rewards from the struggle itself? Listening

to first-hand sources carefully here, one can deal to some degree with the problem identified earlier in this book, regarding the issue of exactly for whom political violence works. Some republicans have expressed disaffection about who gained from the war; as one ex-hunger-striker caustically put it in later years, 'The struggle didn't produce the results we had hoped for but the leadership ended up all right.'[255] Clearly, the Provos were a heterogeneous group operating over many years, so their experiences will have varied significantly. Equally clearly, it seems to me, some leaders and rank-and-file activists did experience some significant rewards (as well as costs) from their struggle. For some, such as long-time PIRA activist Ruairi O Bradaigh, these included the psychological appeal inherent in a politics of uncompromising unwaverability.[256] For others, there was impressive camaraderie and comradeship among republican prisoners,[257] though the boredom, the pain, the loss, the deep unpleasantness, and the negative psychological and health-related effects of incarceration are also very important to note.[258] For, accompanying the camaraderie and purpose, prison for the Provisionals also carried with it much that was deeply negative: the removal of liberty, obviously, but also other suffering, some of it intensely unpleasant;[259] understandably, for some, there emerged personal difficulties with relationships, given so much incarceration.[260] Long-time Sinn Feiner Tom Hartley's elegiac account of Milltown Cemetery (the west Belfast burial space for so many of Belfast's Catholics) refers to 'the deep trauma and hurt suffered by the Belfast Catholic community' during the Troubles, and some of this involved tragic deaths for PIRA members and their friends and relatives.[261]

More positively, prison did exemplify the appeal of defiance and pride in resistance, and this defiant voice was an important element in what the PIRA did through their violence. As one ex-Volunteer put it regarding the Provos, 'they gave a voice to the voiceless at a time that the establishments were doing everything in their power to keep people in their ghettos and on their knees'.[262]

Moreover, there is also compelling evidence of there having been considerable excitement and adventure available through PIRA involvement in itself: 'for a lot of us, it was a big adventure';[263] 'It was an exciting time. I was nineteen, sleeping in ditches, outbuildings or safe houses, always with my clothes on, always armed';[264] 'When you're young, at that age, it's quite exciting.... There was a really exciting aspect to being on the run, living from house to house and travelling about';[265] 'Danger has its own attraction';[266] and there could be a youthful excitement derived from the handling and firing of guns.[267]

There could even be a measure of celebrity involved. As one (admittedly, disaffected and depressed) ex-PIRA man put it: 'Like any big organization, people joined [the PIRA] for different reasons.... 'RA [PIRA] men were celebrities, especially in the seventies.... Some women threw themselves at local celebrities. Some guys joined the 'RA to get off with women and never did ops.'[268] Again (though again from a disaffected ex-Provo): 'In the nationalist community, in republican circles anyway, IRA men have considerable status, and for those Provos who look for sexual advantages from it, there is no shortage of women willing to give more than the time of day to IRA volunteers.'[269]

Most PIRA volunteers did not make much money at all out of being in the organization;[270] and it is not that one can explain the Provisionals through recourse to the inherent rewards discussed above. People could gain comradeship from all sorts of association; the point here is to explain why so many chose the Provos, and that can only be done, ultimately, through reflection on the political goals on which this chapter has mostly focused. But, even beyond the enforced intimacy of jail, there was an incredibly rich comradeship among PIRA activists, as the sources again and again shout out. As one Belfast ex-PIRA man put it, 'You just felt a great comradeship.'[271] Or as another put it regarding involvement in the Provos: 'Now I felt I was one of the boys.'[272] Yet another ex-PIRA volunteer reflected tellingly that, 'Although I was ideologically committed to the cause, for me, in many ways, being in the IRA was almost the objective rather than the means'; conspiratorial 'belonging' and 'comradeship' were, in themselves, rich rewards.[273] Friendship, belief, belonging, purpose, community, and meaning. One ex-Provo described his PIRA years as 'days of certainty, comradeship, and absolute commitment'.[274] Added to this is the fact that PIRA members' actions could gain them influence and standing within their own communities;[275] one ex-PIRA man reflected on how he saw himself after having joined the PIRA with the simple words: 'I felt important.'[276]

IV

The war is over here.

Sinn Fein National Chairperson, Declan Kearney (2015)[277]

Now that the Northern Irish conflict has indeed largely been brought to an end, it's possible to attempt some balanced assessment of what the most lethal player in that conflict—the Provisional IRA—succeeded in bringing about through their armed struggle. And, despite their justified fame as one of the most skilled of the world's clandestine organizations, this chapter has shown just how much evidence one can in fact gather about the PIRA, of different kinds and from people with widely differing perspectives, in order to try to assess the various ways in which different people have considered the Provisionals' violence to have worked. The evidence suggests that they failed to achieve strategic success in terms of their central, primary goals of defending the Catholic community in the north, or achieving a united, independent Irish republic free from British control. Even in terms of the partial achievement of these goals, little support can be given to the idea of their protecting Catholics effectively, although I think a stronger case can be put forward for the PIRA having secured some partial progress towards nationalist ends in terms of necessitating the reforming of the north in a nationalistic direction. Secondary goals have generated mixed results: yes, they achieved much brutal revenge, but in doing so they often deepened rather than eroded sectarian division; yes, some of them enjoyed cultural-nationalist enrichment through the linguistic aspect of their struggle, but socialism was not moved forward to anything like the same degree; yes, resistance was maintained, but non-violent methods were also crucial in doing this. The Provos did help to determine the political agenda, but not in quite the manner that their violence had been intended to do.

Tactically, there were operational successes but also many limitations; they did generate publicity and secure many interim concessions, and they undermined unionist, British, and rival-nationalist opponents (though they did so in ways that also saw some victories for their Irish-based rivals against them).[278] Inherent rewards were there—but these have to be set against the terrible costs paid by so many in the movement too.

Significantly, through so much of this, the effects of PIRA violence are hard to disentangle from other elements of republican struggle (political argument, electioneering, local advice work with the community, journalistic and other writing) and from the work of other actors (constitutional nationalists and indeed the UK state both did much to forward the reform of the north, for example). And some of those who helped to facilitate political compromise and progress came very much from non-PIRA political traditions, and made a decisive contribution to what has now emerged. The unionist politician David Trimble—whose role was critical in producing the 1990s peace deal—made profound concessions in order to make that deal a possibility: in Trimble's own case, this involved bravely trying to

make peace with an organization—the Provisional IRA—which had brutally killed his close political and professional colleague Edgar Graham at
Queen's University Belfast on 7 December 1983.[279]

Some expert observers have written very powerfully about the Provo
campaign as a deep failure. Leading journalist Henry McDonald, for example, has suggested that the settlement achieved through the Northern Ireland
peace process was one 'that could have been realized and bedded down a
very long time ago, well before one of the most futile mini-wars of the late
twentieth century was ever started'.[280] And there are also those who argue
that the state's (especially the security forces') activities in the Northern
Ireland Troubles were successful, and that the PIRA was therefore effectively
defeated.[281] Other voices hostile to the Provos take a different view, it should
be noted. So one experienced ex-Special Branch officer from the RUC, for
instance, has observed the following in interview:

> I wouldn't say PIRA were defeated by the actions of the state. I believe they
> were pragmatic enough to realize that their campaign had brought them to a
> certain point and that they could gain more by switching tactics and moving
> the emphasis to politics backed up by violence when necessary. The leadership
> had obviously been in contact/negotiating with British (and Irish) govern-
> ments over many years, and I have no doubt that a brighter future was out-
> lined to them if they adopted a peaceful course.[282]

Overall, I think the evidence points to the validity of a complex assessment,
and that much of this was hinted at by the inheritances from long Irish pasts.
Long pasts suggested that trying to free Ireland from Britain through violence sat awkwardly with trying to unite Irish people from different religious
and political faiths, Catholic-nationalist on the one hand and Protestant-
unionist on the other. Long pasts suggested that some significant progress
could indeed be made through violence, but probably not the full satisfaction of Irish republican goals. And long pasts hinted that post-revolutionary
disappointment for many would coexist with the satisfactions of what had
been achieved.[283]

It would be wrong to dismiss the Provisional IRA's achievements casually
just because their central strategic aims remained unfulfilled at the end of
their violent campaign. As Lawrence Freedman has suggested, 'The world of
strategy is full of disappointment and frustration, of means not working and
ends not reached'; strategies could even be considered 'ways of coping with
situations in which nobody was in total control'.[284]

Moreover, the PIRA's ending of their campaign, and the emergence of comparative peace in Northern Ireland, were neither inevitable nor anticipated by the crucial actors.[285] Nor is the future open to confident prediction. I have argued in this book for respecting contingency rather than inevitability, and it may yet prove that a united Ireland does emerge in the future, out of a sequence of political events in which the PIRA campaign might then be claimed as having played a major part. The evidence at present allows this as a possibility, rather than compelling us to consider it likely even over a long period. But if we do take a very long timeframe for our analysis, then we humbly have to admit that knowledge of Ireland's future political trajectory is uncertain for any of us, and that a united and independent state might yet emerge. Moreover, there is no doubt that many ex-PIRA figures see their achievements to date as only part of an unfolding process, with political change still very much part of what they seek: 'We have not achieved anything near what we sought to achieve: we have brought about a fairly level playing field in the north; but I don't want to *be* in a northern state';[286] 'Sinn Fein is an Irish republican party. Our strategy to achieve a united, independent Ireland marks us out from other Irish political parties. Our primary political objectives are an end to partition, an end to the union, the construction of a new national democracy, a new republic on the island of Ireland, and reconciliation between Orange and Green.'[287]

But one certainty does poignantly and terribly exist at the heart of this particular Irish story, and that is the undeniably horrific loss that so many people experienced in this conflict, caused by violence from all sides—including the very violent PIRA. That legacy of damage and polarization represents one of the most difficult aspects of Northern Irish politics and life even yet. The fact that so much remains contested about the Northern Irish past (about the killings and maimings and violence within which the Provos played such a leading part) has continued to make Ulster's unionists and loyalists deeply hostile to and untrusting of their Irish nationalist neighbours and of political processes involving them.[288]

And such damage also raises the question of the morality and proportionality of the violence of groups like the PIRA. One sustained, philosophical-scholarly assessment has concluded that 'the IRA's use of terrorism was not (or was not obviously) morally justified'.[289] Opinions on such matters will vary greatly between different readers of this book. But one question for all of us as we reflect on the efficacy of non-state political violence is this: how one should weigh the certainty of the human suffering that it causes, against the uncertainty of what long pasts suggest that such violence is likely to achieve. And we should never forget the voices of those whose lives have been callously destroyed in the process of all this. On Friday 21 July 1972 the PIRA carried out multiple bombings in Belfast in a period of just over one hour, resulting in the death of nine people and the injuring of very many more in what became known as Bloody Friday. The Provisional IRA man who commanded this operation was Brendan Hughes, who later admitted openly that the PIRA had misjudged the likely effects of so many bombs going off in so short a space of time:

> I feel a bit guilty about it because... there was no intention to kill anyone that day. I think we were over-zealous.... the risks were far too high, and... I don't believe they [the British authorities] were capable of handling so many bombs at one time.... I have a fair deal of regret that Bloody Friday took place... a great deal of regret.[290]

Among those killed on Bloody Friday was 14-year-old Stephen Parker, whose body was so badly damaged by a Provo bomb that it was hardly identifiable by his father, Revd Joseph Parker, the latter being understandably devastated by the loss of his precious young son: 'our dearly loved second son Stephen had been killed'; 'facing the greatest crisis in my life, I had to be alone to sort myself out, to come to terms with the unbelievable'.[291]

After Bloody Friday, Brendan Hughes continued as a PIRA man for years, making the choice to carry on repeatedly with that organization's violence in pursuit of the political goals which have been assessed in this chapter. After Bloody Friday, Joseph Parker reacted to the appalling loss of his entirely innocent son by committing himself to reconciliation work between the two communities of the divided north of Ireland ('I was resolved to do my utmost to save others from sharing the same senseless tragedy'). A humane, kind, tolerant, compassionate, caring, gentle man, Revd Parker was a southern-born Irish Protestant, his own preferred political arrangement for his country not being all that divergent from the Provos', ironically: 'At heart I was an Irish nationalist... The Ireland of my dreams was a sovereign thirty-two-county state where being Protestant or Roman Catholic was of no account in one's relationship to the state.' But his preferred methods could hardly have been more divergent from those of the people who had mercilessly killed his son: 'My Ireland, if worthy of sovereignty, must be born of voluntary consent and not the product of the bomb or the bullet.'[292]

3

Hamas and Palestinian Terrorism

I

The Israeli–Palestinian conflict was the catalyst for the rise of modern
international terrorism.

Paul Wilkinson[1]

If, as I have argued, 'Does Terrorism Work?' is a rather controversial question,
then it probably cannot be judged more so than in the case to which we now
turn. Though an unpopular point to make in some settings, the establishment
of the state of Israel arguably embodies one of the most striking examples of
terrorism actually managing to achieve major success. And there have been
few (if any) conflicts more important to the obstreperous history of terrorism than that which has long burned in Israel/Palestine. The origins of the
violence are deep-rooted, extremely tangled, and rich in biblical resonance.
Once part of the Ottoman Empire, Palestine existed as a British Mandate in
the post-First World War period, and the painful enmities of the region had
already become deeply distressing by then. For there are few conflicts more
profoundly embedded in long-term rivalries than that involving modern-day
Israel/Palestine. As I write this, religiously inflected tension over rights of
access and power in Jerusalem are at the heart again of terrorist and counter-terrorist violence in the region; but Jewish struggles with enemies over
Jerusalem possess a centuries-old pedigree,[2] and the roots of a distinctive
Palestinian sense of self go very deep indeed into the past.[3]

In the early 1880s the Jewish community in Palestine comprised around
24,000 people out of a Palestinian population of half a million;[4] this situation was then altered by extensive early twentieth-century Jewish immigration, itself understandably accelerated during the 1930s by Nazi rule in

Germany (though Palestine's Arab population remained far larger at this stage than its Jewish one). The November 1917 Balfour Declaration had seen the UK government commit itself to supporting and facilitating the establishment of a Jewish national home in Palestine, something rendered potent by the fact that by 1918 Britain controlled the entire territory. In 1922 there was formal League of Nations ratification for the British Mandate, at a time when the population breakdown in Palestine was 78 per cent Muslim, 11 per cent Jewish, and 9.5 per cent Christian.[5]

Unsurprisingly, Palestinian hostility towards Jewish immigration developed strongly during the 1930s, and resistance was expressed both violently and through non-violent methods. As noted, that immigration grew dramatically given contemporary events in Germany: in 1932 around 12,500 Jewish immigrants had arrived,[6] while 1933 saw the rate of Jewish immigration from Germany alone reaching 1,000 per month.[7] There was a rather unendearing Palestinian Muslim sympathy for fascism—including Nazi fascism—in the 1930s and 1940s;[8] and the 1936–9 Arab Revolt saw considerable violence against British rule, in demand for independence and in opposition to Jewish immigration.[9] While much attention tends to focus on post-1960s Palestinian activism, there is no doubting the existence for decades before this of an agitating Palestinian popular movement.[10]

The 1930s also witnessed the emergence of violent Zionist struggle, with Irgun—the Irgun Zvai Leumi, or National Military Organization—founded in Palestine in that decade to fight for the establishment of an independent Jewish state, and to protect Jews from their enemies within the Palestinian Mandate. A Zionist terrorist group operating in Palestine during the 1930s and 1940s, the Irgun deployed brutal terrorism to try to undermine British rule in Palestine, violently targeting institutions which represented that rule, and grasping international attention for Zionist grievances and demands as a consequence of these violent acts.[11]

In the wake of the Second World War there was greater international support for large-scale Jewish settlement in Palestine—again, very understandably. Irgun leader Menachem Begin (Figure 9) was sharply aware of the fact that violence seized international attention for one's cause, and the pursuit of Jewish independence undoubtedly and shamingly brought with it terrorist atrocity. On 22 July 1946 Irgun detonated a bomb in Jerusalem at the King David Hotel (headquarters of the British Mandate administration), with ninety-one people—most of them civilians—being killed and over forty more being seriously injured.[12]

Figure 9. Menachem Begin in the 1970s

Again, on 1 March 1947 Irgun killed fourteen British military personnel when they blew up the British Officers' Club in Jerusalem. The years 1947–8 saw Zionists attack Palestinian villages too, and in February 1947 the British declared that the Palestinian problem—a regrettably enduring concept—would be handed over to the United Nations. A November 1947 UN resolution formally ended the British Mandate, partitioning Palestine into two states, one Arab and one Jewish. But fighting very soon erupted between Jews and Arabs; Israel declared independence; the Mandate actually came to an end in May 1948 and Britain withdrew its officials from Palestine, a new Israeli state having now been born; and by October 1948 this state had expanded (despite the significant aggression against it of Egypt, Lebanon, Jordan, Syria, and Iraq) to incorporate 78 per cent of Mandate Palestine, as well as West Jerusalem, with the result that half a million Palestinians fled to what became known as the West Bank and the Gaza Strip, or crossed into neighbouring countries.

British withdrawal having been followed by the devastating expulsion of hundreds of thousands of Palestinians, the Palestinian Arab state portion of the UN partition plan never came into effective being. To the vile atrocity of the Jewish experience of the Holocaust, therefore, was added the catastrophic trauma for the Palestinians of their 1947–9 dispossession, dislocation, and dispersal (al-Nakba, the Catastrophe, as Palestinian memory would have it). So each community in the ensuing antiphonal struggle therefore possessed an entirely understandable sense of appalling and inherited historical loss, and a proportionate sense of the need for expiation. With such painfully entangled roots, the later politics of Hamas and of its enemies becomes more explicable.

As mentioned, Jewish terrorism (which during the years 1945–8 killed 338 British subjects) had seemingly helped to produce the establishment of Israel. The focus of this current chapter will be on the later Palestinian terrorism of Hamas (itself frequently dripping in blood), but no serious analysis even of non-state terrorist violence in the region can ignore the bloody role played in the mid-twentieth century by Jewish terrorism, or ignore its claims to serious success. As one distinguished scholar has pithily put it, 'By 1947 the Irgun had in fact achieved its objectives.'[13] Begin himself (later the Prime Minister of Israel—itself an indication of one level of terrorist success, it could be argued), powerfully testified to the importance of what his group of 'Hebrew rebels' had done 'during our fight for the liberation of our people'; the Irgun had been 'fighting for the liberty and independence, and indeed the survival, of our people'; and, in his zealous view, the violence had worked: 'The revolt was victorious.'[14]

The evidence does suggest that Irgun attacks sped up British withdrawal from Palestine, though other factors played their part too (a point acknowledged even by Menachem Begin himself, and supported by scholarly findings).[15] Post-war UK financial problems and domestic economic challenges made the Mandate seem an expensive as well as troublesome responsibility, while other issues (in India especially) were seriously distracting for Britain, and post-war resource-exhaustion was therefore rendered even more difficult. Moreover, Irgun and other violent proponents of a Jewish state did far more than merely plant bombs, with propaganda and internationally directed argument also playing a role. But the Jewish revolt which had begun on 31 October 1945 might still be considered one of the past's best candidates for a terrorist campaign which centrally worked.

Or did it? I've argued that we should adopt lengthy historical frameworks when answering our central question in this book, and it might be asked therefore whether we should judge the seeming success of Israel's 1940s foundation against the subsequent, extremely troubled history of that state, and the nature of its evolution and character. That character was deeply altered by the 1967 war. Following arms race competition between Israel and nearby Arab states (the two sides respectively supported by Cold War rival superpowers), in the spring of 1967 Syria thought that Israel was planning to attack and consequently asked for assistance from Egypt, which responded. Egyptian President Nasser (himself concerned about the possibility of Israeli attack) ordered troop movements in land bordering Israel, and seemed to be planning for a conflict between the allied Arab states and the Israelis; Israel opted for a Hobbesian, defensive, pre-emptive strike against Syria and Egypt in early June 1967 and destroyed their jet fighters; Jordan then shelled Israel in response to Israel's own attacks on Egypt, and within six days Israel had humiliatingly defeated Jordanian, Egyptian, and Syrian forces, in an embarrassing and lastingly important defeat for the Arab states. This Six-Day War of June 1967 established Israel as the dominant regional military force, as well as witnessing the Israelis expand their territory by occupying the Gaza Strip (from Egypt), the West Bank (from Jordan), East Jerusalem, the Syrian Golan Heights, and the Egyptian Sinai Peninsula; it also shifted the emphasis for Palestinian resistance and struggle very much onto the Palestinians themselves, rather than to any outside Arab states.[16] And Israel now occupied all of the territory which the United Nations had envisaged in the 1940s as due to be allocated to the Palestinians.

And long-term assessment of how far the establishment of Israel worked in achieving what its agents actually sought would have to incorporate the fact that subsequent Palestinian resistance and struggle produced some of the most intense and protracted terrorism in modern history, directed against that Israeli state and its people and its policies. Most famously, this was evident in the tragedy of the 1972 Munich Olympics massacre. On 5 September that year a commando unit from the Palestinian group Black September broke into the Olympic Village in Munich, entered the Israeli team's quarters, shot two Israeli athletes dead, and took nine others hostage. Much of the ensuing hostage crisis effectively took place on television, watched by millions of people: surviving gunman from the massacre, Abu Daoud, argued that the killing eventually of eleven Israeli athletes virtually in front of the eyes of so many viewers forced his political cause 'into the homes of 500 million people'.[17] If there was a profound malignity to this attack, then it also represented a powerfully, deliberately dramatic Palestinian proclamation in violence.

Black September demanded the release of Palestinian prisoners held in Israel. Police surrounded the Olympic Village, and the terrorists and hostages were taken to Fürstenfeldbruck Airport, apparently to be flown to Cairo. Then at the airport, as the Palestinians were about to get onto their plane, the

German authorities opened fire. The Palestinians then shot dead their nine athlete hostages, and five terrorists and one West German police officer were killed in the exchanges. Another three Palestinians were arrested.

The Munich operation did not produce the desired release of the prisoners, and while fame was memorably secured, so too was a public revulsion at such brutality, and something of a welding together of the Palestinian cause with such violent branding. Professor Bruce Hoffman is absolutely right that, 'for the Palestinians, Munich was in fact a spectacular publicity coup';[18] and there was a subsequent boost to Palestinian terrorist recruitment, as well as a much deeper sense in the international community after such acts of violence that something had to be done to remedy the situation of the Palestinians. But, more negatively, such events also established in the international mind an organic connection between Palestinian struggle and blood-stainedly horrific methods.

The contextual violence involving Israel continued long after Munich, of course, including the October 1973 war involving the Israelis, Syria, and Egypt, and the 1978 and 1982 Israeli invasions of Lebanon. In June of the latter year the incursion was masterminded by Israeli Defence Minister Ariel Sharon, with a view to destroying the Palestine Liberation Organization (PLO), whose headquarters were then in Lebanon. The PLO was indeed forced out of Beirut and instead to Tunisia, but the costs to Israel were high, with the Israelis being seen as aggressive and as responsible for some deeply brutal violence. As one leading scholar later noted, 'What the 1982 invasion showed, above all, was the inability of even a powerfully armed state like Israel to defeat terrorism by the use of massive military force.'[19]

The PLO itself had been established in 1964, and it was in 1974 declared by the Arab League to be the only legitimate representative of the Palestinian people. In 1976 pro-PLO candidates won the Palestinian municipal elections in the West Bank, and the awkward balance between terrorism and other forms of political struggle epitomized the group's life under their talented, controversial, long-time leader Yasser Arafat (1929–2004). Ironically, the PLO had early on drawn the lesson from prior Irgun experience that terrorism could help shift state politics and policy in one's favoured direction. For many years Arafat's group dominated the Palestinian terrorist and political world, their hijackings grabbing them international attention and opprobrium simultaneously. In time, Arafat judged that terrorism was more of a liability than an asset in terms of pursuing political goals,[20] but the PLO's 1968 National Charter had declared their aim to be that of liberating

all of the territory of historic Palestine through violent struggle, and establishing an independent Palestinian state; they had also stated the goal of achieving
the repatriation of Palestinian refugees. Fatah (the Palestinian National Liberation Movement set up by Arafat on 10 October 1959, and the group from
which Black September was to spring) had initiated this armed struggle on
1 January 1965 and by the end of the decade had effectively merged with,
and come to dominate, the PLO. But, despite years of violence and some
significant tactical victories and the winning of some interim concessions,
the PLO had not—by the time of Arafat's death in 2004—secured its central
political goal of Palestinian liberation.

By then, the group which was to prove Arafat's nemesis (and which will
form the primary focus of this current chapter) had been born. Early
December 1987 saw the rapid eruption of the First Intifada (literally, a rising
up and shaking off): an unexpected and largely non-violent Palestinian campaign of civil resistance, strikes, riots, and mass demonstrations against Israel
in Gaza and spreading to cover the West Bank. This defiant episode (initially
sparked by the controversial deaths of four Palestinians at an Israeli check-
point on 9 December) entrenched the Palestinian struggle against Israel
very much within Palestine itself, amid the conditions of Israeli occupation
under which Palestinians lived daily; and it prompted the emergence during
the ensuing years of Hamas as a serious rival to the previously pre-eminent
PLO. Behind the Intifada lay a grievance-driven nationalism, aggravated by
economic difficulties: 'The main energizing force of the Intifada was the
frustration of the national aspirations of the 650,000 inhabitants of the Gaza
Strip, 900,000 of the West Bank, and 130,000 of East Jerusalem, who wanted
to live in a Palestinian state and not as stateless inhabitants under a brutal,
foreign military occupation.'[21] As so often with emergent non-state terrorist
campaigns, unwelcome state rule intensified nationalist energy towards the
use of violence against it. The mutually shaping relationship between state
and non-state enemies again and again emerges as having been decisive.[22]

Reading the Intifada as just another phase of anti-Israeli attacks and hostility and subversion, Israel's reaction to this rebellion against occupation
was harsh: their troops used live ammunition, and large numbers of Palestinians
died as a consequence—over a thousand were killed between 1987 and
1991.[23] Here, close attention to historical chronology suggests that we have
an example of state violence (unquestionably political in motivation and
terrorizing for its victims) helping to prompt the strengthening of a non-
state terrorist response in the subsequent Hamas.[24] The Intifada certainly led

to PLO/Fatah dominance being challenged by Hamas, with the latter emerging as a more radical, militant rival in offering Palestinian resistance. As one Hamas leader tellingly put it, the Intifada was 'a phase, and a prelude to a more serious process of getting rid of the zionist presence on this land'.[25] Ominously for Israel, by the spring of 1988, Hamas was already a major player in the Intifada in the West Bank and especially the Gaza Strip.

A very detailed narrative for Hamas is not possible here,[26] but a sketch of the movement is necessary. Compellingly, 'Hamas' is both an acronym for Harakat al-Muqawamah al-Islamiyya (the Islamic Resistance Movement, the IRM), and also an Arabic word meaning 'zeal'. Both are fitting and, as we shall see, the movement's zealous Islamic resistance has involved interlinking elements of terrorism, social welfare work, and electoral politics: as so often, and tellingly, terrorists do not merely practise terrorism. The group was officially founded on 14 December 1987, a stirring Islamic alternative to the PLO, and uncompromising and extremely violent from the start.

A militant, Islamist-nationalist group, Hamas emerged from the long-established Muslim Brotherhood in Palestine. In effect, it was born as the military wing of that Palestinian Muslim Brotherhood, and exemplified a nationalism based on historically rooted dispossession and grievance. The PLO and the Brotherhood had clashed for years in Palestine (intra-communal violence being so frequently a vital theme within the understanding of terrorist activity, and a key inheritance here in this case study).

A Sunni Muslim militia, Hamas from the start called for violence to oppose Israeli occupation. The pre-eminent founder of the group in December 1987 was Sheikh Ahmed Yassin (1936–2004) (Figure 10), the spiritual and symbolic leader of Hamas and—until his arrest in 1989—its undoubtedly leading figure. School-teacher Yassin was eventually killed by the Israel Defence Forces (IDF) on 22 March 2004 (on his way home from dawn prayers at a Gaza mosque). Another crucial leader was the articulate Dr Abdel Aziz al-Rantissi (1947–2004) (Figure 11), who had taken a medical degree at Egypt's Alexandria University and who (after Yassin's death) took over the leadership of Hamas. He himself was in turn killed by the IDF on 17 April 2004.

The group which Yassin and al-Rantissi led was a sharp-edged rival to the more secular PLO, and the latter's post-1960s role as the carrier of the flame of armed Palestinian struggle now became deeply contested. Hamas's means of challenge centrally involved terroristic violence, and a violent reading of jihad: 'There is no solution to the Palestinian problem except through

Figure 10. Sheikh Ahmed Yassin, 6 Oct 1998

Figure 11. Hamas leader Abdel Aziz al-Rantissi

jihad.'[27] The Izz ad-Din al-Qassam Brigades, Hamas's formally military wing, were set up in 1991; but the group's aggressive politics went back to its late 1980s birth. In March 1988 the group had carried out its first military action, with an ambush in Gaza which injured an Israeli water engineer; in February and May 1989 Hamas kidnapped and killed two Israeli soldiers (respectively, Avi Sasportas and Ilan Sa'adon), and in September of that year Israel reacted to this aggressive violence by declaring Hamas an illegal organization.

The First Intifada period witnessed much Palestinian suffering also, however. It seems that between December 1987 and December 1993 the Israeli security forces killed 1,095 Palestinians in the occupied territories; between December 1987 and December 1991 a further 48 Palestinians were killed by Israeli civilians; and during the first three years of the rebellion 359 Palestinians— mostly people suspected of collaboration with the Israelis—were killed by other Palestinians (again, intra-communal violence being a major part of our terroristic tale).[28]

For its part, between the mid-1990s and the mid-2000s Hamas famously used suicide bombings (or martyrdom operations) as a repeated tactic; 'With 217 suicide bombings between 1993 and 2006, Israel and the occupied Palestinian territories provided the most fertile site for suicide bombings in the world before Iraq appropriated that designation after the war that started in 2003.'[29] And during those years there was some strong support among the Palestinian population for this brutal method. Indeed, Hamas's suicide bomb tactic can be read as possessing a decidedly calculated rationale: 'suicide attacks are carefully orchestrated, politically motivated events, reflecting the perpetrating group's strategic goals and objectives.'[30]

Anathema to so many observers across the world, suicide operations seemed an enduringly appealing tactic to Hamas itself. Between February 1989 and March 2000 the group carried out twelve suicide bombings, and nearly thirty violent attacks overall; during the period September 2000–March 2004 they perpetrated fifty-two suicide attacks, killing 288 people; during the same period Hamas carried out 425 violent attacks in total, killing 377.[31] And much of this violence deliberately targeted civilians. So, although the period of the Second Intifada from 2000 onwards witnessed civil resistance by Palestinians[32] as well as the use of terroristic violence, the early twenty-first century has seen considerable and ongoing terrorism deployed by Hamas in pursuit of the organization's various objectives.

II

Thank God that made me a Jihadist in his path
Thank God that has made me join the martyrs' ranks
Thank God that made me part of this holy land
Thank God that made me part of Palestine and its jihadist soldiers...
We are proud that we are engaged in God's path.

A Hamas bomber (2001) in his video-filmed will[33]

What has Hamas wanted?

As with other groups that have practised terrorism, it probably makes sense not to draw too crude a line between individual and group motivation and ambition: they operate at different levels, but they are clearly inter-linked; 'every conscious human action is a mixed outcome of both individual and collective identity'.[34] Hamas's violence has been practised by an organization, but carried out by small-group units or even individuals alone, and so numerous levels of analysis come into play, and the sources used in this chapter will reflect that complexity of process. There is always difficulty in assessing the complicated motives behind people's use of violence, but I hope that sensitivity to the evidence appropriate to these concentric circles of analysis will allow for as full an account as possible.

Hamas's central, primary goal (the attainment of which would signify their strategic victory) is the destruction of Israel and the establishment of an independent, Islamic Palestinian state covering the territory contained in the British Mandate (Israel, the West Bank, and the Gaza Strip). Replacing Israel, liberating historic Palestine from Jewish occupation, ending the oppression of an Israeli-controlled territory, creating a truly Islamic state, and doing so necessarily through violent struggle—all of this has been at the heart of Hamas's fierce, obstreperous, and powerful politics; 'At the top of its agenda are liberating Palestine through a holy war against Israel, establishing an Islamic state on its soil, and reforming society in the spirit of true Islam.'[35] The rich first-hand sources make all this repeatedly clear. In Sheikh Yassin's words from 1997, 'Israel, as the Jewish state, must disappear from the map.'[36] And armed struggle would be crucial in bringing this goal about. As Hamas put it in August 1988, 'Israel understands only the language of force.'[37] Regarding what is seen as unjust occupation, Hamas leader Khaled Meshaal was very clear about the group's thinking: 'Very simply, there is occupation and it calls for resistance. When does resistance stop? When the occupation is finished.'[38] Or, as carefully expressed in 1997 by a formerly senior Hamas figure, Sheikh

Jamil Hamami: 'It is the duty of Hamas and duty of the people of Palestine to go against the occupation—not against Jewishness or Judaism—but against the military occupation.'[39]

Hamas has resisted open, consistent recognition of Israel's right to exist.[40] As one of the group's Gaza-based leaders (Mahmud al-Zahar) put it in 1995, Hamas's aims included 'the establishment of an Islamic state instead of Israel.... We will never recognize Israel.'[41] And the desired state to be established, post-Israel, would be one run according to sharia law: this would be a Muslim society organized in line with what they see as true Islam (and Hamas's thinking has been influenced by, among others, Sayyid Qutb, whom we met in a previous chapter). So the importance to Hamas members of religious faith and religious issues has been significant, and its role must be acknowledged and respected by any serious observer attentive to the sources. In Hamas's manifesto for the January 2006 legislative elections, the group made clear again its goal to 'establish Islamic sharia as the main source of legislation in Palestine'.[42]

As so often when we discuss important terrorist groups, what we find here with Hamas is therefore the politics of nationalism with a terroristic twist. It is a richly Islamic nationalism, possessing an emphatic religious dimension:[43] the sought-after Palestinian nation state is an Islamic one; Hamas 'offers an Islamic solution to the conflict with Israel',[44] and sees its work as embodying something of a religious duty; in the organization's own powerful words, 'the land of Palestine is an Islamic land entrusted to the Muslim generations until judgement day. No one may renounce all or even part of it...Nationalism from the point of view of the IRM is part and parcel of religious ideology.'[45] This fervent interweaving of nationalism and Islam is very evident indeed in the Hamas Charter, which is written in an emphatically Islamic key and whose first article states that, 'The Islamic Resistance Movement draws its guidelines from Islam; derives from it its thinking, interpretations, and views about existence, life, and humanity; refers back to it for its conduct; and is inspired by it in whatever step it takes.'[46] Elsewhere, the Charter piously declares that 'The Islamic Resistance Movement consists of Muslims who have devoted themselves to Allah and truly worshipped him.'[47]

But Hamas's religious version of nationalism is nonetheless open to explanation in terms of the interwoven dynamics of national community, struggle, and power which we could use interpretatively when explaining and analysing nationalism in France, Germany, England, Italy, Spain, Ireland, or elsewhere. With Hamas, communal commitment to territory, people, descent, culture, history, ethical obligations, and an excluding hostility towards opponents is mingled with an instrumental use of violently driven struggle to achieve change, with the inherent rewards of activist struggle as such, and with the politics of (ideally, state) power and freedom.[48] Hamas's Palestinians have pursued aggressively what they consider to be their national rights; and nationalistic motive surely represents the predominant framework to deploy in our analysis of the group.[49] As so often with nationalist struggle, the idea of freedom—of ending unjust and oppressive slavery to another nation, and of establishing proper self-determination and national sovereignty—has been central to Hamas's primary goal.[50]

Partial strategic victory might involve Hamas partly securing their central goal, and there has been (of course) evolution and debate within the movement regarding what might be acceptable. A certain tension has existed between the maximalist ambition of liberating the whole of historic Palestine, and the more limited gaining of an interim or partial solution as embodied in Palestinian state autonomy across Gaza and the West Bank. It is probably the case that the outside leadership (those not based in Palestine) have remained more attached to the former, absolute goal, while the necessarily more pragmatic leaders actually based in the West Bank and Gaza have more easily been able see the value in securing more moderate, short-term goals, while retaining long-term aspirations also.[51] Relatedly, I think that partial strategic success could be detected were it judged the case that Hamas's self-consciously religious violence had served to weaken Israeli determination to hold on to the Palestinian territories.

Partial strategic victory for Hamas might also be identified if their violence could be judged to have secured secondary objectives, and here I would suggest three possible contenders: the sustenance of Palestinian resistance against Israel; the protection or defence of Palestinians against Israeli assault; and the achievement of retaliation or revenge against Israeli opponents.

Even if the Israeli occupation were not brought to an end, resisting it and keeping that flame of nationalistic resistance burning might be seen as a worthwhile attainment, with Hamas at least passing on the faith alive to a future generation, and asserting through violence the case that their nation deserved proper sovereignty and self-determination. Resisting what is seen as an occupying and alien power has (from Basra to Belfast, and across many decades as well as locations) been one of the most persistent and important motivations behind non-state rebel groups. The very name of the organization

that we are considering in this chapter (the Islamic *Resistance* Movement) sets
the tone here, and the ongoing struggle against what is perceived to be illegitimate settlement in and control over Palestinian lands has continued to
drive many Hamas members' motivation. For the faith to survive, there
needs to be transmission to a new generation of the faithful.

Another common theme across terrorist groups evident again here with
Hamas is the secondary goal of protection and defence: 'to defend ourselves', as Hamas political leader Abdel Aziz al-Rantissi clearly put it in June
2002.[52] Hamas has committed itself to the aim of defending the Islamic
territory of Palestine from Israeli occupation, aggression, and domination.
In Sheikh Yassin's own phrasing from June 2003: 'If we do not defend ourselves then who will?';[53] or, as one Hamas communiqué from 2002 emphatically expressed it, the group was committed to 'defending and protecting
our people in [the] face of zionist terrorism'.[54] Regarding Israeli violence,
the voluble al-Rantissi commented of Hamas's campaign of suicide bombings against Israel that, 'in the end, we believe [it] will stop their aggression
against us'.[55] According to this self-comforting reading, Hamas suicide bombing is presented as a way of trying to stop in the future the Israeli violence
which, in the past, had so deeply hurt Palestinian civilians. Abdel Aziz
al-Rantissi again: 'If we did not respond this way, Israelis would keep doing
the same thing.'[56]

Retaliatory hitting back at Israel has also represented a significant sec-
ond-order objective for Hamas (again, the group here fits a wider pattern
across cases, I think).[57] Sheikh Yassin, in 2003: 'We have the right to retaliate
if they kill our civilians and target them.'[58] Abdel Aziz al-Rantissi saw Hamas
violence as embodying both a morally justified revanchism in response to
Israeli violence against Palestinians ('We want to do the same to Israel as
they have done to us'),[59] and also a practical mechanism to deter Israel from
such violence in the future. And the element of vengeance has clearly been
vicious and significant. Sheikh Ahmed Yassin, February 1998: 'We have the
right to do unto them exactly what they are doing to us. So, if they attack
the women and the children on our side, why spare their women and children? . . . They attack our children, we react to their attacks.'[60] Or, as one veteran Hamas military man in Gaza stated in March 2007, 'Hamas wanted to
make [the Israelis] fear every Arab who passed in front of their eyes, to make
them fear us as much as we fear them.'[61] Another experienced IRM member
observed in 2008, regarding Hamas attacks on Israeli citizens: 'We are just
sending a message to tell them: we can act against you. We can harm your

children as you are doing ours.'[62] So a desire to gain revenge for prior wrongs and preceding violence against Palestinians has played a crucial part in motivating some of Hamas's terroristic violence;[63] interwoven with this has been the inherited and re-energized hatred of Jews and of Israel. Broadly, there is much evidence that suicide bombings/martyrdom operations by Palestinians are seen as a way of achieving retaliatory strikes, hitting back against an Israel which has humiliated them, and in a context of frustration and rage in which there is no other way of expressing such emotional response and achieving revenge.[64]

For there has certainly been a strong desire to do deep human damage against a hated, ancient enemy. One very youthful Hamas warrior expressed it clearly by saying: 'I hate Jews, and at any opportunity I have I will kill Jews.'[65] Again, one Hamas military leader has spoken very openly about how those who are anxious to engage in suicide operations keenly 'demand revenge and retaliation'[66] as part of their motivation. Indeed, terrifying Israeli society and striking back at Israelis have been both individual and group imperatives. So two Hamas suicide bombers who attacked a Tel Aviv bar in 2003 asserted, in their joint living will, that they wanted 'to get revenge against Jews and Crusaders'.[67] Scholarly opinion has reinforced this important point: that Hamas has frequently used revenge as a legitimator for its violence against Israel, and has expressed a desire to exact a high price from Israel and Israelis for Jewish violence against Palestinians.[68] Moreover, evidence suggests very strongly that this vengeful violence (suicide bombing, for example) has enjoyed high levels of support among Palestinians in Gaza and the West Bank.[69]

Aiming to avenge damage done by Jews to Palestinians, and to gain revenge for national humiliation, clearly overlaps with other motivations in driving people towards terroristic violence. Most suicide attacks involve group or organizational sanction and planning, with few being entirely solitary operations; and motivations among those comrades responsible can have multiple layers. One academic study of fifteen Palestinian would-be suicide attackers and fourteen organizers of suicide attacks (including Hamas members) demonstrated that both the decision to carry out the suicide attack, and the choice of timing and target, were mostly taken at local level; it also showed that the motivation of these Palestinian suicide bombers was multiple rather than singular, including (most prominently) nationalistic commitment, religious conviction and belief, and what we have here been describing: a strong desire for revenge. So large-scale, civilian casualties were deliber-

ately sought out, the accessibility of such targets being a factor in the decision-making as well.[70] Rage-driven revenge would inflict pain, and would
make Israel and Israelis feel less secure and more under threat. Hamas's Azet
al-Rushuq commented that suicide bombing allowed Palestinians to 'inflict
harm on the enemy', turning 'weakness and feebleness into strength'.[71]

Partial strategic success for Hamas might also be embodied in their violence helping to determine the relevant political agenda. So the group's
desire, for example, to thwart the 1990s Israeli–Palestinian peace process
(which they saw as a sell-out of the Palestinian cause) represented one goal
behind their violence from that period. Part of this involved the intention
to destroy Israeli confidence in the process through using violence in order
to make clear that the peace process was not protecting Israelis. Hamas
tended to view negotiations and the Oslo process (about which, more later
on) as not working, and as a potential threat to their own strength and interests. Could they so determine the agenda as to limit that threat?

Tactical successes could involve terrorism working operationally, particularly in the difficult context of their opponents having endeavoured to harden
potential targets against attack; it could involve the achievement of interim
concessions or of significant publicity for the cause. Regarding the latter, as
one Hamas organizer put it in relation to suicide-operation videos, the aim
was 'to publicize in the world the Palestinian problem and the reasons for
the operation. With regard to the enemy, it is intended to deter and demonstrate that the Palestinians are willing to sacrifice their lives for their freedom.'[72] Did people notice the cause more when people were being killed?
If so, then—as so often—terrorist violence here might be read as a powerfully caustic form of political argument.

Tactical success might be evident also in the undermining of opponents
(whether Israeli or intra-Palestinian). In particular, if Israel could be made
widely to be interpreted as illegitimate, aggressive, and villainous, then violence might be judged by Hamas to have had some positive effect. Again,
violence might serve the tactical purpose of helping Hamas gain and sustain
control over a population; and it might further the goal of organizational
strengthening.

In particular, Hamas challenged the more secular nationalism of the PLO
with an emphatically Islamic species of Palestinian nationalist struggle and
vision. In military terms, Hamas as religious nationalists aimed to outdo
their more secular-nationalist rivals in Fatah, and to gain more and more
popular Palestinian support. As with so much terrorist violence elsewhere,

intra-communal dynamics have been as important as external targets and enmities when assessing and explaining violence, and Hamas has used at times very brutal methods indeed against alleged collaborators and intra-communal opponents.[73] Within the often fractious relationship between Hamas and the PLO and Fatah, violence has formed part of the means of the IRM attempting to challenge for hegemony and dominance and superior legitimacy within the Palestinian struggle.[74] Relatedly, Hamas has aimed to ensure that it is so organizationally strong that it cannot be ignored in any solution or political framework or development in the region.

Beyond strategy and tactics lies the possible realm of terrorism's inherent rewards as such. Palestinian dispossession and domination by Israel have been for many a disgrace and a humiliation; so, for some, the motivation for suicide attacks has therefore involved more a matter of 'realpolitik and despair'[75] than of theological impulsion. Shifting from deference to defiance; regaining agency through struggle and action; securing individual and communal dignity simultaneously—all of this has within it some possible personal and psychological reward, relating to what you become through the very act of resisting.

Added to this might be the emotional returns of engagement with an exalted religious nationalism; and, according to some Islamic tradition, there might be benefits to the individual from martyrdom, including prompt admission into heaven, and immediate remission of sins.[76] More broadly, there might exist the psychological rewards derived from sacrificing oneself for (or devoting one's work and career and activities to) an inherently valuable and noble and holy purpose or cause.

More mundanely, there might be for some people a financial dimension. Palestinian suicide attackers' families have on occasions received money after their death, and there is evidence that in some cases the prospective economic improvement of their families' situation played a role in motivating Palestinian suicide bombers to adopt that tactic.[77]

Drawing all this together, we must recognize the interrelatedness of these various possibilities for success. Multicausality and complexity, rather than mutual exclusivity, are the appropriate colours to paint with here. So the violent pursuit of Hamas's central goal—the religious-nationalist one of destroying Israel and replacing it with an Islamic Palestinian state across the historic territory of Palestine—might increasingly be operationalized with an eye to securing the significant but more limited and partial goal of a state in the West Bank and Gaza, and also the secondary goals of sustaining resistance, defending one's community, and striking back in retaliatory mode at Israel and Israelis. It might simultaneously have the benefit of so determining the agenda as to write oneself into any endgame script, and to write out certain preferences held by one's adversaries. Through all of this, in turn, various kinds of tactical efficacy might possess allure in themselves, while also serving to bring about the above aims; and individual and communal rewards deriving from the struggle itself might yield a further—still interwoven—way in which terrorism might be said to work. Hamas's violence can be read through the goals of the group itself, but entangled with this are activists' individual-level motivations, themselves often complex enough.[78]

III

Palestinian terrorism is the paradigmatic example of terrorism that has worked.

Alan Dershowitz[79]

So: has Hamas terrorism in fact worked? There is some evidence that—in addition to commentators such as Professor Dershowitz—others too have thought that the use of political violence possesses efficacy in this political context. Coinciding with the Second Intifada (a confrontation of Palestinians versus Israelis which began in September 2000), the percentage of Palestinians thinking that violence could achieve what negotiations could not bring about rose from lower than 33 per cent in July 2000 to 59 per cent by July 2001, and to 71 per cent by September 2001.[80] A May 2002 survey found that almost 70 per cent of Palestinians thought terrorist attacks on Israeli targets to be legitimate,[81] and a poll taken in June 2005 found that 66 per cent of Palestinians polled thought that political violence had indeed served to bring about the achievement of Palestinian national objectives.[82] Yet again, a March 2005 poll had found that 75 per cent of Palestinian respondents thought Israeli Prime Minister Ariel Sharon's withdrawal plan for the Israeli Army from Gaza to be a victory for Palestinian (and more particularly, Hamas) violence.[83] Extensive surveys conducted in July 2007 among Palestinians aged between 14 and 34 suggest a complex pattern, with many people supporting *both* violent and civil resistance, but with greater likelihood of actual participation in the latter than the former; large numbers saw terrorism and also non-violent methods as possessing efficacy. But, significantly,

68 per cent of respondents here agreed with the statement that 'Palestinians have tried massive non-violent action in the past and it did not succeed in changing Israel's behaviour.'[84] In one 1994 poll, 33 per cent of Palestinians said that they supported armed attacks against Israeli targets in the occupied territories;[85] and, when asked in December 2001 whether 'armed attacks against Israeli civilians inside Israel so far have achieved Palestinian rights in a way that negotiations could not', an emphatic majority of the surveyed adult Palestinians in the West Bank and Gaza Strip answered 'Yes or definitely yes'.[86]

If we explore this more fully in analysing what has actually happened, then what do we find? Clearly, Hamas has been unable to secure through violence the achievement of its central goal (the destruction of Israel and the establishment of an independent, Islamic Palestinian state covering the historic territory of Palestine). Historians should probably not make too many predictions; but one might tentatively suggest that nobody reading this book is likely to witness this central goal being secured. Careful attention to first-hand sources demonstrates that this has become evident even to Hamas itself. As Abu Shannab, one of the organization's senior Gaza figures, frankly admitted in 2003: 'Forget about rhetoric, we cannot destroy Israel.'[87] The success or otherwise of terrorism is frequently determined by the resolve of the state against which it is primarily directed, the strength of support possessed by such a state, its military and economic capacity, and the degree to which that state prioritizes the prevention of yielding on the terrorist group's particular objectives. In each of these ways, Israel is an enemy unlikely to be shifted on the central, primary goal set out by Hamas.

If strategic success has therefore eluded Hamas, can one make a case for their having secured partial strategic victory through limited but significant progress in the direction of their ultimate goal? The organization has now been noted for exhibiting a certain pragmatism,[88] and it does seem increasingly to distinguish between the short-term goal of a Palestinian state which exists in the Gaza Strip, West Bank, and East Jerusalem, and the longer-term aim of a Palestinian state extending across the whole territory of historic Palestine. In effect, what may emerge is practical acceptance of a coexistence arrangement with Israel. Even if Hamas presents such a prospective deal as temporary, and retains the ultimate goal of a wider Palestinian state as well for the future, it might be that engagement with such a partial victory could lead to more moderated and pragmatic perspectives evolving further, and to the more ambitious goal losing its place at the centre of Hamas gravity.

Partial though such an outcome would prove, it might have involved a weakening of Israeli resolve to hold on to all of its prior Palestinian territory; it would also have involved a weakening of Israel itself (not least in terms of that state's repeated vulnerability to lethal terrorist attacks on its people), and would also fit with what seems to be a sizeable element of Palestinian opinion about the desirability of a compromise arrangement along these lines.[89] And overlaying this development has been the arguable achievement of Hamas violence in helping to Islamize both the Palestinian struggle (in the wake of prior PLO dominance) and therefore also, to some degree, the Israel/Palestine conflict itself as it has been apprehended and defined. Again, therefore, we see what might (perhaps irreverently) be termed an alcohol-free version of the group's central goal: they would be unable to point to the creation of an Islamic state of the kind that, ideally, they would have preferred; but they would be able to celebrate the more fervently Islamic nature of the resistance (and of the wider conflict) which their violence had brought about.

In this partial strategic route, however, we should also identify some negative features, some problems, some obstacles. There can be little doubt that Hamas's often brutal violence has made the relationship between Israel's Jewish majority and its sizeable Palestinian-Arab minority more difficult, polarized, mistrustful, extreme, antagonistic, and crisis-ridden.[90] To the extent that Hamas terrorism has increased both Palestinian militancy and Jewish fears within Israel (and there is evidence that it has indeed done so), then it has surely contributed both to damaging Israel and also to making the prospect of satisfactory compromise and political resolution of the Israel/Palestine problem more elusive and problematic. As so often with terrorist resistance, Hamas's violence has aggravated the problem as well as making it more famous and more urgent of redress. It has certainly reinforced negative stereotypes and hostility between Israel's Jews and Israel's Palestinians,[91] and it is hard to see this deterioration even as a partial strategic success.

I think the evidence is less ambiguous in allowing us to suggest that Hamas's violence has brought about something of its secondary goal of sustaining Palestinian resistance against Israel. The violent movement has succeeded in a long-term sustenance of its own capacity for struggle: it has gathered very significant financial capacity,[92] thereby providing the wherewithal to sustain longer resistance; it has gained significant international support (conspicuously from Iran, but also from within Iraq, Syria, Sudan, and Saudi Arabia) and internationally wide-ranging networks of representation (whether in the United States, Europe, South America, or elsewhere);[93] and in all of this it has brought about for many people a sense that power inheres in the violent struggle.

It might also be argued that Hamas's nationalistic violence has further contributed to the longer-term process of establishing internationally that the Palestinian people are indeed just that: a people, and a people with a strong and long-rootedly historic national identity. There can be little doubt that international perception and opinion have shifted on this issue over the years of post-1960s Palestinian struggle,[94] and I think that the persistence and fame of Hamas violence, together with the determination and commitment evident within it, have contributed brutally to ensuring that shift. Even many who abhor what Hamas have done would now acknowledge that they represent a distinct national group. Moreover, the view held by some Israelis in the immediate post-1967 period, that the Palestinians had become inconsequential,[95] has been demolished by the persistent violence of groups including—though far from exclusively—Hamas.

Has Hamas been able to offer muscular defence of, and protection for, Palestinians? This secondary goal seems to me largely to have eluded them, in relation to what Hamas's terrorism has in practice achieved. There is much that can be said about what Palestinians have gained from the non-terroristic aspects of Hamas's work (social service provision, for example) and to that we will turn later in this chapter. But Hamas's actual terrorism has tended to contribute to tit-for-tat cycles of escalatory violence from which many Palestinians have clearly suffered in terms of injury, loss of life, and damage to property, infrastructure, and the quality of people's day-to-day existence. If we are to address, in historical context and chronology, the problem 'Does Terrorism Work—For Whom?', then the evidence suggests that—for many Palestinians in practice—Hamas violence has brought destruction rather than defence. So, in response to Hamas rocket attacks on Israel, Israel sharply attacked Gaza during late 2008 and early 2009 with tanks and fighter-bombers; well over 1,300 Palestinians were killed as a result, many of them civilians; and this fitted a wider, enduring pattern—Palestinian violence prompting harsh Israeli response, with the latter making Palestinians' lives even more painful.[96] As I write, Palestinian workers in Hamas's Gaza stronghold continue to work and live in very humiliating conditions, some distance from the apotheosis of victory or triumph.

Indeed, some expert assessment has suggested an exacerbation of Palestinian suffering during the period of Hamas's violent career, pointing particularly to the counter-productive effects of the post-2000 shift towards renewed terroristic violence, and to the now prison-like conditions of the Gaza Strip.[97] The experience of mid-2014 certainly pointed in this direction. Whatever the appropriateness of Israeli violence against Gaza in July of that year, there is no doubt that Hamas's continuing terrorism against Israel and Israelis on that occasion prompted lethal, cyclical violence within which Palestinians were the most numerous victims; by the eighteenth day of Israel's 2014 offensive, 825 Palestinians had been killed (over a quarter of them children), with many other people injured and/or rendered homeless.[98] In this sense, one depressing effect of Hamas terrorism has been to reinforce the extent to which violence of political method has become endemic within the region of their operation, with pernicious implications for their own people as well as their opponents.

More success can be identified in relation to the last of Hamas's secondary goals: the achievement of retaliation or revenge against their Israeli opponents. There can be no doubt that Israel and Israelis have suffered greatly as a result of vengeful Hamas violence deliberately targeted against them. Death, injury, and anguish have been accompanied by economic damage,[99] and by the generation of a measure of occasional chaos as well as the creation of insecurity and fear and terror.[100] Palestinian terrorism has caused significant psychological trauma for many Israelis, and has provoked deep insecurity among many people in Israel.[101] To eat away at your enemy's normality and security, and to lash out brutally in violent strikes, might be judged a success—however difficult it is for us to acknowledge this rather depressing part of the answer to our question. And visceral anti-Jewishness has been at the heart of much Hamas motivation.[102] So, during 1994, fifty-five Israeli soldiers and civilians were killed in terrorist attacks; the following year, anti-peace process terrorist attacks by Islamic groups killed forty-five Israeli soldiers and civilians.[103]

Indeed, blood-spattered cycles of violence have long characterized Hamas's work (as is common also in other settings of terrorist campaigns). So when, on 5 January 1996, Hamas's Yahya Ayyash ('the Engineer'—the architect of numerous Palestinian suicide attacks on Israel, and a key Hamas bomb-maker) was killed by the Israelis, Hamas delivered an explicit response: in partial retaliation for Ayyash's death, the group carried out numerous suicide attacks in which fifty-nine Israelis were vengefully killed. And, by then, such a retaliatory pattern had become familiar. On 25 February 1994 Jewish settler

Baruch Goldstein killed twenty-nine Palestinians in a Hebron mosque (Jewish terrorism forming part of our antiphonal story here again); in March 2005, senior Hamas member Musa Abu Marzouq admitted that, 'After the Hebron massacre we determined that it was time to kill Israel's civilians',[104] and in the months following Goldstein's attack, Hamas indeed adopted a policy of suicide bombings in which around forty Israelis were killed and many more were injured. Prior to that, on 23 November 2001, Israelis had killed a senior Hamas leader in the West Bank (Mahmoud Abu Hanoud), and Hamas retaliated by killing thirty-seven Israelis in December 2001. Painfully, repeatedly, terribly, there have been numerous other instances of Hamas seeking and obtaining bloody revenge for Israeli attacks.[105] The seven years of the Second Palestinian Intifada from 2000 onwards saw 1,065 Israelis killed in 30,595 attacks; in March 2002 alone, 82 people were killed and 519 more were injured by Palestinian suicide attacks in Israel.[106] Whatever the broader general goals of Hamas violence, a careful reading of the contextual, chronological reality points to this kind of brutal revenge as being central to what the group's violence has in practice caused. And the issue of whether (in theory) Palestinians have a right to use terrorism, will seem to some observers less pressing than are the life-destroying consequences of their revenge-driven violence when they do so.

There has been strong support at times for retaliatory Palestinian violence against Israel, as was the case during the bloody, tit-for-tat cycle between Hamas and Israel during 2002–3.[107] So there is evidence both that Hamas has been able to inflict serious and retaliatory damage on Israel and Israelis, and also that this has reinforced its popularity among sections of Palestinian society.[108] And one key aspect of this process has been Hamas's seeming capacity to hit back effectively at a stronger enemy. Such revenge can have individual, emotional rewards (as will be discussed later) but it is often achieved on the ground of hitting back representatively and on behalf of the wider, afflicted community. Striking successfully at the reviled Jewish enemy has been one of Hamas's most successful activities, and this fits a wider pattern of Palestinian resistance. In the proud words of the father of one Palestinian suicide bomber (a bomber who had attacked a Jerusalem pizzeria in 2001, killing fifteen people and injuring 130), Ariel Sharon 'is continuing the policy of killing our people, and my son succeeded in carrying out a suitable response'.[109] During this period, as at other times, terrorism contributed to a deepening of the polarization of the Israeli and Palestinian communities.[110]

Partial strategic success might also be evident were Hamas to be shown to have determined the political agenda through their terrorist violence. It has certainly been the case that—during the Second Intifada period, for example—policy responses towards Palestine have focused most sharply on responding to violent attacks and groups rather than to other aspects of the region's politics.[111] And the crucial test of Hamas's capacity to determine political agendas through terrorism lies, arguably, in their desire to thwart what they saw as an unsatisfactory peace process between Palestinians and Israelis. In 1991 Israelis and Palestinians had engaged in negotiations in Madrid (in itself a then dramatic development), and during the early 1990s Fatah and the wider PLO effectively committed themselves to a US-led Middle Eastern peace process which moved jaggedly forward over ensuing years. In 1993 and 1995 the Oslo Peace Accords offered the prospect (indeed, the widespread hope) of some compromise outcome of significance, and the heavily symbolic signing of the September 1993 Declaration of Principles for Interim Palestinian Self-Governance Arrangements in the West Bank and Gaza Strip (DOP), between the PLO and Israel, threatened to marginalize Hamas, who strongly opposed the Oslo peace process and its wider ramifications.[112] So the 1993–2000 Oslo years were also years when Hamas sought through suicide attacks and other violence to ruin, spoil, and derail the peace process.

The Declaration of Principles led to the setting up of the Palestinian National Authority (PA) in 1994. A new Palestinian police force was set up also on the basis of this deal and—despite implementation hurdles—1993–5 saw some other notable developments ensue: the Israeli–Palestinian Economic Cooperation Committee allowed for some coordination in relation to electricity, transport, finance, and water; Israel released large numbers of prisoners; and external actors donated large sums in economic aid for development in the West Bank and Gaza. The September 1995 Israeli–Palestinian agreement which became known as Oslo II allowed for the redeployment of Israeli military forces and the greater empowering of the PA. Indeed, many Palestinians at this stage felt that Oslo would lead to Palestinian statehood, with the PA as the embryonic government.[113]

But, amid these developments, those who opposed the peace process as an unwelcome compromise and betrayal gravitated towards Hamas, whose opposition to Oslo was partly ideological and partly also about intra-Palestinian competition. The formal negotiations between the PLO and Israel had implied a Palestinian recognition of the latter, and were thus anathema to Hamas. The empowering of their intra-Palestinian rivals in the PLO reinforced

Hamas's opposition, not least because dominant PLO authority within the PA would allow for a suppression of Hamas's activity and freedom of operation. We see here, therefore, what we see so often: violent enmity between adherents to the same cause lying at the heart of much terroristic violence, and accompanying hostility towards the extra-communal and more famous enemy. So thwarting, even wrecking, an unacceptably compromising peace process formed part of Hamas's ambition, and they did have some success here. Hamas's 1993–2000 violence did (along with that of groups such as PIJ—Palestinian Islamic Jihad) rather impede the peace process, since the Israeli government repeatedly halted negotiations with the PLO in reaction to suicide attacks in Israeli cities (arguing that the PA had not done enough to stop such attacks from taking place).

Hamas suicide attacks on Israel in 1996 helped to tip an Israeli election towards the right-wing Likud Party, damaging the Oslo process which might have benefited their Fatah rivals. The May 1996 national elections in Israel (which saw the right-wing Likud coalition's Benjamin Netanyahu become Prime Minister, replacing Labour Party Prime Minister Shimon Peres) came in the wake of a series of Hamas suicide attacks on the country; Netanyahu had adopted a harder line on security, and on negotiations with the Palestinians, than had Peres. In this case, success for Netanyahu could perhaps be read as success for Hamas, furthering their intention of damaging the peace process and undermining Oslo.

Hamas welcomed the fact that their Second Intifada violence from 2000 onwards seemed to have diminished the voice of middle-ground moderation in Israeli politics, shifting opinion instead towards the hard-line politics of opposition to compromise; such a development made the unacceptable peace process stumble, and it also generated international condemnation of Israel for its supposed inflexibility.[114] In electoral terms it seems clear that terrorism such as that practised by Hamas has produced significantly greater support for right-wing parties in Israel and an intensification of right-leaning preferences (since voters perceive the right bloc to be more focused on terrorism deterrence); it has therefore helped to thwart the politics of Israeli–Palestinian compromise as embodied in the stuttering peace process.[115]

It was not that the peace process was entirely destroyed, of course (and Hamas were not the only actors opposed to it anyway). Despite the heavy period of 1994–6 suicide bombings against Israel, Israeli–Palestinian talks still moved forward sufficiently for the September 1995 Taba Agreement (Oslo II) to emerge. But the eirenic hopes of many in the 1990s did come in time to be dimmed and disappointed. In late September 2000 a new round of violent conflict between Palestinians and Israel had begun, with the commencement of the Second (or al-Aqsa) Intifada which was to claim thousands of lives.[116] With many Palestinians frustrated at the failure of the peace process to deliver what they thought appropriate, a late September 2000 visit by Likud Party chairman Ariel Sharon to the sacred Haram al-Sharif/Temple Mount in Jerusalem prompted protests and a number of unarmed Palestinians were killed; this led to riots, and to the wider uprising and a deep intensification of enmity. Palestinian support for suicide attacks had been around 25 per cent during the 1990s, but it rose to 75 per cent during the first two years of the al-Aqsa Intifada[117] (a confrontation during which Palestinian groups carried out thousands of attacks). And it seems clear enough that Hamas's violence did play a part in turning peaceful progress into something more frictional; 'suicide attacks were a major factor in the eventual collapse of the Oslo Accord and the breakout of the Second Intifada'.[118]

This is a difficult causal process to trace, of course. As shown above, Hamas violence can help to thwart a peace process; similarly, however, frustration with a peace process which seems not to be delivering the goods can yield greater support for Palestinian violence. So if less violent politics seem efficacious then this can undermine Hamas; but Hamas's violence can make the less violent process seem less efficacious.[119] If Jewish settlement in the occupied territories can be seen to be expanding (and between 1994 and 2000 the number of Israelis settling in the occupied territories in fact tripled),[120] then this can be read both as emerging from Israeli doubts about the peace process which Hamas violence seemed to discredit, and also as the basis for further Palestinian scepticism about the process, which in turn made more Palestinians likely to support Hamas violence. Elements of both processes were involved.

What about Hamas terrorism in terms of tactics? There have clearly been many operationally successful ventures. Grim though it is to concede the point, suicide attacks or martyrdom operations are comparatively cheap, can cause very serious damage, can hit targets which are difficult otherwise to reach, and can have a large and sharp psychological effect. In this and other aspects of its work, Hamas has at times shown some impressive adeptness in terms of methodological sophistication;[121] and it seems that even drastic measures such as Israeli targeted assassinations have not in themselves been the cause for diminishing rates of Palestinian violence.[122] Equally, however, change over time has seen the Israeli state in different ways grow skilful in thwarting Hamas's tactical endeavours. Indeed, it seems likely now that the majority of planned Palestinian terrorist attacks fail to reach completion,[123] due to a mixture of intelligence work and prophylactic measures. Partly for this reason, the tactical effectiveness of suicide attacks seems to have diminished during the early years of the twenty-first century: the number of successful suicide operations by Palestinian groups peaked in 2002, diminishing in number thereafter; and in each of the years 2002, 2003, 2004, 2005, 2006, and 2007, the number of foiled Palestinian suicide attacks was greater than the number successfully completed; so Israeli counter-measures had undoubtedly blunted the previously sharp efficacy of Palestinian suicide attacks.[124]

So there is a mixed tactical-operational picture. Hamas has undoubtedly hit Israel hard, and has shown tactical ingenuity and determination in doing so; but the increasing capacity of Israel to thwart such attacks needs also to be noted, as does the related capacity of Israel to kill senior Hamas figures.[125] It is true that the Israeli record of counter-terrorism has been a mixed one,[126] and the most careful evaluation points strongly to there having been a complicated tactical record on Hamas's part too: neither side can comfort itself with consistent or overwhelmingly tactical-operational efficacy.

There have been interim concessions (including the release of prisoners) won by Palestinian terrorist violence such as that practised by Hamas.[127] And, tactically, the acquisition of publicity has been clear and repeated, with Hamas's violence gaining fame for Palestinian grievances and arguments. As noted in the Introduction to this book, there are difficulties with counter-factual analysis of the past;[128] but it is hard to imagine that an absence of the kind of violence so long practised by groups like Hamas would have left the Palestinian cause, and the grievances associated with it, anything like as prominent or internationally famous and pressing as they have become after that violence. There is compelling evidence that certain forms of violence have prompted international audiences, for example, to listen carefully to the kind of framing arguments deployed by Palestinian terrorist organizations.[129] And there is no shortage of headlines and of press coverage for the aggressive politics for which Hamas has become very famous.[130]

Moreover, the sense that Palestinians possess a genuine grievance, and that their politics have a certain credibility, has almost certainly been reinforced by the sustained violence of groups like Hamas. This is an important point, given that (for example) polling evidence from August 2002 suggested that 78 per cent of Israeli Jews themselves felt that Palestinians had a legitimate right to a state (a remarkable change from prior attitudes).[131] And there is 'broad international recognition of the right of the Palestinian people to a sovereign state that is to include some of the territories still occupied by Israel'.[132] But while it has been impossible, as a result, for people to ignore the cause in whose name Hamas has acted so brutally, that brutality has also involved people identifying the Palestinian cause very much with violence; and it has caused a measure of revulsion at the methods used and at the people possessing the callousness to deploy them. As so often, the achievement of publicity through terrorism is a markedly double-edged process: the cause becomes famous, indeed globally so; but the cause also becomes instantly associated in people's minds with callous killings.

In terms of undermining opponents, Hamas by itself has not been able to damage Israel as much as the organization might have liked. But, in harmony with some other players, it has undoubtedly harmed and degraded Israel's image internationally through the provocation of what is read by many to have been a Draconian state response.[133] Indeed, in facing Hamas terrorism, Israel has frequently found itself in what one scholarly authority has termed 'a no-win situation. On one hand, a failure to respond could embolden its enemies and dishearten its people. On the other hand, tough retaliation could worsen the situation, lead to the deaths of more innocents, and trigger international condemnation.'[134] And Hamas's violence has also enabled it to gain strength against a now-weakened Fatah, although the intra-Palestinian enmity thus produced has arguably weakened and damaged the Palestinian movement as a whole.[135] Still, there can be little doubt that Hamas violence has allowed it to rival the PLO and—among many Palestinians—to outdo and undermine them.

More broadly, might it be argued that Hamas's terrorism has undermined Israel by rendering the status quo unacceptable and unsustainable? Certainly, the group's violence has contributed towards the impossibility of calmly stable politics on Israel's preferred terms, and in that sense Hamas has deepened political discomfort with what is. But it is also true that the largely non-violent First Intifada of the late 1980s had, in Rashid Khalidi's words, 'shaken the comfortable conviction of much of the Israeli public, and of key elements of the Israeli security establishment, that Israel could indefinitely maintain the occupation of the West Bank and Gaza Strip in its then-current form'.[136] That being the case, it is hard to argue that Hamas's violence was necessary to render the status quo problematic, since *non*-violent methods had achieved so much in the same direction.

Hamas violence has helped it to gain and enforce its social control over populations where it already has some strength, and also to secure the constriction of activity within such communities. So its curbing of behaviour which it considers to be unIslamic has been backed up by its intra-communal violence. This has rested at times on very aggressive mechanisms indeed. In June 2007 Hamas's armed forces defeated Fatah in Gaza and took control militarily of that area: this military takeover (which involved executions and torture) allowed for a violence-based control of the Gazan population. The withdrawal of Israeli forces from the Strip in 2005 preceded and rendered possible this development.

Has violence furthered the goal of organizational strengthening? The answer here is complicated. It is true that Hamas's violence, as well as its other activities, has brought about a situation in which it cannot be ignored in any endgame or political settlement. Moreover, as mentioned already, it could be argued that Hamas violence has strengthened the group's market share of support when compared with rival brands of Palestinian resistance (such as that of the PLO and especially Fatah). On the back of a very violent activist history, Hamas has now emerged as the largest Palestinian militant Islamic group, dominating the world of Islamic resistance in the Palestinian territories. During this evolution, Hamas has used violence as one means of gaining further public backing and support,[137] casting itself as the less compromising voice when compromise has seemed to yield inadequate returns, and as the true defenders when rival forces have seemed to vacillate and waver. So, while there have been times of Hamas–Fatah collaboration, dialogue, and near-rapprochement, the rivalry between them has been more telling, and there is clear evidence that Hamas did gain credibility and support by signalling and maintaining a harder line during episodes when the peace process seemed to be moving nowhere for the Palestinians.[138] Even in the early twenty-first century, suicide bombings by Palestinians have had a significant measure of popular support and have arguably served to recruit members to militant Islamic groups in the region.[139]

But there might be limits here too, I think. Some scholars have disputed the importance of competition between rival groups in generating terrorism, in providing a reason for carrying it out; they have pointed out that, for example, the use of suicide terrorism has at times been suspended by Hamas precisely because it was judged to be *losing* them popular support.[140] The picture is cloudy and will vary, of course, from context to context. Despite this, it seems clear that there have been occasions when—in terms of the tactical issue of gaining credibility and support—Hamas violence has yielded some results for the movement. Such a process might, of course, have little to contribute to the achievement of Hamas's ultimate goals: if the group's violence draws in recruits because it seems that Hamas are pursuing the only effective way towards Palestinian victory, but if their violence does not in fact bring such victory about, then the tactical success of gaining support would have to be judged ultimately far less powerful in its effects.

Moreover, Hamas's growth in support and strength has not merely grown out of their violence, and this does subtly complicate the picture. As with so many movements,[141] Hamas has combined violent with non-violent methods. When examined in close context it is clear that their social provision work, and their electoral-political endeavours, have also played a significant causal role in what they have achieved. These three aspects of Hamas's approach (violence, social provision, electoral politics) are interlinked and can be supportive of one another, so any demonstration that the less violent elements have been important does not utterly undermine the role of terrorism. But it does complement it and make the process far more complex.

One of the most distinctive features of Hamas's organizational career has been its commitment to the provision of certain social goods for its Palestinian population in Gaza and the West Bank. Meeting practical needs in the desperate conditions[142] in which many Palestinians find themselves, Hamas has funded and run: hospitals and other medical care; schools, orphanages, kindergartens, and after-school programmes; food distribution centres and money-provision mechanisms; mosques; sports and youth clubs; libraries; and summer camps, care homes, and relief centres. Taken together, this work has created a very important social welfare network, vital for many people in their day-to-day lives in hardship. And, unsurprisingly, it has gained and retained much deep-rooted local support for Hamas, especially when contrasted with what many saw as the more corrupt and nepotistic approach to the community that was typical of the PLO/Fatah. Even before their 2006 electoral success, opinion poll evidence from March 2004 showed that Hamas's support in Gaza had risen to 27 per cent, against Fatah's 23 per cent.[143] In the intriguing words of leading Hamas figure Musa Abu Marzouq from 2006, 'Through its legacy of social work and involvement in the needs of the Palestinian people, the Islamic Resistance Movement (Hamas) flourished as a positive social force striving for the welfare of all Palestinians. Alleviating the debilitative conditions of occupation, and not an Islamic state, is at the heart of our mandate.'[144] Much (if not most) of what Hamas now does lies in this realm of social service provision rather than in actual violence.[145]

This activity can possess an important religious quality. The *dawa* is literally a call to God, the spreading of true Islam; but it can involve both proselytizing preaching and also charitable giving and social welfare work. In this sense, for Hamas, social welfare endeavours can help to attract and recruit people to a particular kind of violent activism, and also towards electoral support and sympathy. As suggested, the three main elements of Hamas's work exist rein-forcingly and so should not be read in isolation from one another: its social organizations have at times helped to recruit for and to finance its military personnel, and the various aspects of Hamas's work—including its brutal vio-lence—have been intimately linked.[146] The group itself certainly seems to recognize that its electoral appeal rests on far more than its reputation for violent resistance and its violent record in practice, although the role of vio-lence within intra-Palestinian rivalry cannot, of course, be ignored.[147]

As the twenty-first century has progressed, so Hamas has grown more and more weighty in its electoral-political role, and its organizational strengthen-ing has in part been based on this kind of activity too. In December 2004 Hamas won around 35 per cent of the individual contests in the municipal Palestinian elections; just over a year later, the group was democratically elected to govern the Palestinian territories. For in the January 2006 Palestinian legislative elections (elections for the parliament of Gaza and the West Bank— the Palestinian Legislative Council), Hamas triumphed against the late Yasser Arafat's Fatah, with the latter now seeming to many to be tired and increas-ingly irrelevant to Palestinians' quotidian struggles. The January elections saw Hamas win 74 seats and their PLO rival Fatah win only 45 (out of a total seat number of 132). Hamas won 44.5 per cent of the vote, only slightly ahead of Fatah's 41 per cent, but nonetheless it became the majority and dominant party in the election and the Council. Hamas had here emphatically won political power, the goal of so many nationalists.

And with its armed, violent takeover of the Gaza Strip in the summer of 2007, Hamas then held effective control of the area both through violence and elections. But the development towards electoral energy (and political power) had been evolving for some time, and should not be read as sudden or utterly recent. Pre-2006, Hamas had taken part in local elections but not in national ones for the Palestinian Council or the Palestinian Authority, since they presented these as illegitimate, being derived from the Oslo pro-cess. Yet the group had been strongly challenging Fatah electorally for some years before this, at what they saw as appropriate levels, and had been put-ting much effort into that electoral work during the 1990s as well as the early twenty-first century.[148] With their shift into more mainstream institu-tional/constitutional politics during 2005–6, they then signalled a major reorientation. The potential exists, of course, for their violence to produce a tension with their democratic political work.[149] But since their involvement in some electoral competition goes back to their earlier years of life, such tensions need not, perhaps, produce a decisive schism.

In assessing how far Hamas terrorism has contributed to organizational strengthening, therefore, we have to note the vital point that Hamas is very much a movement: indeed, an integrated movement yet which has different wings and dynamics. As one of their Gaza leaders put it, 'Hamas is one book. Today you can read the social page, and tomorrow you will read the political page, but they are all Hamas.'[150] I think that its frequent use of tactics such as suicide attacks means that the label of terrorist group is legitimate enough (and, reflecting this, in 1993 it was named by the USA as a terrorist organization). But it is also much more than that. So the problem of definition identified in this book's Introduction is here, I hope, offset by paying historical attention to the full range of what Hamas does in context, instead of adopting an approach which considers merely its violent activism. Far from monolithic or static, Hamas persists in a significant level of violence, but its repertoire of activities extends beyond this, to interlinked social and electoral work which has also played its part in contributing to the movement's survival and popular support. This mixed repertoire has had a deeply Muslim dynamic to it, of course, and much of the claim for international organizational reach lies in this aspect of the group's politics; as Abdel Aziz al-Rantissi confidently and exaggeratedly phrased it, 'Hamas has the widest popular base in the world because Hamas's actions resonate with Muslims from South Africa to India, Pakistan, and China; and from Latin America to the United States and to Europe; all Muslims support what Hamas is doing.'[151]

Finally, what of the inherent rewards available through terrorism? Are there goods which Hamas activists gain from the very act of resistance itself, whether those goods overlap with or exist in partial autonomy from expressed strategic or even tactical goals? Again, contextual attention to a range of evidence points towards a mixed picture, operating variously for different people and at different levels. There are, for example, the material rewards that one might expect. Some Hamas operatives have found paid employment in the charitable aspects of the movement's work,[152] and the interrelated violence has also brought with it some cash rewards: so suicide bombers' families have on occasions received financial assistance and other practical benefits from Hamas.[153]

There have been some clear psychological rewards too: communally, with the shift from humiliated deference to activist-based defiance; and individually, with the exalted status, the glory, the fame, and the celebrity role that can come to you and to your family through suicide-bomber martyrdom,[154] and through the manner in which Palestinian violence has long offered for some people a means of releasing anger at the wrongs one has endured.[155] Here, the different aspects of our framework overlap: emotional rewards achieved through securing the secondary strategic goal of revenge, for example, cannot be utterly dissevered from that strategy. But they do represent a different dimension of the process too. The layers of our framework are not necessarily mutually exclusive of one another, but can exist in complex relationship.

Religio-political self-sacrifice has been highly valued in Palestinian society, with suicide bombers earning prestige, heroism, and honour—for themselves, but also for their families. Abdel Aziz al-Rantissi: 'For Hamas, and Palestinian society in general, becoming a martyr is among the highest, if not *the highest*, honour';[156] and again, 'To die in this way [suicide bombings] is better than to die daily in frustration and humiliation.'[157] Frequently, suicide operations have represented an apotheosis for the martyr, and have bestowed kudos upon their relatives; there has been treatment of suicide bombers as inspirational national heroes, as people to be greatly honoured, venerated, glorified, and celebrated.[158] So suicide-bomb martyrs have been repeatedly hallowed through web sites, posters, murals, films, poems, postcards, and songs. In explaining the appeal and sustenance of suicide attacks by Hamas, therefore, this striking Palestinian culture of celebrating people who martyr themselves in this way has to be remembered in terms of the appeal that this kind of terrorism can succeed in delivering.[159]

For, as well as the individual and small-scale-familial benefits here, there has also been a wider, communal, inherent appeal, Hamas violence being seen by some as replacing Palestinians' humiliating powerlessness, hopelessness, and shame with agency, dignity, power, pride, and self-reliance. As in other struggles, attitudinal resistance can bring its own psychological rewards at numerous levels. And to this must be added the fact that, for some martyrs, a sense of having done Allah's duty, of being right with Allah, in itself has represented a comforting good.

The multi-levelled nature of all this can bring its own complications however. According to a fascinating study by the distinguished terrorism scholar Ariel Merari, Palestinian would-be suicide attackers (people who had intended to carry out suicide attacks but had failed to do so) did possess something of a distinctive personality pattern. None of those studied by Professor Merari were psychotic or psychopathic, and none had a record of being hospitalized in a mental institution. What the majority of them did tend to exhibit, though, was a tendency towards dependent-avoidant personality: a lack of self-confidence, some problems with making decisions independently, a certain willingness to do even unpleasant things in order to please others, an evident reliance on others' views, and a fear of expressing disagreement in case this prompted rejection. Merari claims that there emerged differences in personality type between those who wanted to carry out suicide attacks and others who—though involved in Palestinian terrorism—did not.[160] One inference here might be that for the suicide martyr himself or herself, there can exist on occasions a layer of reward in terms of pleasing comrades and following their direction and strategy; Merari's evidence hints that suicide bombers are more likely to be indecisive followers than decisive, more confident leaders. The rewards of this grisly form of resistance might, therefore, be complex and varied indeed.

Equally, we should not underestimate the costs of Hamas violence for some of those who have been involved in the movement's activism. Imprisonment can form one part of their reality, for example, as can more decisive and brutal punishment.[161] Abdel Aziz al-Rantissi and his mentor Sheikh Yassin were both killed by Israeli missile strike in 2004; likewise, Salah Shehadeh, the founder of the Izz ad-Din al-Qassam Brigades, was killed by Israel on 22 July 2002. If the inherent rewards of Hamas violence form part of our tale, then so too do the often very high and painful costs to be paid for such resistance. And it should also be borne in mind that some very powerful rewards could be, and were, achieved through less brutal means; the First Intifada was essentially non-violent, yet it yielded extraordinary rewards in terms of self-reliance, communal solidarity, and cathartic mobilization.[162]

IV

We must calculate the benefit and cost of continued armed operations. If we can fulfil our goals without violence, we will do so. Violence is a means, not a goal.

Gaza-based Hamas leader Mahmud al-Zahar, 1995[163]

Despite the clandestine nature of terrorism, therefore, there exist multiple sources on which to base a systematic assessment both of what Hamas has wanted, and also of how far it has actually managed to achieve it. Hamas terrorism has not been victorious in the sense of securing the group's central, strategic goal of an Islamic Palestinian state covering the desired territory; but their violence might be judged to have contributed to a long-term process within which Israeli determination to hold onto Gaza and the West Bank has been diluted, and from which autonomy for part of the desired territory might meaningfully emerge. They have unquestionably sustained resistance and have succeeded in inflicting revenge upon their enemies; but the costs here have been high, in terms of producing more violent suffering (rather than protection) for many Palestinians, and in terms of the deeply polarizing consequences of their terroristic endeavours. They have had some success in determining the political agenda (damaging a peace process which they despised), and they have gained some interim concessions as well as huge publicity. That publicity, however, has generated a negative impression of Palestinian politics being associated with cruel violence, and it is also true that Hamas's operational successes have been accompanied by some tactical-operational failures over the years. They have undermined Israeli and also Palestinian opponents, and their violence has allowed them to gain and enforce control over certain populations; but that control has also grown from much of their non-violent work too. Inherent rewards have been there, but so has much torment and suffering as a result of the violent campaign.

Very long pasts indeed lie behind the conflict in which Hamas has been involved, and it would seem unlikely that such enduring enmities will result in clear victory for any combatant or in amiable resolution. Communities in such profound disagreement have here produced a blood-stained palimpsest which is not yet completed. Hamas—whose politics are so different from those of the other Islamic group to which a chapter of this book is devoted[164]—must still (like al-Qaida) be explained in terms of political and historical contexts and reasonable explanation. There seems nothing innately or inevitably violent about the population which produced Hamas. It is hard, for example, to square a culturally inevitable account with the evidence, given that between the 1967 Israeli seizure of the Gaza Strip and West Bank and the mid-1980s, most Palestinians in those places were not actively involved in terrorism against Israel or the IDF.[165] And the early phase of the First Intifada makes clear that there is nothing necessarily violence-prone about Palestinian resistance, since the activity involved in that uprising was largely peaceful or (at most) very punily violent.[166]

Hamas has evolved and changed over time, and there seems to me nothing inevitably determined about people having supported it at the levels at which they have, or about Hamas using violence at particular levels. Like so

many other violent actors, they have been responsive to changing conditions, and ultimately also to the extent of popular support. As one of their
leaders crisply put it regarding assaults on Israeli targets, 'The scale of the
attacks will be determined by the level of popular support for such a
strategy.'[167]

The effects of their violent work have, as noted, been complex. There's
some econometrically assessed evidence that Palestinian terrorism as a whole
has had the effect of 'shifting the entire political landscape toward a more
accommodating position', making Israeli voters and parties more willing in
principle to yield territorial concessions. This still leaves the issue of whether
those concessions to Palestinians actually emerge in practice, however, and it
addresses only one aspect of what a group such as Hamas have fully sought
with their violence. Moreover, it still leaves open the question of whether 'a
more peaceful, diplomatic strategy would have been more effective in
achieving Palestinian goals'.[168] One issue here is whether the Palestinian
movement will ever enjoy sufficient cohesion to sustain longer-term non-
violent politics as its dominant form of activity.[169] The very impressive
Christian Palestinian activist Hanan Ashrawi's brave 1991 declaration that
'Forty years of violence have got us nowhere'[170] indicates one view on this
issue; and the evidence pointing to very significant numbers on both sides of
the Israeli–Palestinian conflict who would prefer a negotiated settlement[171]
suggests that a messy compromise might yet provide the basis for less brutal
futures.

Moreover, if strategy is indeed 'the art of creating power',[172] then there
might be a certain logic in Hamas strengthening the relative weight of their
non-violent work (in social provision, in electoral politics and authority) in
consolidation of the power that they now enjoy. The tension that exists between
the longer-term (and rather distant) ambition to establish a certain type of
Palestinian state over a historic territory, and the more realizable goal of providing a certain kind of life and government and provision for the Palestinian
community in the Gaza Strip and West Bank, maybe does point towards the
good sense of Hamas adopting a more reformist, modest politics.[173] Leading
Hamas figure Khaled Meshaal pointed to Lebanese example in suggesting the
efficacy of violence, as seen by Hamas: 'The zionist enemy…only understands
the language of jihad, resistance, and martyrdom; that was the language that led
to its blatant defeat in south Lebanon and it will be the language that will
defeat it on the land of Palestine.'[174] But the pragmatic instincts of many in the
movement might yet tend away from this kind of logic.

For while it is clear that on some occasions Hamas has carried out acts of violence which cannot have been likely to succeed in terms even of short-term advantage,[175] in the longer term their politics will only be sustainably, centrally terroristic if that mode of operation can be seen to yield strong results. And the record here (as assessed in this chapter) seems too partial to instil great confidence. Aiming at the best end by the best means represents an enduring challenge for us all; in the context of Palestinian political ambition, the historical record suggests that terroristic violence carries with it profound limitations as a method.

Israel/Palestine remains an issue generative of much wider (for example, jihadist) anger and terrorism around much of the world;[176] and the enduring effects of this violent conflict (to which Palestinian terrorists have so significantly contributed) have included profound social disintegration, fragmentation, and damage to Palestinian society itself.[177] If we adopt a very long-term timeframe for our analysis (and this is surely appropriate in a conflict which has already consumed so many lifetimes), then we will concede that the ultimate effects of Hamas's violence will not be known for many years to come. This chapter began by considering long historical roots; those roots suggest that there is much life left in the conflict and its enmities within Israel/Palestine. But if we look closely at the contextual developments that have been involved so far, it seems clear both that Hamas's central goal of destroying Israel and establishing the sought-after state is likely to remain elusive, and also that much of the (admittedly, less ambitious) momentum that Hamas *has* managed to generate in practice has been produced by means other than the terroristic.

It's also vital to remember both the complexity of effect involved in Hamas terrorism, and also the humanity and voices of its victims. In 2002 a Hamas bomb at Hebrew University in Jerusalem killed two of David Harris-Gershon's friends (among the nine people killed in that attack) and very seriously injured his wife. He himself was emotionally and psychologically traumatized by the legacy of the episode; but he sought (without success) to meet the Hamas bomber—Mohammad Odeh—who carried out the attack, and (successfully) to meet with Odeh's family in East Jerusalem. In doing so, and in trying to delve into what had happened in this episode, he retained a clear sense of the vicious cruelty of Hamas's attack on that day in 2002 (a 'murderous act': 'There's no justification for the murder of innocent men, women, and children'). But he also came for the first time to discover the extent of Palestinian grievance and the normality and humanity of the family from which the Hamas bomber had emerged ('being personally affected by the inhumane brutality of Palestinian terror...forced me to consider Palestinians' humanity'). So Odeh's Hamas bomb had hit out vengefully and viciously at enemies, had been a tactical-operational success, and had prompted a humane Jewish American to chronicle very publicly both the detailed cruelty of this brutal terrorist act and also the nature of what had (to him) been a previously invisible Palestinian part of this most tortured of political problems.[178]

4

Basque Terrorism, ETA, and the Spanish State

I

> ETA is a clandestine organization whose only objective is to obtain as rapidly as possible and using all the means possible—including violence—the independence of Euzkadi.
>
> ETA Executive Committee Statement, 1962[1]

ETA's historical inheritances are as significant as the legacies that they will leave to future generations. This is all the more so, given that any proper explanation of terrorist violence has also to engage with those other major phenomena (nationalism, the state, religion, economic development) which make terrorism such a highly significant object of analysis. Moreover, some of these inheritances with which ETA began its career involve very long-term processes indeed, processes without which ETA (Euskadi Ta Askatasuna—Euskadi And Freedom, or Basque Homeland and Freedom) would not be truly explicable.

The effective founder of Basque nationalism itself was Sabino Policarpo de Arana y Goiri (1865–1903). Building on an existing, already impressive sense of Basque identity and distinctiveness, Arana offered a defence of what he interpreted to be a traditional and threatened Basque culture and society. Strongly Catholic, and convinced that Basques represented a long-rootedly distinct people in terms of blood, race, and traditions, he held Basque identity to be significantly separate from that promoted and assumed as Spanish by the modern Spanish state. And he sought the restoration from the past of a perceivedly prior status and condition, rather than the continued process of absorption within Spain. Arana's dominant (if historically rather dubious)[2] vision involved an emphasis on Basque culture as something distinctively expressed in peasant or rural ways; and he looked for Basque national redemption and salvation in the face of a threatening Spanish dominance over Basque culture. Euskadi—the name he generated to refer to the Basque Country—long retained an imprint from his thinking and his inspiration.

As so often, therefore, one cannot really explain the tradition exemplified here (that of an assertive Basque nationalism) without attending also to the dynamics and nature and institutions and beliefs and practices of the more powerful (in this case, Castilian-based) state against which that tradition has been set. And (again, echoing other cases of terroristic violence) there exist very long historical roots to the identities and clashing traditions which have prompted political aggression in a later era.

In effect, Sabino Arana put forward a dichotomous reading of the historical separateness of Basques from the Spanish, and his argument offered to some later enthusiasts a possible legitimization for blood-spilling in defence of the precious Basque nation: for Basque violence could on these terms be seen as involving resistance against prior Spanish aggression, as well as in defence of very long-rooted difference. Despite the flaws in aspects of Arana's nostalgic, historical reading of an occupied and colonized Basque nation,[3] this was a vision of real emotional and cultural power and resonance. If Euskadi was Arana's term for the Basque Country, then his was a compelling ideology of associated struggle and of heroic nationalism.

ETA itself was founded in 1959. But (just as in Israel/Palestine, just as in Ireland, and—let's be honest—just as everywhere else) one cannot properly explain their brutal contemporary violence without at least some engagement with the long and entwined pasts which produced them, and which drew some people from the 1950s onwards to the idea that Basque political violence was both legitimate and necessary. Moreover, attention to long chronologies here undermines any notion of inevitable violence at high levels; it suggests instead the importance of changing combinations of factors which at some moments make terroristic activism seem appropriate to many people, and at other points make it seem far less so. Only such an ultimately synchronic approach will explain the variation over time of Basque political violence, and the causation behind this.

Basque nationalism over its long gestation comprised a strong sense of distinct cultural identity, associated with particular place and also with a form of Catholic religiosity (especially in earlier phases), with a rural self-image, and most crucially with the Basque language. The last of these—Euskara—has been for many Basques a vital element in a profoundly particular cultural identity, and its role appears again and again during the struggle between Spanish centralism and Basque regional identity and nationalism.

Many people see ETA in terms simply of unjustified terrorist violence, reading the problem as one created by such brutal activism and one for which the solution is simply that the group should be defeated and removed from the political scene. This is understandable and, as will become clear, I think that it is hard to make a strong case that ETA's violence has been justified by what it has centrally achieved in historical practice. But it also seems to me that this violence is inexplicable without a recognition that what has occurred is a historically deep-rooted conflict over political legitimacy, between two nationalisms: that of the Spanish state, and that of a section of the Basque community within Spain's borders. To recognize and analyse this reality does not seem to me to legitimize or validate ETA's blood-stained career; it does perhaps offer the best way of understanding it.

In 1659 the Spanish and French monarchs agreed a Pyrenean border between their countries and so the Basque region (which is small—only about 20,000 square kilometres in total)[4] became divided between two states. Basque speakers have called these Iparralde (the northern, French territory, comprising Basse Navarre, Labourd, and Soule, as they are rendered in French; or Nafarroa Beherea, Lapurdi, and Zuberoa, in their Basque versions); and Hegoalde (the southern, Spanish territory most relevant to this current chapter), comprising Vizcaya, Guipuzcoa, Alava, and Navarra (in Spanish); or Bizkaia, Gipuzkoa, Araba, and Nafarroa (as they are in Basque).

Crucially, therefore, the fully considered Basque Country (Euskal Herria, in Basque) consists of land that has long been divided between the Spanish and French states. This version of the nation-without-a-state problem has therefore witnessed two divergent sets of dynamics, and it is the Hegoalde-based context that has pivotally determined the shape of ETA's politics. Moreover, in the modern period of nation-state legitimacy, the Basque Country has never taken the form of a unified and independent entity.

Neither the Spanish nor French states fully or seamlessly absorbed or integrated the Basque identity or people, though the tension was far greater and more acrimonious in Spain. Formally, the Basques of Iparralde became French citizens in 1792, and the Basques of Hegoalde became Spanish citizens in 1876.[5] During the late nineteenth and early twentieth centuries, Iparralde did experience a clerically fuelled Basque opposition to comfortable incorporation into the French state, although even during this period Basque nationalism accelerated more notably in Basque Spain than in the Basque region of France. And the experience of the First World War rather reinforced the process of incorporating Iparralde's Basques into Frenchness, with the centralizing, absorptive process having a greater degree of success here than was typical among Spanish Basques. Indeed, during the late nineteenth and early twentieth centuries, the majority of Basques in Iparralde came to think of themselves effectively as French.

The late nineteenth century saw industrial wealth grow strikingly in the Basque Country (especially in Bizkaia and Gipuzkoa), with Spanish state attempts to imprint Spanishness onto their Basque community taking on much greater significance as a result. But—despite the extensive development of centralized mechanisms, including educational structures—these efforts proved only partially successful. And it is no coincidence that the powerful emergence of organized Basque nationalism in the 1890s coincided with the social transformation, dislocation, and immigration associated with the industrial revolution occurring in the region (particularly in Bilbao).

So the development of the politics of Basque self-determination already displays complex dynamics. There is an inherited sense of group ethnicity; the role of an individual, inspiring entrepreneur in Sabino Arana; the generative tension between a centralizing state and a distinctively regional counter-identity which that state could not fully integrate; and the nostalgic and culturally reactive process of responding to economic disruption. The combination of these factors seems more contingent than inevitable, a judgment reinforced by the fact that there appears no inevitability about the development of nineteenth-century conceptions of self-government towards separatist demands in Spain. Indeed, much of what occurred in the nineteenth-century context there involved the ideal of a Basque self-government which coexisted within (and indeed rather strengthened) the Spanish state.[6] So teleological readings of ETA's pre-narrative would (here, at least) be unmerited. And, decisively, in the Spanish setting with which we are primarily concerned in this chapter, it could be argued that Basque nationalism in Hegoalde emerged as a resentful and reactive response to Spanish nationalism, in a pattern familiar elsewhere in the emergence of nationalist politics of historical weight.[7]

In terms of the intensification of Basque reaction against the supposed incursions of Spanish state power, however, it is necessary to explain the huge and particular significance of the Franco period. The 1936–9 Spanish Civil War itself shaped Basque attitudes powerfully, lastingly, and painfully. The 1930s as a whole were very violent in Spain, with over 2,000 political killings during the years 1931–6,[8] and with the Civil War itself proving horrifically brutal.[9]

The short-lived Spanish Republic of the 1930s saw Madrid's left-wing government offer autonomy to the Basque Country, and so the victory of the anti-Republican Franco forces in the 1936–9 conflict marked an effective defeat also for Basque nationalism. Franco himself saw centrifugal nationalisms in Spain as a threat to Spanish unity, and he favoured the eradication of Basque nationalism as a political force in the country. During the Civil War, Basque nationalism understandably aligned itself with the Republicans and the left, against the Franco-led right. The July 1936 Nationalist military rising against the Spanish Republic had therefore been an ominous eruption for the Basque cause, and when the Nationalist forces emerged victorious after three years of war, that cause had been physically bruised and damaged. The Civil War saw parts of the Basque Country suffering greatly at the hands of Franco's forces,[10] the 1937 Guernica/Gernika raid emblematically reflecting the process: on 26 April that year a lengthy Luftwaffe bombing raid took place on the market town, which was the historic capital of Bizkaia, and a place of symbolic and ancient significance to very many Basques. Although the Luftwaffe carried out the attack, the Francoists were complicit and approving, with waves of aircraft dropping bombs which destroyed the town and killed more than 1,000 people. The atrocity (stunningly evoked in Picasso's extraordinary and famous painting) effectively broke Basque resistance, and the regional government surrendered in June 1937. On 19 June, Franco's forces entered and captured Bilbao and began repressing the population there harshly.

Of course, Basque reactions to the Civil War were not uniform; even then, the Basque region of Spain was heterogeneous rather than monolithic. Around 25,000 Basques were killed during the conflict: of these, approximately 16,000 were anti-Franco, and about 9,000 supportive of his rebellion. But the broad pattern remains that Franco was deeply hostile to the claims and practices of Basque nationalism, and that this left a legacy of huge importance for ETA. For Basque nationalism in Hegoalde had been intensified during the war, and the lasting scars from that traumatic 1936–9 period were further aggravated by Franco's post-Civil War approach to the Basque Country. The war ended on 1 April 1939, with Franco's forces enjoying a decisive victory. As noted, Franco himself was hostile to regional cultures insofar as they seemed to threaten or challenge Spanish central identity, and this shaped his attitude towards the Basque question. Very hostile to Basque national identity, his regime repressed and undermined it and sought to delegitimize Basque nationalism and its associated culture. The Basque language was actively suppressed, being banned from use in public places, and there was a broader post-war persecution of Basque culture and identity.[11]

But what developed in fact was a striking intensification of grievance-driven Basque nationalist politics during the Franco period. Many Basques grew disenchanted with the passivity of an older generation in the face of harsh Francoist repression, and opted for something more militant as a reaction. Eventually in the 1950s ETA was to arise as a violent exponent of this sub-culture of resistance. So Basque identity flourished, despite Francoist attempts at suppression; indeed, the anger against this centralizing, dictatorial state opponent arguably strengthened resolve for some people.

Following the traumatic 1930s Civil War, there was further sustained repression by Madrid during the 1940s and 1950s of Basque culture, language, and civil liberties. The Basque flag was not allowed to be flown; and the language, Euskara, was forbidden in public and in religious activities by a Franco regime which existed in open and painful enmity towards the expression of Basque separateness. Indeed, the 1939–75 period was one during which this Spanish state hostility clashed with a Basque nationalist movement which exhibited some vitality. There also emerged in the 1940s a formal Basque nationalist movement in Iparralde, although again the levels of mobilization and political support there were lower than in the Spanish Basque region. Across much of our period, only a minority of people in the French Basque Country unambiguously identified themselves as Basque; French identity has tended to predominate instead, with considerable indifference (if not hostility) displayed regarding Basque activism and the separatist cause. In contrast, Franco's attempted suppression of Basque national identity within Spain made the latter seem threatened and attacked. But the legacy here was ambiguous for the later development of ETA, who rather gained from the rage felt by many in Hegoalde towards the Madrid-led Spanish state.

As noted, ETA was created in the late 1950s.[12] The group emerged from the ranks of those who represented the next generation of nationalist enthusiasts, after the PNV (the Basque Nationalist Party—in Spanish, the Partido Nacionalista Vasco; in Basque, Euzko Alderdi Jeltzalea) had seemingly been defeated. Founded by Arana himself in 1895, the PNV had been a very powerful political force during the 1930s, keen on a form of Basque Home Rule and acquiring impressive cross-class support. But its comparatively moderate and constitutionalist version of Basque nationalism seemed in the 1950s to have stumbled, leading some younger people (in a pattern familiar from other cases of political violence) to seek more aggressive means for the pursuit of less compromising objectives. ETA (also more left-leaning, politically) sought full Basque independence. And (drawing some inspiration from Jewish, Algerian, Cypriot, and Irish terrorism) it was prepared to wrest it through brutal force if necessary.

So ETA, founded in 1959, described itself as a 'political organization that practises the armed struggle'.[13] But the group can only be understood through recognition of the lengthily wrought inheritance of Basque identity and culture on which it drew, of the sense that ETA zealots had of the vulnerable state of Basque culture and freedom, and of the enduring Basque friction with a centralizing Spanish state. The small body of young men who rejected PNV politics in the 1950s, who broke away from it as dissidents, and who—at the end of that decade—went on to form ETA, did so because they sensed an inevitable failure in less aggressive politics. Initially styling themselves Ekin, these younger radicals transformed themselves into ETA and took tactical inspiration from the Israeli insurgent movement, and from what they read as the efficacy of its political violence[14] (which we considered in the previous chapter). So although ETA did not sustainedly deploy violence until the later 1960s,[15] the assumed necessity and supposed efficacy of force were central to their foundation and intention. And in time, ETA was to kill more than 850 people during its violent political career.[16]

There is some dispute about the nature of the conflict in which ETA has been such a brutal actor. Some emphasize Basque resistance to an encroaching Spanish nationalist state, while others focus more sharply on the problem being ETA's cruel violence itself. As made clear already, my own view is that there has clearly existed a serious and longstanding problem of Spanish legitimacy in the Basque region of Spain for many people who live there, including many who do not support ETA's violence. As with al-Qaida, Hamas, and the Provisional IRA, recognition of the deep political problems from which such groups' violence springs does not necessarily indicate any support for such violence. I myself have never been a supporter of the violence of ETA or of the other three case-study organizations analysed in this book. But it seems to me that analysis of these groups' violent effectiveness requires honest acknowledgement of the political roots beneath their various struggles.

ETA's own struggle was to be bloody enough. Between 1968 and 1975 ETA killed thirty-four people. By March 2003 they had killed 815.[17] Some of this violence was extraordinarily striking. On 20 December 1973 an ETA bomb killed the Spanish Prime Minister, Admiral Luis Carrero Blanco, in

Madrid, generating a huge security response there, and widespread national and international publicity.[18] Much later, a 19 June 1987 ETA car bomb in Barcelona killed twenty-one civilians (including several children);[19] later in the same year, on 11 December 1987, an ETA bombing in Saragossa killed a further eleven people (again, several of them being children).[20]

In addition to such brutal violence, there was always with ETA a political argument and dimension involved. As with so many of the groups that we are considering in this book, such political considerations could prompt schism. In 1974 ETA split into two groupings: ETA *militar* (ETA-m)—a military wing which retained a very strong commitment to violence as the mechanism for achieving independence; and ETA *politico-militar* (ETA-pm)—a politico-military faction which espoused a Marxian political struggle, and which gradually eschewed violence during the 1970s. It is, therefore, the former with which our own discussion increasingly deals and, despite their belief in the necessity and efficacy of terrorism, ETA-m displayed political argument and association also.

In February 1978 the Basque radical organization KAS (Koordinadora Abertzale Socialista or Socialist National Coordinator, a grouping which had been put together in 1976) proposed a set of terms on the basis of which ETA might engage in negotiation with the Spanish state: an amnesty for Basque political prisoners; the legalizing of political parties espousing Basque independence; the withdrawal of the Spanish police from Hegoalde; an acceptance by the Spanish state of the right of self-determination, with Navarre being incorporated into the new Statute of Autonomy (on which, more later); and the amelioration of living conditions for the working class. This KAS alternative was soon enthused over by the newly created Herri Batasuna (HB). Meaning 'Popular Unity' or 'Popular Union', Herri Batasuna was set up as ETA's political party in 1978, and was very much subordinate to the armed wing of the movement. Significantly, however, HB contested Basque elections from 1978 onwards, so what ETA's violence has achieved must be set against what HB's electoral work (admittedly, electoral work organically linked to ETA's campaign) brought about. The party won over 20 per cent of the Basque vote in its first provincial elections in 1979, and secured 15 per cent at its first general election in the same year; so there did then exist serious (though clearly minority) support for HB and—by extension—for its aggressive partners in ETA.

During the 1979–99 period HB contested five more provincial and municipal elections, six autonomous elections, six Spanish legislative elections, and two European contests. Its levels of support varied between 12 per cent and 20 per cent of the Basque vote, a far from negligible proportion (although, again, very clearly a minority of the people on whose behalf ETA claimed to be fighting).[21] In time HB was reincarnated as Euskal Herritarrok ('We the Basque People', formed in 1998), and Batasuna ('Unity', created in June 2001).

Also involved in ETA's political realm of expression was the MLNV, the Movimiento de Liberacion Nacional Vasco or Basque National Liberation Movement. This was an umbrella grouping which included ETA and HB, but also other organizations (such as trade unions) which shared ETA's objectives if not its violent methods. Again, the MLNV was subordinate for a long time to ETA.

If these were the political vehicles, then what of the changing political context within which ETA operated? The decisive shift to note here was that occasioned by the death of Francisco Franco on 20 November 1975. Since 1939, the conservative dictator had ruled Spain in authoritarian manner; prior to his death he had restored the monarchy, which led to King Juan Carlos I becoming his successor. The latter then oversaw Spain's transition to democracy, a development of profound importance for our reflections on the efficacy of ETA violence.

The year 1977 witnessed the first democratic elections in Spain held since 1936. Then in 1978 a new Spanish Constitution was introduced, to be endorsed through a constitutional referendum. The July 1978 draft Constitution stressed the unity of Spain; but it also provided the basis for considerable local autonomy, including opportunities for the Basque region. When the constitutional referendum was duly held in December 1978, in Spain as a whole 67 per cent of the people voted, of whom 88.5 per cent voted yes, thereby emphatically approving the new Constitution; in the Basque Country itself (Araba, Bizkaia, Gipuzkoa), only 45 per cent voted, but of those people an impressive 70 per cent voted yes.[22]

The following year (1979) there was then introduced, under the umbrella of this new Constitution, a Statute of Autonomy for the Basque Country (Alava, Vizcaya, Guipuzcoa); in the referendum held on that Statute (on 25 October 1979), 60 per cent of the Basque electorate voted, of whom a resounding 90 per cent voted yes.[23] The Statute of Autonomy facilitated the setting up of a three-province Basque Autonomous Community (Euskadi), an arrangement which provided for an autonomous Basque police force, for the collection of taxes, for significant control over health and education, for

Basque radio and television stations, and for a real measure of responsibility also in relation to social welfare powers, culture, the administration of justice, and economic decisions; Basque and Spanish were both to be official languages in the region. And, taken together, these were not trivial elements of autonomy. The changes meant that, by the late 1970s, Basques in three of the four Spanish Basque provinces (Navarra/Nafarroa was excluded from the Statute) had been given the right to very considerable autonomy within Spain. The peaceful and in many ways very impressive post-Franco transition to democracy had allowed for the regeneration of regional authority within the country, and for the attempted addressing of historically rooted claims for the necessity of devolved power. In tune with this, in 1980 a Basque parliament was established, with jurisdiction over the provinces of Bizkaia, Araba, and Gipuzkoa.

Yet ETA violence not only continued, despite this transition to democracy. The organization's levels of violence significantly rose. In 1975 ETA had killed 15 people; in 1976 they had killed 18, and in 1977 a further 10. Then in 1978 they killed 65 people, and a further 80 in 1979, and 96 more in 1980.[24] So ETA was bloodily arguing, through its significantly increased violence, both that it represented an important force in Basque and Spanish politics, and also that the shift to democracy had changed far too little to be considered satisfactory. Indeed, there seemed something here of the notion that in a time of already great transition one could violently seize the day and define the political future. Violent methods were continued, in pursuit of more comprehensive goals. And—as the vanguard opposition to Franco within the Basque Country—ETA had brought with it some resistance-based prestige into the new era of democracy.[25]

Accompanying the violence were some attempts to reach an accommodation within the conflict. Exploratory efforts were made soon after Franco's death to see whether some form of dialogue might be generated between the Spanish authorities and the Basque rebels. Indeed, attempts to try to engage in dialogue with ETA have formed a percussive and enduring counter-melody, accompanying the organization's much louder violence. Such moves gained momentum in the 1980s and beyond. Spanish government emissaries met leading figures from HB in October and November 1987. The PSOE (Partido Socialista Obrero Espanol, or Spanish Socialist Workers' Party) having come to power in the 1986 Spanish general election, these overtures then led to talks with ETA representatives in Algiers in early 1989. A January 1989 ETA ceasefire helped the process, and there were six meetings held between two delegations, respectively representing the Spanish government and ETA. In April the talks process broke down, with ETA then returning to its armed struggle.

The 1990s saw a stuttering peace process gain speed, however, and many people's hopes were significantly raised. Arnaldo Otegi had been an ETA member in his youth; from 1998 onwards he was an important spokesperson for Batasuna, and his reflections carry real insight and value for our discussion. For there had been among Basque left-nationalists a rather naive view that, as Otegi himself was to put it, 'ETA was going to resolve everything, that everything depended on the military strength of ETA, that one day ETA would force the state to a negotiating table and an agreement and the next day Basques would live happily ever after.'[26] During the 1990s and beyond, important sections of ETA began to shift its view on this approach. They watched peace processes elsewhere (especially in Northern Ireland) and began to change their orientation towards more realistic goals, perhaps, and in favour of potentially less aggressive methods. So in September 1998 ETA declared a ceasefire, which ended late the following year. The group's violence then commenced again in practice at the start of 2000, during which year ETA killed twenty-three people.

In all of this, it would be misleading to suggest that only ETA carried out terrorizing political violence. As so often in explaining and analysing terrorism, there has existed here an important relationship between state and non-state violence and mutual inter-reaction. During the Franco period, there was much repression of Basque nationalism, and some of this took a violently terrifying form.[27]

After, as well as during, the Franco era, the Spanish state has been strongly resistant to ETA's demands and activities, and has taken a hard line with them. The post-Franco state response to ETA has been comparatively restrained, when set against some 1970s and later state responses to terrorism elsewhere, and political liberties have been impressively sustained for the most part within Spanish democracy. But it is not that the state committed no violence.[28] Most famously, GAL (the Grupos Antiterroristas de Liberacion, or Anti-Terrorist Liberation Groups) were brutal anti-ETA squads with some links to the Spanish state; they killed at least twenty-seven people during 1983–7. In defence of Spanish democracy, it should be recognized that numerous people associated with GAL were prosecuted and incarcerated by the state. But it should also honestly be acknowledged that GAL's work was a callous example of state terrorism.

Important too is the fact that so much non-violent activity was also involved in the Basque case. Though less headline-grabbing than ETA, the non-violent PNV consistently dominated electoral competition in the Basque region, with most Basques and even very many committed Basque nationalists eschewing violence as a tactic.[29] Again echoing so many cases elsewhere in the world, the majority of people here felt that there existed other and better means than terrorism for pursuing their political goals.

For such a transformation to work, of course, there would need to be fruitful engagement with political rivals and opponents. Between 1990 and 2004 Jose Maria Aznar was President of the Partido Popular (the PP, the Popular Party—the main Conservative political party in Spain); during 1996–2004 he was Spanish Prime Minister. Aznar was very keen to defeat ETA using the police and the mechanisms of the law, and to avoid negotiation or dialogue with the terrorists themselves. And the conflict had nearly cost him his own life: in April 1995 (when he was leader of the opposition in Spain), Aznar had almost been killed by an ETA car bomb. After 9/11, he was to use the US-led War on Terror as a way of bolstering his campaign against the group that had nearly killed him. One of the keenest non-American supporters of President Bush's anti-terror campaign, Aznar was (as we saw in the al-Qaida chapter, and our discussion of the 2004 Madrid bombing) enthusiastic that Spain should support the post-2003 war in Iraq. When Aznar was replaced as Prime Minister by the PSOE's Jose Luis Rodriguez Zapatero, the context changed significantly. In 2005 Zapatero effectively commenced a Basque peace process. Initial meetings were held in June and July of that year, and they staggered on after this. Zapatero's regime also kept on pressing ETA through the police and the law. (Attempts to negotiate a deal need not preclude harder pressure being brought to bear by the state on its opponents.) But parallel to such work was a genuine commitment to the political or the peace process.

That process yielded some important, if flawed, outcomes. On 22 March 2006 ETA declared that a permanent ceasefire would begin two days later, and on 29 June Zapatero declared himself willing to have direct dialogue with ETA. But this cessation in violence proved not to be permanent in practice, with a 30 December 2006 ETA bomb at Madrid's very busy Barajas airport ending the ceasefire in shocking fashion, killing two people.[30]

In June 2007 ETA formally ended their ceasefire (claiming that 'The minimum conditions for continuing a process of negotiations do not exist').[31] This statement followed the breakdown of talks which had included

ETA, Batasuna, Spanish government representatives, and international interlocutors. Then on 5 September 2010 ETA claimed that it had ended its
offensive armed actions some months earlier—a significant development
which was complemented when in January 2011 ETA declared another
permanent ceasefire, reaffirmed on 20 October the same year when the
group announced the definitive end of its armed campaign.

On 21 February 2014 an ETA video appeared via the BBC, in which the
organization claimed to demonstrate some decommissioning of weaponry.
Then on 1 March 2014 an ETA communiqué said that the group had begun
to seal its stores of weapons, and that it would decommission all of its arms.
This early 2014 ETA display of putting some of its weaponry beyond operational use prompted positive responses from, among others, Sinn Fein's
Gerry Adams (who called it 'a very significant step forward').[32] To many
observers, ETA's decommissioning did not look like the gesture of a group
whose violence had succeeded. So to what extent had ETA terrorism actually worked?

II

> The only possibility we have of gaining our liberty is through violence.
>
> ETA member, Yoyes[33]

The first thing to do is set out exactly what they had wanted. Strategic victory, securing the organization's central, primary goal, would ideally involve
the attainment of full sovereign independence for a Basque state comprising
all seven provinces of Hegoalde and Iparralde. At root, ETA's violence grew
from a strong sense of the denial of Basque national self-determination, and
the need to put that denial right through force. The group has pursued what
it considers necessary violence in pursuit, centrally, of a nation state independent of the Spanish and French states within which Basque lands currently fall.

Echoing other settings, therefore, the study of ETA involves far more
than merely the study of terrorism: ETA's violence is primarily nationalist
violence, and it must be understood as such. Whether against Franco or
within the admirably democratic Spain which followed him, ETA argued
that force was essential to the securing of an independent Basque state. The
organization knew well that it could not defeat the Spanish state militarily;

but it could apply a kind of Clausewitzean pressure on the Spanish government—a lengthy, attritional war—in an attempt to extract what it judged to be a rightful restoration of historically legitimate national rights and freedoms. Increasingly, their demand for independence has been expressed in terms of the right of Basque self-determination. And, although ideally directed at securing a state covering the whole of the Basque Country, ETA's campaign in practice drew strength from political opinion within the Spanish part of that territory, and focused mainly on Spain's Basque lands.

Etarras (ETA members) are therefore best read as violent nationalists. And their nationalism and its enduring attraction and power are explicable within the framework that we have already encountered, namely the interwoven politics of community, struggle, and power. This detailed pattern[34] works repeatedly in interpreting and explaining the Basque nationalist commitment which is under scrutiny in this chapter. So Dr Cameron Watson's original, fascinating analysis of the emergence of militant Basque nationalism, for example, sustains a focus on what he terms 'universal concerns', places his particular subject in wider, comparative context, and rather confirms the appropriateness of the community, struggle, and power framework for explaining the strength of particular nationalisms. His own Basque nationalists clearly exhibit generative impulses regarding community (in terms of interwoven territory, people, descent, culture, history, ethics, and exclusivism); a commitment to the importance and development of struggle, both as an instrumental means and as something inherently purifying and emancipating in itself; a preoccupation with the means and goal of power; and, ultimately and centrally, a pursuit of freedom.[35] (Indeed, 'Freedom' is written into ETA's very name.) ETA's gruesome violence is what has mainly distinguished them from other actors in Basque and Spanish politics; but in order to understand that vicious violence, we need to identify and recognize it as growing out of deeper, nationalistic, historically rooted convictions.

In a sense, indeed, ETA's violence is about the rivalry between *two* nationalisms: a separatist Basque nationalism, and a Spanish nationalism which has sought (without full success) to centralize identity and power within its wider Spanish state. These are the roots from which is derived the contested political legitimacy of Spain's arrangements for the Basque Country. ETA has considered the Basque region to represent a nation without a state (and one divided between two states which ultimately had no legitimate right to sovereignty over it); their campaign has been a symptom of a long-running conflict between Basque nationalism and Spanish nationalism.

So ETA provides another good example of the fact that when we discuss terrorism, we are often discussing a phenomenon which arises from—and which is integrally linked to—even more significant world-historical forces and the intersections between them: here, again, nationalism and the state. The most significant aspect of terrorism, it might be argued, is that it serves as a lens through which we can more clearly see other, ultimately more important, human realities.

Partial strategic success for ETA might involve their bringing about through violence a watered down version of their ultimate goal: an otherwise unobtainable full independence for only a section of their desired territory, or a diluted version of independence for all or part of the Basque Country. Partial success might also involve the securing through violence of secondary goals. These might involve revenge, the settling of scores (including those against a Spanish state which some Basques saw as the genuinely terroristic actor in the conflict); or the sustenance of committed Basque separatist-nationalist resistance against the more powerful forces of the centralizing Spanish state. Dr Diego Muro has written thoughtfully about ETA violence being used not just instrumentally to achieve Basque independence, but also 'because it reinforces the internal cohesion of the radical community'.[36] Could violence and struggle create more activists, and make activists more committed, thereby intensifying and sustaining necessary resistance to Spanish hegemony?

Secondary goals could also involve the furthering of cultural expression and freedom, even short of a fully sovereign Basque state. ETA's activists have very often expressed a cultural dimension to their politics, and the Basque language (Euskara) has been perhaps the most significant aspect of this. An ETA leader such as Jose Luis Alvarez Enparanza ('Txillardegi') was emphatic about the language being a definitive part of the Basque nation.[37] Indeed, etarras have sometimes expressed the fear that the language might die, with fatal consequences for the Basque nation given its role as one essential basis for distinctive Basque identity. The word Basques have for someone who is Basque is 'euskaldun', the literal meaning of which is 'someone who speaks Basque'.[38] This has again had long roots into the past: the creation in 1918 of the learned society Euskaltzaindia (Academy of the Basque Language) reflected this fact, as has the unalluring tendency of people sometimes to use the Basque language as a device for the exclusion of perceived outsiders to the Basque community.[39] So I do not agree with those scholars who prefer to strip ethnicity of its feeling and emotion;[40] the contextual evidence suggests repeatedly that such inherent aspects of ethnic or national attachment are powerful and that they help to explain its significance. Here, with Basques and language, that seems certainly to be the case.

The cultural aspects of Basque nationalism have partly emerged as a response to powerful Spanish nationalism, and especially the latter's perceived encroachments on traditional and distinctive Basque culture and identity. So the rural was often stressed, as well as ties of racial attachment among native Basques. So too (though, I think, to a diminishing degree as ETA's struggle latterly developed), Catholicism played a constituent part in people's identity and in Basque separatists' long-rooted inheritances from the past. In both Hegoalde and Iparralde the Catholic Church has played historically a vital role in defending and promoting Basque culture.

ETA promulgated an increasingly secular case for Basque independence during the final two decades of the twentieth century, so this issue should not be overstated. But when we assess what it is that has contributed to the distinctive, meaningful formation of Basque identity, there is no doubting that Catholicism has played its part. For many Basques for many decades historically, there was a mingling of the Basque national and the Catholic Christian elements of identity. In its early days, ETA often involved people who were both nationalistically Basque and devotedly Catholic, and who saw the two themes as interwoven;[41] and beyond ETA the long historical tradition of Basque national identity had a strongly Catholic taste to it.[42] For the conservative, Catholic Sabino Arana, the religious dimension to Basque politics had been very important and, while ETA has espoused a formally non-confessional nationalism, Arana was without question an influence on their thinking.[43] The Catholic clergy played a significant part in sustaining and defending Basque dignity and confidence and tradition and, in its early development especially, Basque nationalism was heavily Catholic.

Another secondary goal for some ETA figures concerned socialism. Again, this has rather waned over time. Nor was there ever a neat coextensiveness between socialist commitment and Basque separatism: for many people in Hegoalde, socialism was a Spanish rather than a Basque phenomenon. This was especially true, perhaps, of immigrant workers, many of whom retained cultural allegiances to their original homes, and found Spanish working-class identity more appealing than Basque attachment. In any case, the Basque nationalist phenomenon has tended to be cross-class rather than class-specific. But ETA has had a distinctly socialistic flavour to its politics also. Indeed, the development of a stronger socialist aspect to ETA's evolving politics initially rather diluted the influence of Arana's more racial thinking upon them. Though a secondary goal when compared with the separatist ambition of independence, ETA did espouse leftist politics, with early etarras sympathetic to decolonization struggles elsewhere, some of which carried left-leaning emphases (Cuba, Algeria, India, Israel, Cyprus) and certainly an anti-imperial, anti-colonial tinge. Early ETA activists often read Che Guevara, Mao Tse Tung, Frantz Fanon, and Fidel Castro, so their socialist politics should not be casually dismissed.[44]

Partial strategic efficacy might also be discerned if ETA could be judged to have determined the political agenda, and to have prevented their opponents from securing victory. If, for example, it were concluded that ETA terrorism had made self-government the central issue of debate in the Basque Country, against the wishes of some key opponents, then this might be considered a partial success.

Tactical successes could include operational efficacy, the securing of interim concessions (ETA sought, for example, the repatriation of Basque prisoners who were held in jails around the rest of Spain), the acquisition of publicity through violence, or the undermining of opponents. Regarding the last of these, for example, if the legitimacy and acceptability of the Basque status quo within the Spanish state were thought to have been decisively undermined and threatened and challenged by ETA violence, or if such terrorism had made clear at least that existing political arrangements carried with them destabilizing and very heavy costs, then there might be thought to have been some efficacy to ETA's actions. Likewise, if ETA could provoke the Spanish state into counter-productive reaction then again terrorism might be thought partially to have worked. ETA certainly evinced a belief that their violence would prompt the Spanish state into repressive policies which would, in turn, strengthen people's attachment to and sympathy for the Basque nationalist cause.[45] Thus, while unable to defeat the state militarily (something which, in a literal sense, was always well beyond ETA's capacity), they sought to provoke it into doing things which would backfire against it and which would stimulate more substantial support in the Basque Country for independence.

Tactical efficacy might also be found in ETA violence gaining them or maintaining for them some control over their desired population (and much ETA terrorism was indeed intra-communal—again, a pattern which we find across much of the world with terrorist groups). And tactical success might be identified also if terrorism helped to strengthen ETA and their movement organizationally. If your violence forces a major European government such as that in Madrid to deal with *you* as the interlocutor representing your people, then you might judge your actions to have been somewhat vindicated. ETA certainly exhibited a lengthy possessiveness about the Basque struggle, and had difficulties working with people not under their own sway or control as an organization.[46]

Finally, ETA terrorism might offer some important inherent rewards as such. Among the predominantly male, young, and often single population from which etarras were so frequently drawn, adventure, machismo, and comradeship all seem to have offered some potential attraction.[47] Indeed, listening to first-hand sources, it appears that for some of these people the romance and the excitement of the endeavour played their part in motivating their activities. As one former ETA member rather vividly put it:

> You know, this thing about believing that we could help bring a whole new world into existence overnight. It's one of those exciting things . . . apart from the fact that you might call it romanticism, there was a real over-the-top romanticism. But it's also this . . . really exciting thing, a really awesome feeling, that's for sure. And I couldn't help but being attracted to it. . . . There's also this sense of adventurous spirit, something of that sort is absolutely fundamental.[48]

III

> The Basque people want self-determination, and there will be conflict until they get it.
>
> ETA founding member Jose Luis Alvarez Enparantza (Txillardegi), July 2009[49]

So has ETA terrorism worked?

Regarding strategic efficacy, and the securing of sovereign independence for a Basque state comprising Hegoalde and Iparralde, the answer seems at one level to be rather simple. ETA is a violent secessionist movement which effectively ended its campaign without having been able to achieve the desired secession of the Basque Country from Spain. As one of the world's greatest terrorism scholars has observed, terrorists tend to struggle for political power.[50] On the face of it, in this case, they failed.

Why was it that strategic success eluded them? I think three main reasons suggest themselves: first, the gulf separating ETA's vision on the one hand from the far more complex pattern of political opinion in the Basque

Country on the other; second, the fact that ETA's distinctive activity—carrying out political violence—gradually generated revulsion and a backlash against them, leading to significantly diminishing support; third, the reality that, in contrast to the seeming inefficacy of ETA's violence, there seemed to be more fruitful alternative methods of political activity, which appeared to be yielding practical results for Basque nationalists.

Like so many vanguardist groups practising terrorism, ETA espoused a political vision which was more concentrated and stringent than were the views held by many in the wider community for which they claimed to act. Did most Basques—even most Basques in the Spanish part of the Basque Country—feel that only a fully independent, seven-province Basque nation state was politically acceptable? Damagingly for ETA and for their hopes of strategic success, they did not. In reality, the population of the Basque Country was profoundly divided: between Basques and non-Basques (the latter representing an important part of the actual community); between those who favoured independence and those who found autonomy acceptable; between Basque speakers and non-Basque speakers. This has been and remains a heterogeneous community, and the often very hard-line arguments of ETA about political futures jarred with this reality.

So, in a region like the Bidasoa-Txingudi Franco-Spanish border area, for example, the intermingling complexities of Basque, Spanish, and French identity, and of language negotiation and culture,[51] defy Procrustean compression or ETA-style simplification. More broadly, many Basques now see themselves not as either Basque or Spanish, but as both.[52] So there have been and remain multiple identities within the Basque region of Spain. For these to be simplified away according to a harshly Basque-versus-Spanish dichotomy would clash with the complexity of lived life in the Basque Country. And in practice that clashing has undermined ETA's levels of support and efficacy.

This is not to deny the existence of some tension between Basque and Spanish identity, of course. A 1991 survey saw 62 per cent of young people in the Basque Country declare themselves more Basque than Spanish, and 40 per cent to be only Basque.[53] But the picture is deeply complex and messy, and too much so for ETA to gain the day. In late 2010, 56 per cent of Basques identified themselves as being a mixture of Basque and Spanish; only 31 per cent saw themselves as purely Basque.[54] And Basque political and cultural opinion is fluid, rather than determined and static and inevitable. Not everyone who speaks Basque by any means supports ETA and their vision of nationalism and of how to pursue nationalist goals; instead, heterogeneous views exist,[55] and it is hard to argue that ETA accurately reflects Basque politics, or to see why their version of Basque nationalism should be considered paradigmatic or uniquely authentic.

Indeed, there have been prominent Basques who have opted to engage with Spanish political life, some of them occupying very high positions of state;[56] and to assume a homogeneous Basque sense of self-identity would be crass, not least because it would be to ignore long-inherited, intra-Basque, regional, and sectoral variations.[57] If we take a longer historical view, then the coexistence within Basque nationalist politics for many decades of a separatist instinct among some people, and a more autonomy-focused aspiration among many others, suggests the likelihood of both some separatist enthusiasm enduring, and also of the important, constraining impact of a lasting politics of autonomy rather than independence. As in many other cases, there are large numbers from the constituency in whose name terrorists have carried out violence, who seem likely to be satisfied with less than what the terrorist group has been killing and dying centrally to achieve.

It is not that ETA has lacked notable support. Their problem has been that they did not enjoy sufficient support to make their violence sustainable at a level and in a manner which would coerce the Spanish state as they had hoped it would do towards facilitating their strategic victory. ETA enjoyed enough serious backing to ensure that they had to be taken seriously, and this effect was magnified by their ongoing terroristic violence; but they did not possess enough support to give them the leverage that they would have needed in order to secure strategic victory. With admirable frankness, former ETA prisoner Arnaldo Otegi himself recognized 'very clearly that the majority of the Basques do not share ETA's armed struggle'.[58]

As so often, therefore, popular opinion has, in its variety and complexity, worked against the demands of a terrorist group, and has represented a major problem for ETA in achieving strategic victory. Diego Muro captures the essence of this nicely: 'Basque society is sharply polarized between a hegemonic Basque nationalist half which would like to see increasing autonomy, and maybe independence, and a Basque non-nationalist half which may be happy with more autonomy but wants to remain firmly integrated with Spain.'[59] Basque non-nationalists (whether supporters of the PSOE, of the PP, of other parties, or of none) have grabbed fewer headlines than ETA. But their political voices should be considered no less important for that.

ETA's problems here have been reinforced by the irony—so common across terrorist cases around the world—that what distinguished their political contribution (political violence) has been one of the most decisive factors in actually decreasing their popularity. Across much of Spain, hostility to ETA was always deep and likely to prove enduring. But revulsion at ETA's brutal violence accentuated such enmity, and caused the group also to lose much sympathy in the Basque Country itself.[60] This could be seen sometimes in very direct ways, as when the June 1987 ETA bombing of a Barcelona supermarket (a bombing which killed twenty-one people) was followed by a significant dip in electoral support for Herri Batasuna.[61] Here, as so often, the merciless killing of civilians undermined support for the politics in whose name the violence had been practised. Two of those who died at the Hipercor supermarket were children, which reinforced the horrific effects of the act. In contrast, there is strong evidence that (like Sinn Fein) ETA's political wing gained electorally when there was a ceasefire from the armed part of their nationalist movement.[62] It is true that more scholarly research should and will be done on victims of terrorism than has yet emerged;[63] it is also true that terrorist violence practised against victims has very often undermined those who carried it out, and that seems certainly to be the case with ETA.

For reactions against ETA violence abound. Jose Antonio Ortega Lara was a prison official kidnapped by ETA on 17 January 1996. On 1 July 1997 the Guardia Civil rescued him from the windowless, underground hole in which ETA had been keeping him. Having been held for well over a year in cruelly appalling conditions, Lara emerged as an emaciated, understandably very traumatized man, barely able to stand. There ensued widespread horror at this gruesome behaviour by ETA, popular revulsion here tending to undermine the organization's cause.

Again, on 10 July 1997 ETA kidnapped a 29-year-old PP councillor (Miguel Angel Blanco) from the Vizcayan town of Ermua, saying that they would kill him unless all Basque prisoners were transferred to prisons within the Basque Country. Blanco was indeed killed (ETA shooting him in the head), generating a huge popular wave of revulsion and anti-ETA protest in response. Millions had protested against the kidnapping of this young Basque, calling for Blanco's release. And the very large protests held in reaction to the killing included, significantly, events in the Basque Country itself.

So large-scale moral outrage against their brutal actions damaged ETA's campaign greatly, in a pattern clearly evident from other cases of terrorism around the world.[64] Most Spaniards, and even very many Basques, came to see ETA violence as having been profoundly wrong,[65] resulting in a huge anti-ETA mobilization during the 1990s. Support for ETA violence dwindled partly as a consequence, and had reached very low levels by the time that the group declared their armed struggle at an end in 2011. This process had been developing for some time. Survey evidence (which cannot be considered definitive, but which is in this case strongly suggestive), points to the number of those Basques who totally rejected ETA growing from 23 per cent in 1981, to 61 per cent by 2006. In the period 1978–89 the number of people in the Basque Country who thought ETA to be idealists or patriots apparently dropped from 48 per cent to 23 per cent; during the years 1981–9 the full rejection by Basques of violent methods rose from 35 per cent to 60 per cent; by the year 2000, only 7 per cent of Basques said that they supported ETA's violence.[66] More specifically, in 1979, 17 per cent of the Basque population had said that they thought of ETA as 'patriots'; by 1989, this figure had dropped to 5 per cent.[67] In 1981, 8 per cent of the Basque population had said that they offered total support to ETA; by 1996 this figure had dropped to only 1 per cent, with 51 per cent indeed offering total rejection of the group.[68] Moreover, ETA violence against civilians appears to have played a major part in reinforcing this downward shift in ETA's popularity.[69] And the rise of early twenty-first-century jihadist violence from 9/11 onwards made terrorism seem even less attractive to many people in Spain.[70] Indeed, it became increasingly clear that ETA's violence was preventing it from playing a more engaged role in negotiating some progress regarding the Basque relationship with the Spanish state.[71] Terrorism had become an obstacle.

In particular, many people across Spain shared the view that there was no legitimacy at all in ETA's violence, given the degree of autonomy that had been accorded to the Basque Country since the 1970s. Evidence regarding broader popular attitudes towards ETA suggests that these had become markedly less sympathetic between 1978 and 1989.[72] And the lower and lower levels of support for ETA within the Basque Country became clear even to committed activists themselves. In June 1992 an imprisoned ETA member, Guillermo Arbeloa, referred in correspondence to ETA's 'evident loss of popular support'.[73]

Diminishing sympathy was evident also in the dwindling amount of backing that could be secured for ETA's political party over the years. In the 1989 Spanish parliamentary elections, Herri Batasuna obtained 187,000 votes; in the equivalent elections in 1993, the figure was 175,000 votes; in 1996, only 155,000.[74] For, despite the headline-wresting violence of ETA, it was the majority, mainstream nationalism of the PNV (the constitutional Basque Nationalist Party) which was lastingly dominant within Basque politics. For years, the PNV tended easily to outpoll ETA's political wing; it has proved able impressively to gather votes across different social classes; and it has been for a very long time a crucial political and social institution in the Basque Country.[75]

Part of their success lies in the fact that so many Basque people doubt the efficacy of ETA's brutal methods.[76] Even some who had been centrally involved themselves in the armed struggle eventually began to have serious doubts about the effectiveness or desirability of terrorist violence. Jose Luis Alvarez Santa Cristina (Txelis), for example, had been a leading figure in ETA's political movement. Captured by French police in 1992, he made clear in 1997 that he felt the human costs of ongoing ETA violence to be too high, and that ETA terrorism was actually benefiting the Spanish state and discrediting the Basque cause rather than advancing it.[77] That a figure as ideologically important within the movement as Txelis could come to such a conclusion was extremely telling.

By contrast, it seemed that more moderate goals and peaceful methods did offer possibilities for forward momentum for the Basque cause. The consequences of the 1979 Statute of Autonomy might have taken a long time to have their fuller effect. But there can be little doubt that the considerable autonomy set up under this arrangement, and the dedication to maximizing its possibilities by the non-etarras who engaged with the system, represented key reasons for diminishing ETA support over the decades. When that 1979 Statute was approved, indeed, the only political party in the region to oppose it was Herri Batasuna. And once autonomy had been granted, the reality of power over a wide range of aspects of Basque life reinforced PNV dominance. In time, autonomy undercut separatism and, as elsewhere, a political arrangement was set up which fell far short of what the main terrorist organization wanted, but which offered enough for most of its putative population to accept.

So the normalization of decentralized power within a Spanish framework undermined ETA's absolutism and violence;[78] and many people in the Basque Country were, and are, clearly satisfied with the level of autonomy provided for in the 1979 Statute of Autonomy and the 1978 Spanish Constitution which had preceded and facilitated it.[79]

Could ETA claim that their violence—aimed at full separatism for seven Basque provinces—had helped bring about significant autonomy for the three provinces included in the 1979 Statute? I think this would be a hard argument to sustain on the basis of the available evidence. First, much of ETA's violence (which, as we saw, actually increased after the 1970s shift to democracy) came after the Statute of Autonomy and therefore cannot in any way be seen as causal behind it. And it certainly cannot be claimed that ETA violence determined the Spanish state's shift to democracy after Franco. Second, the effective working of the decentralized administration has been a process against which ETA has set its aggressive face, and so the practical achievements of autonomous Basque power have been in spite of, rather than because of, ETA's armed struggle. The broad legitimacy of the Autonomy arrangement is clear enough;[80] but this has been something lamented and opposed by ETA rather than occasioned by them. It has been the PNV rather than ETA that has been the dominant force in wielding such day-to-day and vital power in the autonomous region.[81]

It could certainly be claimed that the 1959–79 existence of ETA had underlined the depth of disaffection within the Basque region of Spain from an utterly centralized political arrangement. But it is also true that pre-ETA political dynamics and expression had already made that reality abundantly evident. It is hard to see ETA's pursuit of independence as a necessary cause for the autonomy enjoyed today in the Basque region.

Some had hoped that Spain's shift to democracy would speedily end ETA violence, and this proved not to emerge as the political reality (partly because of the historically explicable messiness and slowness of the transformation at ground level from one kind of regime to another after the transition away from Francoism). But the longer-term effects of the late 1970s establishment of extensive, meaningful autonomy for the Basque region *did* have a damaging effect on levels of support for ETA terrorism. As so often, lengthy timeframes are needed for proper understanding of the dynamics of terrorist violence. In committing itself to as full a realization as possible of the potential of the autonomy statute, the PNV adopted what turned out for many people to prove a credible policy. Did the continuation of ETA violence make the success of this PNV project seem more significant for the Spanish state as a way of satisfying Basque aspirations? Perhaps, and it would be wrong to draw an utterly clear line of division between constitutional and violent Basque nationalists. In the early 1980s, for example, it seems that the majority—admittedly, a small majority—of PNV supporters thought that ETA were patriotic idealists.[82] But the overwhelming picture is clear enough. For most Basques in Spain, the partial freedoms and autonomy set up in the late 1970s do suffice and do work, and ETA's terrorism did comparatively little to bring this 1970s deal about or to make it work. Subtle arguments have been offered suggesting that Spain's 1970s shift to democracy was not merely a top-down process, but rather one with complex roots also in longer-term, grass-roots associational and cultural life;[83] one (largely unintended) consequence of this deeper political transition was to lay the foundations for the eventual undermining of Basque terrorism.

Did ETA violence partially work in terms of securing secondary objectives, such as revenge, the sustenance of resistance, cultural expression (whether linguistic or religious), or socialism?

It is true that ETA, over many years, succeeded in causing much vengeful violence against opponents. Such destruction, indeed, might seem to some people to be ETA's main achievement. On one estimate, the organization killed in the region of 830 people between 1968 and 2011, wounding over 2,500 others during this decades-long career.[84] Not only was a huge amount of human damage done here, but ETA killings and maimings reflected and reinforced a deep polarization between people.[85] In ETA's own view, their violence embodied a defensive response to prior Spanish aggression and incursion. As Herri Batasuna's Telesforo Monzon starkly put it, 'It is not ETA that has bred violence. It is violence that has bred ETA.'[86] In shedding so much blood in a struggle which it partly saw as justifiably reactive, ETA did succeed in exacting much revenge.[87]

Did ETA's violence help to sustain a struggle of resistance? Arguably, it lengthily did so in that the cycles of violence, counter-violence, and intensified militancy which long endured were ones which ETA terrorism decisively prompted; and there is some evidence that ETA's armed struggle did reinforce the committed radicalism and cohesive network of some Basque activists, in ways which for decades sustained the kind of vision and struggle that the etarras celebrated.[88] But, in the end, this form of commitment has waned. The eventual diminuendo which marked the conclusion to ETA's endeavours was far too muted to be considered a successful means of passing on this flame of zealots triumphantly to the next generation.

What of the culture wars? As suggested earlier, an understandable focus on ETA violence should not hide from us the wider and deeper politics of nationalism which produced and which explains it. Language has been central to that nationalism. It is true that by the late 1990s there had been a great strengthening of Euskara in the Basque Country, with the decline in the number of Basque speakers being stalled and even reversed. And this process continued into the twenty-first century. In 1996, 22 per cent of the population in Hegoalde had been Basque-speaking;[89] by 2009, 35 per cent of the people in Euskadi were fluent Euskara speakers, with about 50 per cent of the population being able to understand it.[90] Crucially, however, a contextual reading shows that these changes had been brought about centrally through non-violent education work within the Basque Autonomous Community, through education policies and initiatives and subsidies which owed nothing significant to ETA at all. In contrast to Navarre and Iparralde, therefore, there has indeed been a practical advancing of this vital aspect of Basque nationalist ambition in the territory in which significant autonomy within Spain has allowed for peaceful development work to be done. This represents one of the most powerful arguments in favour of the approach adopted by those who embraced and made something of the 1979 Statute of Autonomy.[91] And it does not involve ETA terrorism decisively securing Basque cultural goals. Whatever the difficulties we face in establishing causality in human activity, the evidence firmly points here to there having been no major role played by ETA violence in bringing about language change.

ETA's politics increasingly became divorced from Catholic religion, and there is little therefore to be credited to the violence in positive religious terms (although for a long time there was significant support for the organization from among sections of the Basque clergy). Rather similarly, perhaps, the socialist commitment of ETA has diminished over the years of its struggle.[92] But for those who had espoused a Marxist socialism, politics has certainly not developed in positive directions. Indeed, as time progressed, ETA's socialism became rather eclipsed by an emphasis on its vanguardist, separatist, nationalistic violence.[93] So there was disappointment too in relation to this secondary goal.

Was ETA able sufficiently to determine the political agenda that it achieved partial strategic success of that kind? It is certainly true that years of ETA violence have reinforced the importance within the Basque Country and wider Spanish politics of addressing the relationship between the Basque region and the rest of Spain. But, taking a longer-term view, we would have to note that the profound importance of the tension between Basqueness and Spanish centralism long pre-dated ETA violence; that in other, overwhelmingly non-violent, separatist contexts (Catalonia, for example) the issue of centre-versus-region has been tremendously salient, despite the absence of ETA-style aggression; and that the ultimate shape of what appears to be a largely popular political arrangement is one which ETA long and loudly and very violently opposed. So over time they have been substantially *un*able to determine the political agenda as they would have preferred. There has remained a sense that full Basque separation is not available or necessary, as well as an overwhelming view sustained by most Spanish political parties that ETA was not a legitimate player in representing Basque opinion.[94] Peacefully democratic rather than violent non-state politics were sustained as the way forward. I think that ETA's violence has helped to reinforce the fact that political debate in the Basque Country continues to revolve around the issue of self-government;[95] but they have largely failed to determine the political agenda in a way that ruled out the dominance of alternative, rival politics.

Tactically, has ETA terrorism worked at an operational level? They certainly had some tactical-operational successes. During 1976–86, ETA killed thirteen generals,[96] for example. Spectacularly, on 20 December 1973, the organization killed the Spanish Prime Minister, Admiral Luis Carrero Blanco, in a bomb explosion while he was returning from Mass in Madrid. Carrero Blanco was Franco's right-hand man, and this operation was a striking tactical success. As a consequence of this dramatic attack, indeed, ETA's reputation rose as a force which could actually do things, and the number of people wanting to join the organization notably increased.[97]

But in many other ways and cases the tactical-operational record of ETA has been much less impressive. Even in its earlier days the organization had suffered many tactical blows at the hands of the Spanish state.[98] And during the early 1990s ETA then suffered a series of crucial setbacks against the security forces, with significant figures being arrested and the number of ETA killings going down. From 1992 onwards, it seems that there was a stark decline in the organization's military capacity and strength. As so often in effective counter-terrorism, coordination between various actors was important, for the ability of the Spanish state to counter ETA operationally owed much to improved relations with France. During Franco's rule, the French state had sometimes tolerated ETA members living in France, seeing them as fleeing from a dictatorial regime. But when Spain shifted to democracy this began to change and, during the 1980s and 1990s, there emerged much more cooperation between the two states against ETA, with the result of closing down the previous opportunities which had existed for terrorist sanctuary. An agreement of 14 June 1984 provided for closer cooperation between Spain and France on such issues; and the transfer of ETA suspects from France to Spain grew in the 1980s.

So too did particular tactical successes against the terrorist organization. In April 1986, for example, Domingo Iturbe (Txomin)—ETA's supreme leader—was captured by French police. Again, on 29 March 1992, Franco-Spanish cooperation led the French police to be able to capture several ETA leaders in a farmhouse in Bidart in the south of the country. Those captured included Jose Luis Alvarez Santacristina (Txelis), Francisco Mugika Garmendia (Pakito), and Joseba Arregi Erostarbe (Fiti)—all leading members of ETA's executive committee. This represented a major setback for the group, and rather reinforced the sense that ETA was being, if not militarily defeated, at least forced onto the back foot or even onto the ropes operationally. Cooperation between Spain and France, and intelligence-led police work, were between them severely constraining ETA's capacity for terrorism.[99] During 1988–97 in France there were 823 arrests and 253 imprisonments for activities relating to ETA.[100] Again, in May 2008, the head of ETA's political wing was arrested in Bordeaux.

Indeed, more broadly, anti-ETA police work did much to undermine ETA's operational capacity. During Aznar's time in office, 634 alleged ETA members or sympathizers were detained in Spain and another 331 in France.[101] The list of counter-ETA successes is impressive. One of ETA's key military leaders, Miguel Garikoitz Aspiazu Rubina (Txeroki), was detained in November 2008. Other etarras were similarly apprehended: Jurdan Martitegi (Arlas) in April 2009; Mikel Carrera Sarobe (Ata) in May 2010; and in 2010 as a whole, over 100 alleged ETA members were detained. 27 May 2013 saw a Spanish–French joint operation lead to the arrest of two etarras in the south-west of France; in October 2013, further French–Spanish collaboration led to the detention of leading ETA figures Izaskun Lesaka and Joseba Iturbe.

ETA's operational and other capacities have not been governed entirely by Spanish state policies and interventions, of course, but respond in practice to many different and interlinked factors.[102] But the sustained actions of the Spanish (and, increasingly, also of the French) state did put serious pressure on the organization through the decimation of their ranks with arrests. As noted, it was not that the state had defeated ETA utterly. But it had contained its violence operationally to the point at which ETA's capacity to exert Clausewitzean pressure on the Spanish state had been decisively limited. Here a vital issue was the will of the state actually to face the group down. Where terrorists' state opponents prioritize what is at stake politically, and commit themselves enduringly to facing down their non-state enemies, the likelihood of terrorist efficacy is greatly diminished. Operationally, at least by 2004, ETA had been substantially contained and their actions limited operationally.

What of other tactical considerations? In terms of interim concessions, ETA sought the repatriation of Basque prisoners who were held in jails around the rest of Spain, but they did so without much success. Their violence did prove more effective, however, in generating funds. ETA had long had some success in securing ransom payments through kidnappings and hostage-taking; during 1993–6 alone, kidnappings yielded the group over 2,000 million pesetas.[103] They also did some successful work in terms of securing publicity. Despite having much lower levels of backing than the PNV, for example, they yet seized local, national, and international headlines in ways that dwarfed their constitutional rivals.[104] Violence generated salience, spectacularly so with killings such as that of Admiral Carrero Blanco. But this publicity could work against the group's ideology also. For the publicity secured through terrorism also made many people think that Basque nationalism was somehow identified with such cruel violence. If the association of Basque nationalism with terrorism was one of ETA's enduring achievements,[105] then it might be judged a far from entirely successful tactical endeavour.

Did ETA's violence undermine their opponents? It did make the existing political situation seem uncomfortable, and at times even unsustainable. There was considerable economic damage done, with strong evidence existing of the harm done to the Basque economy by the organization's lasting campaign.[106] More generally, one study suggests that between 1968 and 1991 terrorism in Spain (within which ETA was the most serious agent) reduced net foreign direct investment by 13.5 per cent; another study suggested that between 1993 and 2008 ETA violence cost Spain nearly 700 million euros per year.[107] And profound local polarization accompanied economic damage. Joseba Zulaika's pioneering fieldwork exemplifies this reality powerfully. During 1979–81, Zulaika worked in the Basque village of Itziar: a village of only about 1,000 people, which saw six political murders during 1975–80, five by ETA, and one by the Civil Guards. Such killings generated profound and shocking human divisions and disorientations, documented in Zulaika's brilliant anthropological study.[108]

These are serious effects, as is the broader process of undermining the Spanish state in various ways. ETA deliberately sought to provoke that state into counter-productive overreaction. And here, it did have some success. The ill-treatment of detainees, and the brutal state terrorism practised by

GAL, both undermined Spain's democratic image and reputation in more than minor ways.[109]

Sometimes, this clearly worked well for ETA's tactical campaign. So, for example, the August 1968 ETA killing of Gipuzkoa's police chief (Meliton Manzanas Gonzalez) led to a Spanish military tribunal in Burgos in December 1970 giving six etarras death sentences for the killing (subsequently changed to thirty-year prison sentences), and this in turn generated much negative publicity for what was seen as a dictatorial Spanish state.[110] But it is hard to see this undermining process as having worked ultimately for the non-state group. The legitimacy of the Spanish state and of existing arrangements is much stronger at the end of the ETA war than are the argument and the violence of ETA itself; 'by mid-2008, the inability of ETA to destabilize the Spanish political system had been made apparent'.[111]

Did ETA terrorism enable the group tactically to maintain control over a population? They certainly did carry out, for a very long time, a policy of extortion within their host community. It has been estimated that such extortion earned the organization nearly four million euros each year during 1993–2002, and nearly two million euros a year during 2003–8.[112] This strongly suggests at least some element of coercive authority, derived from the threat of violence. It also relates to our final tactical consideration, that of how far ETA terrorism produced organizational strengthening. The issue is complicated here. ETA's organizational record is far from unproblematic. The movement was long riven with damaging splits and schism;[113] and, although it proved impressively enduring over several decades, its organizational work pre-dated its campaign of systematic violence, and so one cannot assume that terrorism was essential to whatever organizational success the separatists enjoyed. Between 1959 and 1968 ETA built up an organizational, activist structure and got themselves established; they held their first assembly in 1962, long before they began serious violence. Also, as noted, the longer their campaign of terrorism continued, the less alluring the movement seemed to be to many people. Since the mid-1980s the rate of recruitment to ETA appears significantly to have fallen,[114] which hardly suggests that the violence offered unambiguous organizational benefits for the militant Basque separatists.

In another sense, however, could terrorism have offered organizational rewards, with violence ensuring that ETA enjoyed a role as communal interlocutors and representatives of the Basque cause in negotiations and political debate? There is evidence to suggest that even in the early years of Spanish

democracy in the late 1970s, ETA saw its violence as a means towards establishing a place at future negotiations, with the possible implication that
compromise might be necessary at that stage,[115] and with a clear indication
also that terrorism might yield organizational advantage in terms of wider
standing. And there is a long history of Spanish governments engaging in
various forms of exploratory or more full-blooded dialogue with ETA.
Given their minority levels of popular backing among the Basques, this does
indicate some efficacy for the violence. If a major European government
will speak with your representatives, then your organization has gained salience and purchase politically. So, for example, the negotiations in Algiers in
the late 1980s, involving ETA and the Spanish government, or the series of
Geneva and Oslo meetings during 2005–6 (again involving delegations
respectively from the Spanish government and from ETA), reflected a certain standing for the violent non-state group. And that engagement went
beyond what would have been expected for another body with the levels of
support that ETA possessed. It's reasonable to infer that their violence gained
them this dialogue.

Did ETA terrorism work in terms of the inherent rewards of struggle that
it offered to the activist etarras? Looked at in historical context, the emergent picture is mixed in terms of how far terrorism worked for different
people. There has been a certain measure of celebration of ETA members:[116]
this is especially true, perhaps, with their martyrs, but it is the case also with
their prisoner population: 'Political violence became consecrated and the
celebration of the ETA activists, dead, imprisoned, or alive, produced a mystical and emotional aureole around the movement, which penetrated even
into the smallest rural area.'[117] Also, as noted, there was much extortion by
ETA over the years and it would be naive to think that absolutely *all* of that
money went purely to the struggle. Legitimately, in their view, some ETA
activists received a salary. And the sense of purpose from ETA struggle—as
in other activist, violent movements—yielded some clear rewards.

It carried heavy costs too, of course, and these should not be forgotten.
For if we are to overcome the problem of 'Does Terrorism Work—For
Whom?' (which we encountered in the Introduction), then we need to
look in context not just at those in the relevant group who benefited, those
who had a good war; we need also to use our framework to look at the
more bleak aspects of the struggle. Many etarras were imprisoned, some
experiencing torture and other repressive treatment during incarceration. In

early 2010, for example, there were 736 Basque political prisoners in jails in Spain and France, many of them dispersed far from their families. The Spanish governmental policy of sending prisoners to diverse prison locations across Spain caused much hardship for etarras and their families and friends.[118] Again, some etarras were killed by their opponents, some died in violent accidents resulting from the struggle,[119] some were killed by their own former comrades, and there was unpredictability in relation to which people would take which of these contingent rather than predetermined routes. On 10 September 1986, ETA itself killed Maria Dolores Gonzalez Catarain (Yoyes) (Figure 12), a former ETA member who had broken with the group. Yoyes had been a leading figure in ETA in the late 1970s, then publicly broke with the organization in 1981 and became considered a traitor by the group. She was shot dead in her home town (Villafranca de Orditzia) by her former colleagues, in front of her 3-year-old child. As noted, terrorism might be judged to work very differently even for contemporary members of the same organization. Yoyes's fate was profoundly different from that of many of her ex-comrades, and deserves painfully and poignantly to be remembered alongside theirs.

Figure 12. Maria Dolores Gonzalez Catarain (Yoyes)

IV

ETA will try to exist and to struggle in the most appropriate way for the creation of a Basque socialist state, independent, reunified, and Basque-speaking.

ETA communiqué, 21 March 1978[120]

I don't believe that there is an inevitable future for the politics of Basque relationships with Spain. But the available sources are rich enough to make clear that ETA, historically, failed emphatically to secure strategic victory, or even a partial version of their central political goal, through their violence; they couldn't achieve much in terms of cultural or socialistic progress either, or in terms of determining the political agenda (beyond, perhaps, the fact of making self-government seem an even more important issue for the Basque region than would otherwise have been the case). They succeeded in exacting bloody revenge upon many people, and for a time they sustained and intensified Basque nationalist resistance (though with an ultimate fizzling out of their own resistance struggle). Tactically, they had a very mixed record: operational successes were complemented by an increasing incapacity to gain the operational day against the state; financial interim concessions were offset by broad failure regarding sought-after prisoner transfers; publicity was secured, but much of that publicity backfired on them in terms of the popular-opinion reaction to the violent acts being publicized; Spanish enemies were provoked into clumsy overreaction, but the Spanish state ended up being reinforced in the eventual arrangement which seems to have emerged; violence allowed for coercive control over many Basques, but the organization which practised that violence ended up being unable to continue meaningfully, despite having had success in forcing the Spanish authorities to engage directly with it. And inherent rewards existed, but alongside much costly suffering also.

One problem for ETA was the strong degree to which the Spanish state remained committed to the enduring unity of Spain (more fervently committed, I would suggest, than is the case with the UK government in relation to Northern Ireland's place within the union. In the final analysis, and whatever their similarities, each case study is unique). So, while the struggle between centralism and regionalism in Spain is a historically long-rooted one and is unlikely to dissipate utterly any time soon, there seems also a great obstacle in the way of any further progress towards ETA's ideally pre-ferred, separatist outcome.

And that central difficulty for them, politically (that they were unable through violence to move forward toward the kind of self-determination that they sought), needs to be set against the appalling suffering caused over so many years by ETA's violence.[121] Listening to first-hand sources makes clear that many who were ETA activists have candidly now admitted the limitations to what they could achieve. So, for example, former ETA leader Francisco Mugica ('Pagito') was among those incarcerated figures who in August 2004 wrote to the ETA leadership stressing the limited successes of the group's violence to date.[122] And by the early twenty-first century people like Otegi and Antxon seemed to have come to the view that ETA violence was actually impeding rather than facilitating the fulfilment of Basque polit-ical goals. As so often with terrorist groups, there had emerged a profound mismatch between what ETA traditionally demanded, and what its violence put it in a position to be able plausibly to command. So even a very meas-ured and empathetic scholar such as Teresa Whitfield has observed not only that ETA's decisions 'betrayed a callous disregard for human life', but also that they were 'based on a consistent overestimation of the concessions that it might prove possible to force upon a Spanish government at the negoti-ating table'.[123]

As noted in the Introduction, there are problems with counterfactual analysis if the process is pushed too far.[124] But there is a helpful comparison within Spain which suggests that some counterfactual reflection might be of use. Would it have been possible for at least as much progress regarding separatist mobilization to have been achieved by the Basques without vio-lence? The fact that it is now Catalonia (through overwhelmingly a non-violent struggle) which has gained greatest separatist charge within Spanish politics hints that this might indeed have been a possibility.[125]

It is true that Basque and Catalan nationalisms are very different in some ways.[126] But still the point remains: Catalonian nationalist energy and momen-tum demonstrate that violence was not essential for making the issue of regional autonomy within Spain famous or pressing or (for very many people) persuasive. Against the blood-spattered past of ETA's struggle with the Spanish state over so many years, and their ultimate failure to secure their central objectives, this represents a markedly poignant conclusion.

Conclusion

It's entirely understandable that so many people consider terrorism to be utterly heinous, feel that terrorists exist beyond the realm of dispassionate analysis, and think that (to adapt a phrase from the most important of all books) terrorists have drunk too deeply from the wine of violence[1] for them to deserve calmly empathetic analysis. How *could* it be right, patiently to ask how far the callous murderer of a child might have been rational, or even justified, in thinking such an atrocity to be the best way of making morally necessary progress? This book has indeed attempted such calm analysis, but that should not be taken as indicating any necessary endorsement for non-state or for state-based actors who have practised such brutal violence. I think that in some cases it might be judged appropriate to use violence for political ends. Being tough-minded about it, however, most of the cases studied in this book suggest that the terrible human costs of terrorism have been far more certain than have any benevolent outcomes brought about politically by it.

Some readers will wonder whether the four case studies that are assessed in detail in this book are unrepresentative of wider terrorist behaviour (though I have deliberately avoided their all being Islamic, for example, or all being European, or all being nationalistic). But my argument is not that there is a universal pattern; I'm not suggesting that because things happen in a particular way in cases A, B, C, and D, therefore they will happen in the same way in cases E, F, G, and so forth (any more than what occurred in each case study assessed so far has involved neatly mirroring experience between the different groups—in fact, our four case studies involve organizations which are in some ways utterly different from one other). My approach in this book is rather to ask how far there might emerge at least sufficient family resemblances between different cases for us gently to paint some broader shapes (or to decide on some colours in which to paint them, perhaps). Even in order to do that, however, it makes sense to reflect across more than the cases of al-Qaida, the Provisional IRA, Hamas, and ETA. So this Conclusion will, first, look at a wider range of groups from the long terrorist past (through the lenses of our systematic framework); and, second, offer some final reflections about wider patterns which might be thought to have emerged from the book as a whole, regarding the question Does Terrorism Work?

I

The Introduction to this book set out a fourfold framework within which to try systematically to answer our question, suggesting that terrorism might be judged to work in the following ways:

1. strategic victory, with the achievement of a central, primary goal or goals
2. partial strategic victory, in which:
   (a) one partially achieved one's central, primary goal(s)
   (b) one achieved or partially achieved one's secondary (rather than central, primary) strategic goal(s)
   (c) one determined the agenda, thereby preventing one's opponent from securing victory
3. tactical success, in terms of:
   (a) operational successes
   (b) the securing of interim concessions
   (c) the acquisition of publicity
   (d) the undermining of opponents
   (e) the gaining or maintaining of control over a population
   (f) organizational strengthening
4. the inherent rewards of struggle as such, independent of central goals.

So let's consider how this pattern illuminates our reading of a wide range of groups.

As noted in an earlier chapter, a good case might be made that the Irgun's violence expedited British withdrawal from Palestine and the establishment of the state of Israel, which was the central, primary goal of that terrorist organization. It has also to be noted that other factors too pushed in the same direction, and that Irgun terrorism negatively contributed to reinforcing

anti-Jewish attitudes among many people. Moreover, taking a long, historical view (and, as hinted at in this book's Introduction when asking *for whom*
terrorism works, it can take a lifetime and beyond to see what terrorism
really produces), one might note that the troubled, violent, very divided
nature of Israel in the early twenty-first century—and indeed for many
years before that—should be set against the expectations that were held by
those who bombed in order to set up a Jewish homeland. Still, if one removes
the terrorism from this mid-century episode then one of the decisive mechanisms for pressuring the British to decide to leave Palestine is taken away.[2]
And, intriguingly, the Irgun not only believed that violence was necessary,
but indeed drew this lesson from the record of their local enemies: 'Arabs
use terror as a means in their political fight—and they are winning', as an
Irgun communiqué phrased it in 1939.[3]

What of other terrorists? The 1954–62 Algerian struggle for independence witnessed terroristic methods being deployed against the authorities in
a campaign whose scale went beyond what many observers tend to think of
as terrorism. The Front de Libération Nationale (FLN) led the anti-colonial
armed struggle against France from 1954 onwards, and contributed significantly to the French departure. This was reflected by the FLN becoming the
ruling party when independence emerged in 1962; and it was all the more
significant, given that French commitment to involvement in Algeria had
been sustained and very serious. There seems little doubt that FLN violence
did accelerate French withdrawal from the country, although the rebels also
developed other aspects of their work (courts, taxes, welfare provision) in
their attempt to delegitimize the colonial power and its infrastructure. If
terrorism worked here, then it did so as part of a wider set of activities.

Hezbollah (the 'Party of God') is a radical Shi'ite, pro-Iranian movement
formed in Lebanon in the early 1980s. Though it has done far more than
just terroristic violence, there is no doubt that it has carried out some (it was
'the "A-team" of terrorism', as then US Deputy Secretary of State Richard
Armitage put it in 2002).[4] In 1982 Israel invaded Lebanon in order to try to
extirpate the PLO leadership which was then based there, in Beirut. The
PLO did indeed leave the country. But by occupying southern Lebanon for
years, Israel now generated an angered response in the form of another key
opponent: Hezbollah. Indeed, in the words of former Israeli Prime Minister
Ehud Barak: 'When we entered Lebanon...there was no Hezbollah....It
was our presence there that created Hezbollah.'[5]

Hezbollah has been an emphatically religious group. Their February 1985
Programme set out the organization's self-image crisply enough: 'We are the

sons of the *umma* (Muslim community), the party of God (Hizb Allah)...We are an *umma* linked to the Muslims of the whole world by the solid doctrinal and religious connection of Islam...This is why whatever touches or strikes the Muslims in Afghanistan, Iraq, the Philippines, and elsewhere reverberates throughout the whole Muslim *umma* of which we are an integral part.'[6]

Hezbollah sought the expulsion of the USA and its allies from Lebanon, and to establish an Islamic government and state in their country, based on popular endorsement. February 1985:'America and its allies and the zionist entity...have attacked our country, destroyed our villages, massacred our children, violated our sanctities, and installed over our heads criminal henchmen....We have risen to liberate our country, to drive the imperialists and the invaders out of it, and to determine our fate by our own hands.'[7]

And, very famously, they have violently secured some strategic outcomes. On the early morning of Sunday 23 October 1983 a Hezbollah suicide truck-bomber attacked the US Marine barracks in Beirut, with more than 12,000 pounds of explosives. The resulting dead comprised 220 marines, 18 sailors, 3 soldiers, and 5 civilians. On the same day 58 French soldiers were killed by a second suicide-bomb-laden truck at the barracks of French peacekeepers. US and French forces had both been part of a multinational peacekeeping force sent to Beirut to bring stability to Lebanon after the situation created by Israel's 1982 invasion. But, following these devastating 1983 attacks, in early 1984 US President Ronald Reagan chose to withdraw all US combat forces from the country; the French and other international forces left at the same point. One senior US State Department official at the time commented that the longer-term implication of the US withdrawal here was that 'it appeared to terrorists that...all you have to do is hurt the Americans and you will get what you want'.[8] (Osama bin Laden did indeed repeatedly cite this US withdrawal as a sign that America had no spine for a fight and that it could be pushed around through violence.) So Hezbollah became seen as an organization 'which had succeeded in expelling the French and Americans from Beirut in 1983 through the bombing of the French embassy and a US Marine barracks. The success of these Lebanese operations became a model for other terrorists.'[9]

Years later, in May 2000, Israel unilaterally withdrew its own occupying army from southern Lebanon under pressure from Hezbollah fighters (though the scale of what was occurring here—in this later conflict—took it beyond the levels normally associated in people's minds with terrorism).[10]

Still, mixed methods of violence (including terrorism) had prompted the securing of a key goal at crucial times. Another central Hezbollah goal has been to defend Lebanon against Israel, and here the outcomes have been more ambiguous strategically. For example, the war of 2006 (prompted by Hezbollah's capture of Israeli soldiers) did enormous damage to Lebanon (economic disaster, tourist trade disaster, and infrastructural catastrophe— not to mention large numbers of dead and maimed). Indeed, in a television interview given by Hezbollah leader Hassan Nasrallah (Figure 13) on 27 August regarding the war with Israel, Nasrallah admitted that, 'If any of us [on the fifteen-member political-military council] had a one per cent concern that Israel was going to reply in this savage manner we would not have captured those soldiers.'[11]

In assessing Hezbollah's successes, we should note not only that their violence has at times taken the form more of guerrilla war than what people usually consider terrorism, but also that they have by no means utilized only violent means in pursuit of their strategic goals. As one (far from sympathetic) state source has put it, Hezbollah 'is a sophisticated, adaptive, and successful modern non-state actor that has demonstrated the ability to innovate on a large scale. By 2006 Hezbollah had developed major political

Figure 13. Hezbollah leader Hassan Nasrallah

influence within the government of Lebanon.'[12] The group has run hospitals, clinics, orphanages, schools, financial services, housing; it has helped
with the organization of services relating to water and electricity supplies; it
has governed at local level (with some success, efficiency, and professional-
ism), and it has built a strong social fabric of communal support. If Hezbollah's
terrorism has brought it salient strategic successes, then it has done so as part
of a wider repertoire of work. (Here, a contextual historical reading points
clearly to the need for a definition of terrorism which allows for it forming
part of wider campaigns of violent and non-violent activity.)

What of other cases? The chances of an American being killed by terrorists thankfully remain very low ('I calculated the probability of an American
dying in a terrorist attack for 2005, and it is less than one in five million'),[13]
although wider definitions of what constitutes terroristic violence would
write the phenomenon more prominently into the USA's past than is often
assumed to be appropriate ('in fact, violence aimed at inspiring terror in
order to impose political objectives has never lain far beneath the surface of
American life').[14] It seems that nearly 20,000 African-Americans were killed
by the Ku Klux Klan between 1868 and 1871 alone, with thousands more
being killed well into the twentieth century.[15] Was this, to take a very painful
example, not the use of deliberately terrorizing violence for expressly political purpose?

In a politically opposite direction, John Brown (a white abolitionist,
committed to opposing slavery) turned emphatically to terroristic methods
in this cause in the 1850s, thinking that only terror would be effective. He
was captured in 1859 and hanged in December of that year; he saw himself
as acting on God's behalf, and thought that he was fully justified in using
terror against pro-slavers. Brown's group deployed very brutal violence
against pro-slavery families in May 1856 in Kansas, with the ultimate aim of
destroying the slave-holding order altogether. His acts did not spark the
large-scale rebellion that he had hoped for, and though his trial enabled him
to demonstrate the viciousness of the slave-enforcing order, this was (at
best) terrorism succeeding at one remove—where terrorist violence had
failed, the publicity and rhetoric afforded attention by such violence proved
perhaps slightly more efficacious. In this instance, eventually, slavery was
brought to an end through a very different set of dynamics from the small-
scale violence used to pursue it by this American terrorist.[16]

Much later, but also with a small measure of ambiguous outcome, in
post-Second World War Malaya there emerged fierce tension between sections

of the local population and the British rulers. On 16 June 1948 the Malayan People's Anti-British Army (MPABA) killed three European planters and—from February 1949—the MPABA was renamed the Malayan Races' Liberation Army (MRLA). There ensued a communist insurgency against British rule, the latter half of 1948 seeing over 1,200 attacks, with nearly 150 members of the security forces killed. By 1950, the conflict involved greater intensity still, with nearly 5,000 violent incidents, and 942 communist rebels and 889 security force personnel dying. The Emergency came to an end on 31 July 1960, with the MRLA having been contained and depleted; but in 1957 Malayan independence had effectively been secured.

The Malayan counter-insurgency campaign is often seen as having been a success, but it involved in fact rather slow learning. At the start, there was no sense of the importance of winning 'hearts and minds', but rather a pattern of village-burning, poor intelligence, and fatally lethal kinetic methods.[17] This did change, with an increasing emphasis on police-led, intelligence-based counter-terrorism, with counter-terrorism being strengthened by recruitment to the police from the Chinese community itself, and with a shrewd recognition of the importance of credible political and propagandist argument. Overall, far more than terrorism had been involved in this broader insurgency; and the strategic outcomes were in any case mixed.

Involved in Kenya since the nineteenth century, Britain disengaged after a brutal 1950s insurgency (again, anti-British terrorism was deployed, but so was a larger scale of violence than most people consider terrorism to involve; 'terrorism was closely intertwined with insurgencies throughout the twentieth century').[18] The Kenyan Mau Mau rebels carried out much very brutal violence, and not without some effect. Even General Sir Frank Kitson (himself a famous military opponent of the Mau Mau struggle) acknowledged that the Kenyan insurgency had weakened the settler population in Kenya, thereby making more likely the subsequent advancement of African rather than settler power and interests in the country; the Mau Mau's efforts, he judged, 'were not entirely in vain'.[19] But the insurgency was itself defeated by the British, without securing the anti-colonial aim of expelling Europeans and European authority.[20]

Ulster loyalist paramilitaries could perhaps claim that their violence helped to prevent British withdrawal from Northern Ireland, since it presented the grim prospect that British attempts to move in that direction would produce much higher levels of bloodshed rather than peace. In the words of ex-UDA (Ulster Defence Association) leader Jackie McDonald: 'A lot of us would like to believe that if it wasn't for the UDA or the loyalist paramilitaries we would be in a united Ireland now. And there's arguments for and against that. But I think we did an awful lot to keep Ulster British.... The [Provisional] IRA knew they couldn't beat the Ulster people. We just weren't going to go away, we weren't going to give up.'[21] As other former UDA activists expressed it: 'I do believe we did achieve our core objectives'; 'I'll believe to the day I die that our strategy from the middle 1980s brought the [Irish] republican movement to their knees.'[22]

Causation is difficult to establish here, since there was so much else that also worked in favour of Northern Ireland remaining within the United Kingdom (the need for economic stability, the views of the non-violent majority of Ulster's unionists, the reluctance of the UK government to be seen to yield to PIRA violence). But the evidence makes clear—as established earlier in this book—that one reason for the Provisional IRA's shift towards a more modest set of immediate goals, and towards ending their own armed struggle, was the recognition of there being a stalemate in the northern conflict; and part of this relied upon loyalists making clear that their violence would not disappear. In this sense, it seems to me that loyalist violence in Northern Ireland did contribute towards the securing of Northern Ireland's current place within the union. Significantly, however, the kind of Northern Ireland that they produced (one in which ex-PIRA figures have significant influence, and where power is shared between unionists and Sinn Fein) is one containing much that loyalists consider extremely distasteful.

Formed in 1912, the ANC (African National Congress) long pursued majority rights in South Africa. It abandoned non-violence in 1960–1 and did practise some terroristic opposition to the state. In December 1961 leading ANC figures (including Nelson Mandela and Oliver Tambo) set up Umkhonto we Sizwe (Spear of the Nation, shortened to Umkhonto). This group effectively represented the armed wing of the ANC. The governing party in the country since 1994, the African National Congress had also engaged in much less aggressive resistance to the apartheid state as well; and it formally renounced violence in August 1990, saying that its campaign of violent resistance had ended.

How far was it Umkhonto violence which ended apartheid, and how far was this due to other factors? There were international sanctions, and the power inherent in the vast numbers of people suppressed under apartheid made its enduring prospect hard to sustain. As one expert has nicely phrased it, 'Terrorism was a relatively minor element in the final triumph of the

ANC, which benefited from an internationally supported popular uprising in South Africa and arguably took power despite the activities of the MK [Umkhonto], not because of them.'[23]

At the level of strategic victory, therefore, there are undoubtedly claims that can be made about success, albeit that some of what we have just discussed contains much ambiguity. But it is also striking how many terrorist groups and individuals have found their activities resulting in clear failure in terms of their central, strategic goals. In relation to wider political ambitions, violent anarchists of the late nineteenth and early twentieth centuries cannot be judged successful ('they failed miserably');[24] 'the anarchists did not succeed in transforming society by making it non-hierarchical and non-authoritarian';[25] late nineteenth-century anarchist terrorism 'achieved nothing beyond the individual tragedies of those people killed and maimed. They had no significant impact on the domestic or international politics of any of the countries concerned, and certainly did not collapse the social order';[26] 'while anarchists were responsible for an impressive string of assassinations of heads of state and a number of particularly notorious bombings from about 1878 until the second decade of the twentieth century, in the final analysis, other than stimulating often exaggerated fears, anarchism made little tangible impact on either the domestic or the international politics of the countries affected'.[27]

Anarchism did produce some emblematically memorable acts of violence, of course. On 4 May 1886 at the Haymarket Square in Chicago, a bomb was thrown at police during a riot at a labour agitation meeting. Four anarchists were hanged (11 November 1887) for the crime (which killed seven police officers), although those hanged had not been responsible for the bomb itself. It has never been established who actually threw it. Frank Harris's famous novel *The Bomb* is based on this episode, attributing the bomb-throwing to a man motivated by rage at social injustice ('our competitive system is an organized swindle') and at repressive state brutality, as well as by devotion to an inspiring anarchist leader. The character in question, Rudolph Schnaubelt, ends his life in misery and isolation, though convinced that the Chicago bomb-throwing had helped to achieve some progress towards better treatment for the American oppressed, and clear that his own life had been enriched through knowing his bomb-making anarchist mentor.[28] In historical reality, however, anarchist violence pitifully failed to secure its central goals.

From the more recent past, Uruguay had been reasonably peaceful, as a well-established democracy, until the late 1960s. During 1968–72, however, there emerged an upward trend in violence, with a striking rise in the number of terrorist incidents year by year: 1968 (56), 1969 (63), 1970 (129), 1971 (103), 1972 (321).[29] The Tupamaros (the Movimiento de Liberación Nacional, or National Liberation Movement, or MLN) was a Marxist terrorist group, and the most important of the anti-state formations. First established by a set of intellectuals in the early 1960s, until 1969 they mostly concentrated on organization and the development of their ideas, the latter consisting of four main elements: exhausting peaceful attempts at change; recognizing the necessity of force; acting to promote unity; and defining politics by action, rather than merely by ideas. The MLN were responsible for the bulk of anti-state Uruguayan terrorism, but ultimately they were crushed without securing their Marxist, central goal of shifting Uruguay decisively to the left. In early 1972 the Tupamaros began a new offensive against the Uruguayan armed forces; but by late 1972 the state had decisively beaten them. Indeed, the army had been crucial to this process and in June 1973 a coup saw the military take power and run Uruguay for the next twelve years. The MLN's terroristic pursuit of a leftist alternative to Uruguayan democracy had in practice resulted in a harsh military regime which had crushed them.

The German Baader–Meinhof Group (or Red Army Faction, RAF) fitted into a wider existence of Marxist terrorist groups from the late twentieth century in western Europe, some sharing explicitly an anti-imperialist politics which was interpreted globally; so the RAF 'encapsulated the revolutionary spirit and anti-establishment attitudes typical of left-wing terrorists in other western countries at the time'.[30] The central players in the gang were Andreas Baader (1943–77), Gudrun Ensslin (1940–77; Figure 14), and Ulrike Meinhof (1934–76), with Baader and Ensslin being the main driving influences, despite the group's famous name. Their anti-capitalist radical politics was largely that of bourgeois rejectionism rather than proletarian uprising and—drawing some inspirational example from the Tupamaros in Uruguay[31]—the group sought a Marxist promised land, strongly opposed the USA's engagement in Vietnam, adopted deeply anti-Israeli and anti-imperialistic politics, and wanted to provoke the West German state into revealing its supposedly true, fascistic quality and character (and to destabilize and overthrow that state). In each of these central aims and causes they were disappointed.

There was a somewhat Burkean flavour to the RAF's strategic failure ('those who attempt to level, never equalize');[32] and the West German state's legitimacy proved more durable than the revolutionary ambitions of the

Figure 14. The RAF's Gudrun Ensslin in 1972

Baader–Meinhof cult itself. In Baader's own words from January 1972: 'We are here to organize armed resistance to the existing property-based order and the increasing exploitation of the people';[33] and violence was central to their attempt to overthrow liberal democracy in West Germany (Ensslin, on 16 October 1968: 'We have found that words are useless without action').[34] In dismal practice, however, the RAF's violence utterly failed to bring about the central goals that they sought. Similarly, the Italian Red Brigades (Brigatte Rossa) clearly failed to bring about the social upheaval or the revolutionary state that they had centrally wanted, the endurance of the existing Italian state fitting a pattern whereby states tend in fact to outlive their non-state terrorist opponents.[35]

The Greek Revolutionary Organization 17 November (17N) represented another profound strategic failure. A self-consciously revolutionary group, they aimed to use violence to advance the cause of Marxist politics, wanting to uproot the existing political and social system in Greece. Hostile to what they saw as the facade of Greek democracy, and very hostile indeed towards the USA and its imperial influence, they tried to generate resistance and disaffection and to mobilize the public in a Marxist direction. 17N held the belief 'that socialism in Greece could only be achieved through an armed struggle under the leadership of a revolutionary, anti-capitalist vanguard'; but in practice they 'never really managed to affect Greek political and social structures'.[36] There was little real popular sympathy for their methods or their particular version of left-wing politics, and 17N's actions and philosophy gained insufficient purchase on most Greek people, despite the group's notoriety.

Peru's past is strewn with problems of political violence. During the period 1930–68, the military ruled the country for eighteen of thirty-eight years; they also controlled Peru between 1968 and 1980. In the latter year, however, democracy was restored, though the ensuing period witnessed much political violence. The Maoist group Sendero Luminoso (the Shining Path) had been founded in 1970 by its subsequent leader, the cultured philosophy professor Manuel Ruben Abimael Guzmán Reynoso—known as Guzmán (Figure 15). The Shining Path's leftist campaign of terrorism lasted for two decades, beginning in 1980 with operations against the regime in Lima.

Figure 15. Abimael Guzman, leader of the Shining Path, 1992

Initial actions were comparatively minor. But the group soon became a major tactical challenge to the Peruvian state's authority; 'In the space of the first six years of operations, Sendero may have carried out as many as 12,000 terrorist actions, resulting in a possible death toll as high as 10,000.'[37] Guzmán wanted a Marxist revolution in Peru and by the early 1990s his group had brought chaos to the country. Their activities involved an overlapping between terroristic methods (as usually understood) and wider guerrilla resistance (by the early 1990s Sendero were estimated to possess around 10,000 active members, with at least five times that number of supporters).[38]

In 1992 the state's judicial processes were suspended in favour of a more repressive response to the terrorist threat. Much harsh violence (terrorism?) was used by the state in its war with the Shining Path, and on 12 September 1992 Guzmán himself was captured. This decisively helped to defeat the movement. Publicly displayed in humiliating fashion, he called on his followers to end their violence. The Shining Path's campaign was brought to an end, without the central goal of a Maoist state having been secured. Guzmán had launched the 1980 campaign of violence with the declaration that he and his comrades were beginning 'the strategic offensive for world revolution', with the coming half-century destined to see 'imperialism's dominion swept away along with all exploiters'.[39] In practice, even in his Peruvian context, he was unable to bring such heady change near to fruition.

Kashmir has seen high levels of terroristic violence over decades. The Indian state of Jammu and Kashmir is divided into three areas: Ladakh (dominated by Buddhists and Shia Muslims, with fewer than 300,000 people); the Kashmir Valley (Muslim-dominated, with five million people); and Jammu (where Hindus represent a slight majority, and where 4.5 million people live). In Kashmir and Jammu, some Muslims favour independence, others favour absorption into Pakistan, and still others would like greater autonomy but with links still to India. The Jammu and Kashmir Liberation Front (JKLF) deployed violence in pursuit of independence for Indian-administered Jammu and Kashmir: formed in 1964, the group was revivified in the mid-1980s, and aimed centrally for Jammu and Kashmir to be independent of India or Pakistan.

Most Kashmiri armed groups have collapsed (with considerable help from Indian counter-insurgency in suppressing them, it should be said). The 1987–90 insurgency by the JKLF and others in Kashmir began as low-level violence and then escalated. In its early phase, the JKLF's campaign involved quite small numbers of fighters; they became more popular during 1990–2

and achieved a wide measure of support. But the JKLF collapsed and frag-
mented by the mid-1990s, without achieving their central aim. India faced
down the group and its fellow rebels, and Indian counter-insurgency was
broadly successful. The JKLF itself had begun to fragment in the late 1980s;
that schismatic process grew faster in the early 1990s and the organization
withered. By mid-decade, the JKLF had weakened considerably. Political
damage had been done to the region, with high personal and societal costs
from the violence and great instability. But Kashmiri independence had
emphatically not been secured.[40]

Again, the Free Wales Army—or FWA: Welsh separatists of the late twentieth century who sought to use violence to achieve independent statehood—failed miserably in their small-scale efforts.[41] Yet again, the Revolutionary
Armed Forces of Colombia (Fuerzas Armadas Revolucionarias de Colombia,
or FARC) were set up in 1964. Their central (still elusive) aim was the establishment of a Marxist state in their country. Operating more at the level of
a guerrilla organization than is the case with some other groups using terrorism, by 1978 FARC had 1,000 soldiers; by the later 1990s they were
estimated to possess 17,000 troops.[42] Still, their central goal has not been
realized through their violence.

Argentinian guerrilla groups during 1969–79 employed terrorism as well
as guerrilla violence, making clear lines of demarcation difficult. But it is
evident that, while non-state groups enjoyed significant levels of support
during those years, between 1976 and 1983 military juntas ended guerrilla
violence in Argentina (albeit using some morally reprehensible and brutal
methods), without those anti-state groups gaining their central goals.[43]

Sri Lanka's Tamil–Sinhalese war involved different layers of violence,
within which the campaign of the LTTE (the Liberation Tigers of Tamil
Eelam, or Tamil Tigers) undoubtedly carried out some terroristic acts. An
island of twenty million people drawn from three main ethnic groups
(Tamil, Sinhalese, Muslims), from 1948 onwards Sri Lanka was independent.
From the 1970s until 2009 there was sustained violence by Tamils against
the Sri Lankan state, most of it occurring in the northern and eastern parts
of the country. The neo-Marxist LTTE sought an independent Tamil homeland ('Tamil Eelam', a Tamil state in the northern and eastern region of the
country), the existing balance of power within Sri Lanka not suiting their
interests as they would have wished. The state's population make-up favoured
the Sinhalese: 74 per cent Sinhalese, 16 per cent Tamil (comprising 6 per
cent Indian Tamils, 10 per cent Sri Lankan Tamils), 10 per cent Muslims;[44]

and after independence the Sinhala community dominated the state regime and rather discriminated against the Tamil people.

In 1973 the Tamil United Front (TUF, which had been formed in 1972) opted to work towards an independent state; the Tamil United Liberation Front (TULF) was also formed in 1972, and in 1976 this political party started calling for a separate Tamil state, to be achieved through constitutional methods; in 1973 the more radical Tamil National Tigers (TNT) emerged under their founding leader Velupillai Prabhakaran (1954–2009; Figure 16) and was renamed the LTTE in 1976. So—as so often—the main terroristic group emerged not only from a tension over the appropriate boundaries involving nation and state, but also from a wider and complex pattern of other activists.

As noted, the violence in Sri Lanka at times went beyond what most people consider terrorism (with a civil war commencing in 1983). But the LTTE (which had by 1986 become the dominant Tamil separatist organization) did use terroristic methods (including suicide bombings) during its long career. Yet that career ended in brutal defeat, without the establishment of the sought-after Tamil homeland. A fierce 2006–9 campaign ended with the Sri Lankan state killing many of the LTTE (including Prabhakaran himself, shot in the head and killed on 18 May 2009), and securing control of

Figure 16. Tamil rebel leader, Velupillai Prabhakaran, in 2008

the entire island. This crushing state violence involved very brutal methods in 2009 (certainly a case of terrorizing political violence used by a state), and these appear to have included extensive and deliberate violence against civilians.[45] But the Tamil Tigers were duly defeated, and LTTE terrorism failed in terms of its central strategic goal.

The Irish Republican Army from which the Provisionals split in 1969 became known as the Official IRA (OIRA). This latter group carried out considerable violence until 1972, and there is evidence that the OIRA was still active during the 1980s; but it fizzled out without coming close to securing its central goal of a Marxist, independent Ireland.[46] A leading member of the Official republican movement, Tomás Mac Giolla, in 1968 declared that 'The republican socialist ideology is the only one which can unite the mass of the Irish people both Catholic and Protestant', and that a 'new generation of Irishmen are creating a new revolution in Ireland';[47] in fact, his movement failed dismally to achieve anything approaching an Irish revolution, much less one which united Irish Protestants and Catholics.

The Irish National Liberation Army (INLA) also sought to use violence in pursuit of a left-leaning, united, and independent Ireland;[48] and when the group decommissioned its weapons in 2010 it did so without this strategic goal being even remotely close. And again, those militant Irish republicans who have dissented from the Provisionals' latter-day engagement with peace process politics have thus far failed in their central ambition of undoing through violence what they consider the interwoven evils of Irish partition and British sovereignty in Northern Ireland. There is now a large literature on such dissident republicanism, and none of that serious analysis holds out any hope of such small groups achieving through violence what the far stronger Provos could not secure.[49]

Former PIRA man Gerry Bradley captured something of this rather well: 'The war is over and there's little support for starting it again. Guys who want to start it again—what are they going to do different from what we did and why do they think they'll do it any better?'[50] Or, as another ex-Provo aptly phrased it, 'Physical force republicanism has been totally put beyond the Pale and the existence of [dissident republican] groups which misguidedly adhere to this philosophy only plays into the hands of the unionists and Sinn Fein, allowing them to claim the moral high ground.'[51] So, to the extent that republican dissidents are 'committed to the maintenance of an armed campaign in order to achieve a united Ireland',[52] they seem likely to fail in strategic terms. The long history of Irish nationalism's relationship with the UK state offers little to suggest that an entirely harmonious relationship between the two can be arranged while Britain retains sovereignty over Irish territory; disappointingly for dissident republicans, it also offers little evidence that their violence will overcome unionist resistance or achieve a united Ireland.[53]

In 1989 a new constitution opened Algerian politics to greater competition from political parties other than the FLN. In December 1991 the Islamic Salvation Front (the Front Islamique de Salut, or FIS, a group favouring the establishment of a sharia-based Islamic state) emphatically won the first round of parliamentary general elections in the country, but the second round was duly cancelled. The Algerian Army carried out a coup after the FIS election victory, installing their own leader in power. The new regime proclaimed a state of emergency, dissolved FIS-controlled local councils, and jailed FIS founder-members. In response, many Algerian Islamists were (unsurprisingly) enraged and their intensified approach resulted in some of them adopting violent methods, with sections from the FIS (and other, rival groups) resorting to terrorism and wider violence against the government. (This failure to respect an Islamist victory at the polls did not go unnoticed by Osama bin Laden, and he partly blamed the USA for the development: 'When the Islamic party in Algeria wanted to practise democracy and they won the election, you unleashed your collaborators in the Algerian Army on them, and attacked them with tanks and guns, imprisoned them and tortured them—a new lesson from the "American book of democracy".')[54] The Algerian civil war caused vast destruction in the country (and more than 100,000 deaths), without yielding the central, sought-after Islamic state that anti-government rebels aimed to secure.

Aum Shinrikyo (Aum Supreme Truth) was a religiously millenarian cult founded in 1987 by the Japanese mystic Shoko Asahara. The group was responsible for the 20 March 1995 no-warning attack on the Tokyo subway system: here, sarin nerve gas was released on several subway trains, twelve people were killed, and thousands of others were injured. The humanly awful attack gained publicity, but Aum Shinrikyo's goals were impossibilistic (very few would seriously consider Asahara's apocalyptic doomsday predictions realistic), and so their violence could not but achieve strategic failure.

So too the US Marxist group The Weathermen, or Weather Underground, failed utterly in their strategic goal of overthrowing the US government and its—as they saw it, oppressive—influence in the world. Formed in 1969 on the back of American student radicalism, the Weather Underground were—by 1977—effectively defunct, their terrorism having brought their central strategic objective virtually no closer. Also inhabiting the world of US leftist terrorists, the Symbionese Liberation Army (SLA) likewise failed dismally in the strategic realm, their sometimes eye-catching violence from 1973 to 1975 making no mark on the established order in significant fashion. Again, internationally on the far left, the Japanese Red Army (JRA)—a leftist grouping keen to overthrow the Japanese monarchy and government, but also with ties to the Palestinian cause—failed to achieve its central ambitions.

Reinforcing these examples of terroristic strategic failure are several wide-angled surveys of large numbers of groups. So Audrey Cronin's impressive assessment of 450 terrorist groups' campaigns resulted in her judging that 87.1 per cent had achieved none of their strategic aims, that 6.4 per cent had achieved a limited result, that 2.0 per cent had achieved a substantial component of their aims, and that only 4.4 per cent had succeeded in the 'full achievement of [the] group's primary stated aims'.[55] Elsewhere, she has observed, 'Terrorist campaigns rarely achieve their initial goals'; 'Instances of success are rare, especially when judged against a group's stated strategic aims'; 'Very few terror groups achieve their stated strategic aims'. In asking how far terrorist groups have achieved their central goals, therefore, Dr Cronin suggests that 'the overwhelming majority have failed, with only about 6% of groups that rely on terrorism showing full or substantial achievement of their aims'; 'terrorist successes, by which is meant campaigns that achieve long-term objectives and are then ended, are the rare exceptions'.[56] Max Abrahms's scholarly assessment is similar,[57] and is backed up by another significant study (by Jones and Libicki) which considered 648 terrorist groups operating between 1968 and 2006, and which judged that only in 10 per cent of cases did these groups end their campaigns because their goals had been secured.[58]

From a different angle, a similar judgment is offered by Erica Chenoweth and Maria Stephan. Their survey suggested that 'in most cases all types of violent campaigns are likely to be less effective than well-managed nonviolent campaigns'. In terms of central, strategic goals, Chenoweth and Stephan's work suggests that the larger participation typical of non-violent movements leads to greater numbers of points of leverage upon opponents, and therefore to greater success.[59] Early in this book I noted that terrorism is a phenomenon that is centrally focused on the pursuit of political change; the fact that—in terms of groups' main strategic goals—it tends for the most part not to have succeeded in bringing about such desired change, is therefore of high significance for us all in various ways.

But our second level of assessment involved partial strategic victory, whether through the partial achievement of central aims, the securing of secondary objectives, or a determining of the relevant agenda. How might this work beyond our four chapter-long case studies?

In the 1950s EOKA (Ethniki Organosis Kyprion Agoniston, the National Organization of Cypriot Fighters) pursued through violence the central goal of removing the British from Cyprus, and this in itself was indeed achieved (though their interwoven aim of 'enosis', or unifying the island with Greece, was not secured). The organization's campaign ran during 1955–9, beginning on 1 April 1955 with a series of bomb explosions across Cyprus. EOKA targeted the British military, British installations, and British supporters alike. A state of emergency was declared in November 1955; by the spring of 1957 the British had EOKA forces rather on the run, and numerous EOKA leaders had been killed or taken prisoner; but at the end of 1958 a solution (the Zurich Agreement) was reached between the two sides, with the result that Cyprus would become independent in 1959, with a Greek Cypriot President and a Turkish Cypriot Vice-President, and with the government and administration of Cyprus being split 70/30 as with the population, Greek/Turk. Thus EOKA disbanded in 1959 and sovereignty was duly transferred in 1960 to the independent Republic of Cyprus.

On 16 August 1960 Cyprus was declared a state within the Commonwealth, with Archbishop Makarios (Primate of the Orthodox Church of Cyprus, leader of the Greek community in Cyprus, and the embodiment of their political cause) as the first president of this independent state. The other key Greek Cypriot leader had been a Cypriot former soldier in the Greek Army, Colonel George Grivas (Figure 17). During 1951–5 Grivas had laid the foundations for EOKA. Having witnessed what had happened in Palestine, he felt strongly the need for military pressure to be applied to the British in order to bring about their withdrawal: 'it seemed to me that only a revolution would liberate my homeland.'[60]

So the picture here is reasonably complex. The Mediterranean island of Cyprus hosted two rival communities: the majority was Greek Cypriot, the minority Turkish Cypriot, and the latter fiercely opposed unification with Greece. The 1950s struggle was a brutal one and, taking the longer historical view, there was further Greek–Turkish conflict in the 1970s, and the island became partitioned between its Turkish and Greek parts. So we have here, arguably, a partial strategic success: British withdrawal was hastened under the pressure of EOKA's terroristic violence; but unification with Greece, and the unity of the island, were not secured.[61]

Figure 17. George Grivas (EOKA), Nicosia, Cyprus, 25 June 1956

What of secondary goals? Evidence for partial strategic success in terms of revenge is abundant in terrorism's long past. The Irgun and other Jewish terrorists of the 1930s and 1940s repeatedly succeeded in carrying out the violence of revenge (though at very great cost to life and stability in Palestine).[62] In May 1972 the German RAF or Baader–Meinhof group bomb-attacked a US officers' club in Frankfurt, ostensibly in revenge for Vietnam. Ulster loyalists succeeded in exacting much revenge on the northern Catholic community in their part of Ireland (Jackie McDonald: 'Once the [Provisional] IRA started attacking loyalist communities, there was always going to be the UDA. When they started killing ordinary Protestants, then the UFF [Ulster Freedom Fighters] retaliated').[63]

The post-Soviet Chechen struggle against Russia has involved famous terrorism, as part of a wider set of violent and other methods of pursuing Chechen freedom. A combination of national separatism with religious zeal has proved powerful here and, though much of the conflict exceeded what most people interpret as terrorism (the 1994–6 First Chechen War saw over 50,000 Chechens killed; the Second Chechen War of 1999–2002 involved more than 7,000 Russian soldiers dying), there has been terrorism clearly deployed on occasions. And, armed with a historically long-rooted hatred for the Russians, Chechen terrorists have exacted much revenge; the bombings in Moscow on 29 March 2010, for example, killed forty people. 'The heads of Russians will roll, they will pay for what they have done', as one fictional Chechen zealot puts it; 'Revenge, revenge, I want many heads of Russian soldiers,' says another.[64]

Similarly, achieving the secondary goal of sustaining resistance to an unacceptable status quo has been much evident in the wider record of non-state terrorism. Did, for example, Greece's 17N manage to sustain a tradition of resistance, which some later terrorists have subsequently continued and emulated with respect? The collapse of 17N was certainly not the end of Greek revolutionary terrorism, and it could be claimed that the organization did lengthily sustain leftist resistance; the imprisoned Koufodinas, for example, became something of a revolutionary icon.[65] Cross-setting sustenance of resistance can also be telling. The West Bank and Gaza in the early twenty-first century have seen support for Hezbollah among Palestinians, who have been encouraged and even inspired by Hezbollah's efforts and successes against Israel; indeed, Hezbollah has played a role in training and supplying anti-Israeli Palestinians in their sustained resistance.[66]

Irish dissident republicans too have succeeded in sustaining a tradition of (admittedly small-scale) militant resistance to British authority in Northern Ireland. Looking back from 2008 at 1940s Irish republicans, one leading politician from the breakaway group Republican Sinn Fein (RSF) admired their having 'helped to ensure the continuity of the struggle';[67] a similar role was being played in the twenty-first century by RSF itself. So a figure such as Ruairi O Bradaigh, who joined the IRA in the 1950s and who played a significant role in reviving armed struggle with the Provisionals, clearly did succeed in helping to maintain for many years a fluctuating tradition of militant resistance (a tradition which he had inherited from his own parents, and a process which he continued after breaking with the PIRA in 1986 because of what he considered to be their wrongful compromises).[68]

Again, many terrorist groups which have failed to bring about their central, strategic goals have managed through violence to establish the urgency and telling importance of their cause, and of the political problem which has spawned their violence. That Kashmir or the Tamil cause or Chechen rights deserve political attention on international as well as local agendas has been reinforced and partly determined (albeit at terrible human cost) by terroristic violence.

At tactical level there has been a mixed wider picture. Let's start with operational effectiveness. In 1878 a band of Russian anarchists formed Narodnaya Volya (People's Will), a group aiming to overthrow the Tsar. They embarked on a series of terroristic assassination attempts (with senior bureaucrats, and aristocrats, often being the targets); and they tried repeatedly to kill Tsar Alexander II, finally succeeding in doing so on 1 March 1881 with a bomb attack. Elsewhere, US President William McKinley was killed by an anarchist-inspired terrorist in 1901, and anarchists also killed an Italian President in 1894, the Italian King in 1900, and Spanish Prime Ministers in 1897 and 1912. The 1881 International Anarchist Congress in London had looked to encourage the violent 'annihilation of all rulers, ministers of state, nobility, the clergy, the most prominent capitalists, and other exploiters';[69] as we can see, some tactical-operational successes did indeed ensue.

Again, white supremacist John Wilkes Booth succeeded in killing US President Abraham Lincoln on 14 April 1865; the Irgun enjoyed tactical-operational successes but also failures;[70] in Cyprus, the EOKA-related Emergency cost 156 British soldiers' lives, and 238 civilians were also killed by EOKA (though 51 EOKA terrorists were also killed). West European leftists in the late twentieth century succeeded in carrying out large numbers of operations during the 1970s and 1980s: so there were 11,660 left-wing terrorist attacks in West Germany during 1969–87, and 148 deaths in Italy from left-wing terrorist assaults in the same period.[71]

But, certainly in the case of the Baader–Meinhof group, tactical-operational achievements were ambiguous. On 2 April 1968, Baader and Ensslin left firebombs in a shop in Frankfurt, their colleagues doing the same in another shop nearby. Both buildings burned, but the perpetrators were caught by the police within two days. The Frankfurt arson attacks trial began on 14 October 1968, with the four accused each receiving three years in jail; they served fourteen months and were released in June 1969 pending appeal. When that appeal was lost in November 1969, and they were consequently due back in jail, Baader and Ensslin fled over the French border. April 1970 saw Baader recaptured, though on 14 May he was freed in a violent rescue by his comrades.

The group did have some tactical-operational help and support, with striking links in the Middle East;[72] in June 1970 Andreas Baader, Ulrike Meinhof, Gudrun Ensslin, and Horst Mahler arrived in Beirut on their way to a Fatah training camp outside Amman in Jordan; but there developed friction between the Germans and their hosts. The former then returned to

Germany, carrying out bank robberies in September 1970. But Mahler was arrested, and jailed in February 1973 for fourteen years (being released on parole in 1978).

It's important to remember that there were many operations carried out: on 12 May 1972 the RAF attacked Augsburg police HQ with pipe bombs, and on 28 May they set off two car bombs outside the US Army's European HQ in Heidelberg. But (in terms of tactical-operational considerations) the West German police responded powerfully to the RAF challenge. All the leading members of the Baader–Meinhof gang ultimately fell into the hands of police, to be imprisoned; and the group's activities had been penetrated by state agents from the start. There was decisively strong support for the police from the general public against the RAF and—as so often—terrorist conspiracy was countered powerfully through the disruptive effect of key imprisonments.[73]

So on 1 June 1972 Baader, Jan-Carl Raspe, and Holger Meins were arrested in Frankfurt. A week later, Gudrun Ensslin was arrested too. In the same month, Meinhof was captured. In April 1974 Ensslin and Meinhof were moved to Stammheim Prison in Stuttgart; in October of that year Baader, Meinhof, Ensslin, Raspe, and Meins were indicted on five counts of murder, their trial due to occur the following year. Baader and Raspe were also moved to Stammheim. There were hunger strikes (with Holger Meins dying) and these elicited some support; 'In political terms, the imprisoned RAF terrorists managed to acquire more sympathizers than they had had while on the loose.'[74] Even here, however, there was a mixed picture. Among the prisoners' visitors was an ultimately unimpressed Jean-Paul Sartre. (Whatever his public comments, Sartre privately remarked afterwards: 'What an arsehole, this Baader.'[75])

On 21 May 1975 the Baader–Meinhof trial began. It dragged on into 1976 but on 8 May that year Meinhof was found hanging in her cell. In March 1977 the defendants made their last appearance in court, refusing to participate further until the issue was resolved of whether or not their cells were being bugged. On 28 April Baader, Raspe, and Ensslin were found guilty of murder or attempted murder and sentenced to life imprisonment. But on 18 October 1977 in Stammheim Prison, Baader and Ensslin were found dead, and Raspe mortally wounded; nine days later was held the funeral of all three in Stuttgart. So, for the RAF, tactical-operational successes were accompanied by terroristic ineptitude and some effective state counter-terrorism.

For their part, the Red Brigades killed former Italian Prime Minister Aldo Moro on 9 May 1978: twice Prime Minister, and a candidate for President, Moro was a seriously important figure in Italian political life. But the Moro killing also backfired, the authorities engaging in a strong counter-terrorist response with much public sympathy for their effort. Indeed, the police and courts were markedly successful in thwarting the Red Brigades operationally.[76]

The strategically futile 17N in Greece nonetheless achieved some impressive tactical operations. For twenty-seven years, the group carried out a high-profile terrorist campaign without the Greek authorities being able to convict even one member of the gang. On 23 December 1975, 17N even killed the CIA's station chief in Athens (Richard Welch); again, in June 2000, they killed the UK defence attaché in Athens (Stephen Saunders).

The Japanese Red Army or JRA might have failed in their central, strategic ambitions; but their Tel Aviv airport attack, which killed twenty-six people in 1972, did manage to bring about a tactical success of brutal, operational significance.

In the 1980s Hezbollah famously (and lethally) used the operational tactic of suicide bombings. On 11 November 1982 in Tyre they deployed a suicide bomb to attack the Israeli military HQ, killing seventy-four people; on 18 April 1983 a truck containing explosives was driven into the US embassy in Beirut, and killed nearly a hundred; most famously of all, there were the spectacular attacks of October 1983 of which mention has already been made. But there is another dimension to this story also. From 1983 onwards, the tactical efficacy of suicide attacks in Lebanon (the average number of fatalities per attack) decreased; Israeli counter-measures had real effect, and the tactic appealed less to Hezbollah as a consequence.[77]

LTTE leader Velupillai Prabhakaran was seemingly very impressed by Hezbollah's 1983 Beirut truck bombings, the idea that terrorism worked having infectious effect and generating imitation. So suicide attacks became part of the Tamil Tigers' brutal repertoire during the late twentieth century, and this involved the successful carrying out of many operations, tactically. In the words of one recruit to the LTTE, regarding suicide attacks: 'This is the most supreme sacrifice I can make ... The only way we can achieve our eelam [homeland] is through arms. That is the only way anybody will listen to us.'[78]

US domestic terrorism (like its more famous external-jihadist rival) has entered the country's literary consciousness (as in Philip Roth's brilliant creation, the anti-Vietnam 'Rimrock Bomber' Meredith Levov).[79] It has also involved some tactically adept practitioners, such as Theodore Kaczynski, the Harvard-educated Unabomber. Having become a youthful mathematics professor at Berkeley, he engaged in a lengthy mail-bomb campaign, killing three people and wounding more than twenty, over nearly two decades of eccentric violence. His targets were mainly symbols of modern technology (airlines, scientists), since he appears to have thought such developments to be undermining and threatening the human spirit. Hostile to industrial society, Kaczynski was allowed to publish his lengthy manifesto in newspapers, whereupon his brother recognized the writing style and passed identifying information to the police. Only thus was Kaczynski's weird, lengthy, and operationally effective campaign brought to an end.

Timothy McVeigh (a US Army veteran, and a right-wing, anti-government terrorist) seems to have thought that through his 1995 Oklahoma attack on the federal government in the USA he could initiate a racial war in the country. This strategic goal clearly eluded him, but the bombing of the Alfred P. Murrah Federal Building in Oklahoma City on Wednesday morning 19 April 1995 did embody a tactical-operational success. With a rental van full of homemade explosives, McVeigh drove his truck bomb into the building with devastating effects when it was detonated: 168 people were killed. The attack was partly intended to avenge the siege two years earlier of the Branch Davidian compound in Waco, Texas. The Murrah Building housed a variety of federal government agencies, including the federal bureau of Alcohol, Tobacco and Firearms (ATF) from which people had been sent to Waco to enforce firearms legislation. In June 1997 McVeigh was convicted of the Oklahoma attack, and he was executed four years later.

Despite their strategic failure, the INLA enjoyed some tactical-operational successes (including the killing of prominent Conservative Party politician Airey Neave in 1979, within the precincts of the Houses of Parliament in London).[80] More recently, the UK and Irish states have had significant tactical-operational successes against dissident republicans in contemporary Ireland, limiting their effectiveness as a result.[81] And some dissident republican violence has been markedly counter-productive itself. On 15 August 1998 a dissident car bomb in Omagh, County Tyrone, exploded with hopelessly inadequate warnings and as a result thirty-one people were killed and many more were injured. The dead included children and babies and the outrage was widespread, international, and deep. One leading member of the Real IRA (the group which, together with fellow-dissident organization the Continuity IRA, had carried out the attack) was to observe that, when he heard the news of the rising death toll in Omagh, 'I knew we were fucked. I knew there and then the entire army was fucked.'[82]

The carrying out of a terrorist operation can, of course, involve a tactical success which still contributes to a strategic setback. The Egyptian Gamaat Islamiya (Islamic Group) confronted the Egyptian state with terroristic violence during the 1980s and 1990s, attacking government officials but also what they saw as other un-Islamic targets (video stores, the tourist industry, shops selling alcohol). But this campaign in practice turned many people away from, rather than towards, the Islamic Group's cause. In July 1997 the jailed GI leadership announced a ceasefire; but GI dissidents carried out an attack at Luxor on 17 November the same year, killing fifty-eight tourists. This Luxor operation (which succeeded tactically in that it killed so many of its intended targets) so horrified people that it caused a decisive backlash against the terrorists, thereby doing them strategic damage.[83]

The Pakistan-based jihadist group LeT (Lashkar-e-Taiba, or 'Army of the Pious')[84] has also achieved some tactical-operational successes of note. On 11 July 2006 in Mumbai, seven bombs were exploded in a matter of minutes on local trains leaving Churchgate Station; 207 people were killed, and 714 injured. The bombs in this LeT attack had been aimed at commuters on their way home, and it represented a grisly, tactical-operational success. Two years later another LeT attack embodied a similar pattern in the same city. On Wednesday 26 November 2008 a sea-launched assault by ten LeT terrorists was aimed at Mumbai and went on for several days: hotels were targeted, as were a railway station and a Jewish centre. Hostages were taken, western and tourist targets were prioritized, and there emerged horrific scenes. One observer of one of the earliest incidents in the assault (at the Café Leopold) commented: 'I heard continuous machine-gun fire for fifteen to twenty minutes and when it stopped I rushed out to help and I saw nothing but rivers of blood.'[85] The attack did little to further LeT's ultimate goal of ending Indian rule in Kashmir; in killing 172 people, however, it did seize the day in shocking, surprise-based, tactical-operational terms.

Terrorists have often acted in ways that have tactically fallen apart as well, however. In one vivid example, on 23 October 2002 there began a three-day hostage crisis with 800 civilians being held by Chechen terrorists in the Dubrovska Theatre in Moscow. Russian special forces stormed the theatre, all 49 terrorists were killed, and 129 civilians were also killed in or after the raid (which had featured the state's use of anaesthetic gas). And indeed very many terrorist groups have been dismally poor in operational terms. Late twentieth-century Welsh nationalist terrorists, for example, were frequently inept in their tactical-operational work.[86]

Have terrorists succeeded tactically in securing interim concessions through violence and the threat of violence? It's a very mixed record. On the eve of the 1975 Baader–Meinhof trial in Stuttgart, six terrorists took over the German embassy in Stockholm, taking eleven hostages and demanding the release of twenty-six prisoners, including Baader, Meinhof, Raspe, and Ensslin. The West Germans refused this, the terrorists killed a hostage, explosions shook the embassy, and the siege fruitlessly ended. Again, there was the case of Hans Martin Schleyer, the President of the West German Employers' Association, and a board member of Daimler Benz. On 5 September 1977 Schleyer was kidnapped in Cologne by the RAF, his captors demanding the release of all the main Baader–Meinhof prisoners. By mid-September, Schleyer had been moved to a rented apartment in The Hague, and on 19 October 1977 a caller gave information about where his body could be found. The prisoners were not released.

Yet the terrorist record overall has included also considerable success at the tactical level of gaining interim concessions. So the PLO in 1974 was granted observer status at the United Nations, effectively coming to be seen as the legitimate representative of the Palestinian people and cause, in a manner unimaginable had its violence not been carried out in preceding years. Similarly, Black September's hijacking of a German aircraft in the wake of the 1972 Munich attack on the Olympics led to the release from custody of the surviving Munich attackers—an interim concession of powerful significance.

A less equivocal answer can be established, perhaps, regarding the tactical matter of gaining publicity (though the political effects of that publicity can be complex, and it's long been recognized that gaining publicity in itself tends not to be a sole objective—terrorist groups seek publicity in order to further the likelihood of achieving goods beyond media coverage itself).[87] Mau Mau violence in Kenya in the 1950s secured international headlines, but frequently ones which damaged their reputation by stressing what was seen as inhuman barbarity.[88] Very recently, ISIS have been shocking exemplars of the manner in which brutal violence can seize very many headlines around the world.[89] Long before that, anarchist terrorism involved a deliberate aim of securing publicity-based progress, and the headlines were certainly generated. As one distinguished scholar has phrased it, 'there have been groups which killed and bombed in order to express protest rather than in the hope of defeating their enemies. The anarchist propagandists of the deed clearly belong to this category.'[90] 1950s EOKA violence gained such salience that it did prompt the United Nations to consider Greek Cypriots' nationalist demands, making it impossible for the United Kingdom just to say that this was a domestic issue. Terrorism here brought the subject to significant international attention. Likewise, Tamil Tiger suicide bombings made the Tamil cause world-famous; and Salman Rushdie's 1988 novel *The Satanic Verses* occasioned an instance of well-publicized, state-terroristic hostility against its talented author. The novel's opening scene was (ironically) inspired by an instance of Sikh terrorism, and the book caused Rushdie to become the sought-after victim of state terrorism from a Muslim source, with an Iranian fatwa being delivered against him in February 1989 ('terrorism-by-fatwa'; and a terrorism from which the UK state lengthily protected him). The death threat here (on the grounds of supposed blasphemy against Islam) was specific and genuine and long-lasting.[91] What did it (this example of state-sponsored terroristic threat) actually achieve? There was no tactically successful operation against Mr Rushdie (thankfully), although other people were killed in relation to the book; and the wider implications are hard to determine. Rushdie himself observed many years later, 'As to the battle over *The Satanic Verses*, it was still hard to say if it was ending in victory or defeat. The book had not been suppressed, and nor had its author, but the dead remained dead, and a climate of fear had grown up that made it harder for books like his to be published, or even, perhaps, to be written.'[92] But the fatwa-based threat certainly achieved major publicity, magnifying the objections that many felt to publication of a book which they considered to transgress against their religious beliefs.

Again, right-wing Norwegian terrorist Anders Behring Breivik, whom we met in the Prologue to this book, clearly failed to achieve strategic victory in terms of redirecting Norwegian politics onto his favoured path: there has been no prospect of his vision being brought to any serious fruition through his murderous acts. But the secondary goal of lashing out vengefully at the government and at those involved in Labour politics was, tragically, more fully realized through his July 2011 actions. Did he determine the political agenda? No. Did he achieve a certain tactical success in carrying out his two-stage operation, and in securing large-scale publicity? Yes, undoubtedly so.[93] (I suspect that nearly everybody reading this book has heard of Anders Breivik.) But our framework allows us also to recognize the limitations of his work even tactically. There was no organizational leg-acy strengthened, no securing of interim concessions, and no undermining of the Norwegian state. Indeed, the 22 July Centre in Oslo itself rather subverts Breivik's analysis, and reinforces a Norwegian commitment to inclusively democratic politics. Inherent rewards were undoubtedly achieved in terms of fame, but at the cost of very lengthy imprisonment and wide-spread hostility towards the man and his violent crusade.

In April 2015 Dzhokhar Tsarnaev was found guilty by a Boston jury of carrying out the bombing of that city's marathon two years earlier. The attack of 15 April 2013 killed three people and seized attention worldwide. It had been carried out by Tsarnaev and his brother Tamerlan (who was killed by police in the wake of the attack). There can be no doubt about the atrocity securing huge publicity,[94] but—if, as is alleged, the Tsarnaevs were motivated by jihadist enthusiasm—it is hard to see there having been any grander goals achieved.[95]

In the tension between 'system upholders' and 'system destroyers',[96] how far have terrorists managed to undermine their opponents tactically? In the 1930s and 1940s, Irgun violence significantly undermined British authority in Palestine.[97] The 1950s Mau Mau (using terroristic methods as part of a larger insurgency) prompted their British enemy to act in ways that have lastingly damaged the UK's reputation—especially in terms of the British Army's coercive treatment of civilians (although careful analysis presents the complexity of British response here, the restrained as well as the ugly).[98] The FLN's violent campaign in Algeria started in November 1954 and often involved indiscriminate attacks; French reactions were themselves frequently counter-productive in their own harshness: torture by the French caused less benefit than damage to the French cause, generating much counter-productive opinion and effect;[99] more widely, FLN violence prompted harsh, repressive violence from the French, which rather backfired and reinforced anti-French sympathy.[100] Again, EOKA did provoke some hard-edged UK reac-tions. As one British policeman employed in Cyprus during the Emergency in 1958 candidly put it: 'some of the Army and security people were right bastards to the local people.'[101] Yet again, the Uruguyan Tupamaros attempted (and not without some success) to discredit the state police force against which they were in conflict.

Bangladesh-related terrorism in India has also involved a certain under-mining of state security and comfort in the recent period. In late 2014, for example, the Indian authorities expressed concern that Bangladeshi militants were hiding in West Bengal, and that the border district of Jalpaiguri had become a focal point for terrorists. One Indian state government official suggested that 'Jalpaiguri has turned into yet another terror point for JMB [Jamaat-ul-Mujahideen Bangladesh]' and that 'unrecognized madrasas in the state [were] operating as terror-breeding hubs'.[102] On 2 October 2014 two JMB activists had died in the West Bengal town of Burdwan while making bombs; and the Indian authorities were concerned about this part of their state having become a safe haven for the group. Elsewhere, in contemporary Northern Ireland, dissident Irish republicans have been unable through violence to destroy the peace process or to derail Sinn Fein from their post-PIRA politics. But they have created headaches for the UK state through engaging in sufficient violence to make the new Northern Ireland less than fully comfortable in its compromise, post-1998 arrangements.

Does terrorism work in prompting democratic states to stifle their own citizens' civil liberties, and therefore in undermining states by damaging their own political freedom, as security is privileged over liberty? There are instances of this having happened, to be sure. But it is unclear how central a goal this actually is for most serious terrorist groups. And it is also true that—even where concerns are frequently raised, as in the United Kingdom, about such issues emerging amid terrorist threats—the degradation of political freedom and civil liberty has not been extreme, and must be kept firmly in proportion.[103] Still, literary observers are among those who have caught very well the capacity of non-state terrorists to undermine much normal life. John Updike: 'In a land of multiplying security gates, the gatekeepers multiply also.... The enemy has achieved his goal: business and recreation in the west are gummed up, exorbitantly so.'[104]

Tactically, there exist many examples of terrorism facilitating control over certain populations. FARC efforts have moved partly from the achievement of their central aim (establishing a Marxist state in Colombia) towards a greater emphasis on controlling and acting as a government in the territory in which it wields great influence. The LTTE long managed to control the civilian population within their own areas, and terroristic methods were crucial here.[105] Similar patterns could be adduced from twentieth-century Algeria, Kenya, and Cyprus too.

The organizational effects of terroristic violence for terrorist groups themselves have been rather mixed. Narodnaya Volya's 1881 killing of Alexander II actually prompted the secret police to round up and execute the group's main members, and by 1883 Narodnaya Volya hardly existed any more. A tactically operational success here led to a tactically organizational failure. In Palestine, Irgun violence did succeed in writing the group into the enduring political script as a vanguard organization.[106] Organizationally, the RAF in West Germany were ultimately unable to sustain as serious a level of group as they had desired. Following the demise of the first wave, there did emerge a second generation of the movement: after the Stammheim deaths, command of the RAF moved to Brigitte Mohnhaupt, Adelheid Schulz, Sieglinde Hofmann, and Christian Klar. Their campaign of violence ran during 1973–82, this second generation focusing their energies and attacks on the US military presence in Europe. So on 31 August 1981 there was a car bomb attack on the US air force HQ at Ramstein base. But when Klar, Schulz, and Mohnhaupt were all arrested, this closed down the second generation; arrests, and people opting to drop out from this phase of the movement, effectively killed it off.

A third RAF generation carried on a limited campaign until 1998. In August 1985 they set off a car bomb inside the US airbase in Frankfurt, killing two people. On another occasion a roadside bomb was used to kill Karl Heinz Beckurts, a German industrialist. On 10 October 1986 the RAF killed Gerold von Braunmuhl, deputy to Foreign Minister Hans-Dietrich Genscher, and in 1989 they killed Deutsche Bank chief Alfred Herrhausen with a bomb. But in 1992 this latest iteration of the RAF admitted that the world had changed with the collapse of communism, and also that it enjoyed little support for its violence. Consequently, the group said that it would de-escalate its activities, and would stop killing prominent business and government figures. Not all violence ended at this point. But divisions among the few RAF people who remained further weakened them, and on 20 April 1998 the RAF announced that their project was over and that they were dissolving as an organization.

In Italy the Red Brigades declared an end to its campaign in 1984. The group had effectively fizzled out by 1982 and, significantly, it was an imprisoned leadership which announced the end of the group's violent struggle. Greece's 17N for years managed to evade police interruption. But when one of their operatives was badly injured and captured after a failed bombing on 29 June 2002, the group speedily imploded. On 5 September 2002 17N's leader of operations (Dimitris Koufodinas) handed himself in to the police; he had been on the run since the explosion of 29 June which had led to Savvas Xiros (the injured operative) being arrested. In some contrast, Hezbollah's sophisticated organizational approach has made it a key player in Lebanese and wider politics. Iran supports the group with millions of dollars each year, in addition to training and other support.[107] Indeed, Iran spent over $100 million each year between 1982 and 1987 on mosques, schools, hospitals, and charitable ventures linked to Hezbollah.[108] Such support has facilitated a strong organizational set of structures to evolve.

LTTE terrorism helped it to gain organizational dominance over other groups which were active in their own Tamil cause. For numerous other Tamil organizations had been fighting against the Sri Lankan state, yet the LTTE came to dominate among them (their violence helping them to do so). Indeed, not only were many LTTE activists impressive in their work (the Indian High Commissioner to Colombo, J. N. Dixit, commented that 'It would be difficult to come by a more motivated, educated, dedicated, and politicized insurgent or militant group than the LTTE'),[109] but there was significant organizational success for the Tamil Tigers in simply surviving so strongly for so long (nearly forty years), with comparatively impressive discipline.

Elsewhere, the jihadist LeT has retained some impressive measure of organizational cohesion and seriousness.[110] But wide-angled surveys suggest that many terrorist groups from the past have found organizational survival very difficult: 'A careful study of the life spans of the hundreds of groups listed by the MIPT [Memorial Institute for the Prevention of Terrorism] database demonstrates that the average length of time a terrorist group has survived is approximately eight years'; 'careful study of the full empirical record, across regions and types of groups, and over time, indicates that for terrorist groups, longevity is the exception, not the rule'; 'Most terrorism ends because the group employing the tactic fails and eventually disintegrates.'[111]

What of examples regarding our final layer of frameworked assessment, the inherent rewards of terrorist struggle as such? Our understanding of 'for whom' terrorism does or does not work will here require recognition of the ultimate uniqueness of (and within) each case considered. But there may yet exist some family resemblances and shared shapes.

For Irgun members there could be a sense of divinely authorized mission and purpose and meaning, and of altruistic and inspiring sacrifice for the national cause; money was less of a consideration—Irgunists did receive salaries, but rather feeble ones.[112]

Broadly, it seems not to be the case that terrorism emerges primarily from those people in the world who are poor and uneducated.[113] The Baader–Meinhof cult certainly fitted this pattern, with its frequently educated members drawn from comfortable backgrounds. They overlapped with a German student radicalism centred on West Berlin, Munich, Hamburg, and Frankfurt, and they exemplified a politics of alternative lifestyle. Baader and Ensslin were both drug users, and indeed there was much sex and drugs associated with this iconic band (Baader and Ensslin were lovers, and a species of sexual emancipation was interwoven with their revolutionism; in Baader's eye-catching words, 'Fucking and shooting are the same thing').[114] Adventure and egotistical style played their part for the group too. In their on-the-run-robbery phase, the Baader–Meinhof Group loved BMW cars, the latter becoming known for a time as the Baader–Meinhof Wagen. For a brief period, some of the RAF figures certainly did enjoy a radical counter-life, full of adventure and a certain leftist, sanctimonious posturing. So a moral self-righteousness complemented their alienation from conventional bourgeois society, and their terrorism was that of a counter-cultural bohemia.

Baader himself was the rage-filled, intelligent son of a historian and archivist. Self-confident, strong-willed, foul-mouthed, sartorially stylish, autocratic, narcissistic, surly, and possessed of a tendency towards thieving, he had dropped out of school and had a penchant for alternative, commune-based life. Ulrike Meinhof (whose father was an art historian and museum curator) was a left-wing writer and journalist who allowed herself an indulgently patronizing and self-reinforcingly dismissive view of her fellow Germans ('All they can think about is some hairspray, a vacation in Spain, and a tiled bathroom').[115] The rebelliously anti-authoritarian Gudrun Ensslin mixed radical leftism with a fair amount of dope-smoking. And they acquired much money through their aggressive methods, obtaining more than a million Deutsche Marks through bank robberies during just a few months in 1971.[116] Despite the leaders' tragic deaths, there was therefore a set of inherent rewards derived from their cult of violence.

Andreas Baader's lawyer understood Baader himself to echo the hero of Hermann Hesse's *Steppenwolf*, exemplifying a destructive, liberating rejection of bourgeois conformity.[117] Although this perhaps reinforces Hesse's own sense about people misinterpreting his novel ('of all my books *Steppenwolf* is the one that was more often and more violently misunderstood than any other'),[118] it does reflect both the fact that the disturbing novel was then a cult item in left-wing circles, and also the apparent parallels between the book's central character (Harry Haller, the Steppenwolf) and Baader himself. These do exist: Haller, the disordered, angry, disoriented intellectual, a 'hater of life's petty conventions', whose 'sickness of the soul' was 'not the eccentricity of a single individual, but the sickness of the times themselves, the neurosis of that generation' to which he belonged,[119] could in some ways be said to pre-echo Baader's own arrogantly dismissive, bohemian revolutionism. And that revolutionism offered a certain headiness of atmosphere, and an intoxicating exaltation derived from involvement with this bohemian, elitist, terroristic cult.

Attitudinally, 17N violence in Greece seems to have given some of its members a sense of pride in resistance, and of dignity.[120] A certain glamour and kudos was derived also by those who joined and engaged with the Tamil LTTE, many within their community valorizing these warriors' violent struggle.[121] And simple excitement can play its part. Former Weather Underground member Susan Stern commented, regarding her own time in that vanguard group of militants, that, 'Nothing in my life had ever been this exciting.'[122] The emotionally satisfying simplicity of impossibilistic Irish republicanism continues to enthral some in the contemporary dissident struggle, and it will probably do so enduringly for a minority. This involves adherence to a particular kind of Irish republican political principle, seen as being unbreakable unless one is to commit unacceptable apostasy. In these terms, dissidents might be seen as 'the fanatics with hurt in their eyes who stand at the back of meetings and shout . . . about sell-outs and betrayals', as one fictional account has nicely described them.[123] Overlaying this, there have clearly been some dissident Irish republicans whose paramilitary violence has involved them making financial and criminal personal gain,[124] though I do not think that such rewards offer an adequate explanation in themselves for the emergence and sustenance of dissident politics in contemporary Ireland.[125]

First-hand evidence suggests that the appeal of excitement played its part in bringing people into the loyalist UDA (it was, indeed, more 'excitement than anything else, to be truthful', which caused one man to join the organization).[126] Some loyalists also joined in order to make material gains. Ex-UDA leader Jackie McDonald is admirably frank about what some members of his former organization did in terms of pursuing personal, criminal gain. Regarding criminality among some UDA people, and the need for money to provide for prisoners' families and for buying weapons, he observed:

all sorts of things were expensive and it wasn't enough to pay dues, and it wasn't enough to go round the bar with the LPA [Loyalist Prisoners Association] box and get the odds. They had to go into criminality to finance what was going on. And unfortunately, individuals became into procurement, if you like, procuring an awful lot of stuff for themselves. And the organization started to lose its way a bit. I was in prison in '89, and when I came out in '93 on parole, I saw some of the stuff that I saw, I couldn't believe it. People drugged out of their heads. . . . Criminality, drug dealing, and greedy people, and the organization lost its way for a few years.[127]

In Uruguay the MLN or Tupamaros were successful in procuring large amounts of money through robberies and kidnappings. Broadly, the overlap between terrorism and criminality (such as piracy) is a complex one. But it is worth noting that Somali pirates allegedly earn over 150 times their country's national average wage through their piratical activities. The mid-1990s piracy here began in local waters, as an effort by vigilante Somali fishermen to provide protection through violence; by 2010 it had become a major industry (Somali piracy apparently being worth $238 m in that year).[128] In Colombia, FARC has made considerable money from drug-related activities, playing a significant role in the production and exporting of cocaine. Again, in Chechnya in the 1990s, there was profound overlap between terroristic resistance and various clear forms of criminality.[129]

This reflection on wider terrorist examples (across the strategic, the partial strategic, the tactical, and the inherently rewarding) cannot be satisfactorily exhaustive. Any attempt (as here) to present even concise contextual analysis will limit the number of cases which can be considered. Equally, had I taken a different approach, and assessed hundreds of groups, then such consideration would necessarily have been very thin indeed in terms of what could be said and understood about the specific subtleties involved in any one case. (I've spent decades studying the Irish Republican Army; but none of us has the hundreds of lifetimes necessary for developing such decades-long expertise on hundreds of organizations.)

So what I have briefly here tried to adduce so far in this Conclusion is suggestive, reasonably wide-ranging illustration of how our framework of analysis operates beyond the cases of al-Qaida, the Provisional IRA, Hamas, and ETA. This discussion suggests that terrorism has tended most of the time not to bring about its practitioners' central, strategic goals. Even where it has done so, this has often been as part of a wider range of (both violent and non-violent) activities and other factors, has contained some painful ambiguities of outcome, and has been far outnumbered by the cases where terrorism has failed to bring about the achievement of its central, strategic objectives. Partial strategic successes seem more numerous, especially in the realms of revenge and the sustenance of minority-activist resistance. Tactical outcomes vary hugely. There are vast numbers of tactical–operational successes in terrorism's long past; but these have to be set against very many instances of tactical–operational ineptitude, of the state containing and learning well to counter terrorist tactics, and of tactical–operational successes in practice doing their perpetrators considerable political damage.

At tactical level again there is a mixed record in terms of interim concessions gained, and while publicity has been resoundingly and repeatedly achieved across the world, it has often emerged in ways which discredit the cause and the perpetrators associated with the headline-grabbing violence. Tactically, terrorists have frequently undermined their state opponents (with the latter often enough playing clumsily, overreactingly into terrorist hands); and terroristic violence has allowed for considerable influence or even control over local populations too. The organizational effects of violence vary, many of them being negative, in fact. So too, while there are many inherent rewards to be derived from terrorism, these seem—in themselves—not fully to explain why people would choose the alternative lifestyle, or close-bonding cult, of specifically *terroristic* association and activity, rather than to adopt other, much less costly, forms of behaviour.

This discussion does not offer a prescriptive or predictive model for terrorist efficacy. (I don't think history is a predictive business.) But, tellingly, our discussion here of wide-ranging examples does broadly echo the far more extended analyses reached in our four case studies from this book. There are instances where our chapter studies' conclusions partly diverge from what has been summarized in the previous two paragraphs here, with the pattern adumbrated in this Conclusion being echoed only in ultimately unique ways in our four studied cases. And one would expect this, of course, since those four case studies differ even from one another (the PIRA are clearly very different from al-Qaida), and since the closer one can get to the evidence through extended analysis, the more complex the picture will appear to be. But, as we reflect on the interlinked four layers of our analysis (the strategic, the partial strategic, the tactical, and the inherently rewarding), a suggestive shape has, I believe, valuably emerged. I'm not propounding in this book a generalizable theory of terrorist efficacy (as hinted in the Introduction, I'm not convinced about how helpful such a theory would prove in contextual practice). But I do think that the evidence adduced in this book demonstrates sufficient family resemblances between our four case studies, and also across the many other groups considered in this Conclusion, to suggest something more than randomness within this aspect of our blood-stained past. What the past leaves to us for analysis is partial and often very messy, and it rarely allows for utter certainty of judgment[130] about important, evolving, and highly charged issues such as whether terrorism works. Yet this book's historical analysis has gently pointed to there being important echoes across periods and regions.

II

> For all men do all their acts with a view to achieving something which is, in their view, a good.
>
> Aristotle[131]

How, then, should our judgment about the complex efficacy of terrorism affect how we respond in future to this phenomenon?

If the pattern suggested here is accurate, then states should probably focus less on non-state terrorists' central, strategic goals (since these are unlikely to be achieved), and more on other issues instead. Since revenge has turned out to be one of the most likely areas of terroristic success, states should perhaps make more use of this fact. In terms of a battle for public sympathy, it is surely a huge resource for the state to be able to stress that terrorists tend not to bring about their high-sounding, central aspirations (with which many people might have understandable sympathy), but that they do tend far more often to succeed in and celebrate the carrying out of vengeful and callous violence, very often against the defenceless. That non-state terrorists tend not to bring about their central goals (and it is worth reflecting that even the very committed and able activists of Hamas, ETA, al-Qaida, and the Provisional IRA failed to achieve the headline goals of any of those groups) should also encourage states to *overreact* much less often than they tend to do. Despite the fears of cataclysm that terroristic violence can stim-ulate, states do tend to be able to endure (as happened with the USA after 9/11, the UK—and even Northern Ireland itself within it—during the Provos' very sustained long war, Spain while struggling against ETA, and Israel under the threat of Palestinian assault). Calm, measured, patient reac-tion makes most sense, rather than the clumsy overreaction which we have identified at times in each case study (and beyond).

This book has again and again shown that there is a mutually shaping relationship between states (including their own violent, at times terroristic, acts) and their non-state adversaries. It also suggests that states should recognize their own role in generating the problems from which terrorism has emerged as a violent symptom: the Spanish state's treatment of the Basques *had* at times been very prejudicial and harsh; Northern Ireland between the 1920s and 1960s *was* unfair in many ways towards its nationalist inhabitants; US foreign policy *did* include many acts of self-interested crassness in terms of alliances with regimes of very dubious record; Israel *did* long deny the rights and grievances of Palestinian neighbours. The time to solve terrorist crises is, of course, before they arise, and before violence has polarized the relationships that are involved. But it is clear that, in many cases, an outcome far short of what non-state terrorists have killed to achieve would satisfy many within their would-be constituency; these outcomes should be pursued by states if they are judged fair and sustainable. This does not, I believe, give victory to terrorism. Indeed, if a certain set of such arrangements made sense (whether in Ireland, or Israel–Palestine, or Spain, or across the wider Muslim world, or beyond), then we should support their implementation *regardless* of terrorism, but recognizing that the diminution of terrorist violence might be an ensuing benefit. Here, the state/non-state relationship places responsibility upon, but also gives opportunities to, those who govern states.

The arguments in this book tend also to suggest that, rather than focusing on supposed threats to civilization or wars to end evil, states would be much better placed trying to ensure that—at a day-to-day level—tactical operations are as difficult as possible for terrorists to pursue; that the inherent rewards of involvement in terrorism are outweighed (and are publicly made known in advance to be outweighed) by the unappealing and negative consequences of such terroristic involvement; and that the rewards of sustaining non-violent resistance (organizationally as well as personally) are made far more attractive than those secured through the pursuit of more aggressive methods.

Yet again, the implications of this book are that one of the areas of non-state terroristic success might paradoxically be one of its weakest points too. Again and again, the terrorist violence that we have discussed has seized headlines; very often, however, it has done so on the basis of actions which have caused revulsion at the cruelty of the perpetrators. Most victims even of very famous attacks, however, remain appallingly forgotten. How many readers can name the eleven Israeli Olympic athletes killed in 1972, or any of the people killed by the Provisional IRA in the 1974 Birmingham bombs, or more than a handful of those killed during ETA's long war? What terrorism most distinctively does is use shocking violence for political purpose; with sensitive, honest memory of such acts, this violence can in fact help undermine the group carrying it out for its cherished purpose. Yet—from Madrid to London to Washington to Jerusalem and far beyond—those in power in states that are combating terrorism have more often undermined their own legitimacy through dispensing with proper restraint, than they have ensured a sustained case about what thinking about the actuality of terrorist violence can do to make terrorism less likely in the future.

How far terrorism works will depend partly on how well states—in these or other ways—manage shrewdly to respond to it. Non-state terrorism and the state reactions that it generates can transform politics and society (albeit, so very often, not in ways that violent actors on any side anticipate or seek). From June 1914 to September 2001, and before and after both of those epoch-defining months, non-state terrorism *has* instigated huge changes in how humans have lived, and which of them will die, and when, and how. But these have largely been developments which have taken on unintended form, with many of the actual outcomes being as futile and tragic and poignant and unexpected as they have been vicious.

My own inclinations tend to be pessimistic about many things, and I suspect that the next 200 years will witness vast amounts of semi-pointless blood-spilling by state and non-state actors alike. If this book suggests the need for humility, about what we can know in advance regarding what our violence (on all sides) will produce, then it will have served some small good. For that humility would point towards the use of less aggressive political methods by states and by non-state groups alike. In the field of ethnic conflict, scholars have repeatedly studied people's non-terroristic political choices in terms of rational response to changing circumstance.[132] This book aims to locate our understanding of terrorism on similar terrain, though with a recognition that what we are analysing here is not purely rational decision-making by those who engage in terrorism, but rather decision-making that is as rational as is that of other people. Those normal activists who pursue terroristic violence will, in many cases, resist the logic of this book (just as they resist the very label of terrorist itself, and I understand and respect that). But I think the evidence suggests that taking another person's life in one's own political cause is far more certain to produce pain and loss than it is to generate expected and beneficent political change.

The question 'Does Terrorism Work?' implies, of course, consideration of whether it works better or worse than do other methods. And we've touched on that issue at various points in the book. Many observers suspect that terrorists' claims about there being no other available means of effective struggle simplify the actual reality and that—often enough—alternative methods do seem to have been available historically.[133] In policy terms, the logic of this argument is surely to make clear the forward momentum that people can actually, visibly, make down such non-violent routes towards political change. Large numbers of former anti-state groups have made transitions to becoming involved in government and/or in non-violent, constitutional politics; and there have been scholars who have argued that deliberately including such former militants in post-conflict structures of power represents a crucial part of the successful movement from violence to peace.[134] Relatedly, powerful scholarly arguments have been offered suggesting that the establishment of fuller democracy will limit the amount of grievance-driven terrorism that the world experiences, since it will reduce social and political exclusion and lack of recognition.[135] Clearly, this is easier to demand than it is to deliver in practice, and scholars recognize that. But there can be little doubt that one frequent effect of terroristic violence is to provoke states into extensions of state power which infringe civil liberties and limit people's rights,[136] and little doubt either that this can have a deleterious effect on the countering of terrorism. When terrorism prompts liberal-democratic states to erode some of their liberal-democratic features,[137] it shifts them in the opposite direction from that which they should probably follow.

And we might reflect on how far there are other ways in which we can and should find remedies for past grievances. Elazar Barkan has pointed intriguingly to what he calls 'the new global trend of restitution for historical injustices': restitution of what was taken, reparation or payment for that which can't be returned (life, identity), and apology for wrongs committed in the past. Taking restitution, reparation, and apology together, one gets 'a mosaic of recognition by perpetrators for the need to amend past injustices'. Professor Barkan sensibly limits the framework of responsibility: 'I use the concept of historical injustice here in a limited sense to refer to recognition by alleged perpetrators of their own commission of gross injustices over the last fifty years or to demands for such recognition from victims.' And the process he depicts is one to be mutually achieved: 'Restitution as a new system is distinct from past practices in that both sides enter voluntarily into negotiations and agreements; they are not imposed by the winner upon the loser or by a third party.... Restitution agreements as discussed here are distinct from past practices in that both sides voluntarily enter the negotiations and agreements.'[138] I remain somewhat sceptical about this process (not least because the grievances we often encounter in relation to terrorism are ones with roots that are so much deeper than the past half-century). But Barkan's is an elegant and thoughtful and stimulating argument about mutually agreed ways of atoning for wrongs in more fruitful manner than violent exchange.

And one very important point relating to the methods of redress which we deploy is that, as Timothy Garton Ash carefully puts it regarding the pursuit of political change, 'the means you adopt will determine—or at least, very significantly influence—the end at which you arrive.'[139] Related here is the fact that terrorism and other violence cannot easily and cleanly be switched on and off, in societal or in individual memory and action. The damage that we do to each other leaves a lasting re-definition of political relationships, something made even clearer if one takes a long perspective on the legacies of violence.

This raises another major issue which has been implicit throughout this book, concerning morality and political violence. On the morality of terrorism itself, much has now been valuably written.[140] It seems to me that no serious historical analysis can avoid moral assessment in some form (there is much historiographical argument to support this position,[141] and previous generations of historians would have had little hesitation in trying to draw moral implications from their research and writing).[142] The layered framework adopted in this book allows for calm reflection on the various ways in which terrorism might or might not work; hopefully, and despite the pejorative connotations usually associated with the word terrorism, this approach has facilitated a fair-minded assessment of how far brutal methods might indeed have proved to be justified in relation to sought-after goals. And the complex ways in which this book suggests terrorism to have been successful and unsuccessful do, it seems to me, hint at a need for states and non-state adversaries alike to rethink the moral justifications for such violent methods. Very often, what we have seen is the inefficacy of non-compromise, where the pursuit of unattainable victory has sustained campaigns of attritional violence for far longer than its eventual outcomes suggest to have been ultimately justified. 'It is not refusal to compromise but compromise that in political things is the true morality.'[143]

The only serious-minded way, ultimately, of reaching our decisions about how far terrorism can be justified is probably to consider—in closely read context—how far peaceful compromise instead would have allowed for political progress. Views will profoundly differ here, of course. In the opinion of radical philosopher Ted Honderich, just war theory would present a just war as involving an underlying just cause, an appropriate actor waging it, a proportionality of violence deployed, an avoidance of the killing of civilians and non-combatants, a status as method of last resort, an underlying rightness of intention—and 'a probability of succeeding'. Honderich's compelling books do not set out, however, to test this last-named criterion against the record of what humans have actually done in the past, and against the messy but vital test of lived and complex experience. That latter experience has been what this current book centrally and distinctively addresses. Honderich himself espouses the cause of 'the principle of humanity', with its admirable end of 'saving people from bad lives', and he most forcefully focuses on the case of Palestine. He reasonably raises the questions of 'whether an alternative to some particular past campaign of terrorism, say negotiation, would have worked out better', and 'whether terrorism now will secure a certain end or one of a range of ends, or will instead be the worst of things—useless killing, useless suffering, useless wrecking of lives'.

Professor Honderich himself does not, I think, answer these important questions with sufficient attention to how the past has actually unfolded in detail (despite his conclusion that 'terrorism has been the moral right of the Palestinians').[144] My own aim in this book has been to consider complex historical detail in such a way that readers will indeed be able, more clearly, to decide whether (say) ETA or al-Qaida or PIRA or Hamas violence can be judged to have been morally justified after all. The challenge, I think, for those who would argue that it can be so justified is to demonstrate how the less than strategic success of each group can still leave their lengthy campaigns ethically well grounded in historical practice.

Related to morality here is the central notion of empathy. There can now be little doubt that an erosion of empathy provides the basis for some terrible acts, and that this bears relevance both for non-state and state-based violent actors. The acts of carpet-bombing a city in war, or of planting a no-warning bomb in a bar, both reflect a tendency to treat victims cruelly, to ignore their shared humanity, to regard them more as devalued objects than as precious people. This is not to say that terrorism can be explained purely because of its practitioners' empathy erosion. It is, however, to point out that in assessing a phenomenon which has been shown in these pages more likely to achieve brutal revenge than the realization of high-minded, central, political goals, we are (among other things) dealing with a practice which requires that one at least suspend empathy while occasioning vicious violence. The recognition of, and appropriate response to, someone else's feelings and thoughts and interests, which lies at the heart of empathy, is something of profound importance if we are considering both the inhumanity of states (some Israeli violence against Palestinian communities, French actions in Algeria, or British actions in Kenya or in Ireland, for example), and also the behaviour of those non-state terrorists who have peopled our pages in this book.[145] If I am right in arguing that, in responding to terrorism, we need synoptically to consider both non-state *and* state responsibility at the same time,[146] then the importance of not facilitating sustained empathy-erosion becomes clear. The casualness with which we all tend to be comfortable with other people's suffering lies at the heart of the problem of terrorism, and states as well as non-state groups bear responsibility for this tragedy. There is indeed a life-saving dimension to empathy (at the moment of a callous act of violence, the perpetrator has to switch off their empathy);[147] and were appropriate recognition and response employed in how state counter-terrorists and non-state terrorists analysed the world, then much human suffering would be removed.

This leads us to thinking about mercy and, importantly, about religion. At the time of their violence, terrorists tend to be more sharply focused on perceived and actual injustices needing to be righted for their own community than they are on the humanity (and human rights) of those whom they brutally target or damage. Not all terrorism possesses a religious dimension but, after 9/11, very much debate and policy on the subject has focused—rightly or wrongly—on the relationship between religious faith and this form of political violence. Indeed, much alarm has been sounded in recent years about religious terrorism, and some distinguished scholars have argued that there is something very different about 'religious' as opposed to other kinds of terroristic violence.[148] I'm unconvinced exactly how novel this phenomenon—religious terrorism—actually is. Moreover, as this book has suggested, even those whose terroristic violence is indeed partly motivated by religion are people who often interpret that religion as having profound consequences and implications for what the non-religious would consider secular politics (where state borders are drawn; how state power is conducted, and by whom). All sustainably, historically important religions are also about politics, power, identity, economics, society; and the idea that powerful religions can be other than profoundly interwoven with such matters is unhistorical.[149] In this sense, to speak of 'religious' motivation can only make full sense if religion is interpreted as involving a broad world-view. And what is frequently referred to as religious terrorism is also as fully political as it is religious.[150]

Moreover, when thinking of those who are religious and involved in terroristic violence, it is vital to understand the depth and sincerity of much of the religious militancy and altruism that are involved, however bizarre that will initially seem to those of us who abhor the human consequences of al-Qaida or Hamas violence, for instance. And for those of us who would indeed prefer such terrorism to diminish, it is crucial both to appreciate the dynamics of what is really going on in detail (as my al-Qaida and Hamas chapters have tried here to do), and also to respect the importance of debates within the relevant religious traditions, rather than patronizingly to dismiss them. Morality and mercy and humanity are central to the religious trad-itions which have also been cited in defence of much terrorist violence, and those benign strands of thinking continue to offer vital resources if we are prepared to listen to and to use them. Religions are fluid, and the precise shape of their influence depends on the extent to which people are pre-pared to engage with them, and within them, seriously.

So, just as religious literacy is an important element in understanding modern politics effectively,[151] so too it is important if we want to speak sensibly about terrorism. Those people who trust and place their hope in God, who believe in a God who is active in human activity, who pursue a form of religious salvation, are bound to see the world differently from those who do not. And the idea that God is on your side of course changes things utterly for those terrorists who believe it. Things which the secular might consider to involve defeat or unacceptable suffering or loss might, in the eyes of some religious people, be judged to be attractive gain. We have seen in these pages examples of people who have willingly suffered or died for what they took to be a divinely sanctioned cause. Of course, one can take the past seriously as belonging to God, without thinking that God crudely intervenes or that He determines politics in a narrowly prescriptive manner;[152] and it is possible, in any case, to argue that the human past and its purpose are only explicable by reference to Christianity and to God's active role in that process, without at all engaging in a politics of militancy or violence.[153] Most importantly, perhaps, the fact that most religious leaders and believers argue against terrorism remains more salient than most observ-ers tend to admit,[154] especially given the huge and enduring role of religion even in western society (around 270 million people in the USA believe in a God who answers prayer).[155] It has frequently and rightly been pointed out that there is no necessary connection between particular religions and terrorism (even suicide terrorism).[156] It is less frequently pointed out (but is at least as important) that religious beliefs and compassion and leadership and mercy and organizational imperative towards compromise and empathy offer some of our most serious means of trying to limit the popularity of terrorist violence in the future.

Again, the dynamics of some religious traditions can offer important insights as we strive to explain the varied patterns of effectiveness and behaviour across different kinds of terrorist group. Eli Berman has power-fully argued that religious radicals such as Hezbollah, Hamas, and the Taliban have been so lethally effective in tactical terms because of their capacity to weed out shirkers and thus limit defection. The provision of attractive mutual aid services for members, and the insistence on costly prior sacrifices by would-be members of the group, between them make it more difficult and unlikely for members of these radical religious sects to defect, and more attractive and probable for them to remain loyal; so these groups (the argu-ment runs) enjoy a greater capacity to hit high-value targets than do organ-izations more vulnerable to defection.[157]

This current book has argued that, if we are to assess how far terrorism is the best or most appropriate response to perceived suffering and injustice, then we need to assess how far it has worked in practice in the past, rather than making our assessment purely in terms of an abstract set of criteria. Knowing what this book suggests that we know about terrorism's past, we cannot easily separate the intentions of people who have engaged in such violence from what history suggests to be the most probable outcomes in reality—that terrorism is more likely to succeed in producing polarization and revenge than in delivering its higher-sounding central goods, for exam-ple. Equally, given the mutually shaping intimacy between non-state terror-ism and state politics, we need to think humbly about what states do and do not do (and about the frequent casualness that they display about others' suffering) if we do want to diminish non-state violence in the future.

Here, I think Amartya Sen's valuable distinction between realization-focused comparison and transcendental institutionalism points one way for-ward. Professor Sen differentiates between two different approaches to the removal of injustice: one (realization-focused comparison), focusing on people's actual behaviour and influences in practice, and concentrating on preventing or removing egregious injustice; the other (transcendental insti-tutionalism), based on an identification of perfect justice, and the creation of institutions appropriate to such perfection. The former allows for making things (in our deeply imperfect context) relatively less awful, in perhaps more achievable fashion; the latter might be thought to risk counter-productive ambition, and the time-wasting political engineering of supposedly just institutions. I think this dichotomy has relevance to how we approach terrorism and political change. My own argument in this book is that, in order properly to assess whether terrorism is justified, people should engage in a version of realization-focused comparison—looking not at how the world should work if things were ideal, but more at what is most likely to happen (for better or worse or both) if certain courses of action are pursued in practice. The only serious way of making the necessary judgment here is to look at how groups' violence has or has not worked in messy reality over time. In Sen's phrasing, I have favoured a 'focus on actual lives', rather than on abstract conceptions.[158]

And what has emerged is the profound uncertainty of terrorism achieving its central goals, together with a complex pattern of other successes and failures at lower level. What is almost certain (in fact, the historical record suggests it to be certain in all major terrorist campaigns) is that terrible human suffering will ensue from terrorist violence. Taken together, this doesn't mean that such violence is necessarily illegitimate. But weighing the certainty of damage against the much less certain achievement of beneficent outcomes is vital. Every one of the case studies examined sustainedly in this book has involved considerable human suffering being caused; none of them has involved the achievement of the relevant group's central goals. And, contrary to the confidence so often evinced by terrorist activists about violently achieved progress, very many of the political futures that they have helped to create have been far less worthy of celebration than they had anticipated. Indeed, in tune with historians' frequent scepticism about historical watersheds, very much in political life (in our al-Qaida, PIRA, Hamas, and ETA case studies, for example) has actually proved continuous before, during, and after those groups' violent campaigns in pursuit of dramatic change.

Readers' responses here will vary greatly, and understandably so. I look forward to the ensuing debate. Indeed, this book has been intended less to produce consensual agreement, than to contribute substantially to educated discussion about a vital subject. There are limits to what research can change in terms of wider societal attitudes. But there are some topics on which any thoughtful community needs to reflect honestly, and the complex effect of terrorism is surely one of them. Moreover, the difficulties involved in the study of this question (set out at length in the Introduction) are not such as to prevent serious answers from being proposed on the basis of extensive research within a measured framework. Careful historical reflection suggests that binary thinking probably gets in the way of serious argument;[159] as this book makes clear, I don't think the question 'Does Terrorism Work?' can be met with a persuasive and simple 'Yes' or 'No'. It seemed to me that we needed an extended and complex argument on the subject; that this argument should be based on a recognition of the difficulties involved with the question; that it should adopt a methodology and an analytical framework which would enable us to deal with those problems; and that it must combine detailed case studies with a synoptically wide-angled approach. That kind of analysis is, I believe, what the debate has required; and I hope that readers find this book to have moved that discussion helpfully forward.

Notes

INTRODUCTION

1. Later in this Introduction I will more fully address the notorious problems involved in defining 'terrorism'. But it's important at this stage to make clear: first, that although this book focuses primarily on the significant subject of non-state terrorism, I hold that much (indeed, most) terroristic violence has historically been practised by states; second, that although the word carries heavily pejorative meanings for many people, I do not use it in a necessarily condemnatory sense at all; third, that those groups and individuals practising terrorism also do much else, and that (in addition to their terrorism) this non-terroristic activity also deserves assessment. Some people would prefer that we simply do not use the T word at all, and I have some sympathy with that view. But the word is not going to disappear from important public use, and my opinion is that it is better to discuss it fully and honestly than to leave it to those who would use it less responsibly.

2. Documented and analysed in L. Stampnitzky, *Disciplining Terror: How Experts Invented 'Terrorism'* (Cambridge: Cambridge University Press, 2013), pp. 4, 65–6, 78, 179.

3. B. Hoffman, *Inside Terrorism* (New York: Columbia University Press, 2006; 1st edn 1998), p. xv; L. Richardson, *What Terrorists Want: Understanding the Terrorist Threat* (London: John Murray, 2006), pp. 7, 148–9; J. Horgan, *The Psychology of Terrorism* (London: Routledge, 2005), pp. 50, 53, 62–5; D. A. Lake, 'Rational Extremism: Understanding Terrorism in the Twenty-First Century', *Dialog-IO*, 1/1 (2002); M. Sageman, *Understanding Terror Networks* (Philadelphia: University of Pennsylvania Press, 2004), pp. 80–3, 97; M. Sageman, *Leaderless Jihad: Terror Networks in the Twenty-First Century* (Philadelphia: University of Pennsylvania Press, 2008), pp. 17, 62–4; M. Ruthven, *A Fury for God: The Islamist Attack on America* (London: Granta, 2002), p. 28; J. W. Jones, *Blood That Cries Out From the Earth: The Psychology of Religious Terrorism* (New York: OUP, 2008), p. 5; R. A. Pape and J. K. Feldman, *Cutting the Fuse: The Explosion of Global Suicide Terrorism and How to Stop It* (Chicago: University of Chicago Press, 2010), p. 8; M. Crenshaw, *Explaining Terrorism: Causes, Processes and Consequences* (London: Routledge, 2011), pp. 44, 125; R. A. Pape, *Dying to Win: Why Suicide Terrorists Do It* (London: Gibson Square Books, 2006; 1st edn 2005), pp. 23, 27; R. Jackson, L. Jarvis, J. Gunning, and M. Breen Smyth, *Terrorism: A Critical Introduction* (Basingstoke: Palgrave Macmillan, 2011), pp. 207, 209, 215; M. Taylor and E. Quayle, *Terrorist Lives* (London:

Brassey's, 1994), p. 14; D. Pisoiu, *Islamist Radicalization in Europe: An Occupational Change Process* (London: Routledge, 2013; 1st edn 2012), pp. 2–4, 36, 168–9. In pioneering psychological research, Ariel Merari and colleagues have argued that, for Palestinian suicide attackers, there are indeed some distinctive psychological patterns separating different intra-group kinds of terrorist practitioner from one another. This work, however, addresses intra-group differences of role, rather than the central point that I am making here: namely, that terrorists are not characterized by different psychological characteristics or qualities from those that characterize non-terrorists (A. Merari, *Driven to Death: Psychological and Social Aspects of Suicide Terrorism* (Oxford: OUP, 2010)).

4. Quoted in Crenshaw, *Explaining Terrorism*, p. 31.
5. Quoted in Richardson, *What Terrorists Want*, p. 71.
6. Quoted in M. Perry, *Talking to Terrorists: Why America Must Engage with its Enemies* (New York: Basic Books, 2010), p. 133.
7. Patrick Magee, interviewed by the author, Belfast, 5 March 2002.
8. S. Pinker, *The Better Angels of our Nature: The Decline of Violence in History and its Causes* (London: Penguin, 2011), p. 33.
9. A. Guelke, *The Age of Terrorism and the International Political System* (London: I. B. Tauris, 1998; 1st edn 1995), pp. 172, 180.
10. R. Jackson, *Confessions of a Terrorist* (London: Zed Books, 2014), pp. 115, 119, 286.
11. M. Bloom, *Dying to Kill: The Allure of Suicide Terror* (New York: Columbia University Press, 2007; 1st edn 2005).
12. See the very thoughtful discussion in N. Rengger, *Just War and International Order: The Uncivil Condition in World Politics* (Cambridge: Cambridge University Press, 2013).
13. R. English, *Modern War: A Very Short Introduction* (Oxford: OUP, 2013), pp. 37–41.
14. E. Berman, *Radical, Religious, and Violent: The New Economics of Terrorism* (Cambridge, Mass.: MIT Press, 2009), p. 1.
15. E. Stepanova, *Terrorism in Asymmetrical Conflict: Ideological and Structural Aspects* (Oxford: OUP, 2008), pp. 3–4. It is true that President Bush's post-9/11 strategy against terrorism strengthened his popularity in regard to re-election as President of the United States (W. R. Mead, *Power, Terror, Peace, and War: America's Grand Strategy in a World at Risk* (New York: Alfred A. Knopf, 2005), p. 217). But in terms of limiting the amount of terrorist violence actually practised, the record was much less impressive (S. G. Jones, *Counterinsurgency in Afghanistan* (Santa Monica, Calif.: RAND, 2008), p. 116; J. Zulaika, *Terrorism: The Self-Fulfilling Prophecy* (Chicago: University of Chicago Press, 2009), p. 1; P. Wilkinson, *Terrorism Versus Democracy: The Liberal State Response* (London: Routledge, 2006; 1st edn 2001), p. 46; Crenshaw, *Explaining Terrorism*, p. 180; Richardson, *What Terrorists Want*, p. 262; I. Arreguin-Toft, *How the Weak Win Wars: A Theory of Asymmetric Conflict* (Cambridge: Cambridge University Press, 2005), p. 38).
16. A. M. Dershowitz, *Why Terrorism Works: Understanding the Threat, Responding to the Challenge* (New Haven: Yale University Press, 2002), p. 2.

17. R. E. Goodin, *What's Wrong with Terrorism?* (Cambridge: Polity, 2006), p. 124; Zulaika, *Terrorism*, p. 147; Jackson, Jarvis, Gunning, and Breen Smyth, *Terrorism*, pp. 124, 132–5, 139; L. K. Donohue, *The Cost of Counterterrorism: Power, Politics and Liberty* (Cambridge: Cambridge University Press, 2008), p. 351; J. Mueller and M. G. Stewart, *Terror, Security, and Money: Balancing the Risks, Benefits, and Costs of Homeland Security* (Oxford: OUP, 2011).

18. G. F. Treverton, *Intelligence for an Age of Terror* (Cambridge: Cambridge University Press, 2009), p. 24.

19. Pinker, *Better Angels*, p. 344; cf. B. Saul, *Defining Terrorism in International Law* (Oxford: OUP, 2008; 1st edn 2006), p. 314.

20. The brilliant Daniel Kahneman has powerfully made the case regarding the availability heuristic: essentially, our over-reliance on ease of memory when making judgments. If something is easily recalled, if it is very salient, then there is a tendency to make wider assessments based disproportionately on that thing; we often tend to exaggerate the frequency of something on the basis of the ease with which examples of it can be recalled to memory. Likewise, there is a tendency for us easily to focus on dangerously frightening images, which again makes our estimation of the likelihood of terrorism increase. In other words, the frequency and ease with which phenomena like terrorism come to mind make us likely to exaggerate their comparative threat (D. Kahneman, *Thinking, Fast and Slow* (London: Penguin, 2012; 1st edn 2011), pp. 8, 129–30, 138–9, 144–5, 321–4, 333).

21. R. English, *Terrorism: How to Respond* (Oxford: OUP, 2009), pp. 127–31.

22. V. Held, *How Terrorism Is Wrong: Morality and Political Violence* (Oxford: OUP, 2008), p. 22.

23. Stepanova, *Terrorism in Asymmetrical Conflict*, p. 52.

24. Crenshaw, *Explaining Terrorism*, p. 111.

25. S. V. Marsden, 'Successful Terrorism: Framework and Review', *Behavioral Sciences of Terrorism and Political Aggression*, 4/2 (2012).

26. Held, *How Terrorism Is Wrong*, p. 80.

27. Dershowitz, *Why Terrorism Works*, pp. 2, 6, 26, 31, 85, 167.

28. A. H. Kydd and B. F. Walter, 'The Strategies of Terrorism', *International Security*, 31/1 (2006), p. 49.

29. R. A. Pape, 'The Strategic Logic of Suicide Terrorism', *American Political Science Review*, 97/3 (2003), p. 350.

30. A. Merari and S. Elad, *The International Dimension of Palestinian Terrorism* (Boulder, Colo.: Westview Press, 1986), p. 90.

31. D. C. Rapoport, 'The International World as Some Terrorists Have Seen It: A Look at a Century of Memoirs', in D. C. Rapoport (ed.), *Inside Terrorist Organizations* (London: Frank Cass, 2001), p. 54.

32. C. Gearty, *Terror* (London: Faber and Faber, 1991), p. 2.

33. J. R. Schindler, *H-Diplo/ISSF Roundtable Reviews*, 2/8 (2011), p. 12.

34. P. R. Neumann and M. L. R. Smith, *The Strategy of Terrorism: How it Works, and Why it Fails* (London: Routledge, 2008), p. 100.

35. M. Abrahms, 'Why Terrorism Does Not Work', *International Security*, 31/2 (2006), pp. 43–4. Elsewhere, Abrahms—whose contributions to this debate have been vital and extremely valuable—concedes that terrorism is effective in producing harm and fear; maintains that it is ineffective politically, and that such strategic inefficacy is inherent in the tactic itself; but acknowledges that strategic incentives alone do not necessarily explain terrorists' actions (M. Abrahms, 'Response to Peter Krause', *H-Diplo/ISSF* (29 June 2013)).

36. J. J. F. Forest, 'Conclusion', in J. Dingley (ed.), *Combating Terrorism in Northern Ireland* (London: Routledge, 2009), pp. 281, 298. Cf. J. Horgan, *Walking Away from Terrorism: Accounts of Disengagement from Radical and Extremist Movements* (London: Routledge, 2009), p. 26; M. Bloom, *Bombshell: The Many Faces of Women Terrorists* (London: Hurst and Co., 2011), p. 248; A. Silke, 'The Impact of 9/11 on Research on Terrorism', in M. Ranstorp (ed.), *Mapping Terrorism Research: State of the Art, Gaps and Future Direction* (London: Routledge, 2007), p. 83.

37. J. Arquilla, *Insurgents, Raiders, and Bandits: How Masters of Irregular Warfare Have Shaped our World* (Chicago: Ivan R. Dee, 2011), p. 5.

38. L. Weinberg, 'Turning to Terror: The Conditions Under Which Political Parties Turn to Terrorist Activities', *Comparative Politics*, 23/4 (1991).

39. E. Chenoweth and M. J. Stephan, *Why Civil Resistance Works: The Strategic Logic of Non-Violent Conflict* (New York: Columbia University Press, 2011), pp. 17, 74. Cf. A. Roberts and T. Garton Ash (eds), *Civil Resistance and Power Politics: The Experience of Non-Violent Action from Gandhi to the Present* (Oxford: OUP, 2009); M. E. King, *A Quiet Revolution: The First Palestinian Intifada and Non-Violent Resistance* (New York: Nation Books, 2007).

40. M. Abrahms, 'Al-Qaida's Scorecard: A Progress Report on al-Qaida's Objectives', *SICAT*, 29/5 (2006), p. 509.

41. P. Wilkinson, 'Politics, Diplomacy, and Peace Processes: Pathways out of Terrorism?', in M. Taylor and J. Horgan (eds), *The Future of Terrorism* (Abingdon: Frank Cass, 2000), p. 66.

42. Wilkinson, *Terrorism Versus Democracy* (2006 edn), pp. 6, 22, 26, 195; cf. A. K. Cronin, *How Terrorism Ends: Understanding the Decline and Demise of Terrorist Campaigns* (Princeton: Princeton University Press, 2009), pp. 73–93, 203.

43. Richardson, *What Terrorists Want*, pp. 105–6.

44. D. K. Gupta, *Understanding Terrorism and Political Violence: The Life Cycle of Birth, Growth, Transformation, and Demise* (London: Routledge, 2008), p. 191.

45. E. D. Gould and E. F. Klor, 'Does Terrorism Work?', *Quarterly Journal of Economics*, 125/4 (2010), quotations at p. 1460.

46. For valuable, varying reflections on the challenges and possibilities involved in deploying the 'T' word, see A. P. Schmid (ed.), *The Routledge Handbook of Terrorism Research* (London: Routledge, 2011), especially pp. 39–157; Crenshaw, *Explaining Terrorism*, pp. 21–33; Hoffman, *Inside Terrorism*, pp. 1–41; Richardson, *What Terrorists Want*, pp. 19–39; Saul, *Defining Terrorism in International Law*; C. J. Finlay, 'How To Do Things with the Word "Terrorist"', *Review of International*

Studies, 35/4 (2009); A. Richards, 'Conceptualizing Terrorism', *SICAT*, 37/3 (2014).

47. See, for example: A. D. Smith and J. Hutchinson (eds), *Nationalism* (Oxford: OUP, 1994); S. Khilnani, *Arguing Revolution: The Intellectual Left in Post-War France* (New Haven: Yale University Press, 1993); S. Howe, *Ireland and Empire: Colonial Legacies in Irish History and Culture* (Oxford: OUP, 2000); D. Cannadine, *Class in Britain* (New Haven: Yale University Press, 1998); K. Passmore, *Fascism: A Very Short Introduction* (Oxford: OUP, 2002); E. Nimni, *Marxism and Nationalism: Theoretical Origins of a Political Crisis* (London: Pluto Press, 1991); P. Jackson, *Beyond the Balance of Power: France and the Politics of National Security in the Era of the First World War* (Cambridge: Cambridge University Press, 2013).

48. W. Laqueur, *Terrorism* (London: Weidenfeld and Nicolson, 1977), p. 5.

49. English, *Terrorism: How to Respond*, pp. 2–20.

50. Schmid (ed.), *The Routledge Handbook of Terrorism Research*; A. P. Schmid and A. J. Jongman (eds), *Political Terrorism* (Amsterdam: North Holland Publishing, 1988).

51. Distinguished scholars have differed sharply on this point: Louise Richardson argues strongly that the term should be reserved for sub-state actors (Richardson, *What Terrorists Want*, pp. 21–2); but Paul Wilkinson, for example, disagreed (P. Wilkinson, *Terrorism Versus Democracy: The Liberal State Response* (London: Routledge, 2011; 1st edn 2001), p. 17).

52. Richards, 'Conceptualizing Terrorism', p. 222.

53. English, *Terrorism: How to Respond*, p. 24.

54. 'The intent of terrorist violence is psychological and symbolic, not material' (M. Crenshaw, 'Reflections on the Effects of Terrorism', in M. Crenshaw (ed.), *Terrorism, Legitimacy, and Power: The Consequences of Political Violence* (Middletown, Conn.: Wesleyan University Press, 1983), p. 2).

55. English, *Modern War*, pp. 116–18.

56. See, for examples, E. Hobsbawm, *Age of Extremes: The Short Twentieth Century 1914–1991* (London: Penguin, 1994), p. 28; M. Fellman, *In the Name of God and Country: Reconsidering Terrorism in American History* (New Haven: Yale University Press, 2010).

57. M. Amis, *The Second Plane. September 11: 2001–2007* (London: Jonathan Cape, 2008), p. 22.

58. For further doubts about definition according to target or to particular kinds of act, see English, *Terrorism: How to Respond*, pp. 9–12.

59. If guerrilla war is defined as 'an irregular war carried on by small bodies of men acting independently' (*Shorter Oxford English Dictionary: Vol. 1* (Oxford: OUP, 1980; 1st edn 1933), p. 900), then clearly this problem of overlap is evident. Likewise, while civil war might be judged to involve the loss of effective control over a territory by any party (including the state), there exists room for terroristic violence in parts of such a conflict.

60. Crenshaw, *Explaining Terrorism*, pp. 53–4. Cf. A. Gofas, ' "Old" vs. "New" Terrorism: What's in a Name?', *Uluslararası İlişkiler*, 8/32 (2012); O. Lynch and

C. Ryder, 'Deadliness, Organizational Change and Suicide Attacks: Understanding the Assumptions Inherent in the Use of the Term "New Terrorism"', *Critical Studies on Terrorism*, 5/2 (2012); R. Lambert, *Countering Al-Qaida in London: Police and Muslims in Partnership* (London: Hurst and Co., 2011), pp. 19, 44–7.

61. Saul, *Defining Terrorism in International Law*, pp. 3, 21.
62. Compare one scholarly comment on this theme regarding the PIRA: 'Despite the profusion of definitions of terrorism, according to virtually all of them at least some of the Provisional IRA's activities qualify as acts of terrorism' (T. Shanahan, *The Provisional Irish Republican Army and the Morality of Terrorism* (Edinburgh: Edinburgh University Press, 2009), p. 5).
63. 'When it comes to evaluating the effectiveness of terrorism, success is a nebulous concept, often loosely employed and reflecting the intellectual biases of the observer more than the priorities of the group itself (or its constituents)' (Cronin, *How Terrorism Ends*, p. 74).
64. Dershowitz, *Why Terrorism Works*, pp. 24, 28, 36–78.
65. Abrahms, 'Why Terrorism Does Not Work', pp. 46–8.
66. Chenoweth and Stephan, *Why Civil Resistance Works*, p. 14.
67. P. Wilkinson, *Terrorism Versus Democracy: The Liberal State Response* (London: Frank Cass, 2001), p. 218.
68. J. M. Lutz and B. J. Lutz, *Global Terrorism* (London: Routledge, 2008; 1st edn 2004), p. 13.
69. M. J. Moyano, *Argentina's Lost Patrol: Armed Struggle, 1969–1979* (New Haven: Yale University Press, 1995), p. 156.
70. A. Roberts, 'Terrorism Research: Past, Present, and Future', *SICAT*, 38/1 (2015), p. 62; P. Wilkinson, 'Research into Terrorism Studies: Achievements and Failures', in Ranstorp (ed.), *Mapping Terrorism Research*, p. 316; A. B. Krueger, *What Makes a Terrorist: Economics and the Roots of Terrorism* (Princeton: Princeton University Press, 2008; 1st edn 2007), p. 5; R. Jackson, M. Breen Smyth, and J. Gunning (eds), *Critical Terrorism Studies: A New Research Agenda* (London: Routledge, 2009), p. 24; Forest, 'Conclusion', in Dingley (ed.), *Combating Terrorism in Northern Ireland*, p. 281; D. LaCapra, *History and its Limits: Human, Animal, Violence* (Ithaca, NY: Cornell University Press, 2009), p. 91.
71. In this book I refer to 'the past' as that which has happened before now; by 'history', I mean research and writing about the past; I use the term 'historiography' to refer to research and writing about history.
72. Berman, *Radical, Religious, and Violent*, p. 239; Cronin, *How Terrorism Ends*, pp. 2–3, 6; Roberts, 'Terrorism Research: Past, Present, and Future', pp. 63–5; Jackson, Breen Smyth, and Gunning (eds), *Critical Terrorism Studies*, pp. 7, 31, 87, 125, 154; Jackson, Jarvis, Gunning, and Breen Smyth, *Terrorism*, pp. 16, 32–3, 45, 204, 243; P. Staniland, *Networks of Rebellion: Explaining Insurgent Cohesion and Collapse* (Ithaca, NY: Cornell University Press, 2014), pp. 5, 218–19.
73. For a feline, compelling examination of the fluidity and variety of attitudes in even one national history tradition over just one century, see M. Bentley,

Modernizing England's Past: English Historiography in the Age of Modernism 1870–1970 (Cambridge: Cambridge University Press, 2005); for authoritative treatment of cross-national comparisons, see M. Bentley, *Modern Historiography: An Introduction* (London: Routledge, 1999); for an elegant illustration of what can change in approaches to history between periods at an individual-scholarly level, see D. Cannadine, *G. M. Trevelyan: A Life in History* (London: HarperCollins, 1992). More broadly, see P. Paret, *Understanding War: Essays on Clausewitz and the History of Military Power* (Princeton: Princeton University Press, 1992), p. 216; cf. J. Tosh, *The Pursuit of History* (Harlow: Pearson Education, 2010; 1st edn 1984), p. ix.

74. Hobsbawm, *Age of Extremes*, pp. 2–3.

75. See the perceptive comments and analysis in Silke, 'Impact of 9/11', in Ranstorp (ed.), *Mapping Terrorism Research*, pp. 88–91.

76. Tellingly, leading scholars of previous generations ably exemplify this point: R. H. Tawney, *Religion and the Rise of Capitalism* (West Drayton: Penguin, 1938; 1st edn 1926), p. viii; G. R. Elton, *The Practice of History* (Glasgow: Fontana, 1969; 1st edn 1967), p. 22; J. H. Plumb, *The Death of the Past* (Basingstoke: Palgrave Macmillan, 2004; 1st edn 1969), pp. 105–6, 144.

77. 'The most usual ideological abuse of history is based on anachronism rather than lies' (E. Hobsbawm, *On History* (London: Weidenfeld and Nicolson, 1997), p. 7).

78. H. Jordheim, 'Against Periodization: Koselleck's Theory of Multiple Temporalities', *History and Theory*, 51 (2012).

79. J. Burrow, *A History of Histories: Epics, Chronicles, Romances, and Inquiries from Herodotus and Thucydides to the Twentieth Century* (London: Penguin, 2009; 1st edn 2007), p. xvi; G. R. Elton, *Reform and Reformation: England 1509–1558* (London: Edward Arnold, 1977), p. vii.

80. LaCapra, *History and its Limits*, p. 2.

81. K. Jenkins, *On 'What is History?' From Carr and Elton to Rorty and White* (London: Routledge, 1995), p. 20.

82. J. Black and D. M. MacRaild, *Studying History* (Basingstoke: Palgrave, 2000; 1st edn 1997), pp. 19, 23.

83. Elton, *The Practice of History*, p. 41; cf. P. Novick, *That Noble Dream: The 'Objectivity Question' and the American Historical Profession* (Cambridge: Cambridge University Press, 1988), p. 33.

84. L. Jordanova, *History in Practice* (London: Bloomsbury, 2006; 1st edn 2000), p. 56.

85. As one of the first people to use the word terrorist, Edmund Burke, sagely put it in 1790, 'Circumstances (which with some gentlemen pass for nothing) give in reality to every political principle its distinguishing colour, and discriminating effect. The circumstances are what render every civil and political scheme beneficial or noxious to mankind' (E. Burke, *Reflections on the Revolution in France* (Oxford: OUP, 1993; 1st edn 1790), p. 8).

86. Krueger, *What Makes a Terrorist*, p. 72.

87. Tosh, *The Pursuit of History*, pp. 38–9.

88. Tosh, *The Pursuit of History*, p. 69.

89. See the very impressive treatment of this question in regard to religion, nation, class, gender, race, and civilization, in D. Cannadine, *The Undivided Past: History Beyond our Differences* (London: Penguin, 2013).

90. Plumb, *The Death of the Past*, p. 141.

91. Compare one leading scholar's reference to 'history's disciplinary sense of the complexity of social causation' (J. W. Scott, 'Gender', in J. W. Scott (ed.), *Feminism and History* (Oxford: OUP, 1996), p. 155), and another eminent historian's suggestion that 'Most historians will go to some lengths to avoid a "monocausal explanation"' (R. J. Evans, *In Defence of History* (London: Granta, 1997), p. 158).

92. Stepanova, *Terrorism in Asymmetrical Conflict*, p. 57.

93. For valuable reflections on the challenges and opportunities involved in oral history, see L. Abrams, *Oral History Theory* (London: Routledge, 2010).

94. Ranstorp (ed.), *Mapping Terrorism Research*, p. 6; Horgan, *Walking Away from Terrorism*, p. 4.

95. P. Burke, 'Overture: The New History', in P. Burke (ed.), *New Perspectives on Historical Writing* (Cambridge: Polity Press, 1992; 1st edn 1991), pp. 3, 19.

96. G. Prins, 'Oral History', in Burke (ed.), *New Perspectives on Historical Writing*, p. 130.

97. K. M. Fierke, *Political Self-Sacrifice: Agency, Body, and Emotion in International Relations* (Cambridge: Cambridge University Press, 2013), pp. 3, 13.

98. Black and MacRaild, *Studying History*, p. 5.

99. 'The critical attitude to sources dates back to Thucydides' (A. Tucker, *Our Knowledge of the Past: A Philosophy of Historiography* (Cambridge: Cambridge University Press, 2004), p. 68).

100. Cf. 'often one of the most significant scraps of evidence to illuminate a particular historical question is what is *not* actually done or said' (D. MacCulloch, *Silence: A Christian History* (London: Penguin, 2013), p. 1).

101. In my view, the most brilliant treatment of historians' problematic relationship with objectivity remains Novick, *That Noble Dream*.

102. Novick, *That Noble Dream*, p. 1.

103. Jordanova, *History in Practice*, p. 3; M. T. Gilderhuis, *History and Historians: A Historiographical Introduction* (London: Pearson, 2010; 1st edn 1992), pp. 112, 118; K. Jenkins, *Why History? Ethics and Postmodernity* (London: Routledge, 1999), p. 1; A. Marwick, *The New Nature of History: Knowledge, Evidence, Language* (Basingstoke: Palgrave, 2001), p. 48; Bentley, *Modern Historiography*, p. 144. Scholarly difficulties involving objectivity are clearly not restricted to historians; I rather like, for example, one eminent theologian's reference to the hermeneutical 'tension between *critical disinterestedness* and *personal involvement* with the subject matter' (J. D. G. Dunn, *The Theology of Paul the Apostle* (Edinburgh: T. and T. Clark, 1998), p. 8).

104. Evans, *In Defence of History*, p. 46.

105. Black and MacRaild, *Studying History*, p. 19.
106. D. N. Livingstone, *Putting Science in its Place: Geographies of Scientific Knowledge* (Chicago: University of Chicago Press, 2003), p. 11.
107. Even scholars as far apart historiographically as Keith Jenkins and Geoffrey Elton agree that past events exist independently of the historian through whose work we scrutinize them (K. Jenkins, *Re-thinking History* (London: Routledge, 1991), pp. 5, 49; Jenkins, *On 'What is History?'*, pp. 29, 32; Elton, *The Practice of History*, p. 73).
108. Jenkins, *On 'What is History?'*, p. 73.
109. Jordanova, *History in Practice*, p. 11. For a very powerful case study in the importance of recognizing the superior reliability of one historical account over another, see R. J. Evans, *Telling Lies about Hitler: The Holocaust, History, and the David Irving Trial* (London: Verso, 2002); cf. LaCapra, *History and its Limits*, pp. 212–13.
110. Tosh, *The Pursuit of History*, p. 189.
111. Interestingly, recent debates suggest that theoreticians of history are not now quite as anxious as they once seemed to be regarding the supposed problems of relating past events on the basis of present concepts (M. Bevir, 'Why Historical Distance is not a Problem', *History and Theory*, 50 (2011)).
112. In their differing ways, Carr and Evans agree on this: 'when we take up a work of history, our first concern should be not with the facts which it contains but with the historian who wrote it... Study the historian before you begin to study the facts'; 'The facts of history cannot be purely objective, since they become facts of history only in virtue of the significance attached to them by the historian' (E. H. Carr, *What is History?* (Basingstoke: Palgrave, 2001; 1st edn 1961), pp. 16–17, 114); cf. 'Where theory and interpretation come in is where facts are converted into evidence (that is, facts used in support of an argument)... Facts thus precede interpretation conceptually, while interpretation precedes evidence' (Evans, *In Defence of History*, pp. 76–7).
113. English, *Terrorism: How to Respond*, pp. 52–5.
114. Marwick, *The New Nature of History*, p. 15; M. MacMillan, *The Uses and Abuses of History* (London: Profile, 2009), p. 167.
115. Evans, *In Defence of History*, p. 252.
116. Hobsbawm, *On History*, p. 8; cf. R. Spalding and C. Parker, *Historiography: An Introduction* (Manchester: Manchester University Press, 2007), p. 19.
117. G. R. Elton, *Return to Essentials: Some Reflections on the Present State of Historical Study* (Cambridge: Cambridge University Press, 1991), pp. 9, 24; P. Burke, 'Historiography and Philosophy of History', in P. Burke (ed.), *History and Historians in the Twentieth Century* (Oxford: OUP, 2002), p. 242.
118. Tosh, *The Pursuit of History*, p. 239; D. Dworkin, *Class Struggles* (Harlow: Pearson, 2007).
119. R. J. Evans, *Altered Pasts: Counterfactuals in History* (London: Little, Brown, 2014), p. 62.
120. Abrahms, 'Why Terrorism Does Not Work', p. 43.

121. And Max Abrahms's excellent article 'Does Terrorism Really Work? Evolution in the Conventional Wisdom Since 9/11' (*Defence and Peace Economics*, 22/6 (2011)) suggests that empirical research has undermined the theoretically derived assumption that terrorism works. This current book represents a larger-scale engagement with this line of argument, on the basis of lengthier, more fine-grained readings of specific cases.

122. T. Honderich, *Terrorism for Humanity: Inquiries in Political Philosophy* (London: Pluto, 2003; 1st edn 1989), pp. 25, 37.

123. Honderich, *Terrorism for Humanity*, p. 41.

124. T. Honderich, *Humanity, Terrorism, Terrorist War: Palestine, 9/11, Iraq, 7/7* (London: Continuum, 2006), pp. 184–5.

125. Held, *How Terrorism Is Wrong*, pp. 84–7; U. Steinhoff, *On the Ethics of War and Terrorism* (Oxford: OUP, 2007); Goodin, *What's Wrong with Terrorism?*

126. Cf. Held, *How Terrorism Is Wrong*, p. 144.

127. MacMillan, *The Uses and Abuses of History*, pp. 37, 168; cf. Marwick, *The New Nature of History*, p. 36.

128. Jordanova, *History in Practice*, p. 101; Evans, *Altered Pasts*, p. 82.

129. E. Foner, *Who Owns History? Rethinking the Past in a Changing World* (New York: Hill and Wang, 2003; 1st edn 2002), p. 4; cf. Elton, *Return to Essentials*, p. 73.

130. Elton, *The Practice of History*, p. 47; Black and MacRaild, *Studying History*, p. 102.

131. Tosh, *The Pursuit of History*, pp. 31, 33.

132. See, for example, Evans, *In Defence of History*, p. 133.

133. J. C. D. Clark, *Revolution and Rebellion: State and Society in England in the Seventeenth and Eighteenth Centuries* (Cambridge: Cambridge University Press, 1986), p. 164.

134. Kahneman, *Thinking, Fast and Slow*, pp. 218, 259.

135. R. F. Foster, *The Irish Story: Telling Tales and Making It Up in Ireland* (London: Penguin, 2001), p. 34.

136. The pattern whereby 'most, if not all, of what happens is the result of people trying to achieve certain ends, but never possessing the perspective to see what the effects will be' (J. H. Arnold, *History: A Very Short Introduction* (Oxford: OUP, 2000), p. 93).

137. S. Pollard, *The Idea of Progress: History and Society* (Harmondsworth: Penguin, 1971; 1st edn 1968).

138. Evans, *In Defence of History*, pp. 59, 61; Evans, *Altered Pasts*, p. 62.

139. As Roy Foster has sharp-sightedly argued, within an Irish context: 'it is worth noting the anniversaries that do not get commemorated' (Foster, *The Irish Story*, p. 32).

140. B. A. Wurgaft, 'The Uses of Walter: Walter Benjamin and the Counterfactual Imagination', *History and Theory*, 49 (2010); J. C. D. Clark, *Our Shadowed Present: Modernism, Postmodernism, and History* (London: Atlantic Books, 2003), pp. 28–9; Jordanova, *History in Practice*, pp. 102–3.

141. This tension between the counterfactual and the contingent is very well established in Evans, *Altered Pasts*.

142. Strategy is a term now used so very widely that it extends far beyond the instrumental deployment of violence; for a magisterial, wide-angled survey, see L. Freedman, *Strategy: A History* (Oxford: OUP, 2013). But for our purposes here, it is just such a use of violence that is sharply relevant. In line with my previous work, I will therefore define strategy as the art of using military means to achieve specific political ends and policy objectives; tactics operate at a lower level, constituting the detailed, day-to-day choices involved in using organized, armed forces in line with strategic aims (English, *Modern War*, p. 16).

143. Freedman, *Strategy*, p. xi.

144. H. Strachan, *The Direction of War: Contemporary Strategy in Historical Perspective* (Cambridge: Cambridge University Press, 2013), pp. 13–14.

145. Richardson, *What Terrorists Want*, pp. 62–3, 98, 100–1, 113–20, 161, quotation at p. 113.

146. Crenshaw, *Explaining Terrorism*, p. 47.

147. Pinker, *Better Angels*, p. 34.

148. It is hard to see how nuclear terrorism, for example, could work for most groups, the majority of terrorist organizations being likely to think it either beyond them and/or counter-productive (M. Levi, *On Nuclear Terrorism* (Cambridge, Mass.: Harvard University Press, 2007), p. 11). Nonetheless, nuclear terrorism has been a high-priority threat in the view of the US authorities in recent years (Crenshaw, *Explaining Terrorism*, p. 1), and exterminatory terrorism need not be nuclear.

149. Berman, *Radical, Religious, and Violent*, p. 93.

150. Dershowitz, *Why Terrorism Works*, p. 96.

151. Moyano, *Argentina's Lost Patrol*, pp. 57–60.

152. Cf. 'whatever else terrorism might be, it is a highly effective means of gaining attention in the media' (Taylor and Quayle, *Terrorist Lives*, p. 7).

153. C. Townshend, *Terrorism: A Very Short Introduction* (Oxford: OUP, 2002), p. 8.

154. Laqueur, *Terrorism*, p. 109.

155. J. Vittori, *Terrorist Financing and Resourcing* (Basingstoke: Palgrave Macmillan, 2011), p. 13.

156. Krueger, *What Makes a Terrorist*, p. 138.

157. Pinker, *Better Angels*, pp. 344–5.

158. Gearty, *Terror*, p. 10.

159. M. Juergensmeyer, *Terror in the Mind of God: The Global Rise of Religious Violence* (Berkeley: University of California Press, 2001; 1st edn 2000), p. 124.

160. Hoffman, *Inside Terrorism*, p. 173.

161. Richardson, *What Terrorists Want*, pp. 120–4.

162. Cf. terrorism 'critically relies on provoking the target into responding in ways that inadvertently undermine its authority' (Neumann and Smith, *The Strategy of Terrorism*, p. 32); 'Provocation is a classic, well-established strategy of terrorism' (A. K. Cronin, *Ending Terrorism: Lessons for Defeating al-Qaida* (Abingdon: Routledge, 2008), p. 17); Richardson, *What Terrorists Want*, pp. 127–32.

163. Amis, *The Second Plane*, p. 108.

164. Staniland, *Networks of Rebellion*.

165. J. K. Giraldo and H. A. Trinkunas, 'Introduction', in J. K. Giraldo and H. A. Trinkunas (eds), *Terrorism Financing and State Responses: A Comparative Perspective* (Stanford, Calif.: Stanford University Press, 2007), p. 1.

166. Bloom, *Dying to Kill*.

167. J. N. Shapiro, *The Terrorist's Dilemma: Managing Violent Covert Organizations* (Princeton: Princeton University Press, 2013).

168. M. Begin, *The Revolt: Story of the Irgun* (Jerusalem: Steimatzky's Agency, 1977; 1st edn 1952), p. 73.

169. Shapiro, *The Terrorist's Dilemma*, p. 252; Laqueur, *Terrorism*, pp. 89, 103. It is well established that some of those who engage in terrorist activity have done so, at least partly, because of the allure of financial and/or criminal gain (Gupta, *Understanding Terrorism and Political Violence*, pp. xvi–xvii, 12, 65–7).

170. For some, spiritual rewards might emerge from certain kinds of terrorist action (Bloom, *Dying to Kill*, p. 85).

171. Fierke, *Political Self-Sacrifice*, pp. 94–5, 226, 236.

172. Marsden, 'Successful Terrorism', p. 138.

173. B. Acosta, 'Live to Win Another Day: Why Many Militant Organizations Survive Yet Few Succeed', *SICAT*, 37/2 (2014).

174. There have been thoughtful, very helpful attempts previously to set out frameworks for approaching the issue of terrorism's efficacy (such as Sarah Marsden's review article 'Successful Terrorism', and P. Krause, 'The Political Effectiveness of Non-State Violence: A Two-Level Framework to Transform a Deceptive Debate', *Security Studies*, 22/2 (2013)). This current book, however, offers a different approach from that adopted in those articles: partly in setting out a differently layered and more complex framework for analysis and explanation; partly in trying to overcome the difficulties inherent in the question through adopting an explicitly historical methodology; and partly through actually applying the framework at great length, systematically, and in close, first-hand detail to historically researched, nuanced, and contextually rich case studies as they have intricately changed over time. Other first-rate scholarship in the field (such as C. Berrebi and E. F. Klor's powerful article 'Are Voters Sensitive to Terrorism? Direct Evidence from the Israeli Electorate', *American Political Science Review*, 102/3 (2008), or Gould and Klor's 'Does Terrorism Work?') focuses only on one country, and adopts an econometric approach to one aspect of terrorism's effect. Again, therefore, its approach diverges from the one adopted in the current book.

175. P. Saunier, *Transnational History* (Basingstoke: Palgrave Macmillan, 2013).

176. J. M. Banner, *Being a Historian: An Introduction to the Professional World of History* (Cambridge: Cambridge University Press, 2012), pp. 73–4, 87, 128–30, 141–4, 149, 160, 163–7.

177. E. Hobsbawm, *Interesting Times: A Twentieth-Century Life* (London: Penguin, 2002), p. 282.

CHAPTER I

1. M. Scheuer, *Osama bin Laden* (Oxford: OUP, 2011), p. ix.
2. No definitional stance will please everyone regarding the complex terms jihad, jihadism, and Islamism. A central concept within Islam, jihad means striving or struggle, whether the duty of such activity is interpreted within Islamic warfare pursued in order to bring the truth of Islam to humankind, or in terms of an internal and spiritual struggle to obey God's commands as individuals labour against sin and towards perfection. Violent jihad is therefore only one possibility (and one plainly avoided by most Muslims most of the time). In this book I will use the term jihadism to refer to the militant, violent understanding of jihad. So a jihadist is someone actively committed in practice to, and/or active on behalf of, and/or actually engaged in violent jihad. Some might prefer that we define one who practises violent jihad as a mujahid rather than a jihadist; but I will consider jihadis to be people in various ways committed to different possible kinds of jihad, and jihadists and mujahideen as synonymous. Islamist is a wider term, denoting those authenticists who want politics, society, and the state to be ruled in line with strictly applied, scripturally founded Islamic faith and principles; so jihadism will be considered a violent sub-set of Islamism.
3. Amid the overdose of work now existing on al-Qaida, there have emerged some very powerful studies indeed, including: P. L. Bergen, *Holy War, Inc.: Inside the Secret World of Osama bin Laden* (London: Phoenix, 2002; 1st edn 2001); P. L. Bergen, *The Osama bin Laden I Know* (New York: Free Press, 2006); P. L. Bergen, *The Longest War: The Enduring Conflict Between America and al-Qaida* (New York: Free Press, 2011); Scheuer, *Osama bin Laden*; J. Burke, *Al-Qaida: The True Story of Radical Islam* (London: Penguin, 2003); J. Burke, *The 9/11 Wars* (London: Penguin, 2011); B. Hoffman and F. Reinares (eds), *The Evolution of the Global Terrorist Threat: From 9/11 to Osama bin Laden's Death* (New York: Columbia University Press, 2014); M. D. Silber, *The Al-Qaida Factor: Plots Against the West* (Philadelphia: University of Pennsylvania Press, 2012); L. Wright, *The Looming Tower: Al Qaida's Road to 9/11* (London: Penguin, 2007; 1st edn 2006); Sageman, *Understanding Terror Networks*; C. Hellmich, *Al-Qaida: From Global Network to Local Franchise* (London: Zed Books, 2011).
4. 'The Afghan war changed bin Laden' (Bergen, *Longest War*, p. 15).
5. Silber, *The Al-Qaida Factor*.
6. Silber, *The Al-Qaida Factor*, pp. 169–83.
7. Quoted in Scheuer, *Osama bin Laden*, p. 114.
8. Osama bin Laden, 'Declaration of War' (1996), in R. L. Euben and M. Q. Zaman (eds), *Princeton Readings in Islamist Thought: Texts and Contexts from al-Banna to Bin Laden* (Princeton: Princeton University Press, 2009), pp. 448–9.
9. Yeslam bin Laden (28 May 2005), quoted in Bergen, *The Osama bin Laden I Know*, p. 20.
10. Bergen, *The Osama bin Laden I Know*, p. 16.

11. It is important to note that not all Salafis do espouse such violence; for one strong case outlining the role played by Salafis in *countering* terrorism, see A. H. Baker, *Extremists in our Midst: Confronting Terror* (Basingstoke: Palgrave Macmillan, 2011).

12. Though raised in a Wahhabi household, bin Laden was more Salafi than Wahhabi; a branch of Salafism, Wahhabism (based on the teachings of the zealous eighteenth-century Islamic reformer Muhammad ibn 'Abd al-Wahhab), is less tolerant of diversity than Salafism necessarily is, though Wahhabism represents a branch of Salafism and has been a major influence upon it.

13. 'Zawahiri is the ideological brains behind the war launched against America on September 11, 2001' (B. Riedel, *The Search for al-Qaida: Its Leadership, Ideology, and Future* (Washington: Brookings Institutions Press, 2008), p. 16).

14. A. al-Zawahiri, *Knights Under the Prophet's Banner* (2001), in A. al-Zawahiri, *His Own Words: Translation and Analysis of the Writings of Dr Ayman al-Zawahiri* (Old Tappan, NJ: TLG Publications, 2006), pp. 47–50; Sayyid Qutb (1906–66): an Egyptian Islamist ideologue, to whom many jihadists have turned for inspiration; active member of the Muslim Brotherhood; studied English and education in the USA 1948–50, turning very strongly against America while there; was arrested for opposition to Nasser's regime and in 1955 sentenced to fifteen years in prison; tortured while in jail and (unsurprisingly?) became more militantly Islamist during this period; in jail, developed the ideas which became foundational to much later jihadist ideology; released from prison, 1964; arrested again in 1965 on charges of treason; hanged, 29 August 1966 on charges of trying to overthrow the Egyptian government. One of Qutb's earliest supporters had been Zawahiri's uncle, Mahfouz Azzam, so personal connections have complemented the ideological.

15. Wright, *The Looming Tower*, pp. 52–5, quotation from al-Zawahiri at p. 55.

16. Hoffman and Reinares (eds), *Evolution of the Global Terrorist Threat*, p. 3.

17. Osama bin Laden, quoted in Euben and Zaman (eds), *Princeton Readings in Islamist Thought*, p. 434.

18. See Lutz and Lutz, *Global Terrorism*, p. 30.

19. *The 9/11 Commission Report* (2004), p. xv.

20. Zulaika, *Terrorism*, pp. 187, 190.

21. Silber, *The Al-Qaida Factor*, pp. 107–27.

22. B. Hoffman, 'The 7 July 2005 London Bombings', in Hoffman and Reinares (eds), *Evolution of the Global Terrorist Threat*, pp. 192–223.

23. Giraldo and Trinkunas (eds), *Terrorism Financing and State Responses*, p. 18.

24. For contributions to this important debate, see: B. Hoffman, 'The Myth of Grass-Roots Terrorism: Why Osama bin Laden Still Matters', *Foreign Affairs*, 87/3 (2008); M. Sageman and B. Hoffman, 'Does Osama Still Call the Shots? Debating the Containment of al-Qaida's Leadership', *Foreign Affairs*, 87/4 (2008); Hoffman and Reinares (eds), *The Evolution of the Global Terrorist Threat*; P. Neumann, R. Evans, and R. Pantucci, 'Locating al-Qaida's Centre of Gravity:

The Role of Middle Managers', *SICAT*, 34/11 (2011); J. Jordan, 'The Evolution of the Structure of Jihadist Terrorism in Western Europe: The Case of Spain', *SICAT*, 37/8 (2014).

25. A. Bousquet, 'Complexity Theory and the War on Terror: Understanding the Self-organizing Dynamics of Leaderless Jihad', *Journal of International Relations and Development*, 15/3 (2012).

26. K. Chakrabarti, 'Terrorism: Challenges to Politics, Society, and International Relations', *Jadavpur Journal of International Relations*, 11–12 (2006–8), p. 139.

27. Historically long timeframes undoubtedly help here. See A. J. Barker, *The First Iraq War 1914–1918: Britain's Mesopotamian Campaign* (New York: Enigma Books, 2009), pp. xi, 9–10; J. Buchan, *Greenmantle* (Harmondsworth: Penguin, 1956; 1st edn 1916).

28. On the way in which knowledge of anarchism, for example, partly qualifies suggestions about al-Qaida's organizational novelty, see Lynch and Ryder, 'Deadliness, Organizational Change, and Suicide Attacks', pp. 268–9, 271.

29. P. L. Bergen and P. Cruickshank, 'Revisiting the Early Al-Qaida: An Updated Account of its Formative Years', *SICAT*, 35/1 (2012).

30. Much evidence exists about al-Qaida's capacity to think strategically. See, for example, T. Hegghammer and B. Lia, 'Jihadi Strategic Studies: The Alleged Al-Qaida Policy Study Preceding the Madrid Bombings', *SICAT*, 27/5 (2004).

31. Quoted in Scheuer, *Osama bin Laden*, p. 115.

32. Bergen, *Longest War*, p. 8.

33. M. Phillips, *Londonistan: How Britain is Creating a Terror State Within* (London: Gibson Square, 2006), pp. 274–5.

34. Osama bin Laden (4 January 2004), quoted in B. Lawrence (ed.), *Messages to the World: The Statements of Osama bin Laden* (London: Verso, 2005), p. 227.

35. Born in the West Bank in 1959, al-Maqdisi has known numerous people who have played a major role in al-Qaida, he himself applauded the 9/11 attacks and has praised al-Qaida's work, and in his commitment to violent jihad he can legitimately be termed a jihadist (J. Wagemakers, *A Quietist Jihadi: The Ideology and Influence of Abu Muhammad al-Maqdisi* (Cambridge: Cambridge University Press, 2012)).

36. Osama bin Laden (12 November 2001), quoted in Lawrence (ed.), *Messages to the World*, p. 143.

37. Pape and Feldman, *Cutting the Fuse*, pp. 22–3.

38. Quoted in Bergen, *Holy War, Inc.*, p. 19.

39. Osama bin Laden (12 November 2001), quoted in A. Brahimi, *Jihad and Just War in the War on Terror* (Oxford: OUP, 2010), p. 142.

40. Elizabeth Slater, quoted in Bergen, *Holy War, Inc.*, p. 115.

41. Quoted in B. Rubin and J. C. Rubin (eds), *Anti-American Terrorism and the Middle East: A Documentary Reader* (Oxford: OUP, 2002), p. 174.

42. Osama bin Laden (29 December 1994), quoted in Lawrence (ed.), *Messages to the World*, p. 9; cf. Wright, *The Looming Tower*, pp. 75–6, 131.

43. Ayman al-Zawahiri (1 October 2004) in al-Zawahiri, *His Own Words*, p. 234.
44. Baker, *Extremists in our Midst*, pp. 140-1, 144-5, 207.
45. Osama bin Laden (November 1996), quoted in Lawrence (ed.), *Messages to the World*, p. 39.
46. Pape, *Dying to Win*; 'military occupation accounts for nearly all suicide terrorism around the world since 1980' (Pape and Feldman, *Cutting the Fuse*, p. 10).
47. Quoted in Silber, *The Al-Qaida Factor*, p. 27; cf. Baker, *Extremists in our Midst*, pp. 139-41, 145.
48. Bergen and Cruickshank, 'Revisiting the Early Al-Qaida', p. 21.
49. Osama bin Laden, quoted in Wright, *The Looming Tower*, p. 150.
50. Osama bin Laden video speech of December 2001, in K. J. Greenberg (ed.), *Al-Qaida Now: Understanding Today's Terrorists* (Cambridge: Cambridge University Press, 2005), p. 207.
51. Osama bin Laden (March 1997), quoted in Lawrence (ed.), *Messages to the World*, p. 46.
52. R. P. Barnidge, 'War and Peace: Negotiating Meaning in Islam', in J. M. Skelly (ed.), *Political Islam from Muhammad to Ahmadinejad* (Santa Barbara, Calif.: Praeger Security International, 2010), p. 57.
53. J. Davis, 'Introduction', in J. Davis (ed.), *Africa and the War on Terrorism* (Aldershot: Ashgate, 2007), p. 8; Wright, *The Looming Tower*, pp. 187-9, 200.
54. Osama bin Laden, 'Declaration of War' (1996), in Euben and Zaman (eds), *Princeton Readings in Islamist Thought*, p. 451.
55. Osama bin Laden, quoted in Euben and Zaman (eds), *Princeton Readings in Islamist Thought*, p. 429.
56. Ayman al-Zawahiri, *Knights Under the Prophet's Banner* (2001), in al-Zawahiri, *His Own Words*, p. 38.
57. A. Guelke, *The New Age of Terrorism and the International Political System* (London: I. B. Tauris, 2009; 1st edn 1995), p. xiv.
58. Osama bin Laden, quoted in Pape and Feldman, *Cutting the Fuse*, p. 120.
59. Osama bin Laden (20 October 2001), quoted in Lawrence (ed.), *Messages to the World*, p. 109.
60. Osama bin Laden (14 February 2003), quoted in Lawrence (ed.), *Messages to the World*, p. 195.
61. Osama bin Laden, 'Declaration of War' (1996), in Euben and Zaman (eds), *Princeton Readings in Islamist Thought*, p. 436.
62. Osama bin Laden video speech of December 2001, in Greenberg (ed.), *Al-Qaida Now*, p. 207.
63. Quoted in Scheuer, *Osama bin Laden*, p. 69.
64. Riedel, *The Search for al-Qaida*, p. 122.
65. Lawrence (ed.), *Messages to the World*, p. 217.
66. Osama bin Laden (1996), quoted in Scheuer, *Osama bin Laden*, p. 33.
67. Abrahms, 'Al-Qaida's Scorecard', p. 513.
68. Ahmad, quoted in P. Beaumont, *The Secret Life of War: Journeys Through Modern Conflict* (London: Harvill Secker, 2009), p. 99.

69. 26 December 2001, quoted in Lawrence (ed.), *Messages to the World*, p. 153.

70. Osama bin Laden (6 October 2002), quoted in Lawrence (ed.), *Messages to the World*, p. 162. Some observers hold that this October 2002 letter is not in fact from bin Laden (see Bergen, *The Osama bin Laden I Know*, p. xxxiv). It is hard to be anything like certain here. But the sentiment reflected in this particular quotation does resonate with other statements made by bin Laden himself.

71. Quoted in Bergen, *Longest War*, p. 28.

72. Sageman, *Understanding Terror Networks*, p. 1.

73. Sageman, *Leaderless Jihad*, p. 15.

74. The Caliphate disappeared with the end of the Turkish Ottoman Empire in 1924; it embodied an Islamic equivalent to a system such as empire, and had endured from the death of Muhammad in AD 632 until its post-First World War demise; the Caliph, seen as a successor to Muhammad, held the role of rightful political leader of all Muslims.

75. D. Holbrook, *The Al-Qaida Doctrine: The Framing and Evolution of the Leadership's Public Discourse* (London: Bloomsbury, 2014), p. 59.

76. Scheuer, *Osama bin Laden*, pp. 14, 34, 41–3. Though bin Laden explicitly and positively referred to the ideas of Qutb's brother Mohammed (Lawrence (ed.), *Messages to the World*, p. 229), whose public lectures at King Abdul Aziz University he seems to have attended (Wright, *The Looming Tower*, p. 79); and some eminent bin Laden experts see Qutb as highly significant (see Bergen, *The Osama bin Laden I Know*, p. 18).

77. J. Gray, *Al-Qaida and What it Means to be Modern* (London: Faber and Faber, 2007; 1st edn 2003), p. 24.

78. S. Qutb, *Milestones* (New Delhi: Islamic Book Service, 2001), pp. 10–11, 20, 35, 58, 99, 130.

79. Qutb, *Milestones*, p. 111.

80. Quoted in UK Intelligence and Security Committee, *Report into the London Terrorist Attacks on 7 July 2005* (2006), p. 12.

81. Wright, *The Looming Tower*, p. 179; Hoffman and Reinares (eds), *Evolution of the Global Terrorist Threat*, pp. 47, 201.

82. Sageman, *Understanding Terror Networks*, p. 106; Sageman, *Leaderless Jihad*, p. 72; Wright, *The Looming Tower*, p. 306.

83. December 1998, quoted in Brahimi, *Jihad and Just War*, p. 111.

84. 1997, quoted in Bergen, *Holy War*, p. 22.

85. P. Bobbitt, *Terror and Consent: The Wars for the Twenty-First Century* (London: Penguin, 2009; 1st edn 2008), p. 83. Cf. M. R. Habeck, *Knowing the Enemy: Jihadist Ideology and the War on Terror* (New Haven: Yale University Press, 2006), pp. 122–3, 132–3.

86. P. L. Bergen, *Manhunt: From 9/11 to Abbottabad—The Ten-Year Search for Osama bin Laden* (London: Bodley Head, 2012), p. xix.

87. M. Juergensmeyer, *Global Rebellion: Religious Challenges to the Secular State, from Christian Militias to al-Qaida* (Berkeley: University of California Press, 2008), p. 247.

88. Osama bin Laden (12 November 2001), quoted in Lawrence (ed), *Messages to the World*, p. 140.
89. Intelligence and Security Committee of Parliament, *Report on the Intelligence Relating to the Murder of Fusilier Lee Rigby* (2014), pp. 119–26, 129, 131.
90. Hoffman, *Inside Terrorism*, p. 282.
91. M. Ruthven, *Fundamentalism: The Search for Meaning* (Oxford: OUP, 2004), pp. 137, 150–1.
92. F. Reinares, 'The 2004 Madrid Train Bombings', in Hoffman and Reinares (eds), *Evolution of the Global Terrorist Threat*, pp. 29–60.
93. Pape and Feldman, *Cutting the Fuse*, p. 68.
94. Quoted in Jones, *Blood That Cries Out From the Earth*, p. 38.
95. Quoted in Richardson, *What Terrorists Want*, p. 217.
96. Al-Zawahiri, *Knights Under the Prophet's Banner*, p. 200; cf. p. 223.
97. Quoted in Shapiro, *The Terrorist's Dilemma*, p. 38.
98. J. M. Brachman, *Global Jihadism: Theory and Practice* (London: Routledge, 2009), p. 12.
99. S. G. Jones, 'Al-Qaida Terrorism in Afghanistan', in Hoffman and Reinares (eds), *Evolution of the Global Terrorist Threat*, p. 375.
100. A. Wolfe, *Political Evil: What It Is and How To Combat It* (New York: Alfred A. Knopf, 2011), p. 6.
101. M. W. Zackie, 'An Analysis of Abu Mus'ab al-Suri's *Call to Global Islamic Resistance*', *Journal of Strategic Security*, 6/1 (2013).
102. Shapiro, *The Terrorist's Dilemma*, pp. 16, 105–6.
103. Pisoiu, *Islamist Radicalization*, pp. 4, 8, 49, 55, 85–106, 168.
104. As in the troubled case, for example, of Zacarias Moussaoui (Baker, *Extremists in our Midst*, pp. 110, 112–13, 117–18, 178).
105. Jones, *Blood That Cries Out from the Earth*, pp. 137–8.
106. Quoted in Bergen, *Holy War, Inc.*, p. 19.
107. Aimen Dean, interviewed by Peter Marshall (2015), 'The Spy Who Came in from al-Qaida', BBC Radio 4, broadcast on 3 March 2015.
108. 7 October 2001, quoted in Lawrence (ed.), *Messages to the World*, p. 104.
109. Barnidge, 'War and Peace'.
110. Joseph Ratzinger argued that the Islamic model of the state 'is quite obviously exactly the opposite model to pluralist democracy and cannot therefore become its foundational force' (J. Ratzinger, *Church, Ecumenism and Politics: New Essays in Ecclesiology* (Slough: St Paul Publications, 1988), p. 215; cf. p. 162). See the somewhat countervailing view in Euben and Zaman (eds), *Princeton Readings in Islamist Thought*, p. 30.
111. J. Anderson, *Christianity and Democratization: From Pious Subjects to Critical Participants* (Manchester: Manchester University Press, 2009).
112. Burke, *9/11 Wars*, p. 492.
113. A. Guelke, *Terrorism and Global Disorder: Political Violence in the Contemporary World* (London: I. B. Tauris, 2006), p. 133.
114. Abrahms, 'Al-Qaida's Scorecard', pp. 517–23.

115. 12 November 2001, quoted in Brahimi, *Jihad and Just War*, p. 112.
116. M. Burleigh, *Blood and Rage: A Cultural History of Terrorism* (London: HarperPress, 2008), p. 415.
117. Staniland, *Networks of Rebellion*, pp. 109–27; Jones, 'Al-Qaida Terrorism in Afghanistan', in Hoffman and Reinares (eds), *Evolution of the Global Terrorist Threat*, p. 376; Wright, *The Looming Tower*, p. 110.
118. T. Barfield, *Afghanistan: A Cultural and Political History* (Princeton: Princeton University Press, 2010), p. 243.
119. S. Croft, *Culture, Crisis, and America's War on Terror* (Cambridge: Cambridge University Press, 2006), p. 90.
120. D. Antonius and S. J. Sinclair, *The Psychology of Terrorism Fears* (Oxford: OUP, 2012), pp. 94, 102, 132–3.
121. Croft, *Culture, Crisis, and America's War on Terror*, p. 149.
122. E. Hobsbawm, *Globalization, Democracy, and Terrorism* (London: Little, Brown, 2007), p. 135.
123. Strachan, *The Direction of War*, p. 2.
124. Yousef, who masterminded the attack, later claimed to have hoped for a quarter of a million casualties (Bergen, *The Osama bin Laden I Know*, pp. 144–5).
125. Quoted in Hoffman, *Inside Terrorism*, p. 134.
126. Quoted in Bergen, *Holy War, Inc.*, p. 234.
127. 'The September 11 terrorist attacks on the World Trade Center and the Pentagon were a watershed in strategic development and international relations, marking the end of the post-Cold War era' (J. Wanandi, 'A Global Coalition Against International Terrorism', *International Security*, 26/4 (2002), p. 184).
128. Rengger, *Just War and International Order*, pp. 6, 14–26; J. Waldron, *Torture, Terror, and Trade-Offs: Philosophy for the White House* (Oxford: OUP, 2010), p. 189.
129. Antonius and Sinclair, *The Psychology of Terrorism Fears*; cf. Sageman, *Understanding Terror Networks*, p. vii.
130. Antonius and Sinclair, *The Psychology of Terrorism Fears*, pp. 100–2.
131. Croft, *Culture, Crisis, and America's War on Terror*.
132. Antonius and Sinclair, *The Psychology of Terrorism Fears*, pp. 33–5, 86.
133. Waldron, *Torture, Terror, and Trade-Offs*, p. 65.
134. Jackson, Jarvis, Gunning, and Breen Smyth, *Terrorism*, p. 146.
135. Mueller and Stewart, *Terror, Security, and Money*, p. 61.
136. Bergen, *Longest War*, p. 91; cf. Riedel, *The Search for al-Qaida*, p. 1.
137. Mueller and Stewart, *Terror, Security, and Money*.
138. Mueller and Stewart, *Terror, Security, and Money*, pp. 60–1.
139. Bergen, *Holy War, Inc.*, pp. 171–2.
140. Hoffman and Reinares (eds), *Evolution of the Global Terrorist Threat*, p. 30.
141. B. S. Zellen, *State of Recovery: The Quest to Restore American Security After 9/11* (London: Bloomsbury, 2013).
142. This is a point established strongly, for example, in the FBI 9/11 Review Commission Report: *The FBI: Protecting the Homeland in the Twenty-First Century* (2015).

143. In 1839–42 and 1878–80 (Barfield, *Afghanistan*, pp. 110–63). Regarding those two nineteenth-century conflicts, I think it is worth reflecting on Professor Barfield's exact and far from encouraging phrasing: 'The Second Anglo-Afghan War, like the first, began well for the British and ended badly' (p. 141).

144. *The Times* 27 October 2014.

145. Burke, *9/11 Wars*, pp. 252–6, 293–4, 472; Mueller and Stewart, *Terror, Security, and Money*, pp. 30–3; A. Brahimi, 'Crushed in the Shadows: Why al-Qaida Will Lose the War of Ideas', *SICAT*, 33/2 (2010).

146. Bergen, *Longest War*, p. 302.

147. Quoted in Brahimi, 'Crushed in the Shadows', p. 93.

148. Baker, *Extremists in our Midst*, pp. 33–4, 45, 49, 58–9; O. Lynch, 'British Muslim Youth: Radicalization, Terrorism, and the Construction of the "Other"', *Critical Studies on Terrorism*, 6/2 (2013). It is clear that most UK Muslims have been hostile to al-Qaida terrorism (S. Hewitt, *The British War on Terror: Terrorism and Counter-Terrorism on the Home Front Since 9/11* (London: Continuum, 2008), p. 111).

149. S. Croft, *Securitizing Islam: Identity and the Search for Security* (Cambridge: Cambridge University Press, 2012), p. 2.

150. P. Cockburn, *The Jihadis Return: ISIS and the New Sunni Uprising* (New York: OR Books, 2014), p. 9.

151. C. Tripp, *A History of Iraq* (Cambridge: Cambridge University Press, 2007; 1st edn 2000), p. 275.

152. R. Barrett, *The Islamic State* (New York: The Soufan Group, 2014).

153. Cronin, *How Terrorism Ends*, p. 146.

154. Cockburn, *The Jihadis Return*, p. 37.

155. Wagemakers, *A Quietist Jihadi*, p. 22.

156. Ruthven, *Fundamentalism*, p. 87.

157. Pape and Feldman, *Cutting the Fuse*, pp. 180, 184, 188; R. Scruton, *The West and the Rest: Globalization and the Terrorist Threat* (London: Continuum, 2002), pp. 126–7.

158. In the vast and complex and heterogeneous world of Islam, al-Qaida has in fact made comparatively little headway (Burke, *9/11 Wars*, pp. 181, 235); the vast majority of the world's Muslims do not show any support for the group, and even many who might be termed Islamist zealots eschew the use of force (Mueller and Stewart, *Terror, Security, and Money*, pp. 30–1).

159. Wagemakers, *A Quietist Jihadi*, pp. 47–8, 52, 78, 82–4, 240–1, 246.

160. Gray, *Al Qaeda and What it Means to be Modern*, pp. 26, 77–9.

161. Habeck, *Knowing the Enemy*, pp. 47, 53.

162. P. M. Currie, *The Shrine and Cult of Mu'in al-din Chishti of Ajmer* (Oxford: OUP, 2006; 1st edn 1989), p. 1.

163. Bloom, *Bombshell*, p. 242; cf. G. Ramsay, *Jihadi Culture on the World Wide Web* (London: Bloomsbury, 2013), p. 185.

164. Cannadine, *The Undivided Past*, pp. 36–7, 250; Euben and Zaman (eds), *Princeton Readings in Islamist Thought*, p. 2.

165. Quoted in C. Miller (ed.), *'War on Terror': The Oxford Amnesty Lectures 2006* (Manchester: Manchester University Press, 2009), p. 9.

166. Wagemakers, *A Quietist Jihadi*, p. 128; T. Hegghammer, *Jihad in Saudi Arabia: Violence and Pan-Islamism Since 1979* (Cambridge: Cambridge University Press, 2010).

167. John Falding, quoted in *Guardian* 6 July 2006.

168. 'Al-Qaida has always been a terrorist and extremist group, and mass appeal or mobilization... is not a real danger' (Holbrook, *Al-Qaida Doctrine*, p. 28).

169. Including financial support (Hegghammer, *Jihad in Saudi Arabia*, pp. 124–8).

170. B. Lia, 'Al-Qaida's Appeal: Understanding its Unique Selling Points', *Perspectives on Terrorism*, 2/8 (2008).

171. Hoffman and Reinares, 'Conclusion', in Hoffman and Reinares (eds), *Evolution of the Global Terrorist Threat*, p. 635; cf. Brachman, *Global Jihadism*, pp. 10–11.

172. Bergen, *The Osama bin Laden I Know*, p. xxviii.

173. Holbrook, *Al-Qaida Doctrine*, pp. 141–2, 148.

174. Shapiro, *The Terrorist's Dilemma*, pp. 89, 98.

175. *Daily Telegraph* 4 January 2014.

176. 'Jihad in Iraq: Hopes and Dangers', quoted in M. M. Hafez, 'The Origins of Sectarian Terrorism in Iraq', in Hoffman and Reinares (eds), *Evolution of the Global Terrorist Threat*, p. 441.

177. The Conservative Popular Party, Partido Popular.

178. The Partido Socialista Obrero Espanol, or Spanish Socialist Workers' Party.

179. Hoffman and Reinares (eds), *Evolution of the Global Terrorist Threat*, p. 32.

180. It is worth remembering, for example, the comparatively low-level attention that the USA paid to terrorism prior to 9/11 (Wright, *The Looming Tower*, p. 4).

181. Juergensmeyer, *Global Rebellion*, p. 214.

182. May 2004, quoted in Scheuer, *Osama bin Laden*, p. 139. Cf. S. P. Huntington, 'The Clash of Civilizations?', *Foreign Affairs*, 72/3 (1993); S. P. Huntington, *The Clash of Civilizations and the Remaking of World Order* (London: Touchstone, 1998; 1st edn 1997).

183. B. Lewis, *The Crisis of Islam: Holy War and Unholy Terror* (New York: Modern Library, 2003), pp. 25, 137; Jones, *Blood That Cries Out from the Earth*, pp. 162–3; Habeck, *Knowing the Enemy*, pp. 110, 117.

184. Wright, *The Looming Tower*, p. 370.

185. Hoffman, *Inside Terrorism*, p. 132.

186. Pape and Feldman, *Cutting the Fuse*, p. 5.

187. Bergen, *Longest War*, pp. 93–4.

188. English, *Terrorism: How to Respond*, pp. 136–40; J. Argomaniz, *The EU and Counter-Terrorism: Politics, Polity and Policies after 9/11* (London: Routledge, 2011).

189. A. B. Zegart, *Flawed by Design: The Evolution of the CIA, JCS, and NSC* (Stanford, Calif.: Stanford University Press, 1999), pp. 1, 11; cf. pp. 37, 41, 168–9, 184, 190, 194–5, 217, 220–2, 224, 230.

190. D. Omand, *Securing the State* (London: Hurst, 2010), p. 175; Treverton, *Intelligence for an Age of Terror*, pp. 5, 7–8, 56, 76–8, 80–1.

191. *Four Lions* (2010: directed by Chris Morris): a satirical comedy about a rather pathetic group of British jihadists.

192. *Guardian* 9 January 2007.

193. UK Intelligence and Security Committee, *Report into the London Terrorist Attacks on 7 July 2005* (2006), p. 11.

194. Bousquet, 'Complexity Theory and the War on Terror', p. 363.

195. Hegghammer, *Jihad in Saudi Arabia*.

196. Ramsay, *Jihadi Culture on the World Wide Web*, pp. 102, 144.

197. Euben and Zaman (eds), *Princeton Readings in Islamist Thought*, p. 426.

198. *Daily Mirror* 8 January 2015. One of the gunmen apparently mentioned the al-Qaida connection explicitly during the attack, and AQAP subsequently claimed to have been behind the assault on *Charlie Hebdo*.

199. *The Times* 8 January 2015.

200. *Daily Telegraph* 8 January 2015.

201. Bergen, *Manhunt*, pp. 16–18.

202. Sageman, *Leaderless Jihad*, pp. 35–6.

203. S. V. Marsden, 'Media Metrics: How Arab and Western Media Construct Success and Failure in the "Global War on Terror"', *Perspectives on Terrorism*, 7/6 (2013).

204. Davis (ed.), *Africa and the War on Terrorism*, pp. 12, 179–80.

205. Brahimi, *Jihad and Just War*, pp. 99–100.

206. Sageman, *Leaderless Jihad*, p. 91; cf. pp. 138–9.

207. *Sunday Telegraph* 9 October 2011.

208. As noted in: Intelligence and Security Committee, *Report into the London Terrorist Attacks on 7 July 2005* (2006), p. 10.

209. Address by the Director General of the UK Security Service, Andrew Parker (Thames House, London, 8 January 2015).

210. A. Danchev, *On Art and War and Terror* (Edinburgh: Edinburgh University Press, 2011; 1st edn 2009), p. 206.

211. Waldron, *Torture, Terror, and Trade-Offs*.

212. Lambert, *Countering Al-Qaida in London*, p. xiv.

213. C. Gearty, *Liberty and Security* (Cambridge: Polity Press, 2013), pp. 96–7.

214. C. Gearty, *Can Human Rights Survive?* (Cambridge: Cambridge University Press, 2006).

215. Ayman al-Zawahiri (21 February 2005) in al-Zawahiri, *His Own Words*, p. 245.

216. *Washington Post* 16 October 2012, 18 October 2012.

217. Bergen, *Longest War*, pp. 97–108.

218. *Guardian* 4 February 2009.

219. *Daily Telegraph* 4 April 2009; *Observer* 22 February 2009; *New York Times* 24 March 2009; *Guardian* 16 March 2009.

220. Senate Select Committee on Intelligence: Committee Study of the CIA's Detention and Interrogation Program (2014), pp. 2–3.

221. M. O. Slahi, *Guantanamo Diary* (Edinburgh: Canongate, 2015).

222. Barfield, *Afghanistan*, quotation at p. 7.

223. 'The evidence suggests that al-Qaida has played an important role in Afghanistan's insurgency as a force multiplier' (Jones, 'Al-Qaida Terrorism in Afghanistan', in Hoffman and Reinares (eds), *Evolution of the Global Terrorist Threat*, p. 376).

224. I think that a contextualized analysis of the post-2001 Afghan conflict (and indeed of the post-2003 Iraqi conflict too) makes utterly clear that we can only assess what most people would refer to as 'terrorism' by recognizing that it blurs into other categories of violence. What al-Qaida terrorism achieved can only be measured by acknowledging that 9/11 prompted responses which led to civil war and insurgency in both countries, conflicts which themselves witnessed some violence that was clearly terroristic in nature and other, interwoven violence possibly better described under other terms. Here, a historically contextualized approach helps deal with the problem of definition identified in the Introduction.

225. Quoted in *Daily Telegraph* 27 October 2014.

226. Quoted in *The Times* 27 October 2014.

227. Barfield, *Afghanistan*, pp. 251, 317, 325, 333.

228. M. M. Hafez, 'The Origins of Sectarian Terrorism in Iraq', in Hoffman and Reinares (eds), *Evolution of the Global Terrorist Threat*, pp. 436–60.

229. Tripp, *A History of Iraq*, pp. 1, 4.

230. C. Townshend, *When God Made Hell: The British Invasion of Mesopotamia and the Creation of Iraq 1914–1921* (London: Faber and Faber, 2010), pp. xxi–xxii.

231. Tripp, *A History of Iraq*, pp. 267–88.

232. Brachman, *Global Jihadism*, pp. 14, 96.

233. Speaking on 14 December 2011, and quoted in *Guardian* 15 December 2011.

234. Modern war being defined as 'heterogeneous, organized, mutual enmity and violence between armed groups, on more than a minor scale, carried out with political objectives, possessing socio-political dynamics, and focused on the exerting of power in order to compel opponents; it is located in the post-French Revolutionary era of nationalism, during which the interwoven dynamics of national community, struggle, and power have determined a particular form of violent conflict' (English, *Modern War*, p. 16).

235. Intelligence and Security Committee of Parliament, *Report on the Intelligence Relating to the Murder of Fusilier Lee Rigby* (2014), pp. 4, 68, 74–5, 86, 108, 122, 127–9, 139–46, 165–72.

236. *Daily Telegraph* 26 November 2014.

237. 'Al-Qaida is the first truly global terrorist organization in history' (Riedel, *The Search for al-Qaida*, p. ix).

238. Hoffman, *Inside Terrorism*, p. x.

239. B. Hoffman and F. Reinares, 'Conclusion', in Hoffman and Reinares (eds), *Evolution of the Global Terrorist Threat*, pp. 618–22.

240. Sageman, *Leaderless Jihad*, p. vii.

241. Sageman, *Understanding Terror Networks*, p. 51.

242. Neumann, Evans, and Pantucci, 'Locating al-Qaida's Centre of Gravity', p. 826; Jones, 'Al-Qaida Terrorism in Afghanistan', in Hoffman and Reinares (eds), *Evolution of the Global Terrorist Threat*, pp. 385–6.

243. Hoffman, '7 July 2005', in Hoffman and Reinares (eds), *Evolution of the Global Terrorist Threat*, p. 215.

244. Omand, *Securing the State*, p. 89.

245. *Prevent* (2011), pp. 5, 17.

246. Wilkinson, *Terrorism Versus Democracy* (2006 edn), p. 184.

247. M. Eilstrup-Sangiovanni and C. Jones, 'Assessing the Dangers of Illicit Networks: Why Al-Qaida May be Less Threatening than Many Think', *International Security*, 33/2 (2008).

248. Juergensmeyer, *Global Rebellion*, p. 260.

249. Burke, *9/11 Wars*, pp. 196–9.

250. Silber, *The Al-Qaida Factor*, pp. 280–3.

251. UK Ministry of Defence, *Strategic Trends Programme: Future Character of Conflict* (2010), p. 19.

252. On the killing of bin Laden, see Bergen, *Manhunt*; C. Pfarrer, *Seal Target Geronimo: The Inside Story of the Mission to Kill Osama bin Laden* (London: Quercus, 2011).

253. Silber, *The Al-Qaida Factor*, p. 5; cf. Zellen, *State of Recovery*, pp. 87, 135, 163, 225.

254. Silber, *The Al-Qaida Factor*, p. 295.

255. Quoted in *Guardian* 3 May 2011.

256. Bergen and Cruickshank, 'Revisiting the Early Al-Qaida', p. 29; Bergen, *Longest War*, pp. 336–49; Scheuer, *Osama bin Laden*.

257. Bergen, *Longest War*, pp. 81–5; Bergen, *Manhunt*, pp. 40–54.

258. M. Smith and J. I. Walsh, 'Do Drone Strikes Degrade al-Qaida? Evidence from Propaganda Output', *TPV*, 25/2 (2013).

259. Silber, *The Al-Qaida Factor*, pp. 188, 192–3.

260. Mohammed Atta, 'Final Instructions', in Euben and Zaman (eds), *Princeton Readings in Islamist Thought*, pp. 466, 471.

261. Bloom, *Bombshell*, pp. 197–9; Baker, *Extremists in our Midst*, pp. 130–2.

262. Including the fictional: J. Updike, *Terrorist* (London: Hamish Hamilton, 2006).

263. R. English, *Ernie O'Malley: IRA Intellectual* (Oxford: OUP, 1998).

264. Shapiro, *The Terrorist's Dilemma*, p. 40; Bergen, *Holy War*, pp. 30, 83; Wright, *The Looming Tower*, pp. 141–2, 169, 250; Bergen, *The Osama bin Laden I Know*, pp. 154–5; Bergen, *Manhunt*, pp. 55–6.

265. Hegghammer, *Jihad in Saudi Arabia*, pp. 131, 133.

266. Burke, *9/11 Wars*, p. 207; Bergen, *Holy War*, pp. 128–9; Hegghammer, *Jihad in Saudi Arabia*, p. 137.

267. Sageman, *Understanding Terror Networks*.

268. Sageman, *Leaderless Jihad*, pp. 87–8.

269. See the impressively original treatment of this theme in Ramsay, *Jihadi Culture on the World Wide Web*.

270. Ramsay, *Jihadi Culture on the World Wide Web*, p. 117.

271. Quoted in Hoffman, *Inside Terrorism*, p. 94.

272. Holbrook, *Al-Qaida Doctrine*, pp. xvi–xviii, 3, 12, 15, 51–2, 64–6, 73–5, 78, 83, 85–6, 149, 154.

273. *The Times* 12 January 2015.

274. *Daily Mirror* 8 January 2015.

275. *The Times* 12 January 2015.

276. *The Times* 8 January 2015.

277. *Daily Telegraph* 10 January 2015.

278. *Daily Telegraph* 8 January 2015.

279. Holbrook, *Al-Qaida Doctrine*, pp. 111, 129, 131–2.

280. J. Argomaniz and O. Lynch (eds), 'Victims of Terrorism: An Introduction', in *Victims of Terrorism: A Comparative and Interdisciplinary Study* (London: Routledge, 2015), p. 1.

281. J. Githens-Mazer, 'Islamic Radicalization among North Africans in Britain', *British Journal of Politics and International Relations*, 10/4 (2008), p. 552.

282. Al-Zawahiri, *Knights Under the Prophet's Banner*, in al-Zawahiri, *His Own Words*, p. 19.

283. *USA Today/Reno Gazette Journal* 24 September 2014.

284. *USA Today* 25 September 2014.

285. Quoted in Hoffman, *Inside Terrorism*, p. 96.

286. Cronin, *How Terrorism Ends*, p. 194; Wilkinson, *Terrorism Versus Democracy* (2006 edn), p. 40.

287. Bergen, *Manhunt*, p. 36.

288. T. Blair, *A Journey* (London: Hutchinson, 2010), pp. 342, 345, 368.

CHAPTER 2

1. Interviewed by the author, Belfast, 26 November 2012.

2. R. English, *Irish Freedom: The History of Nationalism in Ireland* (London: Pan, 2007; 1st edn 2006).

3. George Harrison, interviewed by the author, New York, 30 October 2000.

4. M. J. Kelly, *The Fenian Ideal and Irish Nationalism, 1882–1916* (Woodbridge: Boydell Press, 2006), p. 2.

5. R. V. Comerford, *The Fenians in Context: Irish Politics and Society, 1848–82* (Dublin: Wolfhound Press, 1985).

6. S. McConville, *Irish Political Prisoners, 1848–1922: Theatres of War* (London: Routledge, 2003), pp. 140–213.

7. *Irish People* 10 February 1866.

8. N. Whelehan, *The Dynamiters: Irish Nationalism and Political Violence in the Wider World, 1867–1900* (Cambridge: Cambridge University Press, 2012).

9. English, *Irish Freedom*, pp. 141–61.

10. D. Fitzpatrick (ed.), *Terror in Ireland 1916–1923* (Dublin: Lilliput Press, 2012), pp. 5–9, 10–19; J. Gantt, *Irish Terrorism in the Atlantic Community, 1865–1922* (Basingstoke: Palgrave Macmillan, 2010).

11. C. Townshend, *Easter 1916: The Irish Rebellion* (London: Penguin, 2005), p. 96; M. Elliott, *Robert Emmet: The Making of a Legend* (London: Profile Books, 2003), pp. 44–67.
12. F. McGarry, *The Rising. Ireland: Easter 1916* (Oxford: OUP, 2010), p. 265.
13. 'Pubic Attitude and Opinion in Ireland as to the Recent Outbreak' (15 May 1916), Bonar Law Papers, House of Lords Record Office, London, BL 63/C/3.
14. Ernie O'Malley, writing in 1923, and quoted in English, *Ernie O'Malley*, pp. 5, 7.
15. R. F. Foster, *Vivid Faces: The Revolutionary Generation in Ireland 1890–1923* (London: Penguin, 2014), pp. 229–30, 246–9, 256.
16. Townshend, *Easter 1916*, p. 218; McGarry, *The Rising*, pp. 59, 157, 159–60, 216, 239, 272.
17. McGarry, *The Rising*, pp. 1, 3, 141.
18. Foster, *Vivid Faces*, pp. 244, 272, 324.
19. R. Fanning, *Fatal Path: British Government and Irish Revolution 1910–1922* (London: Faber and Faber, 2013), pp. 1–6, 356–8.
20. M. Hopkinson, *Green Against Green: The Irish Civil War* (Dublin: Gill and Macmillan, 1988); B. Kissane, *The Politics of the Irish Civil War* (Oxford: OUP, 2005).
21. Ernie O'Malley, writing in 1923, and quoted in English, *Ernie O'Malley*, p. 1. On the revolutionary generation's wider Anglophobia, see Foster, *Vivid Faces*, pp. 18, 72.
22. See the careful treatment in G. Clark, *Everyday Violence in the Irish Civil War* (Cambridge: Cambridge University Press, 2014), pp. 10, 29, 31, 36, 39–40, 43, 45, 48–9, 51, 89–90, 97–100, 102–3, 105–14, 140, 152–3, 167–76, 181, 197–203.
23. R. English, *Armed Struggle: The History of the IRA* (London: Pan, 2012; 1st edn 2003), pp. 128–9.
24. Begin, *The Revolt*, pp. 99, 284–5.
25. K. Conway, *Southside Provisional: From Freedom Fighter to the Four Courts* (Blackrock: Orpen Press, 2014), p. 110.
26. Barron's Report of 15 October 1921, contained in a 'Note on the State of North-West Munster: Memorandum by the Chief Secretary for Ireland [Hamar Greenwood]', National Records of Scotland, Edinburgh, CAB 43/2.
27. Conclusions of a Meeting of the British Representatives to the Conference with Sinn Fein Delegation held at 10 Downing Street, Monday 10 October 1921, at 5 p.m., National Records of Scotland, Edinburgh, CAB 43/1.
28. E. O'Malley, *On Another Man's Wound* (Dublin: Anvil Books, 1979; 1st edn 1936), p. 326.
29. M. Brennan, *The War in Clare 1911–1921: Personal Memoirs of the Irish War of Independence* (Dublin: Four Courts Press, 1980), pp. 80–1.
30. Clark, *Everyday Violence*, pp. 13, 55, 193–5.
31. S. McConville, *Irish Political Prisoners, 1920–1962: Pilgrimage of Desolation* (London: Routledge, 2014), pp. 113–239.
32. P. Hart, *Mick: The Real Michael Collins* (London: Pan Macmillan, 2005); M. G. Valiulis, *Portrait of a Revolutionary: General Richard Mulcahy and the Founding of the*

Irish Free State (Blackrock: Irish Academic Press, 1992); English, *Ernie O'Malley*; M. Ryan, *Tom Barry: Irish Freedom Fighter* (Cork: Mercier Press, 2003).

33. C. Townshend, *The Republic: The Fight for Irish Independence* (London: Penguin, 2013), p. 56; English, *Ernie O'Malley*, pp. 74–5, 84, 89–94, 106–13; Aiken to all Volunteers on Hunger Strike, 30 October 1923, 5 November 1923, Ernie O'Malley Papers, University College Dublin Archives Department, P17a/43.

34. English, *Ernie O'Malley*, pp. 49–50, 63–4, 186–92.

35. The complex formation of that generation is brilliantly, thematically studied in Foster, *Vivid Faces*.

36. Foster, *Vivid Faces*, pp. 7, 23, 25, 27–8, 73, 152, 218, 249, 257, 286, 291, 294–6, 299–302, 319, 331–2.

37. Francis Stuart, interviewed by the author, Dublin, 24 February 1987.

38. Townshend, *The Republic*, p. xv.

39. A. Mitchell, *Revolutionary Government in Ireland: Dail Eireann 1919–22* (Dublin: Gill and Macmillan, 1995).

40. S. Paseta, *Irish Nationalist Women, 1900–1918* (Cambridge: Cambridge University Press, 2013).

41. Townshend, *Easter 1916*, pp. 36, 60, 122; Fanning, *Fatal Path*, p. 186.

42. For a detailed study of the immediate post-Civil War era, see R. English, *Radicals and the Republic: Socialist Republicanism in the Irish Free State 1925–1937* (Oxford: OUP, 1994); cf. the different view in A. Grant, *Irish Socialist Republicanism 1909–36* (Dublin: Four Courts Press, 2012).

43. B. Hanley and S. Millar, *The Lost Revolution: The Story of the Official IRA and the Workers' Party* (Dublin: Penguin, 2009), p. 7.

44. This 1956–62 border campaign 'singularly failed to achieve its objective', partly because of southern republicans' failure to grasp northern realities; and so, 'The IRA had been defeated in 1962' (Hanley and Millar, *Lost Revolution*, pp. 20–2). Cf. B. Flynn, *Soldiers of Folly: The IRA Border Campaign 1956–1962* (Cork: Collins Press, 2009).

45. Conor Murphy, interviewed by the author, Belfast, 16 December 2010.

46. M. Treacy, *The IRA, 1956–69: Rethinking the Republic* (Manchester: Manchester University Press, 2011).

47. The literature on the PIRA is vast. For a wide variety of interpretations, see English, *Armed Struggle*; M. L. R. Smith, *Fighting for Ireland? The Military Strategy of the Irish Republican Movement* (London: Routledge, 1995); M. O'Doherty, *The Trouble with Guns: Republican Strategy and the Provisional IRA* (Belfast: Blackstaff Press, 1998); J. Dingley, *The IRA: The Irish Republican Army* (Santa Barbara, Calif.: Praeger, 2012); H. Patterson, *The Politics of Illusion: A Political History of the IRA* (London: Serif, 1997; 1st edn 1989); E. Moloney, *A Secret History of the IRA* (London: Penguin, 2002); R. Alonso, *The IRA and Armed Struggle* (London: Routledge, 2007); B. O'Brien, *The Long War: The IRA and Sinn Fein 1985 to Today* (Dublin: O'Brien Press, 1993); T. P. Coogan, *The IRA* (London: HarperCollins, 1987; 1st edn 1970); Shanahan, *The Provisional Irish Republican Army*; K. Rekawek,

Irish Republican Terrorism and Politics: A Comparative Study of the Official and the Provisional IRA (London: Routledge, 2011).

48. I don't especially like the acronym PIRA since it tended not to be one used by those who were themselves involved. The latter instead more often referred simply to the IRA. But I'm using PIRA here to avoid confusion regarding other IRAs (before, during, and after the Provisionals), and I hope that readers will understand and accept that decision.

49. Quoted in *An Phoblacht/Republican News* 5 January 1984.

50. S. MacStiofain, *Memoirs of a Revolutionary* (Edinburgh: Gordon Cremonesi, 1975), p. 123.

51. Quoted in *Irish Press* 5 February 1971.

52. George Harrison, interviewed by the author, New York, 30 October 2000.

53. Sinn Fein, the republican political party long associated with the PIRA.

54. Quoted in *Irish News* 2 April 1997.

55. Gerry Bradley, in G. Bradley and B. Feeney, *Insider: Gerry Bradley's Life in the IRA* (Dublin: O'Brien Press, 2009), p. 65.

56. *Irish News* 29 December 1969.

57. Alex Maskey, quoted in B. McCaffrey, *Alex Maskey: Man and Mayor* (Belfast: Brehon Press, 2003), p. 217.

58. P. Magee, *Gangsters or Guerrillas? Representations of Irish Republicans in 'Troubles Fiction'* (Belfast: Beyond the Pale, 2001), p. 9.

59. Ruairi O Bradaigh, quoted in R. W. White, *Ruairi O Bradaigh: The Life and Politics of an Irish Revolutionary* (Bloomington: Indiana University Press, 2006), p. 243.

60. English, *Irish Freedom*, pp. 368–83, 398–420.

61. Quoted in *Irish Times* 18 November 1974.

62. Piece by R. G. McAuley, Long Kesh, 14 March 1977, copy in Linen Hall Library Political Collection Archives, Belfast.

63. *An Phoblacht/Republican News* 14 February 1981.

64. PIRA spokespersons, quoted in *An Phoblacht/Republican News* 17 August 1989.

65. G. Adams, 'To Cherish a Just and Lasting Peace', *Fordham International Law Journal*, 22/4 (1999), p. 1180.

66. G. Adams, *Before the Dawn: An Autobiography* (London: Heinemann, 1996), p. 51.

67. T. McKearney, *The Provisional IRA: From Insurrection to Parliament* (London: Pluto Press, 2011), p. 29.

68. *Republican News* 23 August 1975.

69. *An Phoblacht/Republican News* 14 February 1991.

70. *An Phoblacht/Republican News* 31 December 1992.

71. The east Belfast site of the Northern Irish parliament from the 1930s onwards.

72. PIRA Easter statement, *An Phoblacht/Republican News* 4 April 1996.

73. McKearney, *The Provisional IRA*, p. ix.

74. Conor Murphy, interviewed by the author, Belfast, 16 December 2010.

75. The Social Democratic and Labour Party, a constitutional-nationalist party in Northern Ireland.

76. Conor Murphy, interviewed by the author, Belfast, 16 December 2010.

77. Election Leaflet, Danny Morrison, Sinn Fein, 1984, PRONI, Belfast, D230/12/5.
78. *Republican News* 2 January 1972. Cf. A. Sanders, *Inside the IRA: Dissident Republicans and the War for Legitimacy* (Edinburgh: Edinburgh University Press, 2011), pp. 54–5.
79. *Republican News* 3 January 1976.
80. Quoted in *An Phoblacht/Republican News* 23 June 1979.
81. PIRA New Year Message (1991), *An Phoblacht/Republican News* 3 January 1991.
82. Quoted in O'Brien, *The Long War*, p. 162.
83. Martin McGuinness, speaking in Derry on 24 June 1984, quoted in *An Phoblacht/Republican News* 28 June 1984.
84. English, *Armed Struggle*, p. 142.
85. Gerry Bradley, in Bradley and Feeney, *Insider*, p. 66.
86. E. McGuire, *Enemy of the Empire: Life as an International Undercover IRA Activist* (Dublin: O'Brien Press, 2006).
87. Conor Murphy, interviewed by the author, Belfast, 16 December 2010.
88. *An Phoblacht/Republican News* 25 April 1981.
89. S. Millar, *On the Brinks* (Galway: Wynkin de Worde, 2003), pp. 85, 164; McGuire, *Enemy of the Empire*, p. 124; English, *Armed Struggle*, p. 187; Smith, *Fighting for Ireland?*, p. 224.
90. Ex-PIRA member, quoted in P. Shirlow, J. Tonge, J. McAuley, and C. McGlynn, *Abandoning Historical Conflict? Former Political Prisoners and Reconciliation in Northern Ireland* (Manchester: Manchester University Press, 2010), p. 95. Cf. F. O Connor, *In Search of a State: Catholics in Northern Ireland* (Belfast: Blackstaff Press, 1993), p. 140; D. Morrison, *All the Dead Voices* (Cork: Mercier Press, 2002), p. 66; S. O'Callaghan, *The Informer* (London: Bantam Press, 1998), pp. 54, 76, 81–2; E. Collins, *Killing Rage* (London: Granta, 1998; 1st edn 1997), pp. 30, 32, 36–7.
91. Jackie McDonald, interviewed by the author, Belfast, 31 January 2012.
92. PIRA leader Joe Cahill, speaking on 21 August 1971, quoted in *Irish News* 23 August 1971.
93. Ex-PIRA Volunteer, interviewed by the author, Belfast, 31 October 2001. Cf. Adams, *Before the Dawn*, p. 209; Collins, *Killing Rage*, pp. 50–3.
94. Bradley and Feeney, *Insider*, p. 60.
95. Millar, *On the Brinks*, p. 53.
96. R. O Bradaigh, *What is Irish Republicanism?* (1970), Linen Hall Library Political Collection Archives, Belfast, Sinn Fein (Provisional) Box 1.
97. Quoted in *An Phoblacht/Republican News* 7 November 1985.
98. Adams, *Before the Dawn*, pp. 22–3, 26–7, 233; R. O'Rawe, *Blanketmen: An Untold Story of the H-Block Hunger Strike* (Dublin: New Island, 2005), pp. 4, 96; Millar, *On the Brinks*, p. 54; E. Moloney, *Voices from the Grave: Two Men's War in Ireland* (London: Faber and Faber, 2010), pp. 29, 34–6; Alonso, *The IRA and Armed Struggle*, pp. 45–6; English, *Armed Struggle*, pp. 109–13, 122, 128–9. The situation here varied greatly, of course: some PIRA members had a strongly militant Irish republican flavour to their background, while others did not. Among the latter, see the intriguing accounts by Conway, *Southside Provisional*, and McGuire, *Enemy of the Empire*.

99. R. O'Rawe, *Afterlives: The Hunger Strike and the Secret Offer that Changed Irish History* (Dublin: Lilliput Press, 2010), p. 91.

100. The influence of James Connolly, and the commitment to an explicitly social-istic republicanism, are richly evident in G. Adams, *The Politics of Irish Freedom* (Dingle: Brandon, 1986); cf. Adams, *Before the Dawn*, pp. 64, 73.

101. Danny Morrison, interviewed by the author, Belfast, 26 May 2000.

102. Marian Price, interviewed by the author, Belfast, 28 February 2002.

103. George Harrison, interviewed by the author, New York, 30 October 2000.

104. Gerry Adams, quoted in *An Phoblacht/Republican News* 23 June 1979.

105. L. McKeown, *Out of Time: Irish Republican Prisoners Long Kesh 1972–2000* (Belfast: Beyond the Pale, 2001), p. 144. Cf. O'Callaghan, *The Informer*, pp. 26, 44, 103; O'Rawe, *Blanketmen*, pp. 84–6.

106. Election Leaflet, Paddy Fitzsimmons, Sinn Fein (1983), PRONI, Belfast, D230/11/6/4.

107. *Republican News* May 1971; cf. English, *Armed Struggle*, pp. 235–6.

108. Moloney, *Secret History*, p. 231; Moloney, *Voices from the Grave*, pp. 67, 80, 196, 233; English, *Armed Struggle*, pp. 130–2, 210–11, 346; and, more controversially, Dingley, *The IRA*, pp. x–xi, 23, 51, 81, 109–11, 127, 201.

109. PIRA Easter statement, 1981 (*An Phoblacht/Republican News* 25 April 1981).

110. Quoted in *An Phoblacht/Republican News* 2 February 1989.

111. D. Morrison, *Then the Walls Came Down: A Prison Journal* (Cork: Mercier Press, 1999), p. 213 (4 July 1991).

112. See, for example, Conway, *Southside Provisional*, pp. 17, 101.

113. McKearney, *Provisional IRA*, p. ix; English, *Armed Struggle*, pp. 197, 234–5, 345; Conway, *Southside Provisional*, p. 83.

114. Quoted in T. Hennessey, *Hunger Strike: Margaret Thatcher's Battle with the IRA 1980–1981* (Sallins: Irish Academic Press, 2013), p. 18.

115. Quoted in *Derry Journal* 26 April 2011.

116. Adams, *The Politics of Irish Freedom*, p. 53.

117. M. Sutton, *Bear in Mind these Dead: An Index of Deaths from the Conflict in Ireland 1969–1993* (Belfast: Beyond the Pale Publications, 1994), pp. 2–38.

118. O'Doherty, *The Trouble with Guns*, p. 73; English, *Armed Struggle*, pp. 160, 171, 247, 276–7, 281–3; C. Townshend, *Ireland: The Twentieth Century* (London: Arnold, 1999), p. 208; M. Fay, M. Morrissey, and M. Smyth, *Northern Ireland's Troubles: The Human Costs* (London: Pluto, 1999), p. 178.

119. D. McKittrick, S. Kelters, B. Feeney, and C. Thornton, *Lost Lives: The Stories of the Men, Women, and Children Who Died as a Result of the Northern Ireland Troubles* (Edinburgh: Mainstream, 2001; 1st edn 1999), p. 1494.

120. *The Billy Wright Inquiry—Report* (London: The Stationery Office, 2010), p. 50 regarding Kingsmills and its effect on Wright; cf. McKittrick, Kelters, Feeney, and Thornton, *Lost Lives*, pp. 611–12. On Wright's very brutal career as a loy-alist paramilitary, see C. Anderson, *The Billy Boy: The Life and Death of LVF Leader Billy Wright* (Edinburgh: Mainstream, 2004; 1st edn 2002).

121. M. Mowlam, *Momentum: The Struggle for Peace, Politics, and the People* (London: Hodder and Stoughton, 2002), p. 180.
122. M. McGuinness, *Bodenstown '86* (London: Wolfe Tone Society, 1986), p. 3.
123. PIRA spokesman, quoted in *An Phoblacht/Republican News* 5 September 1981.
124. Adams, *The Politics of Irish Freedom*, pp. 14, 126.
125. *The Belfast Agreement: Agreement Reached in the Multi-Party Negotiations* (10 April 1998), p. 3.
126. *An Phoblacht/Republican News* 30 April 1998.
127. That declaration affirmed that 'the democratic right of self-determination by the people of Ireland as a whole must be achieved and exercised with and subject to the agreement and consent of a majority of the people of Northern Ireland' (Downing Street Declaration, 15 December 1993, reproduced in M. Cox, A. Guelke, and F. Stephen (eds), *A Farewell to Arms? From 'Long War' to Long Peace in Northern Ireland* (Manchester: Manchester University Press, 2000), p. 328).
128. Quoted in *An Phoblacht/Republican News* 6 August 1998.
129. Joe Cahill, quoted in B. Anderson, *Joe Cahill: A Life in the IRA* (Dublin: O'Brien Press, 2002), p. 367.
130. For very different interpretations, see Alonso, *The IRA and Armed Struggle*, and B. O'Leary, 'Mission Accomplished? Looking Back at the IRA', *Field Day Review*, 1 (2005).
131. J. Bew, M. Frampton, and I. Gurruchaga, *Talking to Terrorists: Making Peace in Northern Ireland and the Basque Country* (London: Hurst, 2009), p. 58; S. McDaid, *Template for Peace: Northern Ireland 1972–75* (Manchester: Manchester University Press, 2013), pp. 30–1, 127, 144–9, 154, 161, 166, 172, 175–6, 185.
132. Cf. Abrams, *Oral History Theory*, pp. 4–5.
133. Ex-PIRA Volunteer, interviewed by the author, Belfast, 26 November 2012.
134. Conway, *Southside Provisional*, p. 204.
135. A. McIntyre, *Good Friday: The Death of Irish Republicanism* (New York: Ausubo Press, 2008), p. 7.
136. Ex-PIRA volunteer, quoted in Alonso, *The IRA and Armed Struggle*, p. 151.
137. Strachan, *The Direction of War*, pp. 13–14; Freedman, *Strategy*, p. xi.
138. Morrison, *Then the Walls Came Down*, pp. 91, 96–7 (19 August 1990, 16 September 1990).
139. Ex-PIRA member, quoted in Shirlow, Tonge, McAuley, and McGlynn, *Abandoning Historical Conflict?*, p. 127.
140. McGuire, *Enemy of the Empire*, p. 303.
141. Tom Hartley, interviewed by the author, Belfast, 24 October 2001.
142. J. Powell, *Great Hatred, Little Room: Making Peace in Northern Ireland* (London: Bodley Head, 2008), p. 24.
143. Freedman, *Strategy*, p. 9.
144. On this point, and on the DUP's own quite remarkable shift from uncompromising opposition to collaborative power-sharing, see J. Tonge, M. Braniff,

T. Hennessey, J. W. McAuley, and S. A. Whiting, *The Democratic Unionist Party: From Protest to Power* (Oxford: OUP, 2014).

145. SDLP Press Release, 26 September 1974, Linen Hall Library Political Collection Archives, Belfast, SDLP Box 2.

146. Cahal B. Daly to Secretary of State for Northern Ireland James Prior, 8 May 1984, PRONI, Belfast, CENT/1/12/18 (File: New Ireland Forum).

147. Richardson, *What Terrorists Want*, p. 36.

148. Conor Murphy, interviewed by the author, Belfast, 16 December 2010.

149. English, *Irish Freedom*, pp. 382–3.

150. English, *Armed Struggle*, pp. 165–6.

151. Powell, *Great Hatred, Little Room*, p. 249.

152. J. Powell, *Talking to Terrorists: How to End Armed Conflicts* (London: Bodley Head, 2014), p. 27.

153. Blair, *A Journey*, p. 170.

154. Sanders, *Inside the IRA*, p. 9; K. Rafter, *Sinn Fein 1905–2005: In the Shadow of Gunmen* (Dublin: Gill and Macmillan, 2005).

155. Ex-RUC Special Branch Officer B, interviewed by the author, Belfast, 13 October 2011.

156. English, *Armed Struggle*, p. 399.

157. D. Laitin, *Identity in Formation: The Russian-Speaking Populations in the Near Abroad* (Ithaca, NY: Cornell University Press, 1998), p. 23.

158. R. English, 'Ireland', in M. Flinders, A. Gamble, C. Hay, and M. Kenny (eds), *The Oxford Handbook of British Politics* (Oxford: OUP, 2009), p. 519.

159. McKearney, *The Provisional IRA*, p. 114.

160. Collins, *Killing Rage*, p.7.

161. The tension between these two impulses is evident in Marianne Elliott's magisterial study *Wolfe Tone: Prophet of Irish Independence* (New Haven: Yale University Press, 1989).

162. See the archivally rich treatment in S. Kelly, *Fianna Fail, Partition, and Northern Ireland 1926–1971* (Dublin: Irish Academic Press, 2013).

163. One of the most strident opponents of the Provisionals, UK Prime Minister Margaret Thatcher, was arguably hampered in her own attempts to understand Ireland because, as her biographer puts it, 'She hardly ever sat down to reflect upon the past' (C. Moore, *Margaret Thatcher: The Authorized Biography. Volume One: Not for Turning* (London: Penguin, 2013), p. xi). This was a charge which could not be levelled at the PIRA. But my argument here is that much that they inherited from the past also suggested profound obstacles in the way of their own strategic forward movement.

164. McDaid, *Template for Peace*, pp. 157, 176–7, 186; English, *Armed Struggle*, p. 357.

165. T. K. Whitaker, *A Note on North–South Policy* (11 November 1968), Lynch Papers, National Archives, Dublin, 2001/8/1; Lynch to Heath, 11 August 1970, National Archives, London, PREM 15/101. Eminent politicians' memoirs reinforce this point very strongly: G. FitzGerald, *All in a Life: An Autobiography*

(Dublin: Gill and Macmillan, 1992; 1st edn 1991), pp. 258–9; C. C. O'Brien, *Memoir: My Life and Themes* (Dublin: Poolbeg Press, 1998), p. 7; A. Reynolds, *My Autobiography* (London: Transworld, 2009), pp. 65–8, 204–14. Some will be sceptical about memoir sources, echoing Eric Hobsbawm's concern that 'If you do *not* want to understand the twentieth century, read the autobiographies of the self-justifiers, the counsels for their own defence, and of their obverse, the repentant sinners' (Hobsbawm, *Interesting Times*, p. xii). Despite such stringency, however, I think that the repeated evidence from memoirs such as those just mentioned, and the manner in which they reinforce other kinds of source on this issue, give a certain weight to their significance.

166. Secretary of State's Meeting with No. 10 Policy Unit, 10 May 1984 memo re 9 May 1984 meeting, PRONI, Belfast, CENT/1/13/52A (File: Security and Prison Matters 31 October 1983–31 May 1984).

167. G. McGladdery, *The Provisional IRA in England: The Bombing Campaign 1973–1997* (Dublin: Irish Academic Press, 2006), p. 5.

168. McDaid, *Template for Peace*, pp. 104–6.

169. P. Nash, 'Why Does Britain Remain in Control of the Six Counties?' (9 September 1985), Linen Hall Library Political Collection Archives, Belfast.

170. English, *Armed Struggle*, pp. 303–6.

171. O'Callaghan, *The Informer*; Moloney, *Secret History*, p. 335; Moloney, *Voices from the Grave*, pp. 276, 283–4; McIntyre, *Good Friday*, pp. 179–95; Collins, *Killing Rage*; J. Holland and S. Phoenix, *Phoenix: Policing the Shadows. The Secret War Against Terrorism in Northern Ireland* (London: Hodder and Stoughton, 1997; 1st edn 1996); M. McGartland, *Fifty Dead Men Walking* (London: Blake, 1998; 1st edn 1997); M. Ingram and G. Harkin, *Stakeknife: Britain's Secret Agents in Ireland* (Dublin: O'Brien Press, 2004).

172. Ex-RUC Special Branch Officer A, interviewed by the author, County Down, Northern Ireland, 23 February 2010.

173. Former RUC HMSU Officer, interviewed by the author, Belfast, 25 March 2010.

174. McKearney, *The Provisional IRA*, p. 142.

175. Quoted in A. Sanders, 'Operation Motorman (1972) and the Search for a Coherent British Counterinsurgency Strategy in Northern Ireland', *Small Wars and Insurgencies*, 24/3 (2013), p. 469.

176. Sanders, 'Operation Motorman', p. 484.

177. Ex-RUC Special Branch Officer B, interviewed by the author, Belfast, 13 October 2011.

178. Former RUC HMSU Officer, interviewed by the author, Belfast, 25 March 2010.

179. Whelehan, *The Dynamiters*, p. 136.

180. Gerry Bradley, in Bradley and Feeney, *Insider*, p. 204.

181. *Belfast Telegraph* 21 December 2011.

182. McGuire, *Enemy of the Empire*, p. 43.

183. S. Rimington, *Open Secret: The Autobiography of the Former Director-General of MI5* (London: Hutchinson, 2001), p. 106.

184. Former RUC HMSU Officer, interviewed by the author, Belfast, 25 March 2010.

185. Some serious scholars have downplayed the role of stalemate in producing the Provisionals' move away from political violence in Northern Ireland (see, for example, Shirlow, Tonge, McAuley, and McGlynn, *Abandoning Historical Conflict?*). But since stalemate involves a deadlock from which neither side is able to achieve a decisive victory, and in which the respectively unequal power of the two sides does not allow for one of them to achieve a clear victory, the term seems both apt and telling in regard to what impelled the Provos towards peace.

186. N. O Dochartaigh, 'The Longest Negotiation: British Policy, IRA Strategy, and the Making of the Northern Ireland Peace Settlement', *Political Studies*, 63/1 (2015).

187. Morrison, *Then the Walls Came Down*, p. 71 (6 June 1990).

188. Adams, *The Politics of Irish Freedom*, p. 58; PIRA figure, quoted in Coogan, *The IRA*, p. 604.

189. O'Rawe, *Afterlives*, p. 26.

190. O'Rawe, *Blanketmen*, p. 107; and see the powerful essay by Anthony McIntyre: 'Provisional Republicanism: Internal Politics, Inequities, and Modes of Repression', in F. McGarry (ed.), *Republicanism in Modern Ireland* (Dublin: UCD Press, 2003).

191. Conor Murphy, interviewed by the author, Belfast, 16 December 2010.

192. Rafter, *Sinn Fein*; E. O Broin, *Sinn Fein and the Politics of Left Republicanism* (London: Pluto Press, 2009); B. Feeney, *Sinn Fein: A Hundred Turbulent Years* (Dublin: O'Brien Press, 2002); M. Frampton, *The Long March: The Political Strategy of Sinn Fein, 1981–2007* (Basingstoke: Palgrave Macmillan, 2009); G. Murray and J. Tonge, *Sinn Fein and the SDLP: From Alienation to Participation* (Dublin: O'Brien Press, 2005).

193. Conor Murphy, interviewed by the author, Belfast, 16 December 2010.

194. For a further, sustained argument about this shift from war to peace by the Provisional IRA, see English, *Armed Struggle*, pp. 303–36.

195. Central Secretariat (Stormont Castle) Memorandum: 'Sinn Fein', 12 August 1985, PRONI, Belfast, CENT/1/14/16A (File: Sinn Fein: Policy Group on Non-Violence Declarations etc, 1985).

196. Draft Minute to PS/SOS, 18 June 1985, PRONI, Belfast, CENT/3/18A (File: Approaches to Government by Sinn Fein MPs and Assemblymen, 2 July 1985).

197. Minister's Case 8569: Ms Clare Short MP on Dealings with Sinn Fein, 6 January 1984, PRONI, Belfast, CENT/1/13/35A (File: Sinn Fein—Contacts). Clare Short had written to the Secretary of State the previous month, suggesting that a policy of not corresponding with Gerry Adams might be in contempt of the House of Commons, since Adams was an MP.

198. O'Rawe, *Blanketmen*, pp. 52, 58.

199. See, for example, Conway, *Southside Provisional*, pp. 117, 138, 180, 185–6, 195–6.

200. H. Patterson, *Ireland's Violent Frontier: The Border and Anglo-Irish Relations During the Troubles* (Basingstoke: Palgrave Macmillan, 2013).

201. Even allowing for some unintentional killings, it can safely be assumed that very many of the 1,778 PIRA victims recorded by one reliable source as having been killed by the organization embodied enemies at whom the Provisionals were zealously hitting back. These included 638 British military personnel, 273 Northern Irish police officers, 162 Irish republicans, 28 loyalists, 23 members of the Prison Service, and 642 civilians (McKittrick, Kelters, Feeney, and Thornton, *Lost Lives*, p. 1504).

202. N. Pantling, *Belfast Finds Log: Poems* (Beeston: Shoestring Press, 2014).

203. Marian Price, interviewed by the author, Belfast, quoted in *Independent on Sunday* 2 March 2003. Cf. ex-PIRA man Seanna Walsh's point that there were numerous cases of British state terrorism which decisively influenced the negative response of the nationalist community in the north as the conflict emerged: 'police riots in Derry during civil rights demonstrations, the Falls Curfew, then after that you have internment, Bloody Sunday' (Seanna Walsh, interviewed by the author, Belfast, 18 June 2015).

204. Statement Issued by RUC Headquarters, 20 May 1985, PRONI, Belfast, CENT/3/18A (File: Approaches to Government by Sinn Fein MPs and Assemblymen, 2 July 1985).

205. Election Leaflet, Danny Morrison, Sinn Fein, 1984, PRONI, Belfast, D230/12/5.

206. English, *Armed Struggle*, pp. 303–4.

207. English, *Radicals and the Republic*.

208. See, for example, *An Phoblacht* March 2014.

209. English, *Armed Struggle*, pp. 235–6.

210. English, *Armed Struggle*, pp. 210–11.

211. Seanna Walsh, interviewed by the author, Belfast, 18 June 2015.

212. Hennessey, *Hunger Strike*, p. 427.

213. UDA Lecture Briefing Form, quoted in Sanders, *Inside the IRA*, p. 65.

214. In the elegiac record in McKittrick, Kelters, Feeney, and Thornton, *Lost Lives*, for example.

215. G. Gillespie, *Years of Darkness: The Troubles Remembered* (Dublin: Gill and Macmillan, 2008), pp. 133–7.

216. A. T. Q. Stewart, *The Shape of Irish History* (Belfast: Blackstaff Press, 2001), p. 126; R. English, 'The Interplay of Non-Violent and Violent Action in Northern Ireland, 1967–72', in Roberts and Garton Ash (eds), *Civil Resistance and Power Politics*.

217. C. Lawther, *Truth, Denial, and Transition: Northern Ireland and the Contested Past* (London: Routledge, 2014).

218. Tonge, Braniff, Hennessey, McAuley, and Whiting, *The Democratic Unionist Party*.

302 NOTES TO PAGES 131–137

219. Adams, *Before the Dawn*, pp. 278–9.
220. McKittrick, Kelters, Feeney, and Thornton, *Lost Lives*, p. 1504.
221. *Guardian*: Northern Ireland Datablog—Deaths Since 1969 (accessed 4 March 2015).
222. Gerry Bradley, in Bradley and Feeney, *Insider*, p. 151.
223. Hennessey, *Hunger Strike*, pp. 52, 66.
224. T. Knatchbull, *From a Clear Blue Sky: Surviving the Mountbatten Bomb* (London: Hutchinson, 2009), pp. xi, 214.
225. Blair, *A Journey*, p. 196; Powell, *Great Hatred, Little Room*, p. 249; D. de Breadun, *The Far Side of Revenge: Making Peace in Northern Ireland* (Cork: Collins Press, 2008; 1st edn 2001), pp. 238–45; D. Godson, *Himself Alone: David Trimble and the Ordeal of Unionism* (London: HarperCollins, 2005; 1st edn 2004), pp. 351, 393, 793–8.
226. P. O'Malley, *Biting at the Grave: The Irish Hunger Strikes and the Politics of Despair* (Belfast: Blackstaff, 1990), pp. 197, 207; Hennessey, *Hunger Strike*, p. 426.
227. Morrison, *Then the Walls Came Down*, p. 31.
228. 'Local Effects of the Hunger Strike', Central Secretariat (Stormont Castle) memo, 17 August 1981, PRONI, Belfast, CENT/1/10/66 (File: Hunger Strike).
229. Among others: Adams, *The Politics of Irish Freedom*; Adams, *Before the Dawn*; Conway, *Southside Provisional*; Magee, *Gangsters or Guerrillas?*; McKeown, *Out of Time*; MacStiofain, *Memoirs of a Revolutionary*; Morrison, *Then the Walls Came Down*.
230. For detailed analysis of the prison war, see English, *Armed Struggle*, pp. 187–237, and also the excellent study by Kieran McEvoy: *Paramilitary Imprisonment in Northern Ireland: Resistance, Management, and Release* (Oxford: OUP, 2001).
231. See the original treatment of this subject in F. S. Ross, *Smashing H-Block: The Rise and Fall of the Popular Campaign against Criminalization, 1976–1982* (Liverpool: Liverpool University Press, 2011).
232. McDaid, *Template for Peace*, pp. 1, 9.
233. Conway, *Southside Provisional*, p. 96.
234. Seanna Walsh, interviewed by the author, Belfast, 18 June 2015.
235. Shirlow, Tonge, McAuley, and McGlynn, *Abandoning Historical Conflict?*
236. S. Millar, *Bloodstorm* (Dingle: Brandon, 2008), p. 49.
237. S. Millar, *The Dark Place* (Dingle: Brandon, 2009), pp. 57, 63, 97–8, 101, 194–5, 209.
238. *Report of the Bloody Sunday Inquiry* (2010).
239. Tommy Gorman, interviewed by the author, Belfast, 2 May 2001; cf. P. Taylor, *Provos: The IRA and Sinn Fein* (London: Bloomsbury, 1997), pp. 72, 78–84; Alonso, *The IRA and Armed Struggle*, 47–9.
240. See, for example, the evidence adduced from the records of the King's Own Scottish Borderers from 1970 by A. Sanders and I. S. Wood, *Times of Troubles: Britain's War in Northern Ireland* (Edinburgh: Edinburgh University Press, 2012), pp. 8–9.
241. Lynch to Heath, 7 July 1970, National Archives, London, PREM 15/100; Note of the Prime Minister's Meeting with the Prime Minister of Northern Ireland, 17 July 1970, National Archives, London, PREM 15/101.

242. English, *Armed Struggle*, p. 154.

243. Quoted in Sanders and Wood, *Times of Troubles*, p. 56.

244. Seanna Walsh, interviewed by the author, Belfast, 18 June 2015.

245. A. Cadwallader, *Lethal Allies: British Collusion in Ireland* (Cork: Mercier Press, 2013); cf. S. Bruce, 'Loyalist Assassinations and Police Collusion in Northern Ireland: An Extended Critique of Sean McPhilemy's *The Committee*', *SICAT*, 23/1 (2000).

246. For one recent example, see *The Report of the Patrick Finucane Review*, by the Rt Hon Sir Desmond de Silva QC (December 2012).

247. Mario Biaggi et al. to Secretary of State for Northern Ireland Douglas Hurd, 17 July 1985, PRONI, Belfast, CENT/3/16A (File: NORAID July 1985–August 1985).

248. A. J. Wilson, *Irish America and the Ulster Conflict 1968–1995* (Belfast: Blackstaff Press, 1995); S. McManus, *My American Struggle for Justice in Northern Ireland* (Cork: Collins Press, 2011).

249. Hume addressing his Party Conference in Belfast in 1988, quoted in *Irish News* 28 November 1988.

250. H. McDonald and J. Holland, *INLA: Deadly Divisions* (Dublin: Poolbeg Press, 1994).

251. Fay, Morrissey, and Smyth, *Northern Ireland's Troubles: The Human Costs*, p. 195.

252. J. F. Morrison, *The Origins and Rise of Dissident Irish Republicanism: The Role and Impact of Organizational Splits* (New York: Bloomsbury, 2013).

253. Albert Reynolds, quoted in *Irish News* 14 March 1994.

254. Declan Kearney, interviewed by the author, Belfast, 28 July 2011.

255. Gerard Hodgins, quoted in O'Rawe, *Afterlives*, p. 125.

256. White, *Ruairí O Bradaigh*.

257. Millar, *On the Brinks*, p. 65; Bradley and Feeney, *Insider*, p. 138.

258. Millar, *On the Brinks*, pp. 75, 86, 97, 107–8, 152, 160.

259. McGuire, *Enemy of the Empire*.

260. Conway, *Southside Provisional*, pp. 147–8; McGuire, *Enemy of the Empire*, pp. 37–8.

261. T. Hartley, *Milltown Cemetery: The History of Belfast, Written in Stone* (Belfast: Blackstaff Press, 2014), p. 362.

262. Ex-PIRA Volunteer, interviewed by the author, Belfast, 26 November 2012.

263. Brendan Hughes, quoted in Moloney, *Voices from the Grave*, p. 48.

264. O'Callaghan, *The Informer*, p. 69.

265. Martin McGuinness, quoted in L. Clarke and K. Johnston, *Martin McGuinness: From Guns to Government* (Edinburgh: Mainstream Publishing, 2001), pp. 46–7.

266. McGuire, *Enemy of the Empire*, p. 293.

267. Conway, *Southside Provisional*, pp. 29–30, 50, 75.

268. Gerry Bradley, in Bradley and Feeney, *Insider*, p. 270.

269. Collins, *Killing Rage*, p. 164.

270. Bradley and Feeney, *Insider*, pp. 158–9.

271. Richard O'Rawe, quoted in Sanders and Wood, *Times of Troubles*, p. 43.

272. Collins, *Killing Rage*, p. 96.
273. O'Rawe, *Blanketmen*, pp. 5–6.
274. Conway, *Southside Provisional*, p. 199.
275. Shirlow, Tonge, McAuley, and McGlynn, *Abandoning Historical Conflict?*, p. 19.
276. Collins, *Killing Rage*, p. 16.
277. Keynote Address to the March 2015 Sinn Fein Ard Fheis, Derry (copy in author's possession).
278. Some have argued strongly that the Provos' campaign resulted in strategic failure despite some tactical successes; see Neumann and Smith, *The Strategy of Terrorism*, p. vii.
279. Godson, *Himself Alone*, pp. 69, 76; H. McDonald, *Trimble* (London: Bloomsbury, 2000), pp. 68–71, 252, 322.
280. H. McDonald, *Gunsmoke and Mirrors: How Sinn Fein Dressed Up Defeat As Victory* (Dublin: Gill and Macmillan, 2008), p. x.
281. J. Dingley, 'Introduction', in Dingley (ed.), *Combating Terrorism in Northern Ireland*, p. 2.
282. Ex-RUC Special Branch Officer B, interviewed by the author, Belfast, 13 October 2011.
283. Foster, *Vivid Faces*.
284. Freedman, *Strategy*, pp. 608–9.
285. Powell, *Great Hatred, Little Room*, pp. xii, 1, 3.
286. Seanna Walsh, interviewed by the author, Belfast, 18 June 2015.
287. Gerry Adams, 'Foreword', in D. Kearney (ed.), *Uncomfortable Conversations: An Initiative for Dialogue Towards Reconciliation* (Belfast: Sinn Fein, 2015), p. 3.
288. Lawther, *Truth, Denial, and Transition*.
289. Shanahan, *The Provisional Irish Republican Army*, p. 9.
290. Brendan Hughes, quoted in Moloney, *Voices from the Grave*, p. 105.
291. J. D. Parker, *On the Waterfront* (Durham: Pentland Press, 2000), p. 114.
292. Parker, *On the Waterfront*, pp. 101, 119.

CHAPTER 3

1. P. Wilkinson, 'Politics, Diplomacy, and Peace Processes: Pathways Out of Terrorism?', in Taylor and Horgan (eds), *The Future of Terrorism*, p. 70.
2. B. M. Metzger and M. D. Coogan (eds), *The Oxford Companion to the Bible* (Oxford: OUP, 1993), pp. 349–56. The book of Jeremiah provides a resoundingly powerful example of the centrality of Jerusalem to the biblical account.
3. B. Kimmerling and J. S. Migdal, *The Palestinian People: A History* (Cambridge, Mass.: Harvard University Press, 2003), pp. xv, 59.
4. W. Pearlman, *Violence, Non-Violence, and the Palestinian National Movement* (Cambridge: Cambridge University Press, 2014; 1st edn 2011), p. 27.
5. King, *A Quiet Revolution*, pp. 34–5.
6. Kimmerling and Migdal, *The Palestinian People*, p. 100.

7. King, *A Quiet Revolution*, p. 43.

8. S. Ball, *The Bitter Sea* (London: Harper Press, 2010; 1st edn 2009), p. 21; Kimmerling and Migdal, *The Palestinian People*, p. 142; Pearlman, *Violence, Non-Violence, and the Palestinian National Movement*, pp. 55–6.

9. Kimmerling and Migdal, *The Palestinian People*, pp. 33, 102–31.

10. Kimmerling and Migdal, *The Palestinian People*, pp. 97, 99.

11. The fullest treatment of this now is the magisterial account by Bruce Hoffman: *Anonymous Soldiers: The Struggle for Israel, 1917–1947* (New York: Alfred A. Knopf, 2015).

12. Professor Hoffman's forensic, scholarly analysis (*Anonymous Soldiers*, pp. 290–322) is far more thorough and persuasive here than the more exculpatory account of the Irgun's actions offered by their leader, in Begin, *The Revolt*, pp. 212–22.

13. Hoffman, *Inside Terrorism*, p. 51. Other Jewish terrorists also merit a mention here. In 1940 Abraham Stern split from Irgun to form Irgun Zvai Leumi B'Yisrael (better known as the Stern Gang); they duly started attacking British police and military, and Jewish moderates; Stern himself was killed in a shoot-out in 1942, to be replaced by David Friedman-Yellin; but in November 1944 the Stern Gang (now known as Lehi) were still able to kill the British Minister of State in Cairo, Lord Moyne, prompting a sequence of reprisals.

14. Begin, *The Revolt*, Preface and pp. 25, 331.

15. Begin, *The Revolt*, p. 56; Hoffman, *Anonymous Soldiers*, pp. xi–xii, xv, 93, 472–84.

16. B. Milton-Edwards, *The Israeli–Palestinian Conflict: A People's War* (London: Routledge, 2009), pp. 119–20.

17. Abu Daoud, quoted in Cronin, *How Terrorism Ends*, p. 4.

18. Hoffman, *Inside Terrorism*, p. 69.

19. P. Wilkinson, *International Relations: A Very Short Introduction* (Oxford: OUP, 2007), p. 7.

20. Berman, *Radical, Religious and Violent*, p. 183.

21. B. Morris, *Righteous Victims: A History of the Zionist–Arab Conflict, 1881–1999* (New York: Alfred A. Knopf, 1999), p. 562.

22. This is a theme running through R. English (ed.), *Illusions of Terrorism and Counter-Terrorism* (Oxford: OUP, 2015).

23. R. Singh, *Hamas and Suicide Terrorism: Multi-Causal and Multi-Level Approaches* (London: Routledge, 2011), p. 36; King, *A Quiet Revolution*, pp. 5–8.

24. So, in reference to the difficulty of definition identified in the Introduction, it should be noted that this book's primary focus on non-state terrorism does not preclude recognition either of the existence of state terrorism, or of its role in generating powerful non-state terrorism too.

25. Sheikh Ibrahim al-Quqa, quoted in Morris, *Righteous Victims*, p. 573.

26. For impressively detailed, informative studies, see Singh, *Hamas and Suicide Terrorism*; M. Levitt, *Hamas: Politics, Charity and Terrorism in the Service of Jihad* (New Haven: Yale University Press, 2006); S. Farrell and B. Milton-Edwards, *Hamas: The Islamic Resistance Movement* (Cambridge: Polity, 2010); J. Gunning, *Hamas in Politics:*

Democracy, Religion, Violence (London: Hurst and Co., 2009); S. Mishal and A. Sela, *The Palestinian Hamas: Vision, Violence, and Coexistence* (New York: Columbia University Press; 2006; 1st edn 2000); Y. Alexander, *Palestinian Religious Terrorism: Hamas and Islamic Jihad* (Ardsley: Transnational Publishers, 2002).

27. Hamas Charter, quoted in Singh, *Hamas and Suicide Terrorism*, p. 105.
28. Morris, *Righteous Victims*, p. 596.
29. R. Hassan, *Life as a Weapon: The Global Rise of Suicide Bombings* (London: Routledge, 2011), p. 77.
30. D. K. Gupta and K. Mundra, 'Suicide Bombing as a Strategic Weapon: An Empirical Investigation of Hamas and Islamic Jihad', *TPV*, 17/4 (2005), p. 574.
31. Levitt, *Hamas*, p. 12.
32. J. M. Norman, *The Second Palestinian Intifada: Civil Resistance* (London: Routledge, 2010).
33. Quoted in Levitt, *Hamas*, pp. 132–3.
34. Gupta, *Understanding Terrorism and Political Violence*, p. 45.
35. Mishal and Sela, *The Palestinian Hamas*, p. vii.
36. Quoted in D. Byman, *A High Price: The Triumphs and Failures of Israeli Counter-Terrorism* (Oxford: OUP, 2011), p. 170.
37. Leaflet no. 28 (18 August 1988), quoted in Mishal and Sela, *The Palestinian Hamas*, p. 52.
38. Quoted in K. Hroub, 'Hamas', in J. Peters and D. Newman (eds), *The Routledge Handbook on the Israeli–Palestinian Conflict* (London: Routledge, 2013), p. 233.
39. Quoted in King, *A Quiet Revolution*, p. 270.
40. C. Bell, *Peace Agreements and Human Rights* (Oxford: OUP, 2000), p. 75.
41. Quoted in Hoffman, *Inside Terrorism*, p. 153.
42. Quoted in A. Tamimi, *Hamas: A History from Within* (Northampton: Olive Branch Press, 2007), p. 299.
43. Merari, *Driven to Death*, pp. 128–9.
44. Farrell and Milton-Edwards, *Hamas*, p. vi.
45. Hamas Charter, quoted in Singh, *Hamas and Suicide Terrorism*, pp. 103–4.
46. Hamas Charter, quoted in Alexander, *Palestinian Religious Terrorism*, p. 49.
47. Hamas Charter, quoted in Mishal and Sela, *The Palestinian Hamas*, p. 177.
48. Cf. the extended argument about the manner in which the interwoven politics of community, struggle, and power explain the enduring strength of nationalism, in English, *Irish Freedom*, pp. 11–21, 431–506.
49. Merari, *Driven to Death*, pp. 124, 158.
50. This echoes a wider pattern, of course. 'Where there is a "misfit" between state and nation, violence is often the strategy followed by groups who feel it is the only way to secure a situation in which state power is held by those who share the nationality and... the culture of those subject to that state power. If a national group forms part of a state which does not reflect the identity of that national group, then violence is a distinct possibility' (J. Schwarzmantel, *Democracy and Political Violence* (Edinburgh: Edinburgh University Press, 2011), pp. 6–7).

51. Shapiro, *The Terrorist's Dilemma*, pp. 230–1.
52. Quoted in Farrell and Milton-Edwards, *Hamas*, p. 110.
53. Quoted in Farrell and Milton-Edwards, *Hamas*, p. 145.
54. 12 January 2002 communiqué, quoted in Alexander, *Palestinian Religious Terrorism*, p. 76.
55. Quoted in Brahimi, *Jihad and Just War*, p. 108.
56. Quoted in Juergensmeyer, *Global Rebellion*, p. 71.
57. See the excellent treatment of this theme of revenge in Richardson, *What Terrorists Want*, pp. 100–1, 105, 113–20.
58. Quoted in Farrell and Milton-Edwards, *Hamas*, p. 141.
59. Quoted in Juergensmeyer, *Terror in the Mind of God*, p. 74.
60. Quoted in Gunning, *Hamas in Politics*, p. 201.
61. Quoted in Farrell and Milton-Edwards, *Hamas*, p. 114.
62. Quoted in Farrell and Milton-Edwards, *Hamas*, p. 123.
63. Merari, *Driven to Death*, pp. 89–91, 125–7; Alexander, *Palestinian Religious Terrorism*, pp. 83, 87.
64. Bloom, *Dying to Kill*, pp. 35–6.
65. Quoted in Levitt, *Hamas*, p. 111.
66. Quoted in A. Moghadam, 'Palestinian Suicide Terrorism in the Second Intifada: Motivations and Organizational Aspects', *SICAT*, 26/2 (2003), p. 71.
67. Quoted in Levitt, *Hamas*, p. 209; cf. Singh, *Hamas and Suicide Terrorism*, p. 124.
68. J. Wagemakers, 'Legitimizing Pragmatism: Hamas's Framing Efforts from Militancy to Moderation and Back?', *TPV*, 22/3 (2010), pp. 362–3.
69. L. Weinberg, A. Pedahzur, and D. Canetti-Nisim, 'The Social and Religious Characteristics of Suicide Bombers and their Victims', *TPV*, 15/3 (2003), p. 145.
70. A. Merari, J. Fighel, B. Ganor, E. Lavie, Y. Tzoreff, and A. Livne, 'Making Palestinian "Martyrdom Operations"/"Suicide Attacks": Interviews with Would-Be Perpetrators and Organizers', *TPV*, 22/1 (2010).
71. Quoted in M. M. Hafez, *Manufacturing Human Bombs: The Making of Palestinian Suicide Bombers* (Washington: USIP Press, 2006), p. 26.
72. Quoted in Merari, *Driven to Death*, p. 163.
73. Farrell and Milton-Edwards, *Hamas*, p. 119.
74. Singh, *Hamas and Suicide Terrorism*.
75. Ruthven, *A Fury for God*, p. 101. Cf. Jones, *Blood That Cries Out From the Earth*, p. 36.
76. Hafez, *Manufacturing Human Bombs*, p. 38.
77. Merari, *Driven to Death*, p. 132.
78. Assaf Moghadam has helpfully pointed to the 'pool of personal motivations' behind Palestinians' individual willingness to die in suicide operations, a 'set of motivations—religious, personal, nationalist, economic, and sociological—that play a role in generating and reinforcing individual Palestinians' willingness to die' (Moghadam, 'Palestinian Suicide Terrorism', p. 67).
79. Dershowitz, *Why Terrorism Works*, p. 88.

80. Shapiro, *The Terrorist's Dilemma*, pp. 236–7.
81. Gupta and Mundra, 'Suicide Bombing as a Strategic Weapon', p. 590.
82. Gunning, *Hamas in Politics*, p. 127.
83. Gunning, *Hamas in Politics*, p. 177; cf. J. Beinin and R. L. Stein (eds), *The Struggle for Sovereignty: Palestine and Israel 1993–2005* (Stanford, Calif.: Stanford University Press, 2006), p. 13, and G. Aviad, *The Politics of Terror: An Essential Hamas Lexicon* (Tel Aviv: Contento de Semrik, 2014), pp. 27–8. The Israeli pull-out from Gaza actually occurred in the summer of 2005.
84. Norman, *The Second Palestinian Intifada*, pp. 69–72.
85. Chenoweth and Stephan, *Why Civil Resistance Works*, p. 138.
86. Majorities answered 'Yes or definitely yes' across all educational levels: 56.8% (illiterate); 63.3% (elementary school); 64.8% (middle school); 63.3% (high school); 59.9% (greater than high school) (Krueger, *What Makes a Terrorist*, p. 29).
87. Quoted in Gunning, *Hamas in Politics*, p. 226.
88. Shapiro, *The Terrorist's Dilemma*, pp. 239–40.
89. Beinin and Stein (eds), *The Struggle for Sovereignty*, pp. 14–15.
90. On the wider polarizing effects of Palestinian terrorism, see Berrebi and Klor, 'Are Voters Sensitive to Terrorism?', pp. 292–3.
91. I. Peleg and D. Waxman, *Israel's Palestinians: The Conflict Within* (Cambridge: Cambridge University Press, 2011).
92. Farrell and Milton-Edwards, *Hamas*, pp. 116, 169.
93. Levitt, *Hamas*, pp. 152–4, 167; Hamas's view of international politics has certainly grown much more sophisticated over the years of its struggle (K. Hroub, *Hamas: Political Thought and Practice* (Washington: Institute for Palestine Studies, 2000)).
94. R. Khalidi, *Palestinian Identity: The Construction of Modern National Consciousness* (New York: Columbia University Press, 2010; 1st edn 1997).
95. King, *A Quiet Revolution*, p. 67.
96. Beinin and Stein (eds), *The Struggle for Sovereignty*, p. 9; Khalidi, *Palestinian Identity*, p. xli.
97. Khalidi, *Palestinian Identity*, pp. xxi, xxiv–xxv, 3.
98. *Daily Telegraph* 26 July 2014.
99. Byman, *A High Price*, p. 115.
100. Mishal and Sela, *The Palestinian Hamas*, p. 76.
101. Antonius and Sinclair, *The Psychology of Terrorism Fears*, pp. 36–7, 60; Gupta and Mundra, 'Suicide Bombing as a Strategic Weapon', p. 590.
102. Byman, *A High Price*, p. 98.
103. Wilkinson, *Terrorism Versus Democracy* (2001 edn), p. 83; cf. Tamimi, *Hamas*, pp. 57, 64.
104. Quoted in Farrell and Milton-Edwards, *Hamas*, p. 79.
105. Farrell and Milton-Edwards, *Hamas*, p. 218.
106. Merari, *Driven to Death*, pp. 10, 39.
107. Singh, *Hamas and Suicide Terrorism*, 62.

108. Gunning, *Hamas in Politics*, pp. 139, 192.

109. Shaheel al-Masri, quoted in Singh, *Hamas and Suicide Terrorism*, p. 95.

110. Kimmerling and Migdal, *The Palestinian People*, 209–11.

111. Norman, *The Second Palestinian Intifada*, p. 117.

112. The Declaration of Principles agreement (Oslo I) was signed on the White House lawn on 13 September 1993, by PLO leader Yasser Arafat and Israeli Prime Minister Yitzhak Rabin, with Bill Clinton as the overseeing US President. It saw Israel acknowledge the existence of a Palestinian people and of the PLO as representing them, as well as Israeli acquiescence to emergent Palestinian autonomy in the Israeli-occupied West Bank and Gaza Strip and the removal of Israeli soldiers from some Palestinian areas; in turn, the PLO renounced terrorism and recognized the state of Israel's right to exist. The wider peace process became known as the Oslo process because it had been in the Norwegian capital that it had been reached through prior negotiations between Israel and the PLO.

113. Norman, *The Second Palestinian Intifada*, p. 30.

114. Wagemakers, 'Legitimizing Pragmatism', p. 364.

115. Berrebi and Klor, 'Are Voters Sensitive to Terrorism?'

116. Writing in 2006, Beinin and Stein noted that in the period since September 2000, over 3,200 Palestinians and more than 950 Israelis had been killed in the violence (Beinin and Stein (eds), *The Struggle for Sovereignty*, p. 1).

117. Cronin, *How Terrorism Ends*, p. 55.

118. Merari, *Driven to Death*, p. 36; Hafez, *Manufacturing Human Bombs*, p. 6; Alexander, *Palestinian Religious Terrorism*, p. 2; Kimmerling and Migdal, *The Palestinian People*, pp. 371–2.

119. Bloom, *Dying to Kill*, pp. 25–6.

120. Gunning, *Hamas in Politics*, p. 49.

121. Mishal and Sela, *The Palestinian Hamas*, p. 78.

122. M. M. Hafez and J. M. Hatfield, 'Do Targeted Assassinations Work? A Multivariate Analysis of Israel's Controversial Tactic During al-Aqsa Uprising', *SICAT*, 29/4 (2006).

123. Zellen, *State of Recovery*, pp. 55–7.

124. Merari, *Driven to Death*, pp. 40–1.

125. Farrell and Milton-Edwards, *Hamas*, pp. 106–8.

126. See the thorough, scholarly assessment in Byman, *A High Price*, which records many Israeli achievements and successes in thwarting terrorist groups such as Hamas, but also many flaws in that state's approach towards terrorism over time: neither Israeli 'brilliance' nor a propensity to 'bungle' adequately captures reality on its own here (see especially pp. 3–6, 362, 381).

127. Dershowitz, *Why Terrorism Works*, pp. 37, 39–40, 42–4, 82, 96–7.

128. Evans, *Altered Pasts*.

129. M. Yarchi, 'The Effect of Female Suicide Attacks on Foreign Media Framing of Conflicts: The Case of the Palestinian–Israeli Conflict', *SICAT*, 37/8 (2014).

130. See, from many examples, *New York Times* 4 April 2002; *Washington Post* 30 December 2008; *New York Times* 8 July 2014; *Washington Post* 12 August 2014; *Daily Express* 21 August 2014; *USA Today* 22 August 2014.

131. Kimmerling and Migdal, *The Palestinian People*, pp. xvii, xxvi–xxvii.

132. Stepanova, *Terrorism in Asymmetrical Conflict*, p. 51.

133. Zulaika, *Terrorism*, p. 11; Byman, *A High Price*, pp. 5, 362, 364, 368.

134. Byman, *A High Price*, p. 2.

135. Khalidi, *Palestinian Identity*, pp. xxii, xxxii–xxxv.

136. Khalidi, *Palestinian Identity*, p. xix.

137. Singh, *Hamas and Suicide Terrorism*, 61.

138. Mishal and Sela, *The Palestinian Hamas*, p. 94.

139. Bloom, *Dying to Kill*, p. 19.

140. Merari, *Driven to Death*, pp. 234, 237.

141. Pearlman, *Violence, Non-Violence, and the Palestinian National Movement*, p. 4.

142. Conditions which themselves had deep roots in the past, as well as modern-day sharpness: Kimmerling and Migdal, *The Palestinian People*, pp. 230–1, 246, 302–3.

143. Beinin and Stein (eds), *The Struggle for Sovereignty*, p. 112.

144. Quoted in Tamimi, *Hamas*, p. 287.

145. Berman, *Radical, Religious and Violent*, p. 132.

146. Farrell and Milton-Edwards, *Hamas*, pp. 140, 176; Hassan, *Life as a Weapon*, p. 86.

147. Gunning, *Hamas in Politics*, pp. 182–3.

148. Gunning, *Hamas in Politics*, p. 42; Mishal and Sela, *The Palestinian Hamas*, pp. xv, 90.

149. Gunning, *Hamas in Politics*, pp. 54, 241.

150. Mahmud Zahhar, quoted in Beinin and Stein (eds), *The Struggle for Sovereignty*, p. 114.

151. Quoted in K. Hroub, *Hamas: Political Thought and Practice* (Washington: Institute for Palestine Studies, 2000), p. 3.

152. Levitt, *Hamas*, p. 85.

153. Levitt, *Hamas*, pp. 2, 59–60; Vittori, *Terrorist Financing and Resourcing*, p. 74; Byman, *A High Price*, p. 102; Moghadam, 'Palestinian Suicide Terrorism', p. 72.

154. Jones, *Blood That Cries Out From the Earth*, p. 51.

155. King, *A Quiet Revolution*, p. 83.

156. Quoted in Bloom, *Dying to Kill*, p. 30. Cf. Richardson, *What Terrorists Want*, p. 122.

157. Abdel Aziz al-Rantissi, quoted in Juergensmeyer, *Terror in the Mind of God*, p. 187.

158. Merari, *Driven to Death*, pp. 174–5, 184–8; Hafez, *Manufacturing Human Bombs*, pp. 41, 44.

159. Merari, *Driven to Death*.

160. Merari, *Driven to Death*.

161. Aviad, *The Politics of Terror*, p. 31.

162. Kimmerling and Migdal, *The Palestinian People*, p. 300.

163. Quoted in Hoffman, *Inside Terrorism*, pp. 152–3.

164. J.A. Piazza, 'Is Islamist Terrorism More Dangerous? An Empirical Study of Group Ideology, Organization, and Goal Structure', *TPV*, 21/1 (2009), pp. 65–6; Byman, *A High Price*, p. 204.

165. B. Ganor, 'An Intifada in Europe? A Comparative Analysis of Radicalization Processes Among Palestinians in the West Bank and Gaza Versus Muslim Immigrants in Europe', *SICAT*, 34/8 (2011), p. 589.

166. King, *A Quiet Revolution*, pp. 262–3.

167. Ismael Haniyeh, quoted in Pearlman, *Violence, Non-Violence, and the Palestinian National Movement*, p. 137.

168. Gould and Klor, 'Does Terrorism Work?', pp. 1463, 1508.

169. Pearlman, *Violence, Non-Violence, and the Palestinian National Movement*.

170. Quoted in King, *A Quiet Revolution*, p. 324.

171. Kimmerling and Migdal, *The Palestinian People*, pp. 335–8.

172. Freedman, *Strategy*, pp. xii, 607.

173. Mishal and Sela, *The Palestinian Hamas*, pp. xxiv–xxv, 11–12, 108, 139, 147, 151, 168–70.

174. Quoted in Hoffman, *Inside Terrorism*, p. 155.

175. L. Binder, 'Christmas in Gaza: An Adventitious War?', *TPV*, 21/3 (2009), p. 518.

176. Habeck, *Knowing the Enemy*, pp. 173–4.

177. Beaumont, *Secret Life of War*, pp. 231–2.

178. D. Harris-Gershon, *What Do You Buy the Children of the Terrorist Who Tried to Kill Your Wife? A Memoir* (London: Oneworld Publications, 2013), quotations at pp. 169, 220. I'm grateful to Jasmine English for drawing my attention to this fascinating memoir.

CHAPTER 4

1. Quoted in R. P. Clark, *The Basque Insurgents: ETA, 1952–1980* (Madison: University of Wisconsin Press, 1984), p. 37.

2. M. Keating, 'Northern Ireland and the Basque Country', in J. McGarry (ed.), *Northern Ireland and the Divided World: Post-Agreement Northern Ireland in Comparative Perspective* (Oxford: OUP, 2001), p. 183.

3. C. J. Watson, *Basque Nationalism and Political Violence: The Ideological and Intellectual Origins of ETA* (Reno, Nev.: Center for Basque Studies, 2007), p. 69.

4. W. Douglass and J. Zulaika, *Basque Culture: Anthropological Perspectives* (Reno, Nev.: Center for Basque Studies, 2007), p. 21.

5. C. J. Watson, *Modern Basque History: Eighteenth Century to the Present* (Reno, Nev.: Center for Basque Studies, 2003), p. 112.

6. J. Agirreazkuenaga, *The Making of the Basque Question: Experiencing Self-Government, 1793–1877* (Reno, Nev.: Center for Basque Studies, 2011).

7. L. Greenfeld, *Nationalism: Five Roads to Modernity* (Cambridge, Mass.: Harvard University Press, 1992).

8. J. S. Holmes, *Terrorism and Democratic Stability Revisited* (Manchester: Manchester University Press, 2008; 1st edn 2001), p. 65.
9. The terrible nature of much of that violence is now brilliantly chronicled in P. Preston, *The Spanish Holocaust: Inquisition and Extermination in Twentieth-Century Spain* (London: HarperCollins, 2012).
10. Z. Bray, *Living Boundaries: Frontiers and Identity in the Basque Country* (Brussels: Peter Lang, 2004), p. 165.
11. A. Pérez-Agote, 'Self-Fulfilling Prophecy and Unresolved Mourning: Basque Political Violence in the Twenty-First Century', in B. Aretxaga, D. Dworkin, J. Gabilondo, and J. Zulaika (eds), *Empire and Terror: Nationalism/Postnationalism in the New Millennium* (Reno, Nev.: Center for Basque Studies, 2004).
12. 'On July 31, 1959, a new organization came into existence: Euskadi Ta Askatasuna, or Euskadi And Freedom' (Clark, *The Basque Insurgents*, p. 27).
13. Quoted in T. Whitfield, *Endgame for ETA: Elusive Peace in the Basque Country* (London: Hurst, 2014), p. 41.
14. Watson, *Basque Nationalism and Political Violence*, pp. 201, 211.
15. 'Indeed, the *violent* history of ETA—that moment when it began to use the specific tactic of political violence that had theoretically existed as a possibility since its inception—really began in 1968' (Watson, *Basque Nationalism and Political Violence*, p. 222).
16. ETA's campaign killed 858 people, according to R. Alonso, 'Why Do Terrorists Stop? Analyzing Why ETA Members Abandon or Continue with Terrorism', *SICAT*, 34/9 (2011), p. 696.
17. Bray, *Living Boundaries*, p. 54.
18. *Guardian* 21 December 1973.
19. *New York Times* 20 June 1987.
20. *Los Angeles Times* 12 December 1987.
21. Whitfield, *Endgame for ETA*, p. 65.
22. D. Muro, *Ethnicity and Violence: The Case of Radical Basque Nationalism* (London: Routledge, 2008), p. 120.
23. Muro, *Ethnicity and Violence*, p. 121.
24. Muro, *Ethnicity and Violence*, p. 122.
25. L. Mees, *Nationalism, Violence, and Democracy: The Basque Clash of Identities* (Basingstoke: Palgrave Macmillan, 2003), p. 45.
26. Quoted in Whitfield, *Endgame for ETA*, p. 78.
27. Preston, *The Spanish Holocaust*.
28. Holmes, *Terrorism and Democratic Stability Revisited*, p. 125.
29. Watson, *Basque Nationalism and Political Violence*, p. 27.
30. *USA Today* 30 December 2006.
31. Quoted in *Guardian* 5 June 2007.
32. Quoted in *An Phoblacht* March 2014.
33. Quoted in Hoffman, *Inside Terrorism*, p. 246.
34. Set out in full in English, *Irish Freedom*, pp. 12–21, 110–11, 139–40, 160, 186, 218–23, 305–6, 328–33, 341–5, 372–4, 432–506.

35. Watson, *Basque Nationalism and Political Violence*, pp. 22, 24, 35, 37, 49–50, 53–9, 63, 68–9, 73, 77, 80, 82–3, 89, 100, 109, 111–13, 115–18, 122, 125–6, 152, 163, 165, 175, 188, 190, 199, 211, 217; cf. Muro, *Ethnicity and Violence*.
36. Muro, *Ethnicity and Violence*, p. 8.
37. Clark, *The Basque Insurgents*, p. 33.
38. Bray, *Living Boundaries*, p. 57.
39. Bray, *Living Boundaries*, pp. 101–2.
40. Even when those scholars are superb, as with D. N. Posner, *Institutions and Ethnic Politics in Africa* (Cambridge: Cambridge University Press, 2005), pp. 14, 138–9.
41. Bray, *Living Boundaries*, p. 48.
42. Agirreazkuenaga, *The Making of the Basque Question*, pp. 220, 246.
43. Muro, *Ethnicity and Violence*, p. 207.
44. Clark, *The Basque Insurgents*, pp. 38–9, 59; Muro, *Ethnicity and Violence*, p. 103.
45. Whitfield, *Endgame for ETA*, pp. 41–2; Muro, *Ethnicity and Violence*, pp. 98, 166.
46. Mees, *Nationalism, Violence, and Democracy*, p. 128.
47. Muro, *Ethnicity and Violence*, pp. 8, 140.
48. Quoted in F. Reinares, 'Who are the Terrorists? Analyzing Changes in Sociological Profile among Members of ETA', *SICAT*, 27/6 (2004), p. 475.
49. Quoted in Whitfield, *Endgame for ETA*, p. 32.
50. M. Crenshaw, 'Reflections on the Effects of Terrorism', in Crenshaw (ed.), *Terrorism, Legitimacy, and Power*, p. 25.
51. As illuminatingly examined in Bray, *Living Boundaries*.
52. Muro, *Ethnicity and Violence*, p. 161.
53. Keating, 'Northern Ireland and the Basque Country', pp. 188–9.
54. Whitfield, *Endgame for ETA*, p. 28.
55. Bray, *Living Boundaries*, p. 20.
56. Whitfield, *Endgame for ETA*, p. 61.
57. Agirreazkuenaga, *The Making of the Basque Question*, pp. 101, 109.
58. Quoted in Mees, *Nationalism, Violence, and Democracy*, p. 134.
59. Muro, *Ethnicity and Violence*, p. 4.
60. Bray, *Living Boundaries*, pp. 33, 53–4.
61. Muro, *Ethnicity and Violence*, p. 129.
62. Mees, *Nationalism, Violence, and Democracy*, pp. 142, 147.
63. J. Argomaniz and O. Lynch (eds), *International Perspectives on Terrorist Victimization: An Interdisciplinary Approach* (Basingstoke: Palgrave Macmillan, 2015), pp. viii, 1.
64. Cronin, *How Terrorism Ends*, pp. 94–114. See, for example, Cronin's assessment on p. 94: 'Terrorism can be self-defeating'; 'violence deliberately targeted against civilians repels rather than attracts popular support'.
65. Whitfield, *Endgame for ETA*, p. 284.
66. Keating, 'Northern Ireland and the Basque Country', pp. 196–7.
67. Mees, *Nationalism, Violence, and Democracy*, p. 93; cf. Clark, *The Basque Insurgents*, pp. 170–3.
68. Mees, *Nationalism, Violence, and Democracy*, p. 99.
69. Muro, *Ethnicity and Violence*, pp. 160–1.

70. Muro, *Ethnicity and Violence*, pp. 189, 197–8.

71. Mees, *Nationalism, Violence, and Democracy*, pp. 160–2.

72. Pérez-Agote, 'Self-Fulfilling Prophecy and Unresolved Mourning', p. 183.

73. Quoted in Alonso, 'Why Do Terrorists Stop?', p. 704.

74. Mees, *Nationalism, Violence, and Democracy*, p. 79.

75. C. Ross, 'Nationalism and Party Competition in the Basque Country and Catalonia', *West European Politics*, 19/3 (1996).

76. Whitfield, *Endgame for ETA*, p. 315.

77. Mees, *Nationalism, Violence, and Democracy*, p. 132.

78. R. Alonso, 'Pathways out of Terrorism in Northern Ireland and the Basque Country: The Misrepresentation of the Irish Model', *TPV*, 16/4 (2004), p. 695; cf. Douglass and Zulaika, *Basque Culture*, pp. 134–5.

79. Agirreazkuenaga, *The Making of the Basque Question*, p. 55.

80. Mees, *Nationalism, Violence, and Democracy*, pp. 167, 174.

81. Mees, *Nationalism, Violence, and Democracy*, p. 46.

82. Whitfield, *Endgame for ETA*, p. 68.

83. P. B. Radcliff, *Making Democratic Citizens in Spain: Civil Society and the Popular Origins of the Transition, 1960–78* (Basingstoke: Palgrave Macmillan, 2011).

84. Whitfield, *Endgame for ETA*, p. 29.

85. Bray, *Living Boundaries*, pp. 20, 43, 75, 133, 243.

86. Quoted in Muro, *Ethnicity and Violence*, p. 133.

87. Clark, *The Basque Insurgents*, pp. 86, 105, 113, 123–4, 139.

88. Muro, *Ethnicity and Violence*, p. 8.

89. Watson, *Modern Basque History*, p. 435.

90. Whitfield, *Endgame for ETA*, p. 27.

91. Mees, *Nationalism, Violence, and Democracy*, pp. 50–1.

92. Muro, *Ethnicity and Violence*, pp. 154–5; Mees, *Nationalism, Violence, and Democracy*, p. 76.

93. Muro, *Ethnicity and Violence*, p. 113.

94. Muro, *Ethnicity and Violence*, pp. 144–7.

95. Ross, 'Nationalism and Party Competition'.

96. Holmes, *Terrorism and Democratic Stability Revisited*, p. 92; cf. Clark, *The Basque Insurgents*, pp. 136–7.

97. Bew, Frampton, and Gurruchaga, *Talking to Terrorists*, p. 180.

98. Clark, *The Basque Insurgents*, pp. 50–1.

99. On the importance more generally of intra- and inter-state cooperation and of intelligence-led and police-based counter-terrorism, see English, *Terrorism: How to Respond*, pp. 131–3, 136–40; and see echoes of this in what was effectively done by the Spanish state, in cooperation with other countries, to contain ETA (Whitfield, *Endgame for ETA*, p. 307).

100. Mees, *Nationalism, Violence, and Democracy*, p. 81.

101. Whitfield, *Endgame for ETA*, p. 100.

102. J. Argomaniz and A. Vidal-Diez, 'Examining Deterrence and Backlash Effects in Counter-Terrorism: The Case of ETA', *TPV*, 27/1 (2015), p. 174.

103. Mees, *Nationalism, Violence, and Democracy*, p. 73; cf. Clark, *The Basque Insurgents*, pp. 73, 111, 227–9.
104. Clark, *The Basque Insurgents*, p. 55.
105. Bray, *Living Boundaries*, pp. 71–2.
106. Mees, *Nationalism, Violence, and Democracy*, p. 82.
107. Whitfield, *Endgame for ETA*, p. 30.
108. J. Zulaika, *Basque Violence: Metaphor and Sacrament* (Reno: University of Nevada Press, 1988).
109. P. Woodworth, *Dirty War, Clean Hands: ETA, the GAL, and Spanish Democracy* (Cork: Cork University Press, 2001); Clark, *The Basque Insurgents*, pp. 260–2.
110. Muro, *Ethnicity and Violence*, pp. 105–6.
111. Bew, Frampton, and Gurruchaga, *Talking to Terrorists*, p. 238.
112. Whitfield, *Endgame for ETA*, p. 29.
113. Zulaika, *Basque Violence*, pp. 58, 62, 71–2; Watson, *Modern Basque History*, pp. 329–31; Muro, *Ethnicity and Violence*, p. 108.
114. Reinares, 'Who are the Terrorists?', p. 476.
115. Muro, *Ethnicity and Violence*, p. 127.
116. C. Hamilton, *Women and ETA: The Gender Politics of Radical Basque Nationalism* (Manchester: Manchester University Press, 2007), p. 14.
117. Mees, *Nationalism, Violence, and Democracy*, p. 57.
118. Whitfield, *Endgame for ETA*, pp. 31, 309.
119. Clark, *The Basque Insurgents*, p. 76.
120. Quoted in Clark, *The Basque Insurgents*, p. 106.
121. C. Joyce, O. Lynch, and E. Anton, 'Victims' Issues in Northern Ireland and Spain: A Conceptual and Theoretical Overview', in Argomaniz and Lynch (eds), *Victims of Terrorism*, pp. 61, 69–70.
122. Muro, *Ethnicity and Violence*, p. 184.
123. Whitfield, *Endgame for ETA*, p. 6.
124. Evans, *Altered Pasts*.
125. D. Muro, 'A Catalan Compromise: How to Solve Spain's Secession Crisis', *Foreign Affairs*, 9 November 2014.
126. Ross, 'Nationalism and Party Competition'.

CONCLUSION

1. 'For they eat the bread of wickedness, and drink the wine of violence' (Proverbs 4: 17, King James Bible).
2. See the meticulous treatment in Hoffman, *Anonymous Soldiers*.
3. Quoted in Hoffman, *Anonymous Soldiers*, p. 97.
4. Quoted in M. Levitt, 'Hezbollah Finances: Funding the Party of God', in Giraldo and Trinkunas (eds), *Terrorism Financing and State Responses*, p. 135.
5. Quoted in A. R. Norton, *Hezbollah: A Short History* (Princeton: Princeton University Press, 2007), p. 33.
6. Quoted in Rubin and Rubin (eds), *Anti-American Terrorism and the Middle East*, p. 50.

7. Hezbollah statement, quoted in Pape and Feldman, *Cutting the Fuse*, p. 200.
8. Edward Walker, quoted in Fierke, *Political Self-Sacrifice*, pp. 202–3.
9. Sageman, *Leaderless Jihad*, p. 41.
10. Berman, *Radical, Religious and Violent*, pp. 54–5.
11. Quoted in Norton, *Hezbollah*, p. 154.
12. UK Ministry of Defence, *Strategic Trends Programme: Future Character of Conflict* (2010), p. 18.
13. Krueger, *What Makes a Terrorist*, p. 138.
14. Fellman, *In the Name of God and Country*, p. 1.
15. T. Riley-Smith, *The Cracked Bell: America and the Afflictions of Liberty* (London: Constable, 2010), p. 227.
16. For brilliant treatment of Brown, see Fellman, *In the Name of God and Country*, pp. 14–56.
17. J. Grey, 'Malaya, 1948–1960: Defeating Communist Insurgency', in J. Thompson (ed.), *The Imperial War Museum Book of Modern Warfare: British and Commonwealth Forces at War 1945–2000* (London: Pan, 2003; 1st edn 2002), pp. 73, 75.
18. Cronin, *Ending Terrorism*, p. 52.
19. F. Kitson, 'Kenya, 1952–1956: Mau Mau', in Thompson (ed.), *The Imperial War Museum Book of Modern Warfare*, p. 144.
20. See the excellent treatment in H. Bennett, *Fighting the Mau Mau: The British Army and Counter-Insurgency in the Kenya Emergency* (Cambridge: Cambridge University Press, 2013).
21. Jackie McDonald, interviewed by the author, Belfast, 31 January 2012.
22. Former UDA members, quoted in Shirlow, Tonge, McAuley, and McGlynn, *Abandoning Historical Conflict?*, p. 105.
23. Cronin, *How Terrorism Ends*, p. 92.
24. D. C. Rapoport, 'Preface', in Rapoport (ed.), *Inside Terrorist Organizations*.
25. Gupta, *Understanding Terrorism and Political Violence*, p. 187.
26. Burleigh, *Blood and Rage*, p. 84.
27. Hoffman, *Inside Terrorism*, p. 7. Cf. R. B. Jensen, 'The Pre-1914 Anarchist "Lone Wolf" Terrorist and Governmental Responses', *TPV*, 26/1 (2014).
28. F. Harris, *The Bomb* (Portland: Feral House, 1996; 1st edn 1909), quotation at p. 49.
29. Holmes, *Terrorism and Democratic Stability Revisited*, p. 95.
30. Hoffman, *Inside Terrorism*, p. 75.
31. I. Duyvesteyn, 'The Role of History and Continuity in Terrorism Research', in Ranstorp (ed.), *Mapping Terrorism Research*, p. 63.
32. Burke, *Reflections on the Revolution*, p. 49.
33. Quoted in S. Aust, *Baader–Meinhof: The Inside Story of the RAF* (New York: OUP, 2009; 1st edn 1987), p. 150.
34. Quoted in Aust, *Baader–Meinhof*, p. 37.
35. Cronin, *How Terrorism Ends*, p. 110.
36. G. Kassimeris, *Inside Greek Terrorism* (London: Hurst and Co., 2013), pp. 19–20.

37. G. H. McCormick, 'The Shining Path and Peruvian Terrorism', in Rapoport (ed.), *Inside Terrorist Organizations*, p. 109.

38. Holmes, *Terrorism and Democratic Stability Revisited*, p. 90.

39. Quoted in Crenshaw, *Explaining Terrorism*, p. 56.

40. Staniland, *Networks of Rebellion*, pp. 59–99.

41. J. Humphries, *Freedom Fighters: Wales's Forgotten 'War', 1963–1993* (Cardiff: University of Wales Press, 2008). Wyn Thomas's impressive study of Welsh militancy (*Hands Off Wales: Nationhood and Militancy* (Llandysul: Gomer Press, 2013)) argues that Welsh terrorism perhaps achieved some lesser progress; but his account makes equally clear that the central goal of independence has remained utterly distant in Wales.

42. J. Rochlin, 'Plan Colombia and the Revolution in Military Affairs: The Demise of the FARC', *Review of International Studies*, 37/2 (2011), pp. 720, 722.

43. Moyano, *Argentina's Lost Patrol*, pp. 4–5, 27, 41–2, 84.

44. Bloom, *Dying to Kill*, p. 46.

45. *Independent on Sunday* 17 April 2011.

46. Hanley and Millar, *Lost Revolution*.

47. Quoted in Hanley and Millar, *Lost Revolution*, p. 70.

48. McDonald and Holland, *INLA*.

49. On dissident republicanism, see M. Frampton, *Legion of the Rearguard: Dissident Irish Republicanism* (Dublin: Irish Academic Press, 2011); J. Horgan, *Divided We Stand: The Strategy and Psychology of Ireland's Dissident Terrorists* (Oxford: OUP, 2013); Morrison, *Origins and Rise of Dissident Irish Republicanism*; P. M. Currie and M. Taylor (eds), *Dissident Irish Republicanism* (London: Continuum, 2011); S. A. Whiting, '"The Discourse of Defence": "Dissident" Irish Republican Newspapers and the "Propaganda War"', *TPV*, 24/3 (2012); R. Frenett and M. L. R. Smith, 'IRA 2.0: Continuing the Long War—Analyzing the Factors Behind Anti-GFA Violence', *TPV*, 24/3 (2012); Sanders, *Inside the IRA*.

50. Bradley and Feeney, *Insider*, p. 13.

51. Ex-PIRA Volunteer, interviewed by the author, Belfast, 26 November 2012.

52. Morrison, *Origins and Rise of Dissident Irish Republicanism*, p. 1.

53. English, *Irish Freedom*; A. Edwards, 'When Terrorism as Strategy Fails: Dissident Irish Republicans and the Threat to British Security', *SICAT*, 34/4 (2011).

54. Osama bin Laden, quoted in Miller (ed.), *'War on Terror'*, p. 8.

55. Cronin, *How Terrorism Ends*, pp. 215–16.

56. Cronin, *Ending Terrorism*, pp. 26, 35, 37.

57. Abrahms, 'Why Terrorism Does Not Work'.

58. S. G. Jones and M. C. Libicki, *How Terrorist Groups End: Lessons for Countering al-Qaida* (Santa Monica, Calif.: RAND, 2008).

59. Chenoweth and Stephan, *Why Civil Resistance Works*, pp. 25, 226–7.

60. George Grivas, quoted in Hoffman, *Inside Terrorism*, p. 46.

61. Broadly, I am sceptical about the notion that terroristic and other violence was especially successful in ending empire in the late twentieth century. Stepanova

argues that of the seventy-one self-determination conflicts extant during 1951–2005, separatists won an internationally recognized and independent state through armed conflict in only five cases (Stepanova, *Terrorism in Asymmetrical Conflict*, pp. 49–50); similarly, Hobsbawm's research suggested: 'The truth is that what brought empires to an end was rarely the revolt of their subject peoples alone' (Hobsbawm, *Globalization, Democracy and Terrorism*, p. 79).

62. Hoffman, *Anonymous Soldiers*, pp. 68–9, 80–6, 112, 298.
63. Jackie McDonald, interviewed by the author, Belfast, 31 January 2012; cf. McKittrick, Kelters, Feeney, and Thornton, *Lost Lives*.
64. M. A. Meyers, *Chechnya Jihad* (San Diego: Green Grass Press, 2011), pp. 95, 134.
65. Kassimeris, *Inside Greek Terrorism*, pp. 32, 77–93, 115–17, 119.
66. Norton, *Hezbollah*, p. 93.
67. Des Dalton, quoted in Frampton, *Legion of the Rearguard*, p. 80.
68. White, *Ruairí Ó Brádaigh*.
69. Freedman, *Strategy*, p. 277.
70. Hoffman, *Anonymous Soldiers*, pp. 87, 95–8, 115, 134, 240–1, 247, 255, 345–8, 362.
71. Lutz and Lutz, *Global Terrorism*, p. 187.
72. Wilkinson, *Terrorism Versus Democracy* (2006 edn), p. 25.
73. Aust, *Baader–Meinhof*, pp. 57, 73, 165, 219, 252.
74. Burleigh, *Blood and Rage*, p. 246.
75. Quoted in Burleigh, *Blood and Rage*, p. 247.
76. Crenshaw, *Explaining Terrorism*, p. 199.
77. Merari, *Driven to Death*, p. 31.
78. Vasantha, quoted in Hoffman, *Inside Terrorism*, p. 142.
79. P. Roth, *American Pastoral* (London: Vintage, 1998; 1st edn 1997).
80. McDonald and Holland, *INLA*, pp. 136–40.
81. Frampton, *Legion of the Rearguard*, pp. 141–5.
82. Real IRA Army Council member, quoted in R. Dudley Edwards, *Aftermath: The Omagh Bombing and the Families' Pursuit of Justice* (London: Harvill Secker, 2009), p. 80.
83. Wright, *The Looming Tower*, pp. 256–8.
84. When it was banned in 2002, LeT adopted the name Jamaat-ul-Dawa.
85. Akash Akhinwar, quoted in *Daily Telegraph* 28 November 2008.
86. Humphries, *Freedom Fighters*, pp. 51, 59–60.
87. J. Lodge, 'Introduction', in J. Lodge (ed.), *Terrorism: A Challenge to the State* (Oxford: Martin Robertson, 1981), p. 2.
88. Bennett, *Fighting the Mau Mau*, p. 50.
89. 'Bloodbath at Friday Prayers: Isil Bombers Kill 150 at Yemen Mosques', *Daily Telegraph* 21 March 2015.
90. Laqueur, *Terrorism*, p. 80.
91. S. Rushdie, *Joseph Anton: A Memoir* (London: Jonathan Cape, 2012), pp. 73, 175, 277, 344, 353, 355, 417, 549, 624, 636.
92. Rushdie, *Joseph Anton*, p. 629.

93. *Guardian* 23 July 2011.

94. *New York Times* 15 April 2013; *Rolling Stone* 1 August 2013.

95. *Daily Telegraph* 9 April 2015.

96. In the phrasing of H. Küng, *On Being a Christian* (London: Collins, 1977; 1st edn 1974), p. 54.

97. Hoffman, *Anonymous Soldiers*, pp. 245, 274, 342, 347, 472, 475.

98. Bennett, *Fighting the Mau Mau*.

99. Neumann and Smith, *The Strategy of Terrorism*, p. 20.

100. Crenshaw, *Explaining Terrorism*, p. 29.

101. Derek Snape, quoted in R. Neillands, 'Cyprus, 1955–1959: EOKA', in Thompson (ed.), *The Imperial War Museum Book of Modern Warfare*, p. 176.

102. Quoted in *Hindustan Times* 28 October 2014.

103. C. Gearty, *Civil Liberties* (Oxford: OUP, 2007), pp. 43–9, 54–8, 87, 114–15, 153–4, 158–60, 182, 187–8. Though the dangers of Draconian legislative reaction are almost certainly graver elsewhere, India providing one major example: A. M. Chenoy, and K. A. M. Chenoy, *Maoist and Other Armed Conflicts* (London: Penguin, 2010), pp. 34–5.

104. Updike, *Terrorist*, p. 46.

105. Bloom, *Dying to Kill*, p. 62.

106. Hoffman, *Anonymous Soldiers*, p. 140.

107. Levitt, 'Hezbollah Finances', pp. 137–9; Vittori, *Terrorist Financing and Resourcing*, pp. 60, 102–4.

108. Berman, *Radical, Religious, and Violent*, pp. 3, 51.

109. Staniland, *Networks of Rebellion*, pp. 141–77, quotation at p. 158.

110. C. C. Fair, 'The 2008 Mumbai Attack', in Hoffman and Reinares (eds), *Evolution of the Global Terrorist Threat*, pp. 575–7.

111. Cronin, *How Terrorism Ends*, pp. 75–6, 94.

112. Hoffman, *Anonymous Soldiers*, pp. 70–1, 76–8, 126.

113. Krueger, *What Makes a Terrorist*.

114. Aust, *Baader–Meinhof*, pp. 50, 70, 115, 131, 297 (Baader quotation at p. 70); cf. G. Pridham, 'Terrorism and the State in West Germany During the 1970s: A Threat to Stability or a Case of Political Over-Reaction?', in Lodge (ed.), *Terrorism*, p. 18.

115. Quoted in Hoffman, *Inside Terrorism*, p. 75.

116. Vittori, *Terrorist Financing and Resourcing*, p. 55.

117. Aust, *Baader–Meinhof*, pp. 38–9.

118. H. Hesse, *Steppenwolf* (Harmondsworth: Penguin, 1965; 1st edn 1927), Author's Note (1961), p. 5.

119. Hesse, *Steppenwolf*, pp. 27, 36.

120. Kassimeris, *Inside Greek Terrorism*, p. 30.

121. Bloom, *Dying to Kill*, pp. 63–5.

122. Quoted in Hoffman, *Inside Terrorism*, p. 247.

123. D. Park, *The Truth Commissioner* (London: Bloomsbury, 2009; 1st edn 2008), p. 69.

124. Morrison, *Origins and Rise of Dissident Irish Republicanism*, pp. 193–5.

125. R. English, 'Why Terrorist Campaigns Do Not End: The Case of Contemporary Irish Dissident Republicanism', in English (ed.), *Illusions of Terrorism and Counter-Terrorism*.

126. Former UDA member, quoted in Shirlow, Tonge, McAuley, and McGlynn, *Abandoning Historical Conflict?*, p. 55.

127. Jackie McDonald, interviewed by the author, Belfast, 31 January 2012.

128. *Independent on Sunday* 17 April 2011.

129. C. Moore, *Contemporary Violence: Postmodern War in Kosovo and Chechnya* (Manchester: Manchester University Press, 2010), pp. 106–10.

130. Gilderhuis, *History and Historians*, p. 3.

131. *Politics* (Oxford: OUP, 1995), p. 7.

132. As (brilliantly) in Posner, *Institutions and Ethnic Politics in Africa*.

133. Crenshaw, *Explaining Terrorism*, p. 42; Held, *How Terrorism Is Wrong*, pp. 24, 141; Wilkinson, *Terrorism Versus Democracy* (2006 edn), p. 193.

134. V. Dudouet, H. J. Giessman, and K. Planta (eds), *Post-War Security Transitions: Participatory Peacebuilding After Asymmetric Conflicts* (London: Routledge, 2012), pp. 3–5, 8–9, 267.

135. Schwarzmantel, *Democracy and Political Violence*.

136. Donohue, *The Cost of Counterterrorism*.

137. Schwarzmantel, *Democracy and Political Violence*, pp. 54–5, 68–9.

138. E. Barkan, *The Guilt of Nations: Restitution and Negotiating Historical Injustices* (Baltimore: Johns Hopkins University Press, 2000), pp. x, xix, xxx, 317, 329.

139. T. Garton Ash, 'A Century of Civil Resistance: Some Lessons and Questions', in Roberts and Garton Ash (eds), *Civil Resistance and Power Politics*, p. 388.

140. Goodin, *What's Wrong with Terrorism?*; Honderich, *Terrorism for Humanity*; Honderich, *Humanity, Terrorism, Terrorist War*; Steinhoff, *On the Ethics of War and Terrorism*; Held, *How Terrorism Is Wrong*.

141. D. MacCulloch, *A History of Christianity: The First Three Thousand Years* (London: Penguin, 2009), p. 12; Banner, *Being a Historian*, p. xvii.

142. Black and MacRaild, *Studying History*, p. 7.

143. Ratzinger, *Church, Ecumenism, and Politics*, p. 149.

144. Honderich, *Humanity, Terrorism, Terrorist War*, pp. 22–3, 63, 95, 118.

145. S. Baron-Cohen, *Zero Degrees of Empathy: A New Theory of Human Cruelty and Kindness* (London: Penguin, 2012; 1st edn 2011).

146. R. English, 'The Enduring Illusions of Terrorism and Counter-Terrorism', in English (ed), *Illusions of Terrorism and Counter-Terrorism*.

147. Baron-Cohen, *Zero Degrees of Empathy*, pp. 107, 119–20.

148. Juergensmeyer, *Terror in the Mind of God*; cf. Skelly (ed.), *Political Islam from Muhammad to Ahmadinejad*, p. 11.

149. See, for example, the careful treatment of this theme in MacCulloch, *A History of Christianity*; cf. Lewis, *The Crisis of Islam*, p. 6.

150. D. Veness, 'Low Intensity and High Impact Conflict', in Taylor and Horgan (eds), *The Future of Terrorism*, p. 12; Wilkinson, *Terrorism Versus Democracy* (2006

edn), pp. 10–11; D. E. Jenkins, *God, Politics, and the Future* (London: SCM Press, 1988), p. xv.

151. J. Habgood, *Faith and Uncertainty* (London: Darton, Longman, and Todd, 1997), pp. 199–200.

152. D. English, *God in the Gallery* (London: Epworth Press, 1975), p. 118. And Christianity can be subversive of established order without any recourse to violence (English, *God in the Gallery*, p. 161).

153. C. T. McIntire (ed.), *God, History and Historians: Modern Christian Views of History* (New York: OUP, 1977); R. Clutterbuck, *Handing on Christ: Rediscovering the Gift of Christian Doctrine* (London: Epworth, 2009); W. J. Abraham, *The Logic of Evangelism* (London: Hodder and Stoughton, 1989); Habgood, *Faith and Uncertainty*, p. 33.

154. Jenkins, *God, Politics, and the Future*, pp. 7–8.

155. Riley-Smith, *The Cracked Bell*, p. 84.

156. Richardson, *What Terrorists Want*, pp. 135–6; Bloom, *Dying to Kill*, pp. 2, 79; Pape, *Dying to Win*, pp. 16–17.

157. Berman, *Radical, Religious, and Violent*.

158. A. Sen, *The Idea of Justice* (London: Penguin, 2009), quotation at p. xi.

159. Cannadine, *The Undivided Past*; Danchev, *On Art and War and Terror*, p. 3.

Bibliography

Abraham, W. J., *The Logic of Evangelism* (London: Hodder and Stoughton, 1989).

Abrahms, M., 'Al-Qaida's Scorecard: A Progress Report on al-Qaida's Objectives', *SICAT*, 29/5 (2006).

Abrahms, M., 'Why Terrorism Does Not Work', *International Security*, 31/2 (2006).

Abrahms, M., 'Does Terrorism Really Work? Evolution in the Conventional Wisdom Since 9/11', *Defence and Peace Economics*, 22/6 (December 2011).

Abrahms, M., 'Response to Peter Krause', *H-Diplo/ISSF* (29 June 2013).

Abrahms, M., Chenoweth, E., Miller, N., McClellan, E., Frisch, H., and Staniland, P., 'Correspondence: What Makes Terrorists Tick', *International Security*, 33/4 (Spring 2009).

Abrams, L., *Oral History Theory* (London: Routledge, 2010).

Acosta, B., 'Live to Win Another Day: Why Many Militant Organizations Survive Yet Few Succeed', *SICAT*, 37/2 (2014).

Adams, G., *The Politics of Irish Freedom* (Dingle: Brandon, 1986).

Adams, G., *Before the Dawn: An Autobiography* (London: Heinemann, 1996).

Adams, G., 'To Cherish a Just and Lasting Peace', *Fordham International Law Journal*, 22/4 (1999).

Agirreazkuenaga, J., *The Making of the Basque Question: Experiencing Self-Government, 1793–1877* (Reno, Nev.: Center for Basque Studies, 2011).

Aldrich, R. J., 'US–European Intelligence Co-operation on Counter-Terrorism: Low Politics and Compulsion', *British Journal of Politics and International Relations*, 11/1 (2009).

Alexander, Y., *Palestinian Religious Terrorism: Hamas and Islamic Jihad* (Ardsley: Transnational Publishers, 2002).

Alonso, R., 'Pathways out of Terrorism in Northern Ireland and the Basque Country: The Misrepresentation of the Irish Model', *TPV*, 16/4 (2004).

Alonso, R., *The IRA and Armed Struggle* (London: Routledge, 2007).

Alonso, R., 'Why Do Terrorists Stop? Analyzing Why ETA Members Abandon or Continue with Terrorism', *Studies in Conflict and Terrorism*, 34/9 (2011).

Al-Zawahiri, A., *His Own Words: Translation and Analysis of the Writings of Dr Ayman al-Zawahiri* (Old Tappan, NJ: TLG Publications, 2006).

Amis, M., *The Second Plane. September 11: 2001–2007* (London: Jonathan Cape, 2008).

Anderson, B., *Joe Cahill: A Life in the IRA* (Dublin: O'Brien Press, 2002).

Anderson, C., *The Billy Boy: The Life and Death of LVF Leader Billy Wright* (Edinburgh: Mainstream, 2004; 1st edn 2002).

Anderson, J., *Christianity and Democratization: From Pious Subjects to Critical Participants* (Manchester: Manchester University Press, 2009).

Andrew, C., *The Defence of the Realm: The Authorized History of MI5* (London: Penguin, 2009).

Anthony, D., and Robbins, T., 'Religious Totalism, Violence and Exemplary Dualism: Beyond the Extrinsic Model', *TPV*, 7/3 (Autumn 1995).

Antonius, D., and Sinclair, S. J., *The Psychology of Terrorism Fears* (Oxford: OUP, 2012).

Aretxaga, B., Dworkin, D., Gabilondo, J., and Zulaika, J. (eds), *Empire and Terror: Nationalism/Postnationalism in the New Millennium* (Reno, Nev.: Center for Basque Studies, 2004).

Argomaniz, J., *The EU and Counter-Terrorism: Politics, Polity and Policies after 9/11* (London: Routledge, 2011).

Argomaniz, J., and Lynch, O. (eds), *International Perspectives on Terrorist Victimization: An Interdisciplinary Approach* (Basingstoke: Palgrave Macmillan, 2015).

Argomaniz, J., and Lynch, O. (eds), *Victims of Terrorism: A Comparative and Interdisciplinary Study* (London: Routledge, 2015).

Argomaniz, J., and Vidal-Diez, A., 'Examining Deterrence and Backlash Effects in Counter-Terrorism: The Case of ETA', *TPV*, 27/1 (2015).

Aristotle, *Politics* (Oxford: OUP, 1995).

Arnold, J. H., *History: A Very Short Introduction* (Oxford: OUP, 2000).

Arquilla, J., *Insurgents, Raiders, and Bandits: How Masters of Irregular Warfare Have Shaped our World* (Chicago: Ivan R. Dee, 2011).

Arreguin-Toft, I., *How the Weak Win Wars: A Theory of Asymmetric Conflict* (Cambridge: Cambridge University Press, 2005).

Asal, V., Gill, P., Rethemeyer, R. K., and Horgan, J., 'Killing Range: Explaining Lethality Variance within a Terrorist Organization', *Journal of Conflict Resolution*, 59/3 (2015).

Atienza, J. C., *The Origins, Ideology and Organization of Basque Nationalism, 1876–1903* (Reno, Nev.: Center for Basque Studies, 2006).

Augustine, *City of God* (London: Penguin, 2003 edn).

Aust, S., *Baader–Meinhof: The Inside Story of the RAF* (New York: OUP, 2009; 1st edn 1987).

Aviad, G., *The Politics of Terror: An Essential Hamas Lexicon* (Tel Aviv: Contento de Semrik, 2014).

Baker, A. H., *Extremists in our Midst: Confronting Terror* (Basingstoke: Palgrave Macmillan, 2011).

Ball, S., *The Bitter Sea* (London: Harper Press, 2010; 1st edn 2009).

Banner, J. M., *Being a Historian: An Introduction to the Professional World of History* (Cambridge: Cambridge University Press, 2012).

Barfield, T., *Afghanistan: A Cultural and Political History* (Princeton: Princeton University Press, 2010).

Barkan, E., *The Guilt of Nations: Restitution and Negotiating Historical Injustices* (Baltimore: Johns Hopkins University Press, 2000).

Barker, A. J., *The First Iraq War 1914–1918: Britain's Mesopotamian Campaign* (New York: Enigma Books, 2009).

Baron-Cohen, S., *Zero Degrees of Empathy: A New Theory of Human Cruelty and Kindness* (London: Penguin, 2012; 1st edn 2011).

Barrett, R., *The Islamic State* (New York: The Soufan Group, 2014).

Barth, K., *The Faith of the Church: A Commentary on the Apostles' Creed* (London: Fontana, 1960; 1st edn 1958).

Beaumont, P., *The Secret Life of War: Journeys Through Modern Conflict* (London: Harvill Secker, 2009).

Begin, M., *The Revolt: Story of the Irgun* (Jerusalem: Steimatzky's Agency, 1977; 1st edn 1952).

Beinin, J., and Stein, R. L. (eds), *The Struggle for Sovereignty: Palestine and Israel 1993–2005* (Stanford, Calif.: Stanford University Press, 2006).

Bell, C., *Peace Agreements and Human Rights* (Oxford: OUP, 2000).

Bennett, H., *Fighting the Mau Mau: The British Army and Counter-Insurgency in the Kenya Emergency* (Cambridge: Cambridge University Press, 2013).

Bentley, M., *Modern Historiography: An Introduction* (London: Routledge, 1999).

Bentley, M., *Modernizing England's Past: English Historiography in the Age of Modernism 1870–1970* (Cambridge: Cambridge University Press, 2005).

Bergen, P. L., *Holy War, Inc.: Inside the Secret World of Osama bin Laden* (London: Phoenix, 2002; 1st edn 2001).

Bergen, P. L., *The Osama bin Laden I Know* (New York: Free Press, 2006).

Bergen, P. L., *The Longest War: The Enduring Conflict Between America and al-Qaida* (New York: Free Press, 2011).

Bergen, P. L., *Manhunt: From 9/11 to Abbottabad—The Ten-Year Search for Osama bin Laden* (London: Bodley Head, 2012).

Bergen, P. L., and Cruickshank, P., 'Revisiting the Early Al-Qaida: An Updated Account of its Formative Years', *SICAT*, 35/1 (2012).

Berman, E., *Radical, Religious and Violent: The New Economics of Terrorism* (Cambridge, Mass.: MIT Press, 2009).

Berrebi, C., and Klor, E. F., 'Are Voters Sensitive to Terrorism? Direct Evidence from the Israeli Electorate', *American Political Science Review*, 102/3 (2008).

Bevir, M., 'Why Historical Distance is not a Problem', *History and Theory*, 50 (2011).

Bew, J., Frampton, M., and Gurruchaga, I., *Talking to Terrorists: Making Peace in Northern Ireland and the Basque Country* (London: Hurst, 2009).

Binder, L., 'Christmas in Gaza: An Adventitious War?', *TPV*, 21/3 (2009).

Black, J., and MacRaild, D. M., *Studying History* (Basingstoke: Palgrave, 2000; 1st edn 1997).

Blackbourn, J., 'International Terrorism and Counter-Terrorist Legislation: The Case Study of Post-9/11 Northern Ireland', *TPV*, 21 (2009).

Blair, T., *A Journey* (London: Hutchinson, 2010).

Bloom, M., *Dying to Kill: The Allure of Suicide Terror* (New York: Columbia University Press, 2007; 1st edn 2005).

Bloom, M., *Bombshell: The Many Faces of Women Terrorists* (London: Hurst and Co., 2011).

Bobbitt, P., *Terror and Consent: The Wars for the Twenty-First Century* (London: Penguin, 2009; 1st edn 2008).

Bousquet, A., 'Complexity Theory and the War on Terror: Understanding the Self-Organizing Dynamics of Leaderless Jihad', *Journal of International Relations and Development*, 15/3 (2012).

Bowler, P. J., *Monkey Trials and Gorilla Sermons: Evolution and Christianity from Darwin to Intelligent Design* (Cambridge, Mass.: Harvard University Press, 2007).

Boyce, D. G., *Decolonization and the British Empire, 1775–1997* (Basingstoke: Macmillan, 1999).

Brachman, J. M., *Global Jihadism: Theory and Practice* (London: Routledge, 2009).

Bradley, G., and Feeney, B., *Insider: Gerry Bradley's Life in the IRA* (Dublin: O'Brien Press, 2009).

Brahimi, A. 'Crushed in the Shadows: Why al-Qaida Will Lose the War of Ideas', *SICAT*, 33/2 (2010).

Brahimi, A. *Jihad and Just War in the War on Terror* (Oxford: OUP, 2010).

Bray, Z., *Living Boundaries: Frontiers and Identity in the Basque Country* (Brussels: Peter Lang, 2004).

Brennan, M., *The War in Clare 1911–1921: Personal Memoirs of the Irish War of Independence* (Dublin: Four Courts Press, 1980).

Brill, A. A., *Lectures on Psychoanalytic Psychiatry* (New York: Vintage, 1956; 1st edn 1946).

Brownlow, G., 'Towards an Acceptable Level of Violence: Institutional Lessons from Northern Ireland', *TPV*, 24/5 (2012).

Bruce, S., *The Red Hand: Protestant Paramilitaries in Northern Ireland* (Oxford: OUP, 1992).

Bruce, S., 'Loyalist Assassinations and Police Collusion in Northern Ireland: An Extended Critique of Sean McPhilemy's *The Committee*', *SICAT*, 23/1 (2000).

Buchan, J., *Greenmantle* (Harmondsworth: Penguin, 1956; 1st edn 1916).

Bulley, D., ' "Foreign" Terror? London Bombings, Resistance and the Failing State', *British Journal of Politics and International Relations*, 10/3 (2008).

Burke, E., *Reflections on the Revolution in France* (Oxford: OUP, 1993; 1st edn 1790).

Burke, J., *Al-Qaida: The True Story of Radical Islam* (London: Penguin, 2003).

Burke, J., *The 9/11 Wars* (London: Penguin, 2011).

Burke, P., *History and Social Theory* (Cambridge: Polity Press, 1992).

Burke, P. (ed.), *New Perspectives on Historical Writing* (Cambridge: Polity Press, 1992; 1st edn 1991).

Burke, P. (ed.), *History and Historians in the Twentieth Century* (Oxford: OUP, 2002).

Burleigh, M., *Blood and Rage: A Cultural History of Terrorism* (London: HarperPress, 2008).

Burrow, J., *A History of Histories: Epics, Chronicles, Romances, and Inquiries from Herodotus and Thucydides to the Twentieth Century* (London: Penguin, 2009; 1st edn 2007).

Byman, D., *A High Price: The Triumphs and Failures of Israeli Counter-Terrorism* (Oxford: OUP, 2011).

Cadwallader, A., *Lethal Allies: British Collusion in Ireland* (Cork: Mercier Press, 2013).

Cannadine, D., *G. M. Trevelyan: A Life in History* (London: HarperCollins, 1992).

Cannadine, D., *Class in Britain* (New Haven: Yale University Press, 1998).

Cannadine, D., *Making History Now* (London: Institute of Historical Research, 1999).

Cannadine, D. (ed.), *What is History Now?* (Basingstoke: Palgrave Macmillan, 2002).

Cannadine, D., *The Undivided Past: History Beyond our Differences* (London: Penguin, 2013).

Caplan, N., *The Israel–Palestine Conflict: Contested Histories* (Chichester: Wiley-Blackwell, 2010).

Caridi, P., *Hamas: From Resistance to Government* (New York: Seven Stories Press, 2012; 1st edn 2009).

Carr, E. H., *What is History?* (Basingstoke: Palgrave, 2001; 1st edn 1961).

Chakrabarti, K., 'Terrorism: Challenges to Politics, Society and International Relations', *Jadavpur Journal of International Relations*, 11–12 (2006–8).

Chenoweth, E., and Stephan, M. J., *Why Civil Resistance Works: The Strategic Logic of Nonviolent Conflict* (New York: Columbia University Press, 2011).

Chenoy, A. M., and Chenoy, K. A. M., *Maoist and Other Armed Conflicts* (London: Penguin, 2010).

Childe, V. G., *What Happened in History* (Harmondsworth: Penguin, 1942).

Clark, G., *Everyday Violence in the Irish Civil War* (Cambridge: Cambridge University Press, 2014).

Clark, J. C. D., *Revolution and Rebellion: State and Society in England in the Seventeenth and Eighteenth Centuries* (Cambridge: Cambridge University Press, 1986).

Clark, J. C. D., *Our Shadowed Present: Modernism, Postmodernism, and History* (London: Atlantic Books, 2003).

Clark, R. P., *The Basque Insurgents: ETA, 1952–1980* (Madison: University of Wisconsin Press, 1984).

Clarke, L., and Johnston, K., *Martin McGuinness: From Guns to Government* (Edinburgh: Mainstream Publishing, 2001).

Clausewitz, C. von, *On War* (Harmondsworth: Penguin, 1968; 1st edn 1832).

Cloughley, B., *A History of the Pakistan Army: Wars and Insurrections* (Oxford: OUP, 2006; 1st edn 1999).

Clutterbuck, R., *Handing on Christ: Rediscovering the Gift of Christian Doctrine* (London: Epworth, 2009).

Cockburn, P., *The Jihadis Return: ISIS and the New Sunni Uprising* (New York: OR Books, 2014).

Collins, E., *Killing Rage* (London: Granta, 1998; 1st edn 1997).

Comerford, R. V., *The Fenians in Context: Irish Politics and Society, 1848–82* (Dublin: Wolfhound Press, 1985).

Conway, K., *Southside Provisional: From Freedom Fighter to the Four Courts* (Blackrock: Orpen Press, 2014).

Coogan, T. P., *The IRA* (London: HarperCollins, 1987; 1st edn 1970).

Cox, M., Guelke, A., and Stephen, F. (eds), *A Farewell to Arms? From 'Long War' to Long Peace in Northern Ireland* (Manchester: Manchester University Press, 2000).

Crenshaw, M. (ed.), *Terrorism, Legitimacy, and Power: The Consequences of Political Violence* (Middletown, Conn.: Wesleyan University Press, 1983).

Crenshaw, M., *Explaining Terrorism: Causes, Processes and Consequences* (London: Routledge, 2011).

Croft, S., *Culture, Crisis, and America's War on Terror* (Cambridge: Cambridge University Press, 2006).

Croft, S., *Securitizing Islam: Identity and the Search for Security* (Cambridge: Cambridge University Press, 2012).

Croft, S., and Moore, C., 'The Evolution of Threat Narratives in the Age of Terror: Understanding Terrorist Threats in Britain', *International Affairs*, 86/4 (2010).

Cronin, A. K., *Ending Terrorism: Lessons for Defeating al-Qaida* (Abingdon: Routledge, 2008).

Cronin, A. K., *How Terrorism Ends: Understanding the Decline and Demise of Terrorist Campaigns* (Princeton: Princeton University Press, 2009).

Currie, P. M., *The Shrine and Cult of Mu'in al-din Chishti of Ajmer* (Oxford: OUP, 2006; 1st edn 1989).

Currie, P. M., and Taylor, M. (eds), *Dissident Irish Republicanism* (London: Continuum, 2011).

Danchev, A., *On Art and War and Terror* (Edinburgh: Edinburgh University Press, 2011; 1st edn 2009).

Davis, J. (ed.), *Africa and the War on Terrorism* (Aldershot: Ashgate, 2007).

de Breadun, D., *The Far Side of Revenge: Making Peace in Northern Ireland* (Cork: Collins Press, 2008; 1st edn 2001).

de Lillo, D., *Falling Man* (London: Picador, 2008; 1st edn 2007).

Dershowitz, A. M., *Why Terrorism Works: Understanding the Threat, Responding to the Challenge* (New Haven: Yale University Press, 2002).

Dingley, J. (ed.), *Combating Terrorism in Northern Ireland* (London: Routledge, 2009).

Dingley, J., *The IRA: The Irish Republican Army* (Santa Barbara, Calif.: Praeger, 2012).

Dolnik, A., *Understanding Terrorist Innovation: Technology, Tactics, and Global Trends* (London: Routledge, 2007).

Donohue, L. K., *The Cost of Counterterrorism: Power, Politics and Liberty* (Cambridge: Cambridge University Press, 2008).

Douglass, W., and Zulaika, J., *Basque Culture: Anthropological Perspectives* (Reno, Nev.: Center for Basque Studies, 2007).

Dudley Edwards, R., *Aftermath: The Omagh Bombing and the Families' Pursuit of Justice* (London: Harvill Secker, 2009).

Dudouet, V., Giessman, H. J., and Planta, K. (eds), *Post-War Security Transitions: Participatory Peacebuilding After Asymmetric Conflicts* (London: Routledge, 2012).

Dunn, J. D. G., *The Theology of Paul the Apostle* (Edinburgh: T. and T. Clark, 1998).

Dworkin, D., *Class Struggles* (Harlow: Pearson, 2007).

Eagleton, T., *Holy Terror* (Oxford: OUP, 2005).

Eagleton, T., *Reason, Faith and Revolution: Reflections on the God Debate* (New Haven: Yale University Press, 2009).

Edwards, A., 'When Terrorism as Strategy Fails: Dissident Irish Republicans and the Threat to British Security', *SICAT*, 34/4 (2011).

Eilstrup-Sangiovanni, M., and Jones, C., 'Assessing the Dangers of Illicit Networks: Why Al-Qaida May be Less Threatening than Many Think', *International Security*, 33/2 (2008).

Elliott, M., *Wolfe Tone: Prophet of Irish Independence* (New Haven: Yale University Press, 1989).

Elliott, M., *Robert Emmet: The Making of a Legend* (London: Profile Books, 2003).

Elton, G. R., *The Practice of History* (Glasgow: Fontana, 1969; 1st edn 1967).

Elton, G. R., *Reform and Reformation: England 1509–1558* (London: Edward Arnold, 1977).

Elton, G. R., *Return to Essentials: Some Reflections on the Present State of Historical Study* (Cambridge: Cambridge University Press, 1991).

English, D., *God in the Gallery* (London: Epworth Press, 1975).

English, D., *The Meaning of the Warmed Heart* (London: Methodist Church Home Mission Division, 1987).

English, R., *Radicals and the Republic: Socialist Republicanism in the Irish Free State 1925–1937* (Oxford: OUP, 1994).

English, R., *Ernie O'Malley: IRA Intellectual* (Oxford: OUP, 1998).

English, R., *Irish Freedom: The History of Nationalism in Ireland* (London: Pan, 2007; 1st edn 2006).

English, R., *Terrorism: How to Respond* (Oxford: OUP, 2009).

English, R., *Armed Struggle: The History of the IRA* (London: Pan, 2012; 1st edn 2003).

English, R., *Modern War: A Very Short Introduction* (Oxford: OUP, 2013).

English, R. (ed.), *Illusions of Terrorism and Counter-Terrorism* (Oxford: OUP, 2015).

Euben, R. L., and Zaman, M. Q. (eds), *Princeton Readings in Islamist Thought: Texts and Contexts from al-Banna to Bin Laden* (Princeton: Princeton University Press, 2009).

Evans, R., and Lewis, P., *Undercover: The True Story of Britain's Secret Police* (London: Faber and Faber, 2013).

Evans, R. J., *In Defence of History* (London: Granta, 1997).

Evans, R. J., *Telling Lies about Hitler: The Holocaust, History, and the David Irving Trial* (London: Verso, 2002).

Evans, R. J., *Altered Pasts: Counterfactuals in History* (London: Little, Brown, 2014).

Fanning, R., *Fatal Path: British Government and Irish Revolution 1910–1922* (London: Faber and Faber, 2013).

Farrell, S., and Milton-Edwards, B., *Hamas: The Islamic Resistance Movement* (Cambridge: Polity, 2010).

Fay, M., Morrissey, M., and Smyth, M., *Northern Ireland's Troubles: The Human Costs* (London: Pluto Press, 1999).

Feeney, B., *Sinn Fein: A Hundred Turbulent Years* (Dublin: O'Brien Press, 2002).

Fellman, M., *In the Name of God and Country: Reconsidering Terrorism in American History* (New Haven: Yale University Press, 2010).

Ferguson, N., *Empire: How Britain Made the Modern World* (London: Penguin, 2004; 1st edn 2003).

Fierke, K. M., *Political Self-Sacrifice: Agency, Body, and Emotion in International Relations* (Cambridge: Cambridge University Press, 2013).

Finlay, C. J., 'How To Do Things with the Word "Terrorist"', *Review of International Studies*, 35/4 (2009).

Fishman, B., 'Jihadists Target the American Dream', *CTC Sentinel*, 1/4 (2008).

FitzGerald, G., *All in a Life: An Autobiography* (Dublin: Gill and Macmillan, 1992; 1st edn 1991).

Fitzpatrick, D. (ed.), *Terror in Ireland 1916–1923* (Dublin: Lilliput Press, 2012).

Flinders, M., Gamble, A., Hay, C., and Kenny, M. (eds), *The Oxford Handbook of British Politics* (Oxford: OUP, 2009).

Flynn, B., *Soldiers of Folly: The IRA Border Campaign 1956–1962* (Cork: Collins Press, 2009).

Foner, E., *Who Owns History? Rethinking the Past in a Changing World* (New York: Hill and Wang, 2003; 1st edn 2002).

Foster, R. F., *The Irish Story: Telling Tales and Making It Up in Ireland* (London: Penguin, 2001).

Foster, R. F., *Vivid Faces: The Revolutionary Generation in Ireland 1890–1923* (London: Penguin, 2014).

Frampton, M., *The Long March: The Political Strategy of Sinn Fein, 1981–2007* (Basingstoke: Palgrave Macmillan, 2009).

Frampton, M., *Legion of the Rearguard: Dissident Irish Republicanism* (Dublin: Irish Academic Press, 2011).

Freedman, L., *Strategy: A History* (Oxford: OUP, 2013).

Frenett, R., and Smith, M. L. R., 'IRA 2.0: Continuing the Long War—Analyzing the Factors Behind Anti-GFA Violence', *TPV*, 24/3 (2012).

Fukuyama, F., *After the Neocons: America at the Crossroads* (London: Profile, 2006).

Gabbay, M., 'Mapping the Factional Structure of the Sunni Insurgency in Iraq', *CTC Sentinel*, 1/4 (2008).

Ganor, B., 'An Intifada in Europe? A Comparative Analysis of Radicalization Processes Among Palestinians in the West Bank and Gaza Versus Muslim Immigrants in Europe', *SICAT*, 34/8 (2011).

Gantt, J., *Irish Terrorism in the Atlantic Community, 1865–1922* (Basingstoke: Palgrave Macmillan, 2010).

Gearty, C., *Terror* (London: Faber and Faber, 1991).

Gearty, C., *Can Human Rights Survive?* (Cambridge: Cambridge University Press, 2006).

Gearty, C., *Civil Liberties* (Oxford: OUP, 2007).

Gearty, C., *Liberty and Security* (Cambridge: Polity Press, 2013).

Gelvin, J. L., 'Al-Qaida and Anarchism: A Historian's Reply to Terrorology', *TPV*, 20 (2008).

Gilderhuis, M. T., *History and Historians: A Historiographical Introduction* (London: Pearson, 2010; 1st edn 1992).

Gillespie, G., *Years of Darkness: The Troubles Remembered* (Dublin: Gill and Macmillan, 2008).

Giraldo, J. K., and Trinkunas, H. A. (eds), *Terrorism Financing and State Responses: A Comparative Perspective* (Stanford, Calif.: Stanford University Press, 2007).

Githens-Mazer, J., 'Islamic Radicalization among North Africans in Britain', *British Journal of Politics and International Relations*, 10/4 (2008).

Godson, D., *Himself Alone: David Trimble and the Ordeal of Unionism* (London: HarperCollins, 2005; 1st edn 2004).

Gofas, A., ' "Old" vs. "New" Terrorism: What's in a Name?', *Uluslararası; İlişkiler*, 8/32 (2012).

Goodin, R. E., *What's Wrong with Terrorism?* (Cambridge: Polity, 2006).

Goodwin, J., *No Other Way Out: States and Revolutionary Movements, 1945–1991* (Cambridge: Cambridge University Press, 2001).

Gould, E. D., and Klor, E. F., 'Does Terrorism Work?', *Quarterly Journal of Economics*, 125/4 (2010).

Grant, A., *Irish Socialist Republicanism 1909–36* (Dublin: Four Courts Press, 2012).

Gray, J., *Al Qaeda and What it Means to be Modern* (London: Faber and Faber, 2007; 1st edn 2003).

Gray, W. R., *Embedded: A Marine Corps Adviser Inside the Iraqi Army* (Annapolis, Md: Naval Institute Press, 2009).

Greenberg, K. J. (ed.), *Al-Qaida Now: Understanding Today's Terrorists* (Cambridge: Cambridge University Press, 2005).

Greenfeld, L., *Nationalism: Five Roads to Modernity* (Cambridge, Mass.: Harvard University Press, 1992).

Guelke, A., *The Age of Terrorism and the International Political System* (London: I. B. Tauris, 1998; 1st edn 1995).

Guelke, A., *Terrorism and Global Disorder: Political Violence in the Contemporary World* (London: I. B. Tauris, 2006).

Guelke, A., *The New Age of Terrorism and the International Political System* (London: I. B. Tauris, 2009; 1st edn 1995).

Gunning, J., *Hamas in Politics: Democracy, Religion, Violence* (London: Hurst and Co., 2009).

Gupta, D. K., *Understanding Terrorism and Political Violence: The Life Cycle of Birth, Growth, Transformation, and Demise* (London: Routledge, 2008).

Gupta, D. K., and Mundra, K., 'Suicide Bombing as a Strategic Weapon: An Empirical Investigation of Hamas and Islamic Jihad', *TPV*, 17/4 (2005).

Habeck, M. R., *Knowing the Enemy: Jihadist Ideology and the War on Terror* (New Haven: Yale University Press, 2006).

Habgood, J., *Faith and Uncertainty* (London: Darton, Longman, and Todd, 1997).

Hafez, M. M., *Manufacturing Human Bombs: The Making of Palestinian Suicide Bombers* (Washington: USIP Press, 2006).

Hafez, M. M., 'Jihad After Iraq: Lessons from the Arab Afghans Phenomenon', *CTC Sentinel*, 1/4 (2008).

Hafez, M. M., and Hatfield, J. M., 'Do Targeted Assassinations Work? A Multivariate Analysis of Israel's Controversial Tactic During al-Aqsa Uprising', *Studies in Conflict and Terrorism*, 29/4 (2006).

Hamilton, C., *Women and ETA: The Gender Politics of Radical Basque Nationalism* (Manchester: Manchester University Press, 2007).

Hanley, B., and Millar, S., *The Lost Revolution: The Story of the Official IRA and the Workers' Party* (Dublin: Penguin, 2009).

Harris, F., *The Bomb* (Portland: Feral House, 1996; 1st edn 1909).

Harris-Gershon, D., *What Do You Buy the Children of the Terrorist Who Tried to Kill Your Wife? A Memoir* (London: Oneworld Publications, 2013).

Hart, P., *Mick: The Real Michael Collins* (London: Pan Macmillan, 2005).

Hartley, T., *Milltown Cemetery: The History of Belfast, Written in Stone* (Belfast: Blackstaff Press, 2014).

Hassan, R., *Life as a Weapon: The Global Rise of Suicide Bombings* (London: Routledge, 2011).

Hegghammer, T., *Jihad in Saudi Arabia: Violence and Pan-Islamism Since 1979* (Cambridge: Cambridge University Press, 2010).

Hegghammer, T., and Lia, B., 'Jihadi Strategic Studies: The Alleged Al-Qaida Policy Study Preceding the Madrid Bombings', *SICAT*, 27/5 (2004).

Held, V., *How Terrorism Is Wrong: Morality and Political Violence* (Oxford: OUP, 2008).

Hellmich, C., *Al-Qaida: From Global Network to Local Franchise* (London: Zed Books, 2011).

Hennessey, T., *Hunger Strike: Margaret Thatcher's Battle with the IRA 1980–1981* (Sallins: Irish Academic Press, 2013).

Hesse, H., *Steppenwolf* (Harmondsworth: Penguin, 1965; 1st edn 1927).

Hewitt, S., *The British War on Terror: Terrorism and Counter-Terrorism on the Home Front Since 9/11* (London: Continuum, 2008).

Hewitt, S., *Snitch! A History of the Modern Intelligence Informer* (London: Continuum, 2010).

Hobsbawm, E., *Age of Extremes: The Short Twentieth Century 1914–1991* (London: Penguin, 1994).

Hobsbawm, E., *On History* (London: Weidenfeld and Nicolson, 1997).

Hobsbawm, E., *Interesting Times: A Twentieth-Century Life* (London: Penguin, 2002).

Hobsbawm, E., *Globalization, Democracy and Terrorism* (London: Little, Brown, 2007).

Hoffman, B., *Inside Terrorism* (New York: Columbia University Press, 2006; 1st edn 1998).

Hoffman, B., *Anonymous Soldiers: The Struggle for Israel, 1917–1947* (New York: Alfred A. Knopf, 2015).

Hoffman, B., and Reinares, F. (eds), *The Evolution of the Global Terrorist Threat: From 9/11 to Osama bin Laden's Death* (New York: Columbia University Press, 2014).

Holbrook, D., *The Al-Qaida Doctrine: The Framing and Evolution of the Leadership's Public Discourse* (London: Bloomsbury, 2014).

Holland, J., and Phoenix, S., *Phoenix: Policing the Shadows. The Secret War Against Terrorism in Northern Ireland* (London: Hodder and Stoughton, 1997; 1st edn 1996).

Holmes, J. S., *Terrorism and Democratic Stability Revisited* (Manchester: Manchester University Press, 2008; 1st edn 2001).

Honderich, T., *Terrorism for Humanity: Inquiries in Political Philosophy* (London: Pluto, 2003; 1st edn 1989).

Honderich, T., *Humanity, Terrorism, Terrorist War: Palestine, 9/11, 7/7* (London: Continuum, 2006).

Hopkinson, M., *Green Against Green: The Irish Civil War* (Dublin: Gill and Macmillan, 1988).

Horgan, J., *The Psychology of Terrorism* (London: Routledge, 2005).

Horgan, J., *Walking Away from Terrorism: Accounts of Disengagement from Radical and Extremist Movements* (London: Routledge, 2009).

Horgan, J., *Divided We Stand: The Strategy and Psychology of Ireland's Dissident Terrorists* (Oxford: OUP, 2013).

Howard, M., *Clausewitz: A Very Short Introduction* (Oxford: OUP, 2002; 1st edn 1983).

Howard, M., *Captain Professor: A Life in War and Peace* (London: Continuum, 2006).

Howe, S., *Ireland and Empire: Colonial Legacies in Irish History and Culture* (Oxford: OUP, 2000).

Hroub, K., *Hamas: Political Thought and Practice* (Washington: Institute for Palestine Studies, 2000).

Humphries, J., *Freedom Fighters: Wales's Forgotten 'War', 1963–1993* (Cardiff: University of Wales Press, 2008).

Huntington, S. P., 'The Clash of Civilizations?', *Foreign Affairs*, 72/3 (1993).

Huntington, S. P., *The Clash of Civilizations and the Remaking of World Order* (London: Touchstone, 1998; 1st edn 1997).

Ingram, M., and Harkin, G., *Stakeknife: Britain's Secret Agents in Ireland* (Dublin: O'Brien Press, 2004).

Jackson, P., *Beyond the Balance of Power: France and the Politics of National Security in the Era of the First World War* (Cambridge: Cambridge University Press, 2013).

Jackson, R., 'The Study of Terrorism after 11 September 2001: Problems, Challenges and Future Developments', *Political Studies Review*, 7/2 (2009).

Jackson, R., *Confessions of a Terrorist* (London: Zed Books, 2014).

Jackson, R., Breen Smyth, M., and Gunning, J. (eds), *Critical Terrorism Studies: A New Research Agenda* (London: Routledge, 2009).

Jackson, R., Jarvis, L., Gunning, J., and Breen Smyth, M., *Terrorism: A Critical Introduction* (Basingstoke: Palgrave Macmillan, 2011).

Jenkins, D. E., *God, Politics, and the Future* (London: SCM Press, 1988).

Jenkins, K., *Re-thinking History* (London: Routledge, 1991).

Jenkins, K., *On 'What is History?' From Carr and Elton to Rorty and White* (London: Routledge, 1995).

Jenkins, K., *Why History? Ethics and Postmodernity* (London: Routledge, 1999).

Jensen, R. B., 'The Pre-1914 Anarchist "Lone Wolf" Terrorist and Governmental Responses', *TPV*, 26/1 (2014).

Jones, J. W., *Blood That Cries Out From the Earth: The Psychology of Religious Terrorism* (New York: OUP, 2008).

Jones, S. G., *Counterinsurgency in Afghanistan* (Santa Monica, Calif.: RAND, 2008).

Jones, S. G., and Libicki, M. C., *How Terrorist Groups End: Lessons for Countering al-Qaida* (Santa Monica, Calif.: RAND, 2008).

Jordan, J., 'The Evolution of the Structure of Jihadist Terrorism in Western Europe: The Case of Spain', *SICAT*, 37/8 (2014).

Jordanova, L., *History in Practice* (London: Bloomsbury, 2006; 1st edn 2000).

Jordheim, H., 'Against Periodization: Koselleck's Theory of Multiple Temporalities', *History and Theory*, 51 (2012).

Juergensmeyer, M., *Terror in the Mind of God: The Global Rise of Religious Violence* (Berkeley: University of California Press, 2001; 1st edn 2000).

Juergensmeyer, M., *Global Rebellion: Religious Challenges to the Secular State, from Christian Militias to al-Qaida* (Berkeley: University of California Press, 2008).

Kahneman, D., *Thinking, Fast and Slow* (London: Penguin, 2012; 1st edn 2011).

Kalyvas, S. N., *The Logic of Violence in Civil War* (Cambridge: Cambridge University Press, 2006).

Kassimeris, G., *Inside Greek Terrorism* (London: Hurst and Co., 2013).

Kearney, D. (ed.), *Uncomfortable Conversations: An Initiative for Dialogue Towards Reconciliation* (Belfast: Sinn Fein, 2015).

Kelly, M. J., *The Fenian Ideal and Irish Nationalism, 1882–1916* (Woodbridge: Boydell Press, 2006).

Kelly, S., *Fianna Fail, Partition, and Northern Ireland 1926–1971* (Dublin: Irish Academic Press, 2013).

Khalidi, R., *Palestinian Identity: The Construction of Modern National Consciousness* (New York: Columbia University Press, 2010; 1st edn 1997).

Khilnani, S., *Arguing Revolution: The Intellectual Left in Postwar France* (New Haven: Yale University Press, 1993).

Kimmerling, B., and Migdal, J. S., *The Palestinian People: A History* (Cambridge, Mass.: Harvard University Press, 2003).

King, M. E., *A Quiet Revolution: The First Palestinian Intifada and Non-Violent Resistance* (New York: Nation Books, 2007).

Kissane, B., *The Politics of the Irish Civil War* (Oxford: OUP, 2005).

Knatchbull, T., *From a Clear Blue Sky: Surviving the Mountbatten Bomb* (London: Hutchinson, 2009).

Krause, P., 'The Political Effectiveness of Non-State Violence: A Two-Level Framework to Transform a Deceptive Debate', *Security Studies*, 22/2 (2013).

Krueger, A. B., *What Makes a Terrorist: Economics and the Roots of Terrorism* (Princeton: Princeton University Press, 2008; 1st edn 2007).

Küng, H., *On Being a Christian* (London: Collins, 1977; 1st edn 1974).

Kydd, A. H., and Walter, B. F., 'The Strategies of Terrorism', *International Security*, 31/1 (2006).

LaCapra, D., *History and its Limits: Human, Animal, Violence* (Ithaca, NY: Cornell University Press, 2009).

Laitin, D. D., *Identity in Formation: The Russian-Speaking Populations in the Near Abroad* (Ithaca, NY: Cornell University Press, 1998).

Laitin, D. D., *Nations, States and Violence* (Oxford: OUP, 2007).

Lake, D. A., 'Rational Extremism: Understanding Terrorism in the Twenty-First Century', *Dialog-IO*, 1/1 (2002).

Lake, D. A., *Hierarchy in International Relations* (Ithaca, NY: Cornell University Press, 2009).

Lambert, R., *Countering Al-Qaida in London: Police and Muslims in Partnership* (London: Hurst and Co., 2011).

Laqueur, W., *Terrorism* (London: Weidenfeld and Nicolson, 1977).

Lawrence, B. (ed.), *Messages to the World: The Statements of Osama bin Laden* (London: Verso, 2005).

Lawther, C., *Truth, Denial, and Transition: Northern Ireland and the Contested Past* (London: Routledge, 2014).

Levi, M., *On Nuclear Terrorism* (Cambridge, Mass.: Harvard University Press, 2007).

Levitt, M., *Hamas: Politics, Charity and Terrorism in the Service of Jihad* (New Haven: Yale University Press, 2006).

Lewis, B., *The Crisis of Islam: Holy War and Unholy Terror* (New York: Modern Library, 2003).

Lia, B., 'Al-Qaida's Appeal: Understanding its Unique Selling Points', *Perspectives on Terrorism*, 2/8 (2008).

Livingstone, D. N., *Putting Science in its Place: Geographies of Scientific Knowledge* (Chicago: University of Chicago Press, 2003).

Lodge, J. (ed.), *Terrorism: A Challenge to the State* (Oxford: Martin Robertson, 1981).

Lutz, J. M., and Lutz, B. J., *Global Terrorism* (London: Routledge, 2008; 1st edn 2004).

Lynch, O., 'British Muslim Youth: Radicalization, Terrorism and the Construction of the "Other"', *Critical Studies on Terrorism*, 6/2 (2013).

Lynch, O., and Ryder, C., 'Deadliness, Organizational Change and Suicide Attacks: Understanding the Assumptions Inherent in the Use of the Term "New Terrorism"', *Critical Studies on Terrorism*, 5/2 (2012).

McCaffrey, B., *Alex Maskey: Man and Mayor* (Belfast: Brehon Press, 2003).

McConville, S., *Irish Political Prisoners, 1848–1922: Theatres of War* (London: Routledge, 2003).

McConville, S., *Irish Political Prisoners, 1920–1962: Pilgrimage of Desolation* (London: Routledge, 2014).

MacCulloch, D., *A History of Christianity: The First Three Thousand Years* (London: Penguin, 2009).

MacCulloch, D., *Silence: A Christian History* (London: Penguin, 2013).

McDaid, S., *Template for Peace: Northern Ireland 1972–75* (Manchester: Manchester University Press, 2013).

McDonald, H., *Trimble* (London: Bloomsbury, 2000).

McDonald, H., *Gunsmoke and Mirrors: How Sinn Fein Dressed Up Defeat As Victory* (Dublin: Gill and Macmillan, 2008).

McDonald, H., and Holland, J., *INLA: Deadly Divisions* (Dublin: Poolbeg Press, 1994).

McEvoy, K., *Paramilitary Imprisonment in Northern Ireland: Resistance, Management, and Release* (Oxford: OUP, 2001).

McGarry, F., *The Rising. Ireland: Easter 1916* (Oxford: OUP, 2010).

McGarry, J. (ed.), *Northern Ireland and the Divided World: Post-Agreement Northern Ireland in Comparative Perspective* (Oxford: OUP, 2001).

McGartland, M., *Fifty Dead Men Walking* (London: Blake, 1998; 1st edn 1997).

McGladdery, G., *The Provisional IRA in England: The Bombing Campaign 1973–1997* (Dublin: Irish Academic Press, 2006).

McGuinness, M., *Bodenstown '86* (London: Wolfe Tone Society, 1986).

McGuire, E., *Enemy of the Empire: Life as an International Undercover IRA Activist* (Dublin: O'Brien Press, 2006).

McIntire, C. T. (ed.), *God, History, and Historians: Modern Christian Views of History* (New York: OUP, 1977).

BKCH:McIntyre, A., 'Provisional Republicanism: Internal Politics, Inequities, and Modes of Repression', in F. McGarry (ed.), *Republicanism in Modern Ireland* (Dublin: UCD Press, 2003).

McIntyre, A., *Good Friday: The Death of Irish Republicanism* (New York: Ausubo Press, 2008).

McKearney, T., *The Provisional IRA: From Insurrection to Parliament* (London: Pluto Press, 2011).

McKeown, L., *Out of Time: Irish Republican Prisoners Long Kesh 1972–2000* (Belfast: Beyond the Pale, 2001).

McKittrick, D., Kelters, S., Feeney, B., and Thornton, C., *Lost Lives: The Stories of the Men, Women, and Children Who Died as a Result of the Northern Ireland Troubles* (Edinburgh: Mainstream, 2001; 1st edn 1999).

Mac Laverty, B., *Cal* (London: Vintage, 1998; 1st edn 1983).

McManus, S., *My American Struggle for Justice in Northern Ireland* (Cork: Collins Press, 2011).

MacMillan, M., *The Uses and Abuses of History* (London: Profile, 2009).

MacStiofain, S., *Memoirs of a Revolutionary* (Edinburgh: Gordon Cremonesi, 1975).

Magee, P., *Gangsters or Guerrillas? Representations of Irish Republicans in 'Troubles Fiction'* (Belfast: Beyond the Pale, 2001).

Marsden, S.V., 'Successful Terrorism: Framework and Review', *Behavioral Sciences of Terrorism and Political Aggression*, 4/2 (2012).

Marsden, S.V., 'Media Metrics: How Arab and Western Media Construct Success and Failure in the "Global War on Terror"', *Perspectives on Terrorism*, 7/6 (2013).

Marwick, A., *The New Nature of History: Knowledge, Evidence, Language* (Basingstoke: Palgrave, 2001).

Matesan, I. E., 'What Makes Negative Frames Resonant? Hamas and the Appeal of Opposition to the Peace Process', *TPV*, 24/5 (2012).

Mead, W. R., *Power, Terror, Peace and War: America's Grand Strategy in a World at Risk* (New York: Alfred A. Knopf, 2005).

Mees, L., *Nationalism, Violence, and Democracy: The Basque Clash of Identities* (Basingstoke: Palgrave Macmillan, 2003).

Mendus, S., *Politics and Morality* (Cambridge: Polity Press, 2009).

Merari, A., *Driven to Death: Psychological and Social Aspects of Suicide Terrorism* (Oxford: OUP, 2010).

Merari, A., and Elad, S., *The International Dimension of Palestinian Terrorism* (Boulder, Colo.: Westview Press, 1986).

Merari, A., Diamant, I., Bibi, A., Broshi, Y., and Zakin, G., 'Personality Characteristics of "Self Martyrs"/"Suicide Bombers" and Organizers of Suicide Attacks', *TPV*, 22/1 (2010).

Merari, A., Fighel, J., Ganor, B., Lavie, E., Tzoreff, Y., and Livne, A., 'Making Palestinian "Martyrdom Operations"/"Suicide Attacks": Interviews with Would-Be Perpetrators and Organizers', *TPV*, 22/1 (2010).

Metzger, B. M., and Coogan, M. D. (eds), *The Oxford Companion to the Bible* (Oxford: OUP, 1993).

Meyers, M. A., *Chechnya Jihad* (San Diego: Green Grass Press, 2011).

Millar, S., *On the Brinks* (Galway: Wynkin de Worde, 2003).

Millar, S., *Bloodstorm* (Dingle: Brandon, 2008).

Millar, S., *The Dark Place* (Dingle: Brandon, 2009).

Miller, C. (ed.), *'War on Terror': The Oxford Amnesty Lectures 2006* (Manchester: Manchester University Press, 2009).

Milton-Edwards, B., *The Israeli–Palestinian Conflict: A People's War* (London: Routledge, 2009).

Mishal, S., and Sela, A., *The Palestinian Hamas: Vision, Violence, and Coexistence* (New York: Columbia University Press; 2006; 1st edn 2000).

Mitchell, A., *Revolutionary Government in Ireland: Dail Eireann 1919–22* (Dublin: Gill and Macmillan 1995).

Mockaitis, T. R., *The 'New' Terrorism: Myths and Reality* (Westport, Conn.: Praeger Security International, 2007).

Moghadam, A., 'Palestinian Suicide Terrorism in the Second Intifada: Motivations and Organizational Aspects', *SICAT*, 26/2 (2003).

Moloney, E., *A Secret History of the IRA* (London: Penguin, 2002).

Moloney, E., *Voices from the Grave: Two Men's War in Ireland* (London: Faber and Faber, 2010).

Moore, B., *Lies of Silence* (London: Vintage, 1999; 1st edn 1990).

Moore, C., *Contemporary Violence: Postmodern War in Kosovo and Chechnya* (Manchester: Manchester University Press, 2010).

Moore, C., *Margaret Thatcher: The Authorized Biography. Volume One: Not for Turning* (London: Penguin, 2013).

Morris, B., *Righteous Victims: A History of the Zionist–Arab Conflict, 1881–1999* (New York: Alfred A. Knopf, 1999).

Morrison, D., *Then the Walls Came Down: A Prison Journal* (Cork: Mercier Press, 1999).

Morrison, D., *All the Dead Voices* (Cork: Mercier Press, 2002).

Morrison, J. F., *The Origins and Rise of Dissident Irish Republicanism: The Role and Impact of Organizational Splits* (New York: Bloomsbury, 2013).

Mowlam, M., *Momentum: The Struggle for Peace, Politics, and the People* (London: Hodder and Stoughton, 2002).

Moyano, M. J., *Argentina's Lost Patrol: Armed Struggle, 1969–1979* (New Haven: Yale University Press, 1995).

Mueller, J., and Stewart, M. G., *Terror, Security, and Money: Balancing the Risks, Benefits, and Costs of Homeland Security* (Oxford: OUP, 2011).

Muro, D., *Ethnicity and Violence: The Case of Radical Basque Nationalism* (London: Routledge, 2008).

Muro, D., 'A Catalan Compromise: How to Solve Spain's Secession Crisis', *Foreign Affairs*, 9 November 2014.

Murray, G., and Tonge, J., *Sinn Fein and the SDLP: From Alienation to Participation* (Dublin: O'Brien Press, 2005).

Netanyahu, B., *Fighting Terrorism: How Democracies Can Defeat Domestic and International Terrorists* (New York: Farrar Straus Giroux, 1995).

Neumann, P. R., and Smith, M. L. R., *The Strategy of Terrorism: How it Works, and Why it Fails* (London: Routledge, 2008).

Neumann, P. R., Evans, R., and Pantucci, R., 'Locating al-Qaida's Centre of Gravity: The Role of Middle Managers', *SICAT*, 34/11 (2011).

Nimni, E., *Marxism and Nationalism: Theoretical Origins of a Political Crisis* (London: Pluto Press, 1991).

Norman, J. M., *The Second Palestinian Intifada: Civil Resistance* (London: Routledge, 2010).

Norton, A. R., *Hezbollah: A Short History* (Princeton: Princeton University Press, 2007).

Novick, P., *That Noble Dream: The 'Objectivity Question' and the American Historical Profession* (Cambridge: Cambridge University Press, 1988).

O'Brien, B., *The Long War: The IRA and Sinn Fein 1985 to Today* (Dublin: O'Brien Press, 1993).

O'Brien, C. C., *Memoir: My Life and Themes* (Dublin: Poolbeg Press, 1998).

O Broin, E., *Sinn Fein and the Politics of Left Republicanism* (London: Pluto Press, 2009).

O'Callaghan, S., *The Informer* (London: Bantam Press, 1998).

O Connor, F., *In Search of a State: Catholics in Northern Ireland* (Belfast: Blackstaff Press, 1993).

O Dochartaigh, N., 'The Longest Negotiation: British Policy, IRA Strategy, and the Making of the Northern Ireland Peace Settlement', *Political Studies*, 63/1 (2015).

O'Doherty, M., *The Trouble with Guns: Republican Strategy and the Provisional IRA* (Belfast: Blackstaff Press, 1998).

O'Leary, B., 'Mission Accomplished? Looking Back at the IRA', *Field Day Review*, 1 (2005).

O'Malley, E., *On Another Man's Wound* (Dublin: Anvil Books, 1979; 1st edn 1936).

O'Malley, P., *Biting at the Grave: The Irish Hunger Strikes and the Politics of Despair* (Belfast: Blackstaff, 1990).

Omand, D., *Securing the State* (London: Hurst, 2010).

O'Rawe, R., *Blanketmen: An Untold Story of the H-Block Hunger Strike* (Dublin: New Island, 2005).

O'Rawe, R., *Afterlives: The Hunger Strike and the Secret Offer that Changed Irish History* (Dublin: Lilliput Press, 2010).

Pantling, N., *Belfast Finds Log: Poems* (Beeston: Shoestring Press, 2014).

Pape, R. A., 'The Strategic Logic of Suicide Terrorism', *American Political Science Review*, 97/3 (2003).

Pape, R. A., *Dying to Win: Why Suicide Terrorists Do It* (London: Gibson Square Books, 2006; 1st edn 2005).

Pape, R. A., and Feldman, J. K., *Cutting the Fuse: The Explosion of Global Suicide Terrorism and How to Stop It* (Chicago: University of Chicago Press, 2010).

Paret, P., *Understanding War: Essays on Clausewitz and the History of Military Power* (Princeton: Princeton University Press, 1992).

Park, D., *The Truth Commissioner* (London: Bloomsbury, 2009; 1st edn 2008).

Parker, J. D., *On the Waterfront* (Durham: Pentland Press, 2000).

Parker, M., and Taylor, M., 'Financial Intelligence: A Price Worth Paying?', *SICAT*, 33/11 (2010).

Paseta, S., *Irish Nationalist Women, 1900–1918* (Cambridge: Cambridge University Press, 2013).

Passmore, K., *Fascism: A Very Short Introduction* (Oxford: OUP, 2002).

Patterson, H., *The Politics of Illusion: A Political History of the IRA* (London: Serif, 1997; 1st edn 1989).

Patterson, H., *Ireland's Violent Frontier: The Border and Anglo-Irish Relations During the Troubles* (Basingstoke: Palgrave Macmillan, 2013).

Pearlman, W., *Violence, Non-Violence, and the Palestinian National Movement* (Cambridge: Cambridge University Press, 2014; 1st edn 2011).

Peleg, I., and Waxman, D., *Israel's Palestinians: The Conflict Within* (Cambridge: Cambridge University Press, 2011).

Perry, M., *Talking to Terrorists: Why America Must Engage with its Enemies* (New York: Basic Books, 2010).

Peters, J., and Newman, D. (eds), *The Routledge Handbook on the Israeli–Palestinian Conflict* (London: Routledge, 2013).

Pfarrer, C., *Seal Target Geronimo: The Inside Story of the Mission to Kill Osama bin Laden* (London: Quercus, 2011).

Phillips, M., *Londonistan: How Britain is Creating a Terror State Within* (London: Gibson Square, 2006).

Piazza, J. A., 'Is Islamist Terrorism More Dangerous? An Empirical Study of Group Ideology, Organization, and Goal Structure', *TPV*, 21/1 (2009).

Pinker, S., *The Better Angels of our Nature: The Decline of Violence in History and its Causes* (London: Penguin, 2011).

Pisoiu, D., *Islamist Radicalization in Europe: An Occupational Change Process* (London: Routledge, 2013; 1st edn 2012).

Plumb, J. H., *The Death of the Past* (Basingstoke: Palgrave Macmillan, 2004; 1st edn 1969).

Pollard, S., *The Idea of Progress: History and Society* (Harmondsworth: Penguin, 1971; 1st edn 1968).

Posner, D. N., *Institutions and Ethnic Politics in Africa* (Cambridge: Cambridge University Press, 2005).

Powell, J., *Great Hatred, Little Room: Making Peace in Northern Ireland* (London: Bodley Head, 2008).

Powell, J., *Talking to Terrorists: How to End Armed Conflicts* (London: Bodley Head, 2014).

Preston, P., *The Spanish Holocaust: Inquisition and Extermination in Twentieth-Century Spain* (London: HarperCollins, 2012).

Preston, R., *The Cobra Event* (New York: Ballantine Books, 1997).

Qutb, S., *Milestones* (New Delhi: Islamic Book Service, 2001).

Radcliff, P. B., *Making Democratic Citizens in Spain: Civil Society and the Popular Origins of the Transition, 1960–78* (Basingstoke: Palgrave Macmillan, 2011).

Rafter, K., *Sinn Fein 1905–2005: In the Shadow of Gunmen* (Dublin: Gill and Macmillan, 2005).

Ramsay, G., *Jihadi Culture on the World Wide Web* (London: Bloomsbury, 2013).

Ranstorp, M. (ed.), *Mapping Terrorism Research: State of the Art, Gaps and Future Direction* (London: Routledge, 2007).

Rapoport, D. C. (ed.), *Inside Terrorist Organizations* (London: Frank Cass, 2001).

Ratzinger, J., *Church, Ecumenism and Politics: New Essays in Ecclesiology* (Slough: St Paul Publications, 1988).

Reinares, F., 'Who are the Terrorists? Analyzing Changes in Sociological Profile among Members of ETA', *SICAT*, 27/6 (2004).

Rekawek, K., *Irish Republican Terrorism and Politics: A Comparative Study of the Official and the Provisional IRA* (London: Routledge, 2011).

Rengger, N., *Just War and International Order: The Uncivil Condition in World Politics* (Cambridge: Cambridge University Press, 2013).

Reynolds, A., *My Autobiography* (London: Transworld, 2009).

Richards, A., 'Conceptualizing Terrorism', *Studies in Conflict and Terrorism*, 37/3 (2014).

Richardson, L., *What Terrorists Want: Understanding the Terrorist Threat* (London: John Murray, 2006).

Riedel, B., *The Search for al-Qaida: Its Leadership, Ideology, and Future* (Washington: Brookings Institutions Press, 2008).

Riley-Smith, T., *The Cracked Bell: America and the Afflictions of Liberty* (London: Constable, 2010).

Rimington, S., *Open Secret: The Autobiography of the Former Director-General of MI5* (London: Hutchinson, 2001).

Roberts, A., 'Terrorism Research: Past, Present, and Future', *SICAT*, 38/1 (2015).

Roberts, A., and Garton Ash, T. (eds), *Civil Resistance and Power Politics: The Experience of Non-Violent Action from Gandhi to the Present* (Oxford: OUP, 2009).

Robison, K. R., 'Terror's True Nightmare? Reevaluating the Consequences of Terrorism on Democratic Governance', *TPV*, 22/1 (2010).

Rochlin, J., 'Plan Colombia and the Revolution in Military Affairs: The Demise of the FARC', *Review of International Studies*, 37/2 (2011).

Ross, C., 'Nationalism and Party Competition in the Basque Country and Catalonia', *West European Politics*, 19/3 (1996).

Ross, F. S., *Smashing H-Block: The Rise and Fall of the Popular Campaign against Criminalization, 1976–1982* (Liverpool: Liverpool University Press, 2011).

Roth, P., *American Pastoral* (London: Vintage, 1998; 1st edn 1997).

Rubin, B., and Rubin, J. C. (eds), *Anti-American Terrorism and the Middle East: A Documentary Reader* (Oxford: OUP, 2002).

Rushdie, S., *Joseph Anton: A Memoir* (London: Jonathan Cape, 2012).

Ruthven, M., *A Fury for God: The Islamist Attack on America* (London: Granta, 2002).

Ruthven, M., *Fundamentalism: The Search for Meaning* (Oxford: OUP, 2004).

Ryan, M., *Tom Barry: Irish Freedom Fighter* (Cork: Mercier Press, 2003).

Sageman, M., *Understanding Terror Networks* (Philadelphia: University of Pennsylvania Press, 2004).

Sageman, M., *Leaderless Jihad: Terror Networks in the Twenty-First Century* (Philadelphia: University of Pennsylvania Press, 2008).

Sanders, A., *Inside the IRA: Dissident Republicans and the War for Legitimacy* (Edinburgh: Edinburgh University Press, 2011).

Sanders, A., 'Operation Motorman (1972) and the Search for a Coherent British Counterinsurgency Strategy in Northern Ireland', *Small Wars and Insurgencies*, 24/3 (2013).

Sanders, A., and Wood, I. S., *Times of Troubles: Britain's War in Northern Ireland* (Edinburgh: Edinburgh University Press, 2012).

Saul, B., *Defining Terrorism in International Law* (Oxford: OUP, 2008; 1st edn 2006).

Saunier, P., *Transnational History* (Basingstoke: Palgrave Macmillan, 2013).

Scheuer, M., *Osama bin Laden* (Oxford: OUP, 2011).

Schmid, A. P., 'Frameworks for Conceptualizing Terrorism', *TPV*, 16/2 (2004).

Schmid, A. P. (ed.), *The Routledge Handbook of Terrorism Research* (London: Routledge, 2011).

Schmid, A. P., and Jongman, A. J. (eds), *Political Terrorism* (Amsterdam: North Holland Publishing, 1988).

Schwarzmantel, J., *Democracy and Political Violence* (Edinburgh: Edinburgh University Press, 2011).

Scott, J. W. (ed.), *Feminism and History* (Oxford: OUP, 1996).

Scruton, R., *The West and the Rest: Globalization and the Terrorist Threat* (London: Continuum, 2002).

Sen, A., *The Idea of Justice* (London: Penguin, 2009).

Shanahan, T., *The Provisional Irish Republican Army and the Morality of Terrorism* (Edinburgh: Edinburgh University Press, 2009).

Shapiro, J. N., *The Terrorist's Dilemma: Managing Violent Covert Organizations* (Princeton: Princeton University Press, 2013).

Shirlow, P., Tonge, J., McAuley, J., and McGlynn, C., *Abandoning Historical Conflict? Former Political Prisoners and Reconciliation in Northern Ireland* (Manchester: Manchester University Press, 2010).

Silber, M. D., *The Al-Qaida Factor: Plots Against the West* (Philadelphia: University of Pennsylvania Press, 2012).

Singh, R., *Hamas and Suicide Terrorism: Multi-Causal and Multi-Level Approaches* (London: Routledge, 2011).

Skelly, J. M. (ed.), *Political Islam from Muhammad to Ahmadinejad* (Santa Barbara, Calif.: Praeger Security International, 2010).

Slahi, M. O., *Guantanamo Diary* (Edinburgh: Canongate, 2015).

Smith, A. D., and Hutchinson, J. (eds), *Nationalism* (Oxford: OUP, 1994).

Smith, M., and Walsh, J. I., 'Do Drone Strikes Degrade al-Qaida? Evidence from Propaganda Output', *TPV*, 25/2 (2013).

Smith, M. L. R., *Fighting for Ireland? The Military Strategy of the Irish Republican Movement* (London: Routledge, 1995).

Spalding, R., and Parker, C., *Historiography: An Introduction* (Manchester: Manchester University Press, 2007).

Stampnitzky, L., *Disciplining Terror: How Experts Invented 'Terrorism'* (Cambridge: Cambridge University Press, 2013).

Staniland, P., *Networks of Rebellion: Explaining Insurgent Cohesion and Collapse* (Ithaca, NY: Cornell University Press, 2014).

Steinhoff, U., *On the Ethics of War and Terrorism* (Oxford: OUP, 2007).

Stepanova, E., *Terrorism in Asymmetrical Conflict: Ideological and Structural Aspects* (Oxford: OUP, 2008).

Stewart, A. T. Q., *The Shape of Irish History* (Belfast: Blackstaff Press, 2001).

Strachan, H., *The Direction of War: Contemporary Strategy in Historical Perspective* (Cambridge: Cambridge University Press, 2013).

Sutton, M., *Bear in Mind these Dead: An Index of Deaths from the Conflict in Ireland 1969–1993* (Belfast: Beyond the Pale Publications, 1994).

Svensson, T., 'Frontiers of Blame: India's "War on Terror"', *Critical Studies on Terrorism*, 2/1 (2009).

Tamimi, A., *Hamas: A History from Within* (Northampton: Olive Branch Press, 2007).

Tawney, R. H., *Religion and the Rise of Capitalism* (West Drayton: Penguin, 1938; 1st edn 1926).

Taylor, M., and Horgan, J. (eds), *The Future of Terrorism* (Abingdon: Frank Cass, 2000).

Taylor, M., and Quayle, E., *Terrorist Lives* (London: Brassey's, 1994).

Taylor, P., *Provos: The IRA and Sinn Fein* (London: Bloomsbury, 1997).

Thomas, W., *Hands Off Wales: Nationhood and Militancy* (Llandysul: Gomer Press, 2013).

Thompson, J. (ed.), *The Imperial War Museum Book of Modern Warfare: British and Commonwealth Forces at War 1945–2000* (London: Pan, 2003; 1st edn 2002).

Tonge, J., Braniff, M., Hennessey, T., McAuley, J. W., and Whiting, S. A., *The Democratic Unionist Party: From Protest to Power* (Oxford: OUP, 2014).

Tosh, J., *The Pursuit of History* (Harlow: Pearson Education, 2010; 1st edn 1984).

Townshend, C., *Ireland: The Twentieth Century* (London: Arnold, 1999).

Townshend, C., *Terrorism: A Very Short Introduction* (Oxford: OUP, 2002).

Townshend, C., *Easter 1916: The Irish Rebellion* (London: Penguin, 2005).

Townshend, C., *When God Made Hell: The British Invasion of Mesopotamia and the Creation of Iraq 1914–1921* (London: Faber and Faber, 2010).

Townshend, C., *The Republic: The Fight for Irish Independence* (London: Penguin, 2013).

Treacy, M., *The IRA, 1956–69: Rethinking the Republic* (Manchester: Manchester University Press, 2011).

Treverton, G. F., *Intelligence for an Age of Terror* (Cambridge: Cambridge University Press, 2009).

Tripp, C., *A History of Iraq* (Cambridge: Cambridge University Press, 2007; 1st edn 2000).

Tucker, A., *Our Knowledge of the Past: A Philosophy of Historiography* (Cambridge: Cambridge University Press, 2004).

Updike, J., *Terrorist* (London: Hamish Hamilton, 2006).

Valiulis, M. G., *Portrait of a Revolutionary: General Richard Mulcahy and the Founding of the Irish Free State* (Blackrock: Irish Academic Press, 1992).

Vittori, J., *Terrorist Financing and Resourcing* (Basingstoke: Palgrave Macmillan, 2011).

Wagemakers, J., 'Legitimizing Pragmatism: Hamas's Framing Efforts from Militancy to Moderation and Back?', *TPV*, 22/3 (2010).

Wagemakers, J., *A Quietist Jihadi: The Ideology and Influence of Abu Muhammad al-Maqdisi* (Cambridge: Cambridge University Press, 2012).

Waldron, J., *Torture, Terror, and Trade-Offs: Philosophy for the White House* (Oxford: OUP, 2010).

Walter, B. F., *Reputation and Civil War: Why Separatist Conflicts Are So Violent* (Cambridge: Cambridge University Press, 2009).

Walzer, M., *Just and Unjust Wars: A Moral Argument with Historical Illustrations* (New York: Basic Books, 2006; 1st edn 1977).

Wanandi, J., 'A Global Coalition Against International Terrorism', *International Security*, 26/4 (2002).

Watson, C. J., *Modern Basque History: Eighteenth Century to the Present* (Reno, Nev.: Center for Basque Studies, 2003).

Watson, C. J., *Basque Nationalism and Political Violence: The Ideological and Intellectual Origins of ETA* (Reno, Nev.: Center for Basque Studies, 2007).

Waxman, M., 'Police and National Security: American Local Law Enforcement and Counter-Terrorism After 9/11', *Columbia Public Law and Legal Theory Working Papers* (Paper 08157; 2008).

Weinberg, L., 'Turning to Terror: The Conditions Under Which Political Parties Turn to Terrorist Activities', *Comparative Politics*, 23/4 (1991).

Weinberg, L., Pedahzur, A., and Canetti-Nisim, D., 'The Social and Religious Characteristics of Suicide Bombers and their Victims', *TPV*, 15/3 (2003).

Weinstein, J. M., *Inside Rebellion: The Politics of Insurgent Violence* (Cambridge: Cambridge University Press, 2007).

Whelehan, N., *The Dynamiters: Irish Nationalism and Political Violence in the Wider World, 1867–1900* (Cambridge: Cambridge University Press, 2012).

White, R. W., *Ruairí Ó Brádaigh: The Life and Politics of an Irish Revolutionary* (Bloomington: Indiana University Press, 2006).

Whitfield, T., *Endgame for ETA: Elusive Peace in the Basque Country* (London: Hurst, 2014).

Whiting, S. A., '"The Discourse of Defence": "Dissident" Irish Republican Newspapers and the "Propaganda War"', *TPV*, 24/3 (2012).

Wilkinson, P., *Terrorism Versus Democracy: The Liberal State Response* (London: Frank Cass, 2001).

Wilkinson, P., *Terrorism Versus Democracy: The Liberal State Response* (London: Routledge, 2006; 1st edn 2001).

Wilkinson, P., *Terrorism Versus Democracy: The Liberal State Response* (London: Routledge, 2011; 1st edn 2001).

Wilkinson, P., *International Relations: A Very Short Introduction* (Oxford: OUP, 2007).

Williams, C., *Terrorism Explained: The Facts about Terrorism and Terrorist Groups* (Sydney: New Holland Publishers, 2004).

Wilson, A. J., *Irish America and the Ulster Conflict 1968–1995* (Belfast: Blackstaff Press, 1995).

Wolfe, A., *Political Evil: What It Is and How to Combat It* (New York: Alfred A. Knopf, 2011).

Woodworth, P., *Dirty War, Clean Hands: ETA, the GAL, and Spanish Democracy* (Cork: Cork University Press, 2001).

Wright, L., *The Looming Tower: Al-Qaida's Road to 9/11* (London: Penguin, 2007; 1st edn 2006).

Wright, T., *The Original Jesus: The Life and Vision of a Revolutionary* (Oxford: Lion, 1996).

Wurgaft, B. A., 'The Uses of Walter: Walter Benjamin and the Counterfactual Imagination', *History and Theory*, 49 (2010).

Yarchi, M., 'The Effect of Female Suicide Attacks on Foreign Media Framing of Conflicts: The Case of the Palestinian–Israeli Conflict', *Studies in Conflict and Terrorism*, 37/8 (2014).

Zackie, M. W., 'An Analysis of Abu Mus'ab al-Suri's *Call to Global Islamic Resistance*', *Journal of Strategic Security*, 6/1 (2013).

Zegart, A. B., *Flawed by Design: The Evolution of the CIA, JCS, and NSC* (Stanford, Calif.: Stanford University Press, 1999).

Zellen, B. S., *State of Recovery: The Quest to Restore American Security After 9/11* (London: Bloomsbury, 2013).

Zulaika, J., *Basque Violence: Metaphor and Sacrament* (Reno: University of Nevada Press, 1988).

Zulaika, J., *Terrorism: The Self-Fulfilling Prophecy* (Chicago: University of Chicago Press, 2009).

Picture Acknowledgements

dpa picture alliance/Alamy 14; Bettman/Corbis 17; Can Merey/dpa/Corbis 16; Reuters/Corbis 5; Allison Joyce/Reuters/Corbis 8; Mohammed Salem/Reuters/Corbis 11; EFE/EFE 12; FBI/Public Domain 4; AFP/Getty Images 13; David Levenson/Getty Images 2; Jaime Razuri/Getty Images 15; Stringer/Getty Images 1; Larry Doherty/Victor Patterson 6; Alan Lewis/Photopressbelfast.com 7; REX Shutterstock 3; Israel Sun/REX Shutterstock 9; Sipa Press/REX Shutterstock 10

Index